Pedagogy

Pittsburgh Series in Composition, Literacy, and Culture

David Bartholomae and Jean Ferguson Carr, Editors

Pedagogy

DISTURBING
HISTORY,
1819–1929

EDITED BY

Mariolina Rizzi Salvatori

University of
Pittsburgh Press

Published by the University of Pittsburgh Press, Pittsburgh, Pa. 15260
Copyright © 1996, University of Pittsburgh Press
All rights reserved
Manufactured in the United States of America
Printed on acid-free paper
10 9 8 7 6 5 4 3 2 1

Library of Congress Cataloging-in-Publication Data
will be found at the end of this book.

A CIP catalog record for this book is available from the British Library.

Extracts from Emile Durkheim, "The Nature and Method of Pedagogy," trans. Sherwood D. Fox, are edited and reprinted with the permission of The Free Press, a division of Simon & Schuster, from *Education and Sociology* by Emile Durkheim, translated by Sherwood D. Fox. Copyright © 1956 by The Free Press.

Engenio Montale's "Words," translated by G. Singh, from *Eugenio Montale: New Poems,* is reprinted by permission of New Directions Publishing Corporation.

"Pedagogy and the Academy: 'The Divine Skill of the Born Teachers' Instincts,'" by Mariolina Salvatori, in *Pedagogy in the Age of Politics: Writing and Reading (in) the Academy,* ed. Patricia A. Sullivan and Donna J. Qualley, is reprinted with permission of the National Council of Teachers of English. Copyright © 1994, NCTE.

To Romano, Pia, and Olga
who live my life
whose lives I live
with love

Contents

Preface   *xi*
Acknowledgments   *xix*
Introduction: Chronicle of a Search   *I*

Part One
OF PEDAGOGUES AND PEDAGOGY,
PEDANTS AND PEDANTRY   11

DOCUMENTS

Encyclæpedia Britannica; or, a Dictionary of Arts and Sciences, by a Society of Gentlemen in Scotland	22
Noah Webster, *A Compendious Dictionary of the English Language*	22
Joseph E. Worcester, *A Universal and Critical Dictionary of the English Language*	23
The Encyclopaedic Dictionary, ed. Robert Hunter and Charles Morris	24
The Century Dictionary, ed. William Dwight Whitney	26
Walter W. Skeat, *An Etymological Dictionary of the English Language*	29
Gabriel Compayré, "Pedagogy," in *La grande encyclopédie inventaire raisonné des sciences, des lettres et des arts par une société de savants et de gens de lettres,* trans. Stephen Brett Sutherland	29
A Cyclopedia of Education, ed. Paul Monroe	34
The Encyclopaedia and Dictionary of Education, ed. Foster Watson	38
Dictionary of Philosophy and Psychology, ed. James Mark Baldwin	38
Webster's New Dictionary of Synonyms	39
Meyers Grosses Konversations Lexicon, trans. Thomas Ernst	40
Joseph T. Shipley, *Dictionary of Word Origins*	43
Funk & Wagnalls New Practical Standard Dictionary of the English Language, ed. Charles Earle Funk	45
Grande dizionario enciclopedico, trans. Mariolina Salvatori	45

The New Century Dictionary of the English Language, ed. H. G.
   Emery and K. G. Brewster   48

The Oxford Dictionary of English Etymology, ed. C. T. Onions   49

Oxford American Dictionary, ed. Eugene Ehrlich, Stewart Berg
   Flexner, Gorton Carruth, and Joyce M. Hawkins   50

A Dictionary of Education, ed. Dereck Rowntree   50

Chambers Twentieth Century Dictionary, ed. E. H. Kirkpatrick   51

The Barnhardt Dictionary of Etymology, ed. Robert K. Barnhardt   51

The Oxford English Dictionary   53

Part Two
EARLY ARTICULATIONS OF PEDAGOGY 59

DOCUMENTS

Emma Hart Willard, *A Plan for Improving Female Education*   74

James Gordon Carter, *Essays upon Popular Education with an
   Outline of an Institution for the Education of Teachers*   81

Samuel Read Hall, *Lectures on School-Keeping*   85

Almira Hart Lincoln Phelps, *Lectures to Young Ladies*   95

Calvin Ellis Stowe, "Normal Schools and Teachers' Seminaries"   103

Caleb Atwater, *Essay on Education*   114

"A New Jersey Teacher's Contract" (1841)   121

David Perkins Page, *Theory and Practice of Teaching; or, The
   Motives and Methods of Good School-Keeping*   122

Baynard Rush Hall, *Teaching, a Science: The Teacher, an Artist* 128

Henry Barnard, "Introduction," "Connecticut," and "Topics for
   Discussion and Composition on the Theory and Practice of
   Education"   132

"1872 Rules for Teachers"   142

Karl Rosenkranz, *Pedagogics as a System,* trans. Anna C. Brackett 143

William Bentley Fowle, *The Teacher's Institute; or, Familiar Hints
   to Young Teachers*   155

Karl Rosenkranz, *The Philosophy of Education,* ed. William Torrey
   Harris, trans. Anna C. Brackett   162

Intermezzo   167

_____

DOCUMENTS

George Gary Bush, "The Education of the Freedmen"   173

A. J. Steele, "Normal-School Work Among the Colored People"   177

Albert Salisbury, "Discussion"   182

A. D. Mayo, "The Training of the Teacher in the South"   185

"Report of the 'Chicago Committee' on Methods of Instruction, and
    Courses of Study in Normal Schools," Thomas J. Gray, chairman   190

W. T. Harris, "Letter of Transmittal"   198

Thomas Gray, "The Normal-School Idea as Embodied in the Normal
    School at St. Cloud"   200

J. P. Gordy, "Chairs of Pedagogy"   209

"The Relation Between Theory and Practice in the Training of
    Teachers"   216

Levi Seeley, "The Relation of Theory to Practice in the Training of
    Teachers"   218

Eliphalet Oram Lyte, "The State Normal Schools of the United
    States"   224

                        Part Three
          PEDAGOGY IN THE ACADEMY   233

_____

DOCUMENTS

William T. Harris, "Chairs of Pedagogics"   254

Albert Bushnell Hart, "The Teacher as a Professional Expert" 257

William Harold Payne, Contributions to the Science of Education
    and The Education of Teachers   261

Paul Henry Hanus, "The New Department of Pedagogy at Harvard
    University"   272

Josiah Royce, "Is There a Science of Education?"   275

Charles De Garmo, "The Herbartian System of Pedagogics"   290

Arnold Tompkins, The Philosophy of Teaching   295

Col. Francis Wayland Parker, Talks on Pedagogics   302

Emile Durkheim, "The Nature and Method of Pedagogy"   311

Charles Alexander McMurry and Frank Morton McMurry, The
    Method of the Recitation   317

x CONTENTS

William James, *Talks to Teachers on Psychology* 323

Burke Aaron Hinsdale, *A History of the University of Michigan* 330

Felix Emanuel Schelling, *Pedagogically Speaking: Essays and Addresses on Topics More or Less Educational* 335

Notes *345*
Works Cited *365*

Preface

> At times I think of the right subject matter of the book to be written as something that already exists: thoughts already thought, dialogue already spoken, stories already learned, places and settings seen; the book should be simply the equivalent of the unwritten world translated into writing. At other times, on the contrary, I seem to understand that between the book to be written and things that already exist there can be only a kind of complementary relationship: the book should be the written counterpart of the unwritten world; its subject should be what does not exist and cannot exist except when written, but whose absence is obscurely felt by that which exists, in its own incompleteness. . . .
>
> If I think I must write *one* book, all the problems of how this book should be and how it should not be block me and keep me from going forward. If, on the contrary, I think that I am writing a whole library, I feel suddenly lightened: I know that whatever I write will be integrated, contradicted, balanced, and amplified, buried by hundreds of volumes that remain for me to write.
>   —Italo Calvino, *If on a winter's night a traveler,* tr. William Weaver

Over the years, I have transformed these passages from *If on a winter's night a traveler* into a kind of talisman. I have appropriated Calvino's words and made them appropriate to my project. In careful handwriting I copied them onto a sheet of paper that since then—a bit smudged, a bit faded—sits pasted on top of the first of what are now several boxes of more or less chronologically arranged documents on pedagogy. Calvino's passages—or, should I say, the sustaining strategies the passages allowed me to weave—served me well. Every time I opened any of these boxes to reread the documents, to rearrange them, to add new ones, every time I posited the possibility of alternative lines of inquiry, I drew strength from my reading of Calvino's paradox: "If I think I must write *one* book, all the problems of how this book should be and how it should not be block me and keep me from going forward. If, on the contrary, I think that [my work may lead others to write on this subject so as to inaugurate] a whole library, I feel suddenly lightened: I know that whatever I write will be integrated, contradicted, balanced, amplified, buried by [all the] volumes that remain [to be written]."

Like the subject matter of Calvino's book—of any book—the subject matter of the books (the library) on pedagogy that wait to be written already exists; but unlike Calvino's, the thoughts, dialogues, stories, places, and settings of the book(s) I want to make possible (for me or others) to write have already been "written," have already been recorded, though they are not widely read. Thus, as far as my project is concerned, the philosophical and theoretical issues that "the already existent" subject matter of pedagogy forces me to confront have little to do with how to demonstrate and to celebrate the perennial virtuality of the unwritten. The philosophical and theoretical issues that confront me have to do with how to propose a reading of dominant accounts of education in the United States that will highlight how and why they leave the subject matter of pedagogy, its past, unwritten. Why this past, about which important and interesting records abound, is generally passed over in silence, discarded, ignored, or distorted is a question that any discipline concerned with the formation, reception, and exchange of knowledge might profitably engage.

A project of this scope is an ambitious and difficult one, particularly in the ambit of current critiques of what it means to write about history, and especially when, as in the present case, that history is framed by and frames the foreignness, the ex-centricity of the subject who tries to write about it. Therefore, in this volume, I settle for a modest goal: a provisional beginning. What I submit to my readers is a selection of excerpted documents that testifies to pedagogy's past. In the introduction and in the essays that precede the four groups of documents, I begin to make visible some of the questions that have compelled me to look for that past, have enabled me to give it a voice—as the German hermeneuticist Hans-Georg Gadamer (1975, 1976) would say—and to recognize the relevance of the stories it can tell. Hopefully, these initial questions, and the additional questions they might lead to (mine and others'), will productively complicate current reductive constructions of the nature and the function of pedagogy.

The more challenging goal—the pedagogy library housing several volumes that will integrate, contradict, balance, and amplify *this* beginning—is a collective one, and one for which I do hope this volume might function as a catalyst.

The textual field within which I have been working is constituted by remarkably different materials: dictionary and encyclopedia entries; addresses to legislatures on the establishment of normal schools; government documents on normal school history; National Education Association (NEA) proceedings on the status of normal schools in the South; arguments for the establishment of courses in pedagogy at the university; and theoretical constructions of pedagogy by its proponents and its critics.

How I have entered and transversed this field—what I have looked for and seen, what I have found or not found, the connections I have established—is to a large extent a function of my cultural assumptions about pedagogy and the questions such assumptions have compelled me to raise. Why are *pedagogy* and *pedagogue* such contested terms in U.S. culture at large, but especially in the university milieu? Why did pedagogy as a university discipline live such a brief life? Why has pedagogy come to be generally identified as *practice,* either divorced from *theory* or inadequate to contest or revise it? How does this opposition construct theory's and theorists' field of influence and responsibility? How, on the other hand, does this opposition construct the function and the status of teachers as *practitioners?* What accounts for either the tradition of vituperation that has marked the use of these terms, or the attempts to replace them with *education* and *educators* in the 1890s? And after decades of being out of fashion, what on the other hand accounts for their recent reversal of fortune (in the 1970s to 1990s) signaled, for example, by their presence in titles of papers given at Modern Language Association meetings in the last ten years, or in titles of influential books by publishers that do not specialize in composition or education (two contexts with which pedagogy is usually automatically associated)? What changes have occurred in our understanding of pedagogues and pedagogy that justify the current ubiquitousness of these terms in journals of composition, education, literature, and other disciplines? What new understandings about knowing, teaching, and learning justify and authorize allowing pedagogy, this itinerant discipline, back into the halls of the academy?

I have divided the materials that have enabled me to engage these and other questions into four clusters. For each cluster I have composed an introductory essay that proposes a particular reading of them.

In "Introduction: Chronicle of a Search," I give an account of what motivated this study, of the questions that led me to enter this textual field, of a few crucial turning points in the investigation I undertook.

In "Part One: Of Pedagogues and Pedagogy, Pedants and Pedantry," taking issue with widespread cultural constructions of *pedagogue* as a synonym for *pedant,* and of *pedagogy* as a synonym for *pedantry,* I call attention to some of the ways in which U.S. dictionaries and encyclopedias can be said both to reflect and to shape these negative associations, and consequently both to reflect and to shape pedagogues' and pedagogy's disciplinary and institutional marginalization. The dictionary and encyclopedia entries I have collected record a lengthy tradition of condescension toward pedagogy and pedagogues. In light of this tradition, I argue, current positive and constructive uses of these terms—in the field of radical education, in English studies, and in other disciplines—risk being written off as a matter of trend, as fad, unless the reasons for their present valorization and (more importantly) their past deprecation are carefully researched, theorized, and historicized.

In "Part Two: Early Articulations of Pedagogy," I suggest a reading that acknowledges the crucial role of normal schools in constituting and disseminating the study of pedagogy as the teaching of teaching, as the study of theories *and* practices of teaching considered necessary to adequately prepare teachers for their profession. I focus on the period that goes approximately from the 1820s, which mark the establishment of the first private normal schools, to the 1880s, which mark the establishment of courses in pedagogy at the university level. Out of the many texts examined, I select and excerpt those that give a sense of the terms and the ways in which the need for normal schools and the teachers they would provide were argued. To assess how the work planned for normal schools would actually be carried out in schoolrooms, I have identified and analyzed texts that record theoretical constructions of pedagogy designed for that purpose.

Many rich and problematic stories echo through these texts. There is the story of the extraordinary expectations placed on teachers and the general cultural reluctance to provide for their intellectual preparation (in the form of adequate preparatory institutions) and material needs. There is the story of teachers who unwittingly participated in setting up expectations they could not ultimately meet as they claimed for themselves powers that, being natural ("tact," "talent") or divine ("inspiration"), could not be adequately taught. And there is the story of early normal school professors who, attentive to the intersection of theory and practice in their teaching, provide early rigorous theorizations of pedagogy as "reflexive praxis" (a concept I develop in the introduction). Their work disputes those totalizing narratives that, in the 1880s, began to argue for the inadequacy of normal schools "to educate" teachers (cf. Payne in part three) because of their exclusive and limiting reliance on "methods" (which reduced teachers to mere implementors of somebody else's theories). As all these stories intersect, they raise provocative questions about the reasons for the waning of these institutions, about the silence that came to cloak pedagogy's disciplinary past, and about whether or not university professors of pedagogy enriched its theory and practice, as it was claimed they would.

Between part two and part three is a transitional section. The cluster of documents from the 1888 *NEA Proceedings* that I group in "Intermezzo" brings to the foreground some of the challenges that normal school professors of pedagogy, especially in the South, were still facing and trying to address toward the end of the century. Read individually, or side by side with the excerpts from the *Second Year-Book of the National Society for the Scientific Study of Education* and the government reports on the history of normal schools, these documents complicate representations of normal schools and their faculty as a- or anti-theoretical. To the extent that they remind us, disturbingly, of earlier discussions of the problems and the promises of teacher education, these documents urge us both to reflect on the magnitude of the challenges confronting proponents of pedagogy throughout the nineteenth century (our challenges are no less daunting) and to resist dismissive constructions of pedagogy, of its practitioners, and of the work done within its original institutional sites.

In "Part Three: Pedagogy in the Academy" I try to understand and to reconstruct the debate about pedagogy's "nature" and its rights to academic citizenship. The terms of the debate, which took place in the last two decades of the nineteenth century, were whether pedagogy could or should be defined as *art* or *science*. The definition, as we shall see, was neither inconsequential nor disinterested. Those who defined pedagogy as art argued that to teach well was a matter of instinct, tact, and inspiration. Their argument was an attempt to invalidate the need for a systematic study of pedagogy, so that pedagogy neither could nor should be granted disciplinary status. In opposition to this definition of pedagogy, another emerged, pedagogy as science, wherein science was appealed to in order to justify pedagogy's disciplinary status and to secure the right to academic citizenship for it and for its proponents.

Cast in these terms, the debate was not productive. It generated acrimony, factions, and institutional divisions. Nevertheless, it is important to return to it, since the oppositions that it generated inhibited a necessary and penetrating exploration of the function of pedagogy in every discipline that concerns itself with the construction and sharing of knowledge.

The period I have chosen to investigate goes from the 1820s to the 1920s. The first date allows me to record the establishment of the first private normal schools and to consider a time when the need for rigorous theoretical constructions of pedagogy became apparent (See Samuel R. Hall, part two). As to the 1920s . . . frankly, that date allows me to include and spotlight the excerpt from Felix E. Schelling's *Pedagogically Speaking* (1929). At the very beginning of this study, when I tried to identify texts on pedagogy, the title of his book was one of the very few that would use *that* word (cf. the introduction). I recall my excitement and my expectations when I came across that title, and later my perplexity at Schelling's vituperative statements about pedagogy and pedagogical matters. Perplexing at first, his text was nevertheless instrumental in leading me to consider different investigative lines to follow.

All things considered, however, I could have included some of his statements in the introduction, and let go of them. But I did not, and this is why: I want the specific bias of his perspective on pedagogy and pedagogues to be assessed and engaged by readers at the very end of my study, in light of the documents I have collected. Schelling, who in 1914 served as MLA president, was a respected and engaging scholar. How many students and colleagues did he inspire to view pedagogy in his terms? How many respected, engaging, and influential scholars today take a similar position toward pedagogy? With what consequences, and for whom? As the last document in this volume I hope the excerpt from Schelling's text will bring the reader both back—to the 1890s, to trace and reexamine the theoretical sources and the institutional interests that constructed the views of pedagogy Schelling so eloquently expressed—and forward, to the 1990s, to assess whether and how pedagogy's status in the academy has changed, and how much more it ought to change.

The historians of education who most helped me in understanding and finding my bearings through the textual field within which I have been working are Lawrence A. Cremin (especially *American Education: The National Experience, 1783–1876; American Education: The Metropolitan Experience, 1876–1980;* and *The Transformation of the School: Progressivism in American Education, 1876–1957*); Merle L. Borrowman (in particular *Teacher Education in America: A Documentary History* and *The Liberal and the Technical in Teacher Education*); Walter S. Monroe (*Teaching-Learning Theory* and *Teacher Education, 1890 to 1950*); and Sol Cohen, who in *Education in the United States: A Documentary History* (5 vols.) provides a mine of invaluable and exciting information about the rich U.S. educational past. The textual fields of these authors and mine often intersect and overlap, but our readings of the materials are different, since the questions about pedagogy I raise do not concern them.

Ed School: A Brief for Professional Education, by Geraldine Jonçich Clifford and James W. Guthrie, has proven most encouraging and inspiring. This work began as an institutional history of the Department of Education at Berkeley and became in the process a comparative study of ten leading schools of education. As far as I know, Clifford and Guthrie are the only historians of education sensitive to the ways in which pedagogy has been written off even within departments and schools of education. (An interesting study in contrast is provided by Robert H. Beck's *Beyond Pedagogy: A History of the University of Minnesota College of Education*—a telling title.)

The work by Marrou, Bonner, and Lodge—historians of Greek and Roman culture—and by lexicographers Urdang and Landau has sustained me at moments when, as I attempted to imagine the chapter on dictionaries and encyclopedias (a particularly difficult one to compose), I doubted the advisability of doing so. The complex theorizations of pedagogy responsible for the influential work of Ann E. Berthoff, Louise Rosenblatt, and David Bartholomae; the extraordinary work produced by those graduate students in our department who have chosen to meet pedagogy's challenge; the encouragement and advice of Jean Ferguson Carr, a colleague who has a passion for historical work—have all challenged me to pursue this project. At the same time, the search for composition's past recently undertaken by John Brereton, Robert Connors, and JoAnn Campbell, and the close-up look at the materials at the base of one's theoretical argument that Gerald Graff and Michael Warner dared publish in *The Origins of Literary Studies in America: A Documentary Anthology*, have persuaded me of the usefulness of publishing these documents as a way of making visible the "origins" of my argument. Some of the questions Graff raises in *Professing Literature: An Institutional History* (see especially "The Generalist Approach"), I believe, complicate and can be productively complicated by the argument I construct and the documents I make available in *Pedagogy: Disturbing History*.

Finally, Raymond Williams's *Keywords: A Vocabulary of Culture and Society*, which does not include *pedagogue, pedagogy, pedants,* or *pedantry,* has encouraged me to do the work I did in part one and throughout this book to suggest the relevance of the history of these terms to an understanding of U.S. education, culture, and society. Later in the process of constructing this book, the volume *Critical Terms for Literary Study* (edited by Frank Lentricchia and Thomas McLaughlin) encouraged me to persevere. The fact that, for example, *pedagogy* is not one of the critical terms whose invisibility needs to be made visible (3); and even more, the fact that pedagogy in McLaughlin's introduction is never named as the place, the context, the *forma mentis* that produces the exciting and reflexive questions he raises about theory (all I could think, as I was reading it, was, "these are the questions that pedagogy as reflexive praxis would demand that theorists, teachers, and scholars engage at all times") suggested that perhaps the time is right for the kind of work I offer here.

Acknowledgments

As I try to imagine what it will feel like when I finally hold this book in my hands, I think of all the people, occasions, and contexts that are part of it but that no system of citation can adequately record. I am indebted to Ann E. Berthoff and Louise M. Rosenblatt, strong theorists, resilient women whose understanding of pedagogy has inspired and sustained me. And I am indebted to David Bartholomae, William E. Coles, and Marcia Landy, whose work has shaped and continues to shape mine in ways they might not recognize.

Much of what became this project began about fifteen years ago in spirited and reflexive talks about teaching held at lunchtime on the seventeenth floor of the Cathedral of Learning at the University of Pittsburgh. Though this meeting place is no more, the people with whom I met hold a special place in my mind and my heart. Carolyn Ball, Paul Bové, Stephen Leo Carr, Laura Dice, Aeleen Frisch, Kathryn T. Flannery, Paul Kameen, Shawn Monagle, Margaret Shaw, Monette Tiernen: thank you—the ideas you gave me, the thoughts you made me think run deep through this book.

My work in print is always intimately connected with my work in the classroom; this book is an extension of and a return to a very special course I teach: the literacy and pedagogy seminar, which over the years has provided me with opportunities to clarify and to revise my conceptualization of pedagogy. Carolyn Ball, Ellen Bishop, Donna Dumbar-Odum, Rashmi Bathnagar, Claire Connors, Jeff Galin, Linda Jordan, Barbara McCarthy, Richard Miller, Christine Ross, Julia Wagner, Patricia Wysor, and, later on, Nancy Atkins, Kit Ayars, Gary Calpas, Pow Chee Chen, Bianca Falbo, Angela Farkas, Phillip Flynn, Jack Giles, Jean Grace, John Nichols, Wayne C. Peck, Lisa Schwartz, Ann Stafford, Stephen B. Sutherland, Julie Turner, Matthew Willen, James Zukowski: I am grateful for what you taught me. Special thanks to those of you who brought the work you did in the seminar to bear on your dissertations.

Several friends have sustained my work on this project since its very inception. Marilyn DeMario, Paul Kameen, Patricia Donahue, Kathryn Flannery, Jean Ferguson Carr, Mike Rose, and Phillip Smith read rough drafts, listened to emerging thoughts, contributed insights, urged me not to give up; Anna

xix

Maria Bartoletti energized me with her enthusiasm: I couldn't ask for more precious friends and colleagues. Several people made invaluable contributions as research assistants: Christine Ross, incomparable finder, always knew where to look and what to look for; Liz Marshall and Paula Noyes gave generously of their time and intelligence; Steve Sutherland, an integral part of this project, provided smart advice and loving support.

I owe a special debt of gratitude to my editors: David Bartholomae, who in his rare intellectual honesty never painted a less than realistic picture of the difficulties my project might encounter but gave me, nevertheless, his trust and encouragement; and Jean Ferguson Carr, for the glee on her face when we talked about this book, for knowing before I did the shape it would take, for helping me to imagine how to give my research provisional closure; to the University of Pittsburgh Press readers, Geraldine Clifford and John Brereton, for their insightful comments and for suggesting that this book be published; to Kathy McLaughlin and Catherine Marshall, at the University of Pittsburgh Press, for their courtesy and hard work.

Most of the research for this book was done at Rollins College, in Winter Park, Florida, thanks to special borrowing privileges from Dr. Grant, and to the interest, support, and generosity of Gertrude F. Laframboise, archives specialist, and Dr. Kathleen J. Reich, director of archives and special collections. Trudy and Kate let me enter the archives, and became my friends at a time of dislocation. And finally, this book could not have been put together without the emotional and time investment of Olga Salvatori who many times saved her mother and her mother's writing from what seemed to be inevitable computer-induced death.

Most of all, thanks to Romano, Pia, Olga, John, Giulia, and Maria Rosaria for their love, confidence, and support.

Pedagogy

Introduction

Chronicle of a Search

Throughout my research for this project, and in twenty years of professional life, I have been struck over and over again either by a widespread, peculiar, and unrestrained hubris on the part of the academy toward pedagogues and things pedagogical—in which case what pedagogy and pedagogues do, can do, should do, is defined *for* them; or by a lack of knowledge about and understanding of what even the terms mean. That there are historical precedents for this does not justify continuing this uncritical tradition, particularly at times, like the present, when a widespread circulation of the terms marks an apparently heightened awareness of pedagogy's potential to address the intricate educational issues that confront us.

A glance at how the term and the concept of *pedagogy* (less frequently, pedagogue and pedagogist) has been deployed in academic discourse in the last twenty years or so points out considerable confusion about its nature and function, and a peculiar lack of attention to the historical reasons responsible for that confusion. Since (approximately) the 1970s, its valorization has taken place *mainly* within the field of composition and radical education (though patterns are changing, now), which might have to do with the publication of Paulo Freire's *The Pedagogy of the Oppressed* (1968). Generally speaking, even in these fields, the term is often used to refer to "teaching," or "practice," in which case the expression *pedagogical practice* seems redundant. More and more frequently, however, the term *pedagogy* seems to be deployed to designate a theoretically informed alternative to mechanical conceptualizations of teaching or instruction. In this case, the expression *pedagogical practice* suggests a teacher's commitment to teach in ways that are consistent with, in fact that are the enactment of, her theories of reading, writing, and thinking. A need to widen pedagogy's sphere of influence seems to be signaled by the proliferation of such phrases as *liberatory pedagogy, critical pedagogy,* and *radical pedagogy*. But the fact that pedagogy's positive valence is pegged on the adjective—critical, liberatory, radical—seems to underscore its perceived conceptual inadequacy (cf., for example, Simon 1992). Moreover, even when the term or concept *pedagogy* is invoked by "radical educators" as an alternative to approaches to teaching dominant in the academy, the past that led to pedagogy's demise is often so de-historicized that their move runs the risk of losing credibility.

1

A case in point. In *Getting Smart: Feminist Research and Pedagogy With/in the Postmodern,* the issue of pedagogy is at the center of Patti Lather's project:

> Like [Gayatri] Spivak (1989b), I position pedagogy as a fruitful site for learning strategies of a postmodern praxis. *In the interest of accessible language,* I had given thought to replacing the word pedagogy with the word teaching in the title of this book until I read David Lusted's 1986 article in *Screen* entitled, "Why Pedagogy?" Lusted defines pedagogy as addressing "the transformation of consciousness that takes place in the intersection of three agencies—the teacher, the learner and the knowledge they produce" (p. 3). According to Lusted's definition, pedagogy refuses to instrumentalize these relations, diminish their interactivity or value one over another. It, furthermore, denies the teacher as neutral transmitter, the student as passive, and knowledge as immutable material to impart. Instead, the concept of pedagogy focuses attention on the conditions and means through which knowledge is produced.
>   Arguing for the centrality of the issue of pedagogy to both cultural production and the popularization of critical analyses, Lusted sees the disattention, the 'desperately untheorized' (p. 3) nature of pedagogy as at the root of the failure of emancipatory objectives. While he cites Stuart Hall and Michael Young, Lusted appears unfamiliar with *the American literature on radical pedagogy,* a small but vibrant literature in both feminism (e.g., Culley and Portuges, 1985; Bunch and Pollack, 1983; Shrewsbury, 1987) and Neo-Marxism (Giroux, 1983; Shor, 1980; Freire, 1985). Nevertheless, Lusted brings to the center stage of cultural studies the interactive productivity as opposed to merely transmissive nature of what happens in the pedagogical act. (1991, 15, emphasis mine)

It seems odd that in the language necessary for Lather to construct her quite *smart* feminist critique with/in the postmodern, *pedagogy* should prove to be a troublesome term. It is not clear whether Lather is concerned that the term might make her work inaccessible because of its recondite meaning, or because of the negative valence it carries. The decisive factor in Lather's adoption of the term was, she states, a 1986 essay—"Why Pedagogy?"—by David Lusted, a British theorist of film studies, who convinced her of the necessity to adopt the term so as to identify a teaching that is other than merely transmissive (that is, other than the "banking concept of education" Freire described in 1968 in *The Pedagogy of the Oppressed*).[1]

To read Lusted's essay is to recognize that although Lusted, like Lather, constructs a cogent argument for pedagogy, that argument is peculiarly dehistoricized. In the opening paragraphs, Lusted elegantly summarizes several "stories" of pedagogy and misconceptions that have contributed to its lamentable reputation. Having asked "*Why should pedagogy* be of interest to anyone?" he rehearses some of the reasons why it is not:

Few are familiar with the term. Even aficionados gag on its pronunciation and falter on its spelling. Where the word is familiar at all, it's most often in the shape of "pedagogue," conjuring mental images of the mortar-board and cane, Bash Street Kids and Mr. Chips (Michael Redgrave rather than Peter O'Toole), connoting pedantry and dogmatism.

Indeed, even among elite realms of thought, pedagogy is taken as coterminous with teaching, merely describing a central activity in an education system. The invisibility of pedagogy in education and cultural production generally is well matched by the imprecision of dictionary definitions which relate pedagogy variously to teaching as an agency, a profession or a practice.

Within education and even among teachers, where the term should have greatest purchase, pedagogy is under-defined, often referring to no more than a teaching style, a matter of personality and temperament, the mechanics of securing classroom control to encourage learning, a cosmetic bandage on the hard body of classroom contact.

So, is there any useful purpose in investigating a term so incoherent and unacknowledged?

Why is pedagogy so important? (Lusted 1986, 3).

According to Lusted, the term *pedagogy* (rather than *teaching, education, or instruction*) is important because "it draws attention to the *process* through which knowledge is produced." Though he is specifically concerned with examining and redefining the function of pedagogy in film, TV, and culture studies education, what he says is eminently applicable to any scene of instruction:

The central question here is how adequate the theorization of film, TV, culture in general can be without a consciousness of the conditions which produce, negotiate, transform, realize and return it *in practice*. What pedagogy addresses is the process of production and exchange in this cycle, the transformation of consciousness that takes place in the interaction of three agencies—the teacher, the learner and the knowledge they together produce. (3)

Lusted's conceptualization of pedagogy assigns pedagogues an important role. Insofar as pedagogy's function *is not* the transmission of immutable knowledge but instead "the interaction of three agencies—the teacher, the learner and the knowledge they together produce," pedagogues ought to be theorists who rigorously and responsibly practice the theories they espouse. Moreover, they ought to understand that they and their theories are not the sole "origins" or repositories of knowledge (knowledge is produced by the interaction of three agencies), and they need to practice that belief with intellectual integrity. This means, among other things, that pedagogues need to begin their investigations "where students are," not in condescension or as a beginning to be quickly left behind, but with a passion and an intellectual curiosity about how students think and the language they use to think, that might lead them to recognize in their students' work telling examples of knowledge formation. By assigning to teachers, learners, and the knowledge they *together* produce the role of agencies, Lusted deftly destabilizes the hierarchical system that assigns differential powers, values, and roles to theorists and teachers, teachers and students, theoretical knowledge and practical knowledge, and teachers' knowledge and students' knowledge.

What leads Lusted to this exciting and (potentially) powerful conceptualization of pedagogy? Nothing more, nothing less, I think, than the fact that the future of TV, film, and culture studies and their responsibility to educate depend, as he astutely points out, on methods of teaching that demystify the "process through which knowledge is produced." I fully agree. Unless teachers are able and willing to demystify the processes of knowledge formation and reception that constitute different theories (a function remarkably different from the "implementation of theory function" that teachers are usually assigned), theories will remain sophisticated bodies of knowledge inaccessible to and unaffected by those (students, the public) whose consciousness they are supposed to transform. Theories and theorists become hermetic, incapable of sharing the knowledge they can produce—which depletes rather than strengthens theories' and theorists' function.[2] This is a point that I have repeatedly argued—in print as well as in the classroom—in my work, work that is both shaped by and shapes my conceptualization of pedagogy as *reflexive praxis*.[3] What I particularly value about this definition of pedagogy is the inextricability of theory and practice that *praxis* conveys.[4] But because *praxis* can become inflexible, and blind to the possibility that the *nexus* of theory and practice might become an imprisoning knot, I think it is necessary for pedagogy to be reflexive. This means that a teacher should be able and willing to interrogate the reasons for his or her adoption of a particular theory and be alert to the possibility that a particular theory and the rigorous practice that enacts it might be ineffectual, or even counterproductive, at certain times or in certain contexts.[5]

Lusted's insight about the radical transformative power of pedagogy is valuable. Unfortunately, teachers, at any level, cannot become by fiat the kind of pedagogues Lusted expects them to be. The theorization and valuation of teaching that would make that possible is dependent on a radical transformation of what teachers' preparation and teachers' responsibilities, within every discipline, are assumed to be. And the potential for such transformation depends on a cogent and rigorous critique of the various ideological rationalizations that, especially in large research universities, mainly assign and confine pedagogy qua teaching, and its hygiene, to devalued members of the academy. If pedagogy is to fulfill the function Lusted (re-)claims for it, the coercive and constitutive power that the academy has had in articulating such intellectually devalued functions for it (pedagogy as transmission of knowledge, teaching style, cosmetic bandage, etc.) and in demarcating its space of operation needs to be unravelled. Because Lusted does not expose how pedagogy's diminished functions came to be constructed, his attempt to assign a positive valence to a term that, as he points out, is still burdened with negative traces is ultimately puzzling. And it could be ineffectual, since the reasons and myths responsible for pedagogy's and pedagogues' peculiar reputation are left in place, readily available to whoever will want to oppose or abort the educational changes necessary to accomplish Lusted's encomiable goals.

Like Lusted, I am aware of the "imprecision of dictionary definitions" of pedagogy, its "invisibility in education and cultural production," and the differences that mark its various discourses. But having tried to conjecture the reasons for the imprecisions, and the invisibility, and the differences, I am in a position to suggest that Lusted's and Lather's and many other radical educators' critique of current educational practices would gather strength if they could contest and unravel the apodictic force of stories that, for example, automatically and uncritically reinscribe the close identity between a pedagogue and a pedant; or feed the notion that pedagogy is either an art so pure, so high, as to be unteachable, or a craft so lowly, so mechanical that any manual could teach it. I believe it is important to expose how and where these "stories" were produced so as to make it difficult for pedagogy's critics not to confront their own perhaps unself-conscious vested interest in continuing to assign to it merely a transmissive, didactic, and ancillary role. It is my hope that this book might contribute to the beginning of such a critique.

To this end, I have collected documents that bring together for the first time in one volume cultural, theoretical, institutional, and political constructions of pedagogy, constructions that are either scarcely known or not widely circulated among both proponents and critics of pedagogy. These texts, and the further texts they can lead us to uncover or to produce, should complicate current conceptualizations of pedagogy, especially those that sustain the distinction—ossified over time into an increasingly untenable stereotype—between the intellectual preparation, and the concomitant function, that sets the scholar apart from the teacher. This separation of functions, often invoked to demarcate a hierarchy of intellectual capabilities and connected powers, had its historical reasons.[6] In the 1880s, for example, it served to justify the establishment of departments of pedagogy at the university level as centers for the education of teachers that would advance the "liberal" discovery and production of knowledge. These new and supposedly more sophisticated and comprehensive departments of pedagogy were advertised as being different from and in opposition to departments of pedagogy in normal schools, the first publicly funded institutions for the preparation of teachers that for complex economic, political, and ideological reasons came to be identified essentially with "pragmatic" and "professional" (a term with a hint of the mercenary) goals.[7] My research suggests that in the following decades, however, for equally complex economic, political, and ideological reasons, the distinction between the liberal (with its supposedly exclusive attention to scholarship) and the professional (with its supposedly exclusive attention to teaching) also demarcated, within universities, the opposition between departments of English and departments of pedagogy. The latter, housed initially within departments of philosophy and psychology, later became departments of education and subsequently schools of education.

Since then, it seems, this opposition has been kept firmly in place, one of the most lamentable consequences being that it has allowed and continues to allow many university professors of English to be dogmatically critical and dismissive of *all* work done in *all* schools of education, especially of "teacher preparation," which gets to be constructed not only as the main function and responsibility of such schools, but also as a marker of difference between the "mission" of schools of education and of departments of English.[8] In the name of this difference English departments have historically legitimated a lack of systematic attention in their various graduate programs to (a) courses that will prepare graduate students to fulfill their teaching responsibilities at the college and university level in their areas of expertise as well as in areas about which they might have less specialized knowledge; (b) and in undergraduate programs to courses that might begin to prepare undergraduates who plan to go on to teach high school English. The devastating irony, as I see it, is that although university departments of English are *in* the business of teaching, indeed are kept in the business *by* teaching, very few elect to make teaching, and even less the teaching of teaching, *their* business and responsibility.[9]

As a member of a department of English—though fortunately of one that does make teaching and the teaching of teaching its business—I am interested in calling attention to some of the questionable rationales that historically have allowed English departments to look at teacher preparation with suspicion, derision, and condescension. I am interested in calling into question the widely circulated and anachronistic assumption that thorough and scholarly knowledge of subject matter constitutes automatic and sufficient preparation for teaching it. And I am interested in asking that we consider, squarely and honestly, what the consequences are, and for whom, of constructing pedagogy as something so "natural" or "elementary" as to make the study of it superfluous or arbitrary. And, finally, I am interested in suggesting that it might be both timely and productive for English departments to pay closer attention to those institutional and ideological moves that by replicating reductive conceptualizations of pedagogy do not make pedagogy worthy of those *collective critical investigations* that in the last twenty years or so have so effectively called into question the disciplinary marginalization of so many other subjects of study.

I believe an investigation of the historical precedents that foster dismissive attitudes toward pedagogy must begin with the recuperative gesture, one that aims at recapturing a version of pedagogy's past that will make such dismissals problematic and self-indicting.

A composite text, the documents I have selected in this volume can be emplotted to tell different, even competing stories—stories that, hopefully, will lead to critical interrogations of what gets to be called, praised, or dismissed as pedagogy. How I came to look for, to select, and to arrange these documents into a plot structure that, as the title of this volume suggests, both represents and can be deployed as a "disturbing history" of pedagogy, is itself as story of, and for, critical interrogations and analyses. It is a story of a research that was propelled and framed by certain persistent questions that only recently have I begun to read as potentially positive markers of my cultural deracination, as an Italian in an American English department.

Unclearly formulated at first, belying a brooding sense of uncertainty about the nature of what I knew and its value in a foreign academic context whose historical formation, cultural traditions, and biases I was in no position then to fully comprehend, these questions, markers of a difference I tried to suppress, haunted me for years.

I began to ask them when, as a foreign graduate student in a Department of English, I was disoriented, and often silenced, by negative responses to my professed interest in pedagogy. In no uncertain terms, mentors and colleagues who cared about my professional future told me to be careful about my choices, lest I be identified as a "School of Education" person—a warning that at the time did not fully register, both in terms of what it meant and how it had come to mean what it meant. Though at the time I neither had the courage nor the authority to fully articulate it for my own and others' benefit, I was operating from within a conceptualization of pedagogy that made it the sine qua non of *any* teacher's professional life: I conceived of pedagogy as an always already interconnected theory and practice of knowing, that in order to be effective must "make manifest" its own theory and practice by continuously reflecting on and deconstructing it.[10] What my skeptical interlocutors mostly named as pedagogy, I realized, was—within my conceptual frame-work—actually didactics, an integral part of pedagogy that, when divorced from the theory of knowing that motivates it, produces approaches to teaching that shun a teacher's and a student's critical reflexivity on the act of knowing and promote the reduction of somebody else's method of knowing into a sequential schematization of that method (Salvatori 1988, 1989, 1991).[11]

It was only when I chose to become involved with the study and the teaching of composition that my interest in pedagogy became both valued and expected. But its being valued and expected, I was soon to find out, signified one thing to compositionists and something else to literary theorists. Moreover, my conceptualization of pedagogy, of what pedagogy could and should be, usually struck most people in both fields as being either idealistic, or foreign, ex-centric or extravagant.

When I was about to conclude that my questions were both anachronistic and nonautochthonous, that I was approaching the issue of pedagogy with speculative and evaluative criteria that were ultimately inapplicable because determined by my foreign cultural formation, I "sighted" a rare entry on pedagogy. The entry, written by E. N. Henderson, professor of philosophy and education at Adelphi College, for the 1913 edition of *A Cyclopedia of Education,* confirmed the plausibility of the questions I had been asking. The entry acknowledges what I had all along suspected and had begun to problematize: the connotation of "lack of esteem, if not contempt" historically associated with both the status of the *pedagogue,* usually a slave, and with the education of children, a task generally assigned to servants and women since it was deemed not to require special education. More importantly, the entry suggested a direction for my research that I had not imagined it would take. According to Henderson, even when the nascent science of child psychology gave pedagogy new status and, in the last decades of the nineteenth century, contributed to pedagogy's acceptance as a university subject and discipline, so persistent were the negative connotations attached to the term that is was thought advisable to substitute the term *education* for *pedagogy.* "The newer 'education' differs from the old 'pedagogy' in two respects. First it includes *more than method in teaching and school management;* second it is *more scientific"* (Henderson 1913, 622, emphasis added).

To know that *pedagogy* had been renamed *education* proved extremely helpful for my research. To begin with, it helped me to make sense of the unexpected difficulty I encountered in my first attempts even to identify titles that would display the word pedagogy. But more importantly, it helped me to construct that difficulty as an area of investigation that became this book's project.

As I tried to uncover the reasons for this particular renaming, I found myself turning and returning to two specific protracted moments in the history of American education. The two periods are, approximately, the 1840s–1850s and the 1880s–1890s. The first period roughly corresponds to the theorization of the function and the establishment of the domain of public normal schools. The second period roughly coincides with the theorization of the function and the establishment of the domain, at the university level, of chairs and departments of pedagogy, which after 1990 were renamed departments of education and later became schools of education.

Most historical accounts and synopses of American education, I discovered, connect these two periods in casual and progressive terms: they date the beginnings of a systematic theory of education, i.e., pedagogy, to the 1840s, and locate those beginnings in normal schools; but they also single out the 1880s–1890s as the period that marks the coming of age of education as a science in the universities. These accounts, in other words, pay normal schools and pedagogy an ambiguous tribute. While they recognize in normal schools' theories and practices of pedagogy the historical antecedents of education, they also construct those antecedents as already and always in need of remediation. More disturbingly, from my perspective, by paying little attention to the terminological change, or by recording it as relatively inconsequential, these celebratory accounts simultaneously cover over and reproduce the reasons and the conditions that marked the reduction of pedagogy's function and domain, from a discipline and field of study to mere teaching, mere implementation.

As I read these historical accounts, I kept questioning—unconsciously at first, and later from a consciously framed oppositional stance—the obscure(d) relations between what I saw as an uncritically accepted and disseminated terminological substitution, and the indictment of normal schools marked by that substitution.[12] By disrupting the naturalizing logic both of available historical documents (Henderson's entry is a case in point) and of more concealed ones, I found myself hypothesizing an alternative account both of normal schools' work, and of the coming of age of education as a science. Part two and part three, respectively, map out such readings.

Historical research in these two sites, however, did little to alleviate my disorientation about another renaming, the synonymization of *pedant* for *pedagogue,* and of *pedantry* for *pedagogy.* Once more it was an encyclopedia that suggested a path to follow. *The Encyclopedia and Dictionary of Education* (1922) offers no entry on either pedagogy or pedagogue; however, it records "PEDAGOGICAL INSTITUTE, CHILE" and immediately below, "PEDANTRY."[13] I was struck by what the encyclopedia included as much as by what it left out. To find out whether or not this might have been an isolated case, I began to look for similar significant absences, replacements, connections, and confusions in other dictionaries and encyclopedias. As I did so, I began noticing interesting patterns, which then led me to focus specifically on the differences between, on the one hand, American and British sources and, on the other, Italian, French, and Spanish ones.[14] That search produced the argument that I map out in the introduction to part one concerning some of the possible reasons for this synonymy, its consequences, and the role of dictionaries in shaping pedagogy's and pedagogues' cultural and institutional marginalization.

Part One

Of Pedagogues and Pedagogy, Pedants and Pedantry

There is nothing so pedantic as pretending not to be pedantic.
—William Hazlitt, *The Plain Speaker*

Pédanterie, n.f. Langue class caractère, attitude du pédant: La pédanterie est un vice d'esprit et non pas de profession.
—*Logigue de Port-Royal,*
quoted in *Grand Larousse Encyclopédique*

words
are everyone's property and in vain
do they hide in dictionaries,
for there is always a rouge
who digs up the rarest
and most stinking truffles.
—Eugenio Montale, "Words"

In my early attempts to trace and to understand the formation and the dissemination of negative constructions of pedagogy, I turned to dictionaries and encyclopedias.[1] I did not set out to undertake an exhaustive investigation: I simply wanted to gather some evidence of what I suspected were corruptions or transformations of meaning that would explain why in U.S. culture (or at least in particular sectors of it) pedagogy is frequently written off as nonscholarly, technocratic, implementational, and a- if not anti-theoretical. My initial desire was to set things straight: I wanted to expose what I saw as a fundamental etymological or conceptual (or both) "error" in U.S. usage of the term, an error that might be responsible for the circulation of what I considered inadequate and ultimately limiting constructions of pedagogy. As the boundaries of my investigation widened, from dictionaries and encyclopedias to the few texts on pedagogy I was able to locate, to the times and institutions within which those texts were written, learned, and taught (see part two), to other times and institutions in which those texts were targets of derision (see part three), and to other sites; and as my research criteria became sharper and more organized, my focus shifted from *demonstrating that* to *demonstrating why*. I moved, that is, from wanting to demonstrate that common understandings of pedagogy in the United States were at variance with their European antecedents, to *conjecturing* which possible forces might have contributed to shaping such understandings and to *hypothe-sizing* why the reasons for these differences have not so far been deemed worthy of inquiry. What I began to realize, with increasing clarity and confidence, was that the cultural construction of pedagogy as not worthy of scholarly research was itself in need of scholarly research.

As I routinely returned to the first data of my research, the dictionary and encyclopedia entries on pedagogy, the function of these educational apparatuses in reporting, constructing, disseminating, and controlling a particular capital of knowledge became more and more perceptible: I began to pay methodical attention to how the language of dictionary and encyclopedia entries wove a network of covert and overt links within and between their various definitions, between those definitions and the specific historical circumstances they referred to, and within historical narratives of education. As I worked with these texts, I began to see how dictionaries—both commercial and scholarly—had participated in shaping pedagogy's cultural and institutional marginalization in this country.

In the following pages, I try to reconstruct the reading that led me to this conclusion. I focus, especially, on the nexus of synonymity that certain entries establish between *pedant* and *pedagogue, pedantry* and *pedagogy,* and on the same or other entries' relative inattentiveness to recording the representation of the pedagogue as a slave valued by and valuable to those who owned him because of the knowledge he could teach.

I offer the following reading as a possible way of moving through and making sense out of the various entries I collect in this section. It is my hope that this reading will generate further readings of the documents I have collected in this volume, that it might lead to the uncovering of more documents about pedagogy's past, and that it might produce responses that will lead to productive revisions and complications of my argument. It is also my hope that, as an important corollary, this reading might function as a reminder of how difficult it is to test and to contest the authority of dictionaries and encyclopedias, a difficulty that in most classrooms is too frequently insufficiently attended to and theorized.

The following cluster of current dictionary entries offers a provocative text about how dictionaries shape and transmit meanings and values, while they also reflect actual usages.[2]

pedagogue. 1. A teacher; schoolteacher. 2. A person who is pedantic, dogmatic, and formal. Also *pedagog, paedagogue.* [ME *pedagoge*⟨L *paedagog(us)*⟩⟨GR *paidagogos* a boy's tutor].

pedagogy. 1. The function or work of a teacher; teaching. 2. The art
or method of teaching.
> *The Random House Dictionary of the English Language,* 1967

pedagogue, n. a pedantic, dogmatic teacher. Also *pedagog.*
pedagogy, n. the art or science of teaching.
> *The Random House Dictionary,* paperback edition, 1980

pedagogue, n. 1. A schoolteacher; educator. 2. One who instructs in
a pedantic or dogmatic manner [ME pedagoge ⟨OFr⟨Lat paeda-
gogus⟨Gk paidagogos: pais, boy + agogos, leader⟨agein, to lead].
pedagogy, n. 1. The art or profession of teaching. 2. Preparatory
training or instruction.
> *The American Heritage Dictionary,* 1969

pedagogue, n. A schoolteacher [⟨GR paidagogos, teacher, trainer (of
boys)]
pedagogy, n. The art, profession, or study of teaching.
> *The American Heritage Dictionary,* paperback edition, 1970

The first *RHD* entry (1967) provides two definitions of *pedagogue.* The
first definition, a denotative one, marks the use of the term as a noun desig-
nating the occupation of teachers in general, schoolteachers in particular
(rather than, for example, college and university professors). The second
definition, a connotative one, charges the term with negative qualities (pedantic, dogmatic, formal). However, such negative qualities are not specifically ascribed to teachers, but rather to a person, any person, who displays
them.[3]

The second *RHD* entry (1980) constructs a different picture. By eliding
the generic "person" (cf. "A person who is pedantic"), and by collapsing the
space between two definitions that serve two different functions (denotative
and connotative), this entry produces a synthetic definition that limits the
attribution of pedantry and dogmatism *to teachers only* (see Landau on *genus,*
quoted above in n. 2). At the same time, the definition suggests that a teacher
is only called a pedagogue if/when he is pedantic, but a pedagogue is always
already a pedantic teacher (see Landau on *differentia,* quoted above in n. 2).

Like the first *RHD* entry, the first *AHD* entry (1969) provides both a denotative and a connotative definition of *pedagogue.* The *AHD* entry, however,
introduces *educator* as an alternative to, or additional meaning for, schoolteacher. Compared with the *RHD* entry, the *AHD* entry seems to expand,
rather than contract, the semantic field of the term, since *educator,* in its
general meaning, is a term applicable to any teacher, from grade school to

the university level. But when the entry on *pedagogue* is juxtaposed to the entry on *pedagogy* in the same dictionary, a possible interesting clue surfaces about the formation and the implications of this particular meaning (i.e., pedagogue as educator):

> **pedagogy:** n. 1. The art or profession of teaching. 2. Preparatory
> training or instruction.

As practitioners of pedagogy, pedagogues are located within the space of preparatory schools (teachers' colleges, departments and schools of education). To juxtapose this entry with the entry on pedagogy from *A Cyclopedia of Education* (in this volume) is to foreground the paradox that *pedagogy,* a term from which "educators" at the turn of the century had deliberately distanced themselves in an effort to improve their status in the academy, is reassociated with them (cf. the introduction and part two). In light of dominant constructions of normal schools, teachers' colleges, and departments and schools of education, the lexicographic definition can be read as an organized signification that records and perpetuates a highly charged hierarchical difference.

Both the *Random House* and the *American Heritage* dictionaries establish a semantic link with *pedant* in the second definition of *pedagogue.* However, in their paperback editions, it is clear that *AHD* and *RHD* operate according to different rules (at least in this case) as to which meanings should or can be retained in the inevitable process of reduction that produces paperback editions. Sidney Landau remarks in *Dictionaries: The Art and Craft of Lexicography,* that "desk dictionaries" and "paperback or 'pocket' dictionaries" not only contain many fewer entries than college and unabridged dictionaries; they differ from them, respectively, because etymologies, if and when given, "are in telescoped form" and definitions "are often little more than strings of synonyms" (19). Given their distribution and the nonspecialized readership they are targeted for, it seems to me that in the case of *pedagogue,* *AHD*'s decision to withold its association with *pedant* results in articulating an etymologically more accurate definition of this term than the one *RHD* forges and disseminates.

It is plausible to argue that the different views and expertise of lexicographers (see, for example, *AHD*'s definition of pedagogy, one that historicizes it in a closer past) might be partially responsible for the lack of agreement on definitions of *pedagogue* and *pedagogy.* But it is also important not to underestimate the effect that policy and managerial decisions have on the ordering of meanings (whether "obsolete" meanings are to precede or to follow "common" ones), or the effect that the fusion of primary and secondary and denotative and connotative meanings may have had on the formation of these definitions. (The argument is obviously not confined to the terms in question.)

A cursory comparison of the *Oxford English Dictionary*'s and *The Century Dictionary*'s entries on *pedagogue* suffices to foreground the consequences that inevitable decisions about the size of a dictionary may have on dictionaries' functions as cultural authorities and legislators. By recording meanings in historical order, the *OED* offers, *first,* nonnegative definitions of *pedagogue* ("A man having the oversight of a child or youth"; "an attendant who led a boy to school"), and positive ones (pedagogue as a metaphor for divine law; see, also, St. John's example under *pedagogic*). It is only under the *second* meaning that the *OED* simultaneously expands (in relation to the term's original historical usage) and limits (in relation to its future usages) the application of the term to schoolmasters, teachers, and preceptors, and that it records current contemptuous and hostile uses of the term and its association with pedantry, dogmatism, or severity. The *CD,* the American contemporary of the *OED* and its competitor, telescopes into one meaning the historical definition of the term, elides its positive religious usage, and highlights instead its current usage as a contemptuous synonym for *schoolmaster,* that is, "dogmatic and narrow-minded teacher."

The influence of the *CD* on subsequent American dictionaries may explain widespread contemptuous understandings of pedagogue. But the question of how pedantry and dogmatism came to penetrate the semantic field of *pedagogue* and contributed to the diffusion of that contemptuous meaning still needs to be answered. The *OED*'s and *CD*'s entries on *pedant* suggest a possible explanation.

The *OED* gives as uncertain the Italian origin of *pedante*:

> The origin of the It. is uncertain. The first element is app. the same as in peda-gogue, etc.; and it has been suggested that *pedante* was contracted from a med.L. *paedagogant-em*, pr. ppl. of *paedagōgāre* to act as a pedagogue, to teach (Du Cange); but evidence is wanting.
>
> (*OED* 1988–1928)

Though the *OED* also records the use of *pedant* as a synonym for *pedagogue* ("a schoolmaster, teacher, or tutor"), it clarifies that such usage is not necessarily derogatory ("often without implication of contempt"). The *OED*'s second meaning for pedant refers to a *person* rather than a schoolteacher.

The *CD* gives an etymological analysis of the term that coincides with the *OED*'s; however, it stresses neither the uncertainty of the Italian term's origin nor the isomorphism between *peda*gogue and *ped*ant. Moreover, it cites these authoritative illustrative examples for the term:

A domineering pedant *o'er the boy.*

Shak., *L. L. L.,* iii. 1. 179. (CD 1899)

He loves to have a fencer, a pedant, *and a musician seen in his lodgings a-mornings.*

B. Jonson, *Cynthia's Revels,* ii, 1. (CD 1899)

It is worth pondering about the extent to which Shakespeare's and Jonson's influence might have affected the decisions of those lexicographers who subsequently chose not to factor in the uncertainty of the etymological link between pedant and pedagogue, thus contributing to a transhistorical overlapping of the terms and to disseminating negative definitions of pedagogue.

If we look at how French, Italian, and Spanish—three of the European romance languages within which *peda*gogue and *ped*ant are of common usage—record these terms, we notice a different evaluation. Although dictionary and encyclopedia entries in these languages acknowledge the lexicographic link *peda-* as *probable,* they neither readily juxtapose nor blur the two terms.

Grand Larousse Encyclopédique, for example, defines pedantry as "a vice of the spirit, not of the profession" (un vice d'esprit et non pas de profession). Rather than being a synonym for schoolmaster or teacher, then, a pedant denotes a "person who expounds knowledge which is often superficial and who condescendingly corrects others" (personne qui fait étalage d'une science souvent superficielle, qui reprend les autres sur un ton plein de suffisance). In its pejorative connotation, a pedant is "a man of the academy rather than a man of the world" (l'homme de collège, par opposition à l'homme du monde). The same source defines pedagogue as a "servant who instructs, raises children" (maître qui instruit, qui élève des enfants), but also as "a person who has [knows] the art of teaching" (personne qui a l'art d'enseigner). In its pejorative connotation, a pedagogue is defined as one who "parades his knowledge, and/or adopts a dogmatic tone" (celui qui fait parade de sa science, qui adopte un ton dogmatique). The entry also records the use of "principalis paedagogus" as the title for the heads of the colleges in the ancient university of Paris; and, it points out, the pejorative connotation attached to the term is to be traced to the criticism of medieval universities by Renaissance humanists.

DeVoto and Oli's *Dizionario della lingua italiana* records a rare use of *pedante* as a term of encomium: "a person whose elevated diction demonstrates knowledge of and respect for linguistic traditions and rules" (una eletta accu-

ratezza nel rispetto della tradizione linguistica e nell'esercizio dello stile). Deserving attention is the fact that DeVoto and Oli give as *archaic* the use of
pedant for preceptor, or instructor, and trace this convergence of meanings
to the popularity of a sixteenth-century comic character who would speak a
language replete with literary otiosities and Latinisms. (See entries on "Pedante" and on "Pedantesca, lingua, poesia.")

The *Diccionario enciclopedico abbreviado*'s definition of pedant, as a noun, is:
"a teacher who taught grammar to children, going home" (Maestro que ensen-
aba a los niños la gramatica, yendo a las casas). The definition stresses the
literal meaning of "going on foot" (ped-ante) but does not charge it negatively.
On the other hand, the *Diccionario*'s definition of pedant as an adjective connotes ridiculous conceit, and vain and inopportune display of fake or actual
erudition (aplicase al que por ridiculo engreimiento se complace en hacer ino-
portuno y vano alarde de erudicion, tengala o no en realidad). However, it
does not suggest that these characteristics are exclusive to teachers.

Even on the basis of this cursory comparative analysis, it is evident that in
French, Italian, and Spanish cultures, surely because the etymological differences are more readily and widely perceivable, the meanings of pedagogue
and pedant are less likely to be *confused* (as in "fused together"). In the case
of these terms, French, Italian, and Spanish dictionaries and encyclopedias, by
simultaneously recording and disseminating their differentiated origins, contribute to a more affirmative valuation of pedagogues, their discipline, and
their profession.[4]

Of my observations so far, Landau (*Dictionaries: The Art and Craft of Lexicography*) might argue that they exemplify the "pedantic," unjustified, inappropriate response of anybody who, having a special interest or expertise in
a particular field, expects knowledge of that field to be adequately and amply
represented in dictionaries. Insofar as the charge of pedantry is often levied
against those who perceive and can trace the consequences of certain intellectual and linguistic imprecisions, I choose to run the risk of being dismissed
as a pedant.

Discussing anti-Black or anti-Semitic (and elsewhere, sexist) accusations
raised against lexicographers for their inclusion of terms deemed offensive,
Landau's explanation for such decisions is that "the lexicographer can only
claim to be objectively reporting usage. The language expresses bias toward
these and other groups because large numbers of people over protracted
periods of time have felt the need to express these biases. The inclusion of
offensive terms in a dictionary is a record of this fact" (295). Landau's argument, typical of lexicographers, needs to be complicated. Precisely because,
as he himself points out, dictionaries are often granted unconditional author-

ity, the incredible responsibility that dictionaries carry needs to be carefully and sensitively handled; they are not supposed to prescribe usages, only to record them. Yet recorded negative or incorrect usages not only reflect and reveal widespread practices, they also justify and reinforce their continued dissemination and reproduction (for a similar argument, cf. Kenneth Cmiel 1990, 227–32). If to make such a choice puts lexicographers in an untenable position, then perhaps teachers could contribute to checking some of the problems that a lexicographer's commitment to recording usages can give rise to. Students and the public at large could be alerted to various sets of restrictions that make dictionaries approximate and fallible—not quite the objective canonizing apparatuses they are often believed to be.

The formation and dissemination of the lexical and semantic confusion between *pedant* and *pedagogue* in U.S. dictionaries is in and of itself an interesting phenomenon, one that invites reflection on dictionaries' role and function in communicating knowledge. But even more interesting are the consequences of that confusion, insofar as it grants the figure of the pedant extraordinary prominence within the language of and about education, a prominence that overshadows, indeed covers over, the representation of the pedagogue as a figure of trust, affection, and respect.[5]

Historical accounts of the role and status of the pedagogue in Greek and Roman cultures portray him as a trusted slave who supervised, in loco parentis, the activities and behavior of the young boy (and often of the whole family's brood, including girls, in which case he was given the assistance of a nurse or handmaid) at home, in school, and on his way from one to the other.[6] Though the description identifies his task as specifically "the one who leads the child" from home to various teaching establishments and back, he was also and above all the one who led the child in moral and civic matters. To the Athenians, the pedagogue was an "educational agent" who exercised full control over his charge from when the boy was six until he was eighteen (Eby and Arrowood 1940, 235). A "mixture of nurse, footman, chaperon, and tutor" (Freeman, quoted in Eby and Arrowood 1940, 235), the pedagogue was often a respected figure "among well-regulated families, as on the stage in Greek tragedy" (Bonner 1977, 38). According to Marrou, "in Hellenic Greek παιδαγωγός loses its etymological sense of 'slave companion' and begins to take on the modern meaning of the word 'pedagogue'— someone who is an educator in the full sense of the word" (1956, 144). To be sure, available accounts do not warrant asserting that pedagogues were consistently worthy of trust and respect; however, they justify calling into question characterizations that consistently and categorically demean them.

With the spread of the Roman Empire, Greek pedagogues became an important part of Roman education.[7] Such was their reputation as protectors, trainers in good manners, and supervisors and directors in matters of school that Roman parents did not hesitate entrusting their children to them. Though the Romans also had a tradition of custodial care for their children, one that trusted household slaves carried out, Greek pedagogues, particularly in wealthy families, increasingly took over that task because of their advantage over slaves born in Roman households: they spoke and, often (if they were well educated), they could teach Greek. Not all pedagogues were equally qualified to be good (language) teachers; but this clearly had less to do with their being pedagogues than with their having a limited education.

As a sign of appreciation for their services, Romans would often grant freedom to their pedagogues, who would then be able to offer their services for pay. One of the training establishments where they practiced their skills was the *paedagogia,* ironically a school for the proper training of young slaves, the *paedagogiani.* In their function as teachers of these slaves, the freed pedagogues were called "pedagogues of the slave-staff" (*paedagogi puerorum*). Not infrequently, those who were taught within these establishments would eventually open and run schools of their own when they received freedom later in life (Bonner 1977, 45–46).

There is, then, a lot more to be said about pedagogues than the common tale of their being just escorts of children or pedantic schoolteachers: and yet these are the two representations that most commonly circulate in U.S. culture. It might be interesting to speculate whether early practices of slavery in this country might have had something to do with the fact that many dictionaries elide knowledge of the pedagogue-teacher as a (former) slave. (Frederick Douglass eloquently exposed white people's fear of educated freedmen.) Whether or not there is a connection, and whether or not it might be possible to document it, it seems at least appropriate to argue that the absence, in U.S. culture, of an affectionate and respectful aura around the pedagogue may have made it possibly more easily and unproblematically to dismiss the role and the function of pedagogues. The attribution of pedantry to pedagogues—through the etymological convergence of *pais* and *peda*—may have turned to farce and ridicule, and thus deflected attention from, the enslaved condition of early pedagogues, their knowledge, and the possibility for that knowledge to be deployed as currency toward (relative) freedom. An investigation of the ideological, cultural, and economic blockages that might have filtered and impeded the rooting of this concept in U.S. soil is an important subject of study—but it exceeds the scope of this volume and certainly of this chapter.

The dictionary and encyclopedia entries I have discussed so far record two of the most widely circulated constructions of pedagogues and pedagogy in U.S. culture: (a) the devaluation of the terms when they are understood as synonyms for pedants and pedantry, and (b) the lack of esteem for the professional education of teachers often conveyed by the use of pedagogues and pedagogy as negative epithets for practitioners and practices of teacher education. To say that in contrast with American entries, French, Spanish, and Italian definitions accord pedagogues and pedagogy greater estimation, which is connected with greater etymological precision, is not to set up an invidious cultural comparison nor a charge of willful semantic aberration. Rather, it is to encourage a break from past practices by advocating critical precision in the use of terms and concepts chosen to describe the fundamental activities of the teaching profession, and to suggest the importance and the usefulness of exposing the subtle and insidious processes by which these cultural representations, inimical to teachers, have acquired widespread cultural authority. Can these processes be rechannelled? And if so, how? Is the mobilization of counterhegemonic definitions and interpretations of pedagogy sufficient, in and of itself, to bring to crisis devalued conceptualizations of pedagogy that are in circulation? What kinds of political, economic, cultural, and institutional changes must obtain for these conceptualizations to be granted credibility and to bring about change?

As I stated earlier, current positive usages of the terms *pedagogue* and *pedagogy* can be read as signs of a renewed appreciation of the role of teachers and of the function of teaching, especially in academic contexts that for ideological, economic, and institutional reasons have for (too) long assigned them secondary importance. But as positive and constructive as these usages are, they risk being written off as a matter of trend, of fad, unless the reasons for their current valorization, but more importantly, for their past deprecation are not carefully researched, theorized, and historicized.

In part two I begin to map out an area of investigation for such a project by collecting, and suggesting a way of discussing, documents that challenge the conceptual and institutional devaluation of normal schools as sites of learning that were compromised, as Henderson's entry suggests, by their theoretical and practical concern with pedagogy.

Documents

In this section I have collected what I consider significant and representative examples of dictionary and encyclopedia entries on *pedagogue, pedagogy, pedant,* and *pedantry.* In my introductory essay, I suggest how these educational apparatuses have participated in shaping pedagogy's cultural and institutional marginalization. Here I offer some of the materials that have helped me to formulate my hypothesis and come to my particular (provisional) conclusion. As I share these sources with my readers, I invite them to test and engage my argument as well as to propose alternative lines of investigation. And I invite them to return to these entries and the argument I weave out of them as they read on, but especially at the end, when the significance of individual entries and of the different representations of pedagogy they offer can be best appreciated in light of the other documents and of the readings I provide for them.

The entries can be read without the interpretive frame I provide. They can be used, for example, in undergraduate and graduate classrooms as a way of reflecting on, teaching, and theorizing the kind of reading that such authoritative sources as dictionaries and encyclopedias require; a reading that must test their authority, when necessary; a reading that in most classrooms is infrequently attended to and taught. A careful examination of these entries should disclose interesting differences—differences that a teacher can present as a provocative text about how these repositories and guardians of knowledge choose to go about their crucial function of shaping and transmitting meanings and values, while also reflecting actual usages.

I have arranged the documents chronologically to call attention to certain historical and cultural variations in the use of these terms. My main focus is U.S. sources, although I have examined British sources to establish lines of influence, and Italian, Spanish, Portuguese, French, and German ones to establish lines of divergence and to locate possible etymological origins for the widespread U.S. association between pedagogues and pedants.

Given the length of the foreign entries on pedagogy (a significant clue about its place in those cultures) and the limits of space I have had to reckon with, I have only provided brief (translated) excerpts from them. These entries are fascinating to read in their entirety and to compare with earlier and later editions. They are well worth a much more extended analysis and independent publication. For now, I hope the glimpses I offer of them will suffice.

From: *Encyclopædia Britannica; or, a Dictionary of Arts and Sciences, Compiled upon a New Plan. In which the different sciences and arts are digested into distinct treaties or systems; and the various technical terms, &c. are explained as they occur in the order of the alphabet. Illustrated with One Hundred and Sixty Copperplates. By a Society of Gentlemen in Scotland* (1761)

pedagogue, a tutor or master, to whom is committed the discipline and direction of a scholar.

pedant, is used for a rough unpolished man of letters, who makes an impertinent use of the sciences, and abounds in unseasonable criticisms and observations.

pedarian, in Roman antiquity, those senators who signified their votes by their feet, not their tongues; that is, such as walked over to the side of those whose opinion they approved of, in divisions of the house.

From: Noah Webster, *A Compendious Dictionary of the English Language* (1806)

ped'agogue, *n.* a schoolmaster, teacher, pedant

ped'agogue, *v. i.* to teach or tell superciliously

ped'agogy, *n.* the office of a pedagogue, discipline

ped'ant, *n.* one vainly ostentatious of learning

pedant'ic, *a.* like a pedant, conceited, vain, proud

pedant'ically, *ad.* in a pedantic manner

ped'antism, ped'antry, *n.* pedantic behavior

From: Joseph E. Worcester, *A Universal and Critical Dictionary of the English Language: To which are Added Walker's Key to the Pronunciation of Classical and Scripture Proper Names, Much Enlarged and Improved; and a Pronouncing Vocabulary of Modern Geographical Names* (1846)

pĕd-ạ-gŏg′ịc, *a.* Same as *pedagogical. Warton.*

pĕd-ạ-gŏg′ị-cạl, [pĕd-ạ-gŏj′ẹ-kạl, *Sm. R. Wb.;* pĕd-ạ-gō′jẹ-kạl, *Ja.;* pĕd-ạ-gŏḡ′ẹ-kạl, *K.*] *a.* Belonging to a schoolmaster. *South.*

pĕd′ạ-gọ-gĭṣm, [pĕd′ạ-gọ-jĭzm, *R. Wb.;* pĕd′ạ-gŏg-ĭzm, *Sm. K.*] *n.* Office or character of a pedagogue.

pĕd′ạ-gŏgue, (pĕd′ạ-gŏg) *n.* [παιδαγωγός.] One who teaches boys; a schoolmaster; a pedant. *Sir M. Sandys.*

pĕd′ạ-gŏgue, (pĕd′ạ-gŏg) *v. a.* [παιδαγωγέω.] To teach, as a pedagogue. *Prior.*

pĕd′ạ-gŏḡ-y, *n.* [παιδαγωγία.] The employment of a schoolmaster; teaching. *White.*

pē′dạl, [pē′dạl, *S. W. P. Ja.;* pĕd′ạl, *K. Sm.*] *a.* [*pedalis,* L.] Belonging to a foot. *Brande.*

pĕd′ạnt, *n.* [*pédant,* Fr.] A schoolmaster; a vain pretender to learning; one full of pedantry; a man vain or awkwardly ostentatious of his learning.

pẹ-dăn′tic, pẹ-dăn′tị-cạl, *a.* [*pédantesque,* Fr., from *pédant.*] Relating to pedantry or a pedant; resembling a pedant; ostentatious of learning.

pĕd′ạn-try, *n.* Character or quality of a pedant; awkward or vain pretension to learning; ostentation of learning; an obstinate addiction to the forms of some profession or line of life, with contempt of other forms.

†**pĕd′ạn-ty,*** *n.* An assembly of pedants. *Milton.*

pĕd′dle,* *v. a.* To carry about and sell; to retail, as a peddler. *Smart.*

pĕd′dlẹr,* *n.* One who peddles.

pĕd′ẹ-răst,* *n.* One addicted to pederasty. *Burney.*

pĕd′ẹ-răs-ty,* *n.* Unnatural love for boys. *Ash.*

From: *The Encyclopaedic Dictionary, a New, Original, and Exhaustive Work of Reference to All English Words, Their Origin, Development, Orthography, Pronunciation, Meaning, and Legitimate or Customary Use; Being also a Comprehensive Encyclopaedia of All Arts and Sciences, With Condensed Encyclopaedic Definitions of 50,000 Important Words and Topics, With Numerous Illustrations* (1896), Robert Hunter and Charles Morris, editors

pĕd-a̤-gŏǵ'-ĭc, *a.&s.* (Fr. *pédagogique,* from Gr. παιδαγωγικός (*paidagōgikos*), from παιδαγωγός (*paidagogōs*) = a pedagogue (q.v.); Ital. & Sp. *pedagogico.*)
A. *As adj.:* Pertaining or belonging to a pedagogue; suited for or characteristic of a pedagogue.
*B. *As subst.:* [PEDAGOGICS].

pĕd-a̤-gŏg-ĭc-a̤l, *a.* (Eng. *pedagogic;* -al.) The same as PEDAGOGIC (q.v.)

"That way forsooth was accounted boyish and pedagogical."—Wood: Athenæ Oxon; Chillingworth.

pĕd-a̤-gŏǵ-ĭcs, *s.* [PEDAGOGIC.] The art or science of teaching; pedagogy.

pĕd'-a̤-gŏǵ-ĭṣm, pĕd'-a̤-gŏg-uĭṣm, *s.* [Eng. *peda-gogue; -ism.*] The occupation, manners, or character of a pedagogue.

"Ink doubtless, rightly apply'd with some gall in it, may prove good to heal this tetter of pedagoguism."—Milton: Apol. for Smectymnuus, § 6.

pĕd'-a-gŏgue, *s.* [Fr., from Lat. *pœdagogus* = a preceptor, from Gr. παιδαγωγός (*paidagōgos*), from παῖς (*pais*), genit. παιδός (*paidos*) = a boy, and ἀγωγός (*agōgos*). = leading; ἄγω (*agō*) = to lead; Sp., Port., & Ital. *pedagogo.*]
*1. *Class. Antiq.:* A slave who led his master's children to school, places of amusement &c., until they became old enough to take care of themselves. In many cases the pedagogues acted also as teachers.
2. A teacher of young children; a school-master. (Used generally in contempt or ridicule.)

"Perhaps you will think me some pedagogue, willing by a well-timed puff, to increase the reputation of his own school."—Goldsmith: The Bee No. 6.

*pĕd'-a-gŏgue, v.t. [Lat. *pœdagogo,* from Gr. παιδαγωγέω (*paidagó-geö*) = to be a pedagogue (q.v.).] To teach as a pedagogue; to instruct superciliously.

"Wise Greece from them receiv'd the happy plan, And taught the brute to *pedagogue* the man."—*Somerville: To the Earl of Halifax.*

*pĕd'-a-gŏ̆ğȳ, s. [Fr. *pédagogie,* from Gr. παιδαγωγία (*paidagōgia*), from παιδαγωγός (*paidagōgos*) = a pedagogue (q.v.); Sp. & Ital. *pedagogia.*] The art or occupation of a pedagogue; pedagogism.

"He [Thomas Horne] was, for his merits and excellent faculty that he had a *pedagogy,* preferr'd to be master of the school at Eaton."—*Wood: Athenæ Oxon.,* vol ii.

pĕd'-ant, ped-ante, s. [Fr. from Ital. *pedante;* Sp. & Port. *pedante;* ultimate origin doubtful.]

*1. A schoolmaster, a pedagogue.

"A *pedant* that keeps a school i' th' church."—*Shakes.: Twelfth Night,* iii.2.

2. One who makes a vain display of his learning; one who puts on an air of learning; a pretender to superior knowledge.

"However, those *pedants* never make an orator."—*Goldsmith: Polite Learning,* eb. xiii.

pĕ-dăn'-tĭc, *pĕ-dăn'-tĭc-ạl, a. [Eng. *pedant; -ic, -ical*] Pertaining or relating to pedants or pedantry; making a vain display of learning; using farfetched words or expressions; characterized by pedantry.

"Then would, unroofed, old Granta's halls *Pedantic* inmates full display."—*Byron: Granta.*

pĕ-dăn'-tĭc-al-lȳ, adv. [Eng. *pedantical; -ly.*] In a pedantic manner; like a pedant.

*pĕ-dăn'-tĭc-lȳ, *pĕ-dăn'-tĭck-lȳ, adv. [Eng. *pedantic; -ly.*] In a pedantic manner; pedantically.

*pĕd'-ant-ĭşm, s. [Eng. *pedant; -ism.*]

1. The office or manners of a pedagogue.

2. Pedantry.

*pĕd'-ant-ĭze, v.i. [Eng. *pedant; -ize*] To act the pedant; to make a vain display of learning; to use pedantic expressions.

*pĕd'-ant-ŏc'-ra-çў, *s.* [Eng. *pedant;* Gr. κρατέω (*krateō*) = to rule. The rule or sway of a pedant or pedants; a system of government funded on mere book-learning. (*J. S. Mill*)

*pĕd'-ant-rў, *s.* [Fr. *pédanterie.*] [PEDANT]

1. The manners, acts, or character of a pedant; a vain display of learning; habitual use of pedantic expressions.

"*Pedantry* is all that schools impart, But taverns teach the knowledge of the heart."—*Cooper: Tirocinium, 212.*

2. Obstinate adherence or addiction of the forms of a particular profession, or of some particular line of life.

*pĕd'-ant-ў, *s.* [Eng. *pedant; -y*] Pedants collectively; a pedant.

"The *Pedanty* or household school-master" *Lennard: Of Wisdome,* bk. i., eb. xxxix.

From: *The Century Dictionary: An Encyclopedic Lexicon of the English Language* (1899), William Dwight Whitney, editor

pedagogue (ped'a̱-gog), *n.* [Also sometimes (with ref. to Greek usage) *pædagogue;* ⟨ F. *pédagogue* = Sp. Pg. It. *pedagogo,* ⟨ L. *pædago-gus,* ⟨ Gr. παιδαγωγός (see def. 1), ⟨ παῖς (παιδ-), a child, a boy or girl, ⟨ ἄγειν, lead, conduct, ἀγωγός, a guide or conductor. In def. 2, ⟨ OF. *pedagoge,* m., a schoolroom; cf. *pedagogy.*] 1. A teacher of children; one whose occupation is the instruction of children; a schoolmaster: now used, generally with a sense of contempt, for a dogmatic and narrow-minded teacher.

Among the Greeks and Romans the pedagogue was originally a slave who attended the younger children of his master, and conducted them to school, to the theater, etc., combining in many cases instruction with guardianship.

Time was, when th' artless *pedagogue* did stand
With his vimineous sceptre in his hand,
Raging like Bajazet o'er the tugging fry.
    Brome, On the Death of his Schoolmaster.

The *pædagogue* with the youngest son and the prostrate Niobide may be supposed to be on the right.—*A. S. Murray,* Greek Sculpture, II. 322.

2†. A schoolroom, or an apartment set apart as a schoolroom.

Another part [of the university] is what they call the *pedagogue,* which is for noblemen and gentlemen; there are six youths in each room, with a master over them.—*Pococke,* Description of the East, II. ii. 231.

pedagogue (ped'a-gog), *v. t.;* pret. and pp. *pedagogued,* ppr. *pedagog-uing.* [⟨ *pedagogue, n.*] To teach; especially, to teach with the air of a pedagogue.

This may confine their younger Stiles,
Whom Dryden *pedagogues* at Will's;
But never could be meant to tye
Authentick Wits, like you and I.
> *Prior,* To Fleetwood Shepherd, l. 81.

Grave eastern seers instructive lessons told;
Wise Greece from them receiv'd the happy plan,
And taught the brute to *pedagogue* the man.
> *Somerville,* To the Earl of Halifax.

pedagogy (ped'a-gō-ji), *n.* [Formerly also *pædagogy;* = F. *pédagogie* = Sp. *pedagogia* = Pg. It. *pedagogia,* ⟨ Gr. παιδαγωγία, the training or guiding of boys, education, ⟨ παιδαγωγός, a peda-gogue: see *pedagogue.*] 1. The art of the pedagogue; the science of teaching; pedagogics.

The tendency to apply the exact methods of science to problems of edu-cation is one of the most hopeful signs of present *pedagogy.*—*Science,* VI. 341.

2. Instruction; discipline.

He delivers us up to the *pædagogy* of the Divine judgments.—*Jer. Tay-lor,* Works (ed. 1835), I. 826.

The Jews were a people infinitely delighted with pompous and busy su-perstition, and had ordinances accordingly whilst they remained under that childish *pedagogy.*—*Evelyn,* True Religion, II. 181.

There was a sacrifice for the whole congregation prescribed in the Mo-saic *Pædagogy.*—*C. Mather,* Mag. Christ., Hist. Boston, 1698.

pedant (ped'ant), *n.* [= D. G. Dan. Sw. *pedant,* ⟨ F. *pédant* = Sp. Pg. *pedante,* ⟨ It. *pedante,* a teacher, schoolmaster, pedant; contracted ⟨ L. *pædagogan(t-)s,* ppr. of *pædagogare,* teach, ⟨ *pædagogus,* a teacher, pedagogue: see *pedagogue.*] 1. A schoolmaster; a teacher; a pedagogue.

A domineering *pedant* o'er the boy.
> *Shak.,* L. L. L., iii. 1. 179.

He loves to have a fencer, a *pedant,* and a musician seen in his lodging a-mornings.—*B. Jonson,* Cynthia's Revels, ii. 1.

2. A person who overrates erudition, or lays an undue stress on exact knowledge of detail or of trifles, as compared with larger mat-

ters or with general principles; also, one who makes an undue or inappropriate display of learning.

Such a driveller as Sir Roger, so bereft of all manner of pride, which is the characteristic of a *pedant,* is what one would not believe would come into the head of the same man who drew the rest of the play.—*Steele,* Spectator, No. 270.

He [James I.] had, in fact, the temper of a *pedant,* a *pedant's* conceit, a *pedant's* love of theories, and a *pedant's* inability to bring his theory into any relation with actual facts.—*J. R. Green,* Hist. Eng. People, vii. 3.

pedantic (pē-dan′tik), *a.* [⟨ *pedant* + *-ic.* Cf. D. G. *pedantisch* = Sw. Dan. *pedantisk.*] Of, pertaining to, or characteristic of a pedant or pedantry; overrating the importance of mere learning; also, making an undue or inappropriate display of learning; of language, style, etc., exhibiting pedantry; absurdly learned: as, a *pedantic* air.

We borrow words from the French, Italian, Latine, as every *Pedantick* Man pleases.—*Selden,* Table-Talk, p. 64.

He was a man of gallantry, and despised all that wore the *pedantic* appearance of philosophy—*Goldsmith,* The Bee, No. 2.

He [Baron Finch] had enjoyed high fame as an orator, though his diction, formed on models anterior to the civil wars, was, toward the close of his life, pronounced stiff and *pedantic* by the wits of the rising generation.—*Macaulay,* Hist. Eng., vii.

pedantry (ped′an-tri), *n.* [= D. G. *pedanterie* = Sw. Dan. *pedanteri,* ⟨ F. *pédanterie* = Sp. *pedantería* = Pg. It. *pedanteria;* as *pedant* + *-ry.*] 1. The manners, acts, or character of a pedant; the overrating of mere knowledge, especially of matters of learning which are really of minor importance; also, ostentatious or inappropriate display of learning.

Pedantry proceeds from much reading and little understanding. A pedant among men of learning and sense is like an ignorant servant giving an account of a polite conversation.—*Steele,* Tatler, No. 244.

Pedantry consists in the use of words unsuitable to the time, place, and company.—*Coleridge,* Biographia Literaria, x.

The more pretentious writers, like Peter of Blois, wrote perhaps with fewer solecisms, but with more *pedantry,* and certainly lost freedom by straining after elegance.—*Stubbs,* Medieval and Modern Hist., p. 153.

2. Undue addiction to the forms of a particular profession, or of some one line of life.

There is a *pedantry* in manners, as in all arts and sciences; and sometimes in trades. *Pedantry* is properly the overrating any kind of knowledge we pretend to. And if that kind of knowledge be a trifle in itself,
the *pedantry* is the greater.—*Swift,* On Good Manners.

From: Walter W. Skeat, *An Etymological Dictionary of the English Language* (1910; 1st ed. 1879–1882)

pedagogue, a teacher, pedant. (F.—L.—Gk.) In Caxton's Golden Leg-
end, St. Eutrope, § I.—MF. *pedagogue,* 'a schoolmaster, teacher,
pedant;' Cot.—L. *pædagogus,* a preceptor.—Gk. παιδαγωγός, at
Athens, a slave who led a boy to school, hence, a tutor, instructor.—
Gk. παιδ-, stem of παῖς, a boy; and ἀγωγός, leading, guiding,
from ἄγειν to lead. β. The Gk. παῖς is for παΓις, i. e. *pau-is,* from
a probable √PEU, to beget, whence L. *pu-er,* a boy, Skt. *pu-tra-,* a
son. The Gk. ἄγειν, to lead, is cognate with L. *agere,* whence E.
Agent, q. v. **Der.** *pedagog-ic; pedagog-y,* MF. *pedagogie* (Cot.).
PEDAL, belonging to the foot. (L.) '*Pedal,* of a foot, measure or
space;' Blount's Gloss., ed. 1674. '*Pedalls,* or low keyes, of or-
gans;' Sherwood, index to Cotgrave. Now chiefly used as a sb., as
the *pedal* of an organ, i.e. a key acted on by the foot.—L. *pedālis,*
1) belonging to a foot, (2) belonging to a foot-measure (whence the
old use, as in Blount).—L. *ped-,* stem of *pēs,* a foot; cognate with
E. **Foot,** q.v.

Pedant, a schoolmaster, vain displayer of learning. (F.—Ital.—Gk.?)
In Shak. L. L. L. iii. 179.—MF. *pedant,* 'a pedant, or ordinary
schoolmaster;' Cot. Borrowed from Italian (Littré).—Ital. *pedante,*
'a pedante, or a schoolemaster, the same as *pedagogo;*' Florio. β
Pedante is a pres. participial form as if from a verb **pedare,* which,
as Diez suggests, is probably not the MItal. *pedare,* 'to foote it, to
tracke, to trace, to tread or trample with one's feete' (Florio), but
rather **pædāre,* an accommodation of the Gk. παιδεύειν, to instruct, from παιδ-, stem of παῖς, a boy. See **Pedagogue.** Diez cites
from Varchi (Ercol., p. 60, ed. 1570), a passage in Italian, to the
effect that 'when I was young, those who had the care of children,
teaching them and taking them about, were not called as at present
pedanti nor by the Greek name *pedagogi,* but by the more honour-
able name of *ripititori*' [ushers]. **Der.** *pedant-ic, pedant-ic-al, ped-
ant-ry.*

From: Gabriel Compayré, ''Pedagogy,'' in *La grande
encyclopédie inventaire raisonné des sciences, des lettres et
des arts par une société de savants et de gens de lettres,* trans.
Stephen Brett Sutherland (1910)

pedagogy. I. Pedagogy has had some difficulty getting recognized: in
France at least, since, abroad, it has long been in favor. The word
''pedagogy'' all but shared the unfortunate fate of the word ''pedagogue,'' which, Littré said a few years ago, ''is most often taken
amiss.'' Even today they say it sounds bad to French ears. One uses
it only reluctantly. In primary teaching programs, among the materials taught in normal schools, we clearly see pedagogy and the
history of pedagogy unmistakably represented. But it is no longer
the same in higher education; and in those of our universities where
pedagogy is taught, either under a professorial chair (as in Paris),
or in classes and lectures (as in Lyon and Toulouse), it is officially
called ''science of education,'' not ''pedagogy.'' Yet pedagogy
claims to be precisely the science of education. It is not a case of
defining it, as Littré does, as ''the moral education of children'': it
encompasses all parts of education, physical, intellectual, as well as
moral. It is true that pedagogy is at once a science and an art, and
that it joins general and philosophical principles of education with
practical rules, methods and procedures of discipline and education;
and this no doubt explains why our universities, where the teaching
of education must remain above all theoretical, have still not accepted the name ''pedagogy.'' But the usage has gained more and
more acceptance—for want of another technical term that would
have been desirable, but is impossible to coin from the long word
''education''—so that ''pedagogy'' has been made the synonym
for the practical science of education, with its own double character: that of studying and raising children all at once; in the same
way that logic, at the same time science and art, studies and directs
reason, just as politics studies and governs men.

Noone would contest the fact that pedagogy exists. It has its history. Huge treatises, a multitude of journals, and entire dictionaries
such as M. Buisson's *Dictionnaire de pédagogie* are devoted to it. It
is taught in almost all countries. There are courses in pedagogy as far
away as the one at Japan's Imperial University in Tokyo. In American
universities, where they prefer to simply call it ''Education,'' there
are ''Departments of the science and art of teaching'' almost every-

where. There is even a doctorate in pedagogy in the United States, and, as preparation for it, the lower degrees of "bachelor" and "master of pedagogy." In certain normal schools (Philadelphia and Albany) the two years of study are dedicated solely to various parts of pedagogy, to the exclusion of all general, literary or scientific education: these are schools of pure pedagogy. Old universities, like Harvard, offer their students several courses in the history of theories and practices of education, in the application of psychology to education, and in the theory of teaching. And the most newly created universities are distinguished by their singular enthusiasm for the new science. Clark University, with its rigorously scientific character, has a school for pedagogical research: its president, Mr. Stanley Hall, publishes its results in an important periodical, *The Pedagogical Seminary*. Pedagogy, like all self-respecting science, has recourse to experimentation, and at the young Leland Stanford University in California Professor Earl Barnes has established a kind of experimental school for children between two and twelve years; something like a service for observing children, analogous to services that care for sick children which have always been organized in hospitals. With the same intention, the University of Lille in France has just created an "education laboratory." In Brussels, in the free University just as in the new University, there are courses in pedagogy. Almost all the Italian universities teach pedagogy, which is associated with the teaching of philosophy and anthropology or even literature. Finally, in Germany, where noone fears the word "Padagogik," there are at least eight universities where it is possible to study the science or practice of education: in Berlin and Strasbourg the renowned Frederic Paulsen and Theobald Ziegler give only theoretical lessons; it is the same in Gottingue; but in Leipzig, Iena, Heidelberg, Giessen and Halle practical exercises are added to theoretical teaching: students work in seminaries for practical pedagogy, for instance, in Iena they work in the seminary directed by Professor Rein.

There are such multiple proofs of pedagogy's vitality that one may consider it to be a definitely constituted science. Like all derived sciences, whose fate is tied to the advancement of the fundamental knowledge that they presuppose, pedagogy is still imperfect and always changing. Along with a rather large number of acquired truths which would withstand any critique, pedagogy also presents us with ongoing controversies and the problems involved in solving them. Granted, in the principles it proposes as general rules for the formation of intellect [esprit] and in the methods and processes it recommends for application, it has not always attained the degree of exact precision that would produce an incontestable certitude. . . .

As long as the fundamental sciences on which pedagogy depends remain themselves indecisive and uncertain, this state of indecision and incertitude will endure. These sciences are: psychology, physiology, ethics and sociology. Is it necessary to highlight this dependence? The science which claims to establish the laws of education, which would instruct and raise the child and form the man, cannot with certainty construct its inductions and deductions unless other sciences have taught it what man is, what child is—in body, in soul, in his individual nature and also in what he must be in terms of his destiny, his social role. Different pedagogical prescriptions correspond to different psychological conclusions: an idealist like Malebranche will not think about education in the same way as a sensualist like Locke. . . .

The path of education is being lit by the yet uncertain light of child psychology, a young science which is only the first chapter of a general psychology. We know the importance it has already acquired; it was first established by the observations of Darwin, extended in Germany by Preyer, and has been cultivated by a great number of psychologists in France, Italy, and in the United States—where it has become popular as ''Child study''. . . .

Study of the child is so much the order of the day that a new science, called ''pedology,'' needs to be classified and take its place in the catalogue of the sciences. We have already determined its object and its limits: it would be a pure science, free of practice and application: it would study the child, first in history and then in present times, among the uncivilized and civilized peoples; it would not disregard the study of abnormal and disabled children who lack certain wits, criminals, those abandoned vagabonds, etc.: but it would insist above all on the normal child, examined even before birth, describing in detail and from infancy its anatomy and physiology, feelings and perceptions, emotions and whims by analyzing its games, language and activity. To tell the truth, it does not seem that pedology, *paidology* as Americans spell it, could legitimately claim to constitute a distinct science: it is more like a dictionary of childhood, in which one might compile many facets of this subject; a collection of scientific fragments borrowed from history, psychology, physiology, and other disciplines. Its complex design encompasses so many things that no single expert could keep abreast of it or engage in such disparate kinds of research. In order to assure its own future, pedagogy must not count on pedology, even though it might thereby gain a few useful facts: it must count on the special sciences that we have enumerated; education cannot achieve its ideals except to the extent that pedagogues have first learned from the preliminary sciences about man's nature (physical and mental), his destiny, and his social role. . . .

In order to be understood and studied profitably, pedagogical doctrines therefore need to be placed back into the milieu in which they first arose. They are neither fortuitous opinions, nor inconsequential events. On one hand, they have their causes and principles: the moral, religious and political beliefs that they faithfully reflect. On the other hand, they engender, in practice, scholarly institutions that shape minds and establish customs. The education of a people is at once the outcome of all it believes and the source of what it will one day become.

A brief review of the history of education will demonstrate that pedagogy has always and everywhere been ''conditioned,'' so to speak, by the intellectual and moral state of society. ''In all countries,'' it is correctly said, ''the direction of education depends on the idea that these countries have of the perfect man''. . . .

One teaches only that which one knows, and the pedagogy of any given period always corresponds to what is known and understood at that time. . . .

It is not within the scope of this article to sketch an outline of pedagogy as it is currently constituted or the scientific facts about human nature and the work and experiments of past generations. We will at least try to trace the framework, the divisions, indicating at each point some of the truths that appear to be established.

There is no need to demonstrate the distinction between theoretical and practical pedagogy: the one considers the subject of education, i.e., the human being, studied according to the laws of his spontaneous development and scholarly cultivation; the other envisions the *object* of education, i.e., methods of instruction, rules of discipline and the distribution of knowledge. . . .

Practical pedagogy has hardly completed its task when it has resolved all the questions of method, didactics, or discipline that we have just discussed. It's not enough for pedagogy to tell us what to teach and how to teach it. It still has to tell us whom we need to teach. In other words, it has to distinguish between different orders of instruction, institutions which measure the quantity and quality of studies according to the conditions, needs, aptitudes and sex of the individuals. . . .

We are far from exhausting all aspects of a large ensemble of facts and ideas about pedagogy. Our aim was above all to show that if the science of education has not yet been finalized it is at least possible and in the process of being formed. We must hope that the day will soon come when a scientific schematization will finally be accomplished. The future of humanity largely depends on the development of pedagogy. Undoubtedly one can say about it, as about logic, that the best pedagogy is the one that does not become conceited, is not wrapped up in itself and acknowledges the limits of its own power. We are not forgetting that heredity, environment, and all the so-called secret collaborators of education play their role, often a decisive one, in the formation of mind and character. But this is not the equivalent to an admission of powerlessness, which would be as humiliating as it is troubling; because it all comes back to saying that liberty can do nothing against fatalism, and that it is impossible to eliminate or at least reduce the hand of chance in human destiny. On the contrary, let us remain convinced that the beneficial action of pedagogy will grow more and more, that illuminated by science it will become the world's teacher, always being the strongest expression of human will and thought struggling against the blind forces of nature.

From: *A Cyclopedia of Education* (1913), Paul Monroe, editor

pedagogy.—Pedagogy is commonly understood to mean the science and art of teaching. The word is derived from the Greeks, among whom a pedagogue was the person, usually, if not always, a slave, who attended the young boy, going with him to and from school, carrying his materials for study, looking out for his wants and exercising authority over him. It is supposed that the pedagogues were often such slaves as would be useless for other tasks, and that they were not held in much respect even by the children who were placed in their charge. The name thus acquired in ancient times a connotation of lack of esteem, if not of contempt, which it has not entirely shaken off in modern usage.

A somewhat similar meaning became attached to the derived
term, "pedagogy." Since the Renaissance educational reformers
have drawn more and more attention to the significance of the process of education as contrasted with that of the subject matter taught.
The study of this process has been for several centuries referred to
as pedagogy. The philosopher Kant (*q.v.*) denominated his lectures
on education as *Über Pädagogik*. They dealt especially with the
formation of habit, and moral training and instruction. Thus defined, pedagogy concerned that aspect of education commonly held
to be most childish and least interesting, a phase of life relegated to
nurses, mothers, and pedagogues, and felt to have little in it to command the thoughtful attention of the strong in mind or will. In fact,
the management and instruction of children was from the fathers'
or schoolmasters' point of view thought to resolve itself into an
authoritative display of superior power. Learning was treated as a
matter of application on the part of the pupil. Application was regarded as a question of will, and will as to be governed by com-
mands. But to command children was held, on account of their
weakness and lack of resources, not to require great strength or to
merit much thought or esteem.

But while, on account of its derivation from the word pedagogue
and its application to an art held in little honor, the term pedagogy
at first failed to carry the implication of a profound science, nevertheless the existence of the ideal of such a study and its resolute
pursuit by a few reformers eventually gained for it a richer content
and a higher standing. In the beginning its practical influence was
felt especially in the elementary schools. The nineteenth century
brought with it in the more advanced nations of the world an extraordinary expansion of the facilities for elementary education.
The preparation of teachers for this work came to be in the hands
of normal and training schools. These institutions devoted themselves largely to the pedagogy of the subjects taught in the common
schools and to the problems of school management. It came to be
an accepted principle that elementary teachers should know not
only the subjects they were to teach, but also the art of their craft.

Eventually the idea that the scientific study of education should
not be confined to the problems of the elementary school led to the
establishment of departments of pedagogy in colleges and universities. The University of the City of New York (now New York University) offered such courses in 1832. The same institution

established a School of Pedagogy in 1890 and offered the degree of Master and Doctor of Pedagogy. The New York State Normal College at Albany gives the degree of Bachelor of Pedagogy. Many universities, especially in the western part of the United States created professorships in pedagogy in the last two decades of the nineteenth century. See EDUCATION, ACADEMIC STUDY OF.

The introduction of the study into higher education led to new difficulties in regard to the term pedagogy. It was felt to be essentially a normal school subject, concerned especially with the problems of the elementary school and "rule-of-thumb" methods of teaching the subjects of its curriculum. The specialists of the universities were prone to regard the power to teach as due primarily to knowledge of subject matter. In addition to this they admitted the importance of natural aptitude and of experience, but rejected the efficacy of methods. Many ridiculed outright the pretensions of "pedagogy," and resented its injection into the curriculum of higher education. Some even went so far as to criticize the entire influence of pedagogy on elementary education, on the ground that in its emphasis on interest it had demoralized the work of the school, giving us "soft" pedagogy.

Much of this criticism of pedagogy as a university subject had, doubtless, validity, and in consequence it was necessary to modify and expand its content in order to secure for it a permanent foothold and equality of rank. To mark the change there grew up a tendency to substitute the word *education* for *pedagogy* as a title for the department and for professorships. Thus the term "pedagogy" has to a considerable extent passed out of vogue. The newer "education" differs from the older "pedagogy" in two respects. First, it includes far more than method in teaching and school management; second, it is more scientific. Taking up the first point, we note that all the educational functions and agencies of society are considered; the history and administration of education are taken into account; the care of the body is brought before the attention as well as the care of the mind, and the education of defectives as well as of the normal child; the educational ideals and the curriculum are treated both in general and in detail and the relation of education to general welfare is investigated. A good illustration of the expansion of the field is seen in the transition from the history of pedagogy such as we find in Compayré's volume with that title, to present-day history of education. Then the subject confined itself for the most part to the ideals and methods that have prevailed in the schools, together with some account of the conceptions and work of educational reformers. Now the historian of education tries to relate the processes and agencies of education to the institutional, economic, social, and cultural movements of history.

The second change that has come about with the transition from pedagogy to education lies in the more thoroughgoing and scientific methods employed to-day. On the one hand, a far wider range of underlying sciences is brought into requisition in the treatment of educational problems. Thus not only psychology and philosophy, but also biology, physiology, sociology, and economics are brought to bear on the work. On the other hand, the propagation of opinions, ''armchair'' pedagogy, has been replaced by resolute search for facts through historical research, through comparative study, through the use of experiment and statistical methods. The department of education brings to scientific research a set of interesting practical problems and to the schoolmaster a mass of incontrovertible facts and conclusions that cannot fail to prove of practical use.

It is interesting to note that the term pedagogy bids fair to be revived in the title ''experimental pedagogy.'' This science springs not so much from the desire of the schoolmaster or the educational reformer to establish teaching on an unshakable basis, as from the tendency on the part of experimental psychology to reach out into new fields, especially those where its methods and principles can be made to bear on the practical world. But, although somewhat different in its origin from genetic and educational psychology, which began as attempts to get a scientific basis for teaching rather than new problems for science, experimental pedagogy naturally tends to include both these forerunners. E.N.H.

See EDUCATION, ACADEMIC STUDY OF; EXPERIMENTAL EDUCATION; PSYCHOLOGY, EDUCATIONAL; PHILOSOPHY OF EDUCATION; also CHILD STUDY

pedantry is the undue display of learning, the presentation of material in a didactic fashion, or a finicking adherence to rules and technicalities. The pedant has been a stock comic character in literature because of his pompousness and lack of humor, his parade of knowledge without sense, and his remoteness from the everyday world.

Pedantic writing is characterized by polysyllabic words and circumlocution. It is most likely to be found in specialized fields of knowledge—where the necessary technical words seem to attract unnecessarily long and obscure companions. Authority and official position also seem to stimulate pedantry.

Grammar is a favorite haunt of the pedant. He is equipped with rules, which he is convinced came before practice, and effectiveness and lucidity, charm, wit, grace and the fine excesses that surprise us with delight are nothing to him. His sole delight is to pounce upon the violation of one of his rules.

From: *The Encyclopaedia and Dictionary of Education, a Comprehensive, Practical and Authoritative Guide on All Matters Connected with Education, Including Educational Principles and Practice, Various Types of Teaching Institutions, and Educational Systems Throughout the World* (1922), Foster Watson, editor

Pedagogic Institute, Chile.—(See Chile, The Educational System of.)

pedantry.—As defined in the *Century Dictionary,* a pedant is "a person who overrates erudition, or lays undue stress on exact knowledge of detail or of trifles, or who makes an undue or inappropriate display of learning." Steele, in *The Tatler,* says pedantry proceeds from much reading and little understanding. Swift, in *Good Manners,* says that there is a pedantry in manners as in all arts and sciences, and that properly it is "the overrating any kind of knowledge we pretend to." The word is derived from *peadogogus* (a teacher).

From: *Dictionary of Philosophy and Psychology* (1928), James Mark Baldwin, editor

pedagogics [Gr. παιδαγωγία, the training or guiding of boys]: Ger. *Pädagogik;* Fr. *pédagogie;* Ital. *pedagogia.* The theory and art of teaching as a profession, involving the scientific application of the sciences of mind, body, and society, to the work of education.

Since pedagogics is an applied science, depending upon civilization for its ends, and upon psychology for its methods, it is natural, first, that different nations and different stages of civilization should vary in their ideals of the purposes of education; and second, that

psychologists should vary in their method of approach to the study
of educational problems according to their several ways of studying
the mind. The main problems in pedagogics pertain (*a*) to the construction of the curriculum; (*b*) to the methods of teaching; (*c*) to
the development of character.

There are three chief standpoints from which these problems are
viewed: (1) The *a priori* method, which, following the lead of rational psychology, considers the necessary constitutive elements of
the mind, the character and the institutions of civilization (see Rosenkranz, *Philos. of Educ.*); (2) the *a posterori* method, which, ignoring largely the *a priori* aspects of mind and society, gives its
main attention to the content of the studies and the processes of the
mind (see Herbart, *Sci. of Educ.*); (3) the method of the child study,
or actual observation of children. It is evident that a complete pedagogics must take all these varying methods of approach into consideration, since each emphasizes important aspects of the ends and
methods of education.

Literature: Rosenkranz, Philos. of Educ.; Herbart, Sci. of Educ.
(Eng. trans.); Parker, Talks on Pedagogics; Harris, Psychol. Founda-
tions of Educ.; Froebel, Educ. of Man; Bain, Educ. as a Science;
Rein, Outlines of Pedagogics; A. Angiulli, La Pedagogia (1882);
R. Ardigò, La Scienza dell' Educazione (1893).

Pedagogy: see PEDAGOGICS

From: *Webster's New Dictionary of Synonyms* (1968; 1st ed. 1942)

pedantic, academic, scholastic, bookish are comparable as terms of
   derogation applied to thinkers, scholars, and learned men and their
   utterances. **Pedantic** often implies ostentatious display of knowledge, didacticism, and stodginess ⟨his opinions were as *pedantic* as
   his life was abstemious—*Froude*⟩ It may also connote undue attention to scholarly minutiae and small interest in significant issues
   ⟨much *pedantic* mistaking of notions for realities, of symbols and
   abstractions for the data of immediate experience—*Huxley*⟩ **Academic** rarely carries implications of disagreeable personal characteristics but it does stress abstractness, lack of practical experience
   and interests, and often the inability to consider a situation realistically ⟨there is so much bad writing . . . because writing has been

dominated by . . . the *academic* teachers and critics—*Ellis*⟩ **Scholastic** is less fixed in its implications than the others, for sometimes the allusion is to philosophic Scholasticism and sometimes to modern education. As a rule it implies dryness, formalism, adherence to the letter, and sometimes subtlety ⟨it is very able, but harsh and crabbed and intolerably *scholastic*—*Laski*⟩ **Bookish** often suggests learning derived from books rather than from actualities ⟨the Greeks had a name for such mixture of learning and folly, which might be applied to the *bookish* but poorly read of all ages—*Adler*⟩ ⟨the gestures of Mr. Lutyens's heroes are a trifle *bookish,* too seldom of the dusty streets—*Times Lit. Sup.*⟩ and sometimes it implies a decided literary or rhetorical quality ⟨*bookish* words⟩ ⟨*bookish* interests⟩

From: *Meyers Grosses Konversations Lexicon* (1943), Thomas Ernst, translator

pedagogue (Greek: paidagogos, "guide of boys"), among the ancient Greeks guardian of boys, usually an educated slave who sometimes also functioned as a teacher; nowadays, it generally designates an educator or a schoolman.

pedagogy (Greek) according to its etymology the "art or science of the pedagogue," that is, of the guidance of boys, education of boys; nowadays meaning as much as the instruction of education, educational science, the theory of education and of instruction, being the most important means of school education. One can only speak of educational science with regard to the higher cultural development of a people. Thus pedagogy as science did not actually bloom, until the heyday of Greek philosophy. In Greece, the Dorian and Ionian tribal customs (Lycurgian and Solonian constitution) as well as the rich talents of the Hellenic people for physical and intellectual education (gymnastics and music) constituted a fortunate empirical foundation for pedagogy. . . .

The pedagogical ideas of the Age of Enlightenment were also voiced, contemporary to or following Rousseau, by the so-called Philanthropists in Germany, above all Johann Bernhard Basedow (died 1790). They inveighed against the external form of education and instruction of their time; they considered the teaching method of the Grammatici (philologists) nothing but a blind groping in the dark. They did not promise an improved method because they were the first to actually consider methodology, something new within education. The pupil is to be led from his proper perceptions—in a natural manner, without the means of force or rote memory—to his proper understanding. Since this method is natural, children will learn with enjoyment and love; for this reason, any form of punishment, especially physical is abolished. Preference is given to the mother tongue; the tyrannical rule of Latin is opposed. . . .

Besides Basedow, among the philanthropists particular mention must be made of J. H. Campe, author of the German "Robinson", E. Chr. Trapp, one Salzmann, founder of the educational institute in Schnepfenthal, as trustees of pedagogical theory; furthermore Guts Muths because of his contributions to the instruction of gymnastics and geography. Through their efforts, education became the primary focus of German interest. Rousseau's influence on Kant's pedagogical views is unmistakable, as much as Kant's influence on the discussion around the turn of the 18th to 19th century. Pedagogical traces are unmistakable in Lessing, Goethe, and Schiller; Herder and Richter (Jean Paul) directly and felicitously participate in the pedagogical debate. The attention also shifted more and more to the education of the people as a national task and duty of the state. In the same year in which Rousseau's "Emile" was published, La Chalotais ("Essai d'éducation nationale," 1763) ushered in the concept of national education in France. F. E. v. Rochow, dean of the cathedral (died 1805), was also influenced by the Philanthropists, although his famous school reform on his estate Rekahn near Brauschweig focused on the real needs of life. Most of the Philanthropists' practical endeavors (Philanthropines) bloomed for only a short period of time; their stimuli, however, proved to be very effective. The so-called Socrateans further developed the tendencies of the philanthropists and strove for an enlightened form of religious instruction according to the Socratic-heuristic method. From this circle, J. L. v. Mosheim (died 1755), G. F. Dinter (died 1831), the Kantian Grüsse (died 1808), G. F. Seiler (died 1807), H. Stephani (died 1850) have to be mentioned. Even Catholic Germany did not completely oppose the spirit of the pedagogical century and produced a number of careful reformers like Abbot J. V. Felbiger in Silesia and Austria (died 1788), Bishop Kindermann, Ritter V. Schulstein in Bohemia (died 1801), the dean of the cathedral B. Overberg in Münster (died 1826), H. Braun (died 1792) and Bishop J. M. Sailer in Bavaria (died 1832), J. B. Graser (died 1841) in Franconia, J. M. Vierthaler (died 1827) in Salzburg and Vienna, and others.

The founder of the new pedagogy, Johann Heinrich Pestalozzi (died 1827), based his ideas on the concepts of Rousseau, with the difference, however, that he considered general human education to be the basis for the specific education of a certain class and profession and not opposed to it. His first goal and task was the higher development of man's natural powers; based on perception, the basic tenets of his methods are continuous progress while retaining a indelible remembrance of the material studied, and a continuously parallel development of the faculties of understanding and speech, judgement and volition. He calls number, form, and language the basic forms of intellectual perception, from which he derives the topics and rules of instruction. Instruction and education are always closely interrelated and put into the service of a magnificently-conceived education of the whole people. Soon, early stages of instruction were informed by Pestalozzi's pedagogy (elementary method); his indirect influence was, and is, incalculable. Among the disseminators and developers of his ideas, special mention must be made of the brothers Zeller, v. Türk, Plamann, Fröber, Blochmann, Harnisch, Dieserweg with regard to practical application, Fichte, Herbart with regard to theory. Fichte (died 1814), who in the winter of 1807/08 gave his famous addresses to the German people, recommended in them the pedagogy of Pestalozzi as the best instruction to provide the debased (''sunken'') nation with a renewed and healthier life. With that, he emphasized the national element in education, which takes second place to philanthropic and cosmopolitan elements with Pestalozzi. During the years of introspection and rebirth, through medication of the Baron of Stein, Nicolovius, Wilhelm v. Humboldt, Süvern, and others, the pedagogy of Pestalozzi found its second home in the seminars and schools (Volksschule) of Prussia.

J. F. Herbart (died 1841) expanded and deepened the pedagogy of Pestalozzi by basing it more clearly than Pestalozzi had done on the scientific foundation of ethics and psychology. He divides all of education into three activities: instruction, government and discipline, or also into instruction and education in the narrower sense, and demands the closest cooperation between education and instruction, which would be without purpose if separated. According to Herbart, the ultimate goal of education is virtue. The instruction has to directly awaken the pupil's versatility of interests, discipline, and strength of ethical character. Herbart may be called the founder of speculative pedagogy; among present pedagogues, he has a faithful following far beyond the German borders. F. Exner (died 1853) contributed to the dissemination of Herbart's pedagogy in Austria, which even up to the present is still in widespread use there. In Germany, it was popularized by K. B. Stoy (died 1885), while Ziller (died 1882) developed it in his own particular manner and tightly organized the Herbart school (since 1868) in the "Society for Scientific Pedagogy." Among the living exponents of Herbart-Ziller, W. Rein is known and influential as a writer and the director of the pedagogical seminar at the University of Jena; E. V. Sallwürk, on the other hand, follows Herbart, but opposes Ziller's trend. Next to Herbart, among the great philosophers of Germany, it was especially Schleiermacher (died 1834) who developed pedagogy. Following them, E. Beneke (died 1856) sought to further develop speculative pedagogy in close contact with his psychological system. Like Herbart, Beneke opposes the traditional idea of the so-called faculty of the soul and teaches that personal development occurs through the traces of outer impressions left on a few basic faculties which, in the beginning are merely sensitive. Neither one developed a real following; however, they left their traces in scientific pedagogy. After them, many others approached pedagogy in a systemic and philosophical manner and gained more or less influence thereby. For example, the followers of Schelling, J. J. Wagner, who equates education with the stimulation of the young mind, and J. B. Graser, the Hegelians Rosenkranz and Thaulow, the practically-oriented pedagogues A. H. Niemeyer, F.H.C. Schwarz, H. Grafe, the theologians K. Palmer, G. Baur, V. Zezschwitz, and others.

The lives and works of the pedagogues in the present are so rich and varied that they can no longer be systematically surveyed. This applies especially to the history of pedagogy, which has grown more and more to be an independent and extremely fruitful branch of general cultural history.

From: Joseph T. Shipley, *Dictionary of Word Origins, An Authoritative Guide to the Better Use, Understanding, History and Background of the English Language* (1945)

pedagogue A modern schoolmaster may not be quite a slave to his pupils; but the first *pedagogue* was a slave, who led his young master to school (Gr. *paidogogos*, from *pais, paid*—, boy + *agein*, to lead. Thus a *demagogue* leads the people—sometimes astray: from Gr. *demos*, the people, whence *democracy, q.v.* So also does an *agitator*, from L. *agere, agit*—, to stir, to lead, from Gr. *agein*. A *synagogue* is a place where persons—now, only Jews—are led together: Gr. *syn*, together.) It. *pedagogo* was shortened (by slang) into *pedant;* both these words show the scorn of the layman for those in spite of whom he learned (hence, Shaw's ''Those that can, do; those that cannot, teach'').

Confusion arises from the fact that the L. word for foot is *pes, ped*—*;* Gr. *pedon*, ground. Medicine uses the Gr. forms; thus *pediatrician* and *pediatry* deal with boys (children: grammatically as well as dramatically the male embraces the female): *podiatry* (Gr. *pous, pod*—, foot) deals with the *pedal* extremities. *Podagra* (Gr. *agra*, trap) is the medical name for the gout. A *chiropodist* was first one that cared for the hands and feet (Gr. *chiro*—, *cheiro*, from *cheir*, hand: *chiromancy*, divination by the hand; *cp. necromancy*). The word *chirurgeon* was long an Eng. word, from Gr. *cheirourgos*, from *cheir*, hand + *ergon*, work; via OFr. *surigien* it was gradually replaced by its easier-to-pronounce doublet, *surgeon*.

A fellow the soles of whose feet are facing yours when he is standing (some 8,000 miles away) is at the *antipodes*. G. *podion*, foot in the sense of base, gives us (in the L. form) *podium*—from which the Philharmonic is being delightfully conducted as I stay away and write; applied (in its plural, *podia*) to the imperial seat at theatre, it became OFr. *puie*, balcony, whence ME *puwe*, whence Eng. *pew*.

The combinations from L. *ped*— are numerous; *e.g. pedometer, pedestrian*. *Impede* (L. *in*+*ped*) is to catch the foot in something; hence, to hinder. L. *expedire* is to get the foot out again (of a trap); hence Eng. *expedite*, to speed up; *expedient*, that which helps the foot along, as with our *expeditionary* force. A *pedlar*, or *peddler*, however, although a person that goes about on foot, traces his descent through the A.S. *ped*, basket; hence, a man that thus carries his wares.

The interlinkings can be carried further. Thus in Gr. *podagra* (Eng. *podagra*, gout) the *agra*, trap, catching, is related to Gr. *agein*, to bring, to lead, as in *pedagogue*. And Gr. *pous, podos,* foot (Gr. *peza,* ankle), is probably related to Gr. *pedilon,* sandal, *pedias, pediad—,* level, flat (Gr. *pedion,* plane, whence Eng. *pedion,* flat surface of a crystal), whence Gr. *pedon,* oarblade and its plural *peda,* rudder. This word, through It. *pedota,* helmsman, became It. *pilota* and Eng. *pilot,* a guide in a different field from the *pedagogue.*

From: *Funk & Wagnalls New Practical Standard Dictionary of the English Language* (1946), Charles Earle Funk, editor

·**ped,** ·**pede** Combining forms from Latin *pes, pedis,* foot, used to mean footed, as in quadru*ped,* centi*pede,* etc.
1) **ped·, pedi·** Combining forms from Latin *pes, pedis,* foot, used to mean foot, feet, of the feet, etc., as in *pedi*cure.
2) **ped·, pedo·** Combining forms from Greek *pais, paidos,* child, used to mean of or pertaining to children, as in *peda*gogy, *pedol*ogy, etc.

ped'·a·gog *noun* 1 schoolmaster; especially, a pedantic, narrow-minded teacher. 2 In ancient Greece and Rome, a slave who attended children to school. Also PED'·A·GOGUE. [⟨Gr. *paidagōgos* ⟨PED- + *agō,* lead]

ped·a·gog'·ic (-gŏj'·ĭc) *adj.* 1 Pertaining to the science or art of teaching. 2 Of or belonging to a pedagog; affected with a conceit of learning. Also PED·A·GOG'·I·CAL.—PED·A·GOG'·I·CAL·LY *adv.*

ped·a·gog'·ics (-gŏj'·ĭcs) *noun* The science and art of teaching; pedagogy.

ped'·a·gog·ism (-gōg·ĭzm) *noun* The nature, character, or business of teachers or a teacher.

ped·a·go'·gy (-ji) *noun* The science or profession of teaching; also, the theory or the teaching of how to teach. . . .

ped·ant (-unt) *noun* 1 A scholar who makes needless and inopportune display of his learning, or who insists upon the importance of trifling points of scholarship. 2 [Obs.] A schoolmaster; teacher. [⟨F. *pédant* ⟨It. *pedante*]—PE·DAN·TIC *adj.*—PE·DAN·TI·CAL·LY *adv.*

ped·ant·ry *noun* [·RIES *pl.*] 1 Ostentatious display of knowledge. 2 Undue and didactic adherence to forms or rules in presenting knowledge.

From: *Grande dizionario enciclopedico* (1954), Mariolina Salvatori, translator

pedagogy. . . . Pedagogy has been recently constituted into a science. Until the "Risorgimento" (eighteenth and nineteenth centuries), the meaning of the term was still a matter of dispute. For example, A. Rosmini, G. A. Tayner and A. Franchi used the term pedagogica to name the science, and pedagogia to name the art of education, whereas L. A. Parravicini called pedagogica the art of education, and pedagogia its science. In its historical evolution, this science has increasingly affirmed its autonomy from such other disciplines as ethics, religion, psychology, sociology—disciplines with which it has occasionally been confused, or which at given times have tried to rule it. Pedagogy's indebtedness to these disciplines, which it contributed to develop and sharpen, is undeniable. Nevertheless, pedagogy's particular structure, methods, and goals must be acknowledged. . . .

   Pedagogy is a philosophical science, since it draws its norms from philosophical sciences; however, it is not exclusively philosophical, since it must reckon with biological data, empirical psychology, as well as the results and the history of educative experience. . . .

   An integral part of Pedagogy is the doctrine or methods or methodology. Methodology teaches that in the process of education it is not appropriate to shift ideas, topics, approaches abruptly and erratically, without considering how they are connected with one another and how they are affected by the personalities of teachers and learners. An educator's moves should be gradual, reflexive, and appropriate to the particular historical conditions and pedagogical ideals. When the doctrine of methods establishes how to attain knowledge, morality, aesthetic attitudes, piety, it is called general didactics. When, on the other hand, it establishes the particular steps by which to teach individual disciplines and cultural abilities such as reading, writing, language, nomenclature, mathematics, history, geography, natural sciences, philosophy, drawing, singing, manual work, gymnastics, it is called special didactics. It is clear that a method cannot be determined a priori, apart from its science and art, independently of the individual teacher or student, or else abstractions would determine life, human activities would follow extrinsic rules, individuality and spontaneity would be harnessed within formulas and pre-conceived systems. To conceive of methods in this fashion is to suggest that the content and the form of education are independent of each other, that learning can be imagined apart from those who teach and those who learn. . . . One must then reject, from the start, "pedagogic pedantry" or "pedagogism," which by turning pedagogy into abstract precepts, thwarts the educative freedom of both teachers and learners; the use of learning manuals which by substituting for the original texts of a culture, and the living sources of knowledge, make it impossible to grasp the spirit inherent in the process of history; and finally, the formalistic interpretation of programs which by constituting teaching as the pouring in of various notions prevents learners from understanding its synthetic unity and provides them with an alibi for intellectual laziness. . . .

pedant, the. A comic character in early seventeenth century plays by Flaminio Scala, although its characteristic traits date back to prior times. Similar to the "Dottore" (Doctor) in its pretentious behavior, it nevertheless lacks the humor of that character ("maschera"). The Pedant preaches moral maxims without practicing them, and is often mocked by those who must submit to his preachings. He speaks in affected Tuscan, but also occasionally in Sicilian or Roman dialect.

pedantic (pedantesque), language, poetry. The word "pedant" dates back to the sixteenth century. Probably because of a humorous phonetic link between Latin pes, pedis (= foot) and Greek παῖς, παιδός (= child) it meant "a man who leads (on foot) children to school" and became a disparaging synonym for "pedagogue," "school teacher"; it then came to mean "punctilious and servile imitator of the ancients," "one who writes in antiquated style." Pedantic was and is called a literary form that rigorously conforms to strict precepts without any trace of geniality or originality. When the figure of the pedant, both the literatus and the pedagogue, became an object of derision, the pedant's stilted language generated another literary form which was called pedantic (pedantesque) since it objectified the most visible defects of the category. To speak pedantically, then, meant to speak a vulgar language replete with unusual Latinisms, citations, trite sententiae and Latin phrases.

Pedant pedagogues, since Plautus (their prototype is Lysidus in Le Bacchidi), were traditionally blamed for many defects: empty and inconsistent doctrines, obtuse minds, rough and vexing traits, know-it-all-ness, presumption, arrogance.

The antecedents of such unfavorable portraits can be found in Horace, Juvenal, Martial. But aversion and contempt for pedants increased in the Renaissance as a result of customs that in courtly life degraded the literati to mere servants, or elevated them to arbitrary heights. Typically, parodic pedantic literature dates back to the fifteenth century or to the beginning of the sixteenth. Such literature displayed fervid, fanatic and exclusive admiration for antiquity, classical languages, especially Latin, and grammar. In reaction to it, students coined a pedantic language, a deformation of the vulgar language by means of unimaginable Latinisms and inappropriate Latin expressions. This language is not to be confused with "macheronic Latin" ("latino meccheronico") which is instead a corruption of Latin by means of vulgar idioms and grossly Latinized vulgar forms. The first examples of intentional, parodic literature are to be found in drama. Beside a few essays in imitation of Plautus (for example, the pedant Polinico in B. Dovizi's Calandra, first performed at Urbino in 1513 and in Rome in 1514), we have a comedy by Francesco Belo, Il Pedante (written in 1529, published in 1538), already remarkably different from its classical antecedents; Aretino's comedy Il Marescalo; G. Bruno's Candelaio (1583); G. B. Della Porta's Fantesca; several novellas by Della Porta and other authors. . . . But the masterpiece of pedantic literature are the verses written by Count Camillo Scrofa, or Scroffa (midsixteenth century).

From: *The New Century Dictionary of the English Language, Based on Matters Selected from the Original Century Dictionary and Entirely Rewritten, with the Addition of a Great Amount of New Material, and Containing the Great Mass of Words and Phrases in Ordinary Use.* 12,000 quotations, 4,000 pictorial illustrations (1959), H. G. Emery and K. G. Brewster, editors

ped-a-gogue (ped′a̱-gog), *n.* [F. *pédagogue,* ⟨L. *pædagogus,* ⟨Gr. παιδαγωγός, ⟨παῖς (παιδ-), child, + ἀγωγός, leading, ⟨ἄγειν, lead.] A teacher of children; a schoolteacher: now usually implying pedantry, dogmatism, or narrow-mindedness.—**ped′a-go-guish** (-gog-ish), *a.* Like or befitting a pedagogue; pedantic.—**ped′a-go-guism** (-gog-izm), *n.* The occupation, character, or ways of a pedagogue; the system of pedagogy.—**ped′a-go-gy** (-gō-ji or -goj-i), *n.* [Gr. παιδαγωγία.] The function, work, or art of a teacher; teaching; pedagogics.

ped-ant (ped′a̱nt), *n.* [F. *pédant,* ⟨It. *pedante,* teacher, pedant; origin uncertain: cf. *pedagogue.*] A schoolmaster† or teacher†; one who makes an excessive or tedious show of learning or learned precision; one who possesses mere book-learning without practical wisdom (as, "He [James I.] had the temper of a *pedant;* and with it a *pedant's* love of theories, and a *pedant's* inability to bring his theories into any relation with actual facts": Green's "Short Hist. of the Eng. People," viii. 2).—**pe-dan-tic** (pē-dan′tik), *a.* Pertaining to or characteristic of a pedant; exhibiting pedantry; resembling a pedant; tediously or absurdly learned: as, "There was nothing *pedantic* in their discourse" (Smollett's "Humphry Clinker," June 10); "They regulated verse by the most *pedantic* and minute laws" (Hallam's "Literature of Europe," i. 1. § 43); "He was often considered rather a *pedantic* than a practical commander, more capable to discourse of battles than to gain them" (Motley's "Dutch Republic," iii. 1). Also **pe-dan′ti-cal.—pe-dan′ti-cal-ly,** *adv.*—**pe-dan′ti-cism** (-sizm), *n.* A pedantic notion or expression; a piece of pedantry.—**ped′ant-ism,** *n.* Pedantry; a pedanticism.—**ped′ant-ize,** *v. i.; -ized, -izing.* To play the pedant; display pedantry.

ped-an-toc-ra-cy (ped-ạn-tok′rạ-si), *n.;* pl. *-cies* (-siz). [F. *pédantocra-tie:* see *pedant* and *-cracy.*] Government by pedants or a pedant; a system of government conducted by pedants.—**pe-dan-to-crat** (pē̠-dan′tō̠-krat), *n.*—**pe-dan-to-crat′ic,** *a.*

ped-ant-ry (ped′ạnt-ri), *n.;* pl. *-ries* (-riz). The character or practice of a pedant; an undue display of learning.

From: *The Oxford Dictionary of English Etymology* (1966), C. T. Onions, editor

pedagogue pe·dəgɔg instructor of youth. xiv (Trevisa).—L. *pædagō-gus*—Gr. *paidagōgós* slave who took a boy to and from school, f. *paid-, país* boy (cf. PAEDO-) + *agōgós* leading, *ágein* lead (see ACT). So **pe·dagogy³** -gɔgi, -gɔdʒi. xvi, **pedago·gic**. xvii; after F.

pedant pe·dənt †schoolmaster xvi (Sh.); person who overrates book-learning xvi.—F. *pédant*—It. *pedante,* of obscure origin; the first el. is presumably that of PEDAGOGUE, to which has been added the prp. ending *-ante,* -ANT. In xvi–xvii also †*pedanti(e),* *-ee,* direct from It. Hence **peda·ntic** pidæ·ntik. xvii; corr. to F. *pédantesque,* It. *pedantesco;* -ICAL xvi (Sh.). **pe·dant**RY. xvii; after F. *pédanterie* or It. *pedanteria* (used by Sidney).

From: *Oxford American Dictionary* (1980), Eugene Ehrlich, Stewart Berg Flexner, Gorton Carruth, and Joyce M. Hawkins, editors

ped-a-gŏgue, *n.* (*ped-ă-gog*) a person who teaches in a pedantic way.

ped-a-go-gy, *n.* (*ped-ă-goh-jee*) teaching, the art of teaching. **ped-a-gog-ic, *adj.*** (*ped-ă-goj-ik*), **ped-a-gog′i-cal, *adj.***

ped-ant, *n.* (*ped-ănt*) a person who parades his learning or who insists unimaginatively on strict observance of formal rules and details in the presentation of knowledge. **Ped′ant-ry. *n.*,** **pe-dan-tic** (*pi-dan-tik*) *adj.* **pe-dan′ti-cal-ly, *adv.***

From: *A Dictionary of Education* (1981), Dereck Rowntree, editor

pedagogical method: see **teaching technique.**

pedagogium: a class established at Halle in Germany by August Hermann Franke (1663–1727) to prepare teachers for his and other schools; this pedagogical class was composed of the most gifted and pious of his theological students.

pedagogy: (1) the art, practice, or profession of teaching; (2) the systematized learning or instruction concerning principles and methods of teaching and of student control and guidance; largely replaced by the term *education.*

pedagogy of action: the science or procedure of teaching through purposeful activities, analyzable into the following steps, each of which involves initiation, evaluation, and choice by the child: (*a*) purposing—setting up of goals; (*b*) planning—preparing means necessary to realize the goals; (*c*) execution—performing the means; (*d*) judging—evaluating the extent of realization of the goals and the process. *See* **activism.**

pedagogy, therapeutic: correction of disabilities, particularly in the academic area, through specialized educational techniques.

pedantry: bookishness or ostentatiousness with respect to learning. (Applied to scholarship, it denotes preoccupation with minute matters of no practical significance. In the teacher, it denotes rigid insistence on formalism in instructional procedures often to the detriment of the pupil's genuine development as a person.). . .

pedology (pe·dol′ə·ji): the study of the complete child, his life, growth, ideas, and very being; places emphasis on the learner and his capacities and needs.

pedophilia (ped′ō·fil′i·ə): the desire on the part of adults for sexual relations with children.

From: *Chambers Twentieth Century Dictionary* (1983), E. H. Kirkpatrick, editor

pedagogue *ped′ə-gog, n.* a teacher: a pedant.—*v.t.* to teach.—*adjs.* **pedagogic** (*-gog′, -goj′*), **-al.**—*adv.* **pedagog′ically.**—*n.sing.* **ped-**

agog′ics (*-gog′, -goj′*) the science and principles of teaching—*n.* **ped′agoguery** (*-gog-ə-ri*) a school: schoolmastering: pedagoguishness.—*adj.* **ped′agoguish** like a pedagogue.—*ns.* **ped′agoguishness; ped′agog(u)ism** (*-gizm, -jizm*) the spirit or system of pedagogy: teaching; **ped′agogy** (*-gog-i, -goj-i*) the science of teaching: instruction: training. [Partly through Fr. and L. from Gr. *paidagōgos,* a slave who led a boy to school—*pais, paidos,* boy, *agōgos,* leader—*agein,* to lead.]

pedant *ped′nt, n.* a schoolmaster (*Shak.*): an over-learned person who parades his knowledge: one who attaches too much importance to merely formal matters in scholarship.—*adjs.* **pedantic** (*pidant′ik*), **-al** schoolmasterly: of the character or in the manner of a pedant.—*adv.* **pedant′ically.**—*v.t.* **pedant′icise, -ize** (*-i-sīz*) to make pedantic, give pedantic form to.—*n.* **pedant′icism** (*-i-sizm*) a pedant's expression.—*v.i.* **ped′antise, -ize** to play the pedant.—*v.t.* to turn into a pedant.—*ns.* **ped′antism** pedantry: pedanticism; **pedantoc′racy** government by pedants; **pedant′ocrat.**—*adj.* **pedantocrat′ic.**—*n.* **ped′antry** the character or manner of a pedant: a pedantic expression: unduly rigorous formality. [It. *pedante* (perh. through Fr. *pédant*); connection with **pedagogue** not clear.]

From: *The Barnhardt Dictionary of Etymology* (1988), Robert K. Barnhardt, editor

pedagogue (*ped′əgog*) *n.* teacher. Before 1387 *pedagoge* teacher of children, in Trevisa's translation of Higden's *Polychronicon;* borrowed from Old French *pedagogue, pedagogien,* from Latin *paedagōgus* a slave who took children to and from school and generally supervised them; later, a teacher, from Greek *païdagōgós* (*paîs,* genitive *paidós* child; see FEW + *agōgós* leader, from *ágein* to lead; see AGENT).—**pedagogical** (*ped′əgoj′əkəl*) *adj.* of teaching. 1619, formed in English from French *pédagogique* + English *-al*[1], or from English *pedagogue* + *-ical,* modeled on Greek *paidagōgikós* pedagogic, from *paidagōgós* teacher.—**pedagogy** (*ped′əgō′jē*) *n.* teaching. 1583, instruction, discipline, training; borrowed from Middle French *pédagogie,* from Greek *paidagōgíā* education, from *paidagōgós* teacher; for suffix see -Y[3].

pedal *n.* 1611, lever (on an organ) worked by the foot, in Cotgrave's *Dictionary;* borrowed from French *pédale,* from Italian *pedale* treadle or pedal, from Late Latin *pedāle* (thing) of the foot, from neuter of Latin *pedālis* of the foot (in size or shape), from *pēs* (genitive *pedis* FOOT.—*v.* 1866, to work a pedal; from the noun.

pedant *n.* 1588, a teacher or tutor, in Shakespeare's *Love's Labour's Lost;* borrowed from Middle French *pédant,* from Italian, or borrowed directly from Italian *pedante* teacher, schoolmaster, pedant. The meaning of a person who displays or emphasizes minor points of learning in an unnecessary or tiresome way, is first recorded in Nashe's *Have With You to Saffron-Walden* (1596).

The origin of Italian *pedante* is uncertain. It is suggested, by Bloch-Wartburg, that *pedante* was formed from the root of Greek *paideúein* to teach, at a period of the early Renaissance when it was still the fashion to pronounce Greek *ai* with the sound represented by *e* in *let.* On the other hand, and according to Corominas, the word had the early meaning of "foot soldier" and was humorously identified with *pedagogo* PEDAGOGUE in allusion to the fact that a teacher of children is always on his feet.

—**pedantic** *adj.* characteristic of a pedant. About 1600, in Donne's *Works;* formed from English *pedant* + *-ic.*

—**pedantry** *n.* pedantic quality. 1612, in Donne's *Progress of the Souls;* formed from English *pedant* + *-ry,* possibly modeled on French *pédanterie* or Italian *pedanteria.*

The Oxford English Dictionary, 1st ed. (1888–1928)

pedagogue (′pɛdəgɒg), *sb.* Forms: 4–6 pedagoge, 6–8 pedagog, 6–8 (9 in sense 1) pædagogue, 7 pædagog, 6–pedagoge. [a. OF. *pedagoge* (Oresme 14th c.), also *pedagogue* (14th c. in Littré), ad. L. *pædagōgus,* a Gr. παιδαγωγός a trainer and teacher of boys, f. παῖς, παιδο- boy + ἀγωγός leader.]

1. A man having the oversight of a child or youth; an attendant who led a boy to school. *Obs.* exc. in reference to ancient times.

1483 CAXTON *Gold. Leg.* 191/1 He durst not for his pedagoge or his governour whyche was wyth hym. **1542** UDALL *Erasm. Apoph.* 183 Alexander . . had many pædagogues, nourturers and schoole maisters. **1637–50** Row *Hist. Kirk.* (Wodrow Soc.) 206 The careles education of the children of noble men, . . the sending them out of the countrey, under the charge of pædagogues suspect in religion. **1770** LANGHORNE *Plutarch*

(1879) I. 203/1 The office of a pedagogue of old was . . to attend the children. *a* **1855** J. J. BLUNT *Right Use Early Fathers* Ser. I. ii. (1869) 29 The *Paedagogue* of Clemens Alexandrinus contains a number of precepts which the *Paedagogue* (who gives a name to the treatise) is supposed to impart to his pupil as he takes him to school.

†b. *fig.* (chiefly in reference to St. Paul's use of παιδαγωγός in *Gal*. iii. 24.)

1538 STARKEY *England* II. iii. 206 The law . . as Sayn Poule sayth dymely, . . ys the pedagoge of Chryst. **1582** N. T. (Rhem.) *Gal*. iii. 24 The law was our Pedagogue in Christ. [WYCLIF vndirmaister, TINDALE scolemaster, 1611 Schoolemaster.] **1609** BIBLE (Douay) *1 Kings* Comm., S. Paul teaching that the whole law was a pedagogue guiding men to Christ. *a* **1633** AUSTIN *Medit.* (1635) 268 The Law . . is but the Pedagogue to the Gospel. **1653** BINNING *Serm.* (1845) 22.

2. A man whose occupation is the instruction of children or youths; a schoolmaster, teacher, preceptor. Now usually in a more or less contemptuous or hostile sense, with implication of pedantry, dogmatism, or severity.

1387 TREVISA *Higden* (Rolls) VI. 7 Sigebertus . . ordeyned scoles of lettrure . . , and assignede pedagoges and maistres for children. **1494** FABYAN *Chron.* v. cxxxiii. 117 [He] ordeygned ouer them scole masters and pedagoges. **1596** NASHE *Saffron-Walden* Epistle Dedicat. **1613** SIR E. HOBY *Counter-snarle* 39 As if I were now to learne of such an Hipodidascalian Pedagogue to measure my phrase by his rule and line. **1660** PEPYS *Diary* 25 July, A Welsh schoolmaster, a good scholar but a very pedagogue. **1735** SOMERVILLE *Chase* II. 96 Cow'd by the ruling Rod, and haughty Frowns Of Pedagogues severe. **1875** GLADSTONE *Glean.* VI. v. 145 Without . . any assumption of the tone of the critic or the pedagogue.

†b. An assistant teacher; an usher. *Obs.*

1563–7 BUCHANAN *Reform. St. Andros Wks.* (1892) II The studentis . . salbe . . onder cure of the principal or sum regent or pedagogis lernit and of jugement, quha sal haif cure of thayr studie and diligens. **1613** R. CAWDREY *Table Alph.* (ed. 3), *Pædagogue*, vsher to a Schoole-maister.

†3. A schoolroom or school building. *Obs.*–¹

1745 POCOCKE *Descr. East* II. II. 231 Another part [of the university of Halle] is what they call the pedagogue, which is for noblemen and gentlemen; there are six youths in each room, with a master over them.

Hence **pedagogue** *v. trans.*, to instruct as a pedagogue; **pedagoguery** (ˈpɛdəgɒgrɪ), (*a*) a pedagogic establishment; (*b*) the occupation of a pedagogue; **pedagoguing** (ˈpɛdəgɒgɪŋ) *vbl. sb.*, the acting as, or following the occupation of, a pedagogue (*attrib.* in quot.); **pedagoguish** (ˈpɛdəgɒgɪs) *a.,* characteristic of a pedagogue.

1689 PRIOR *Epist. F. Shepherd* 82 This may confine their younger Stiles, Whom Dryden *pedagogues at Will's. **1724** WELSTED *Wks.* (1787) 130 To pedagogue a man into this sort of knowledge. **1820** SYD. SMITH *Ess.* (ed. Beeton) 209 The children are . . to be taken from their parents, and lodged in immense *pedagogueries. **1872** F. HALL *Recent Exempl. False Philol.* 31 It is not because of any poverty of matter for remark in the headlong sciolism of the one and in the piddling pedagoguery of the other. **1883** T. C. HADDON in W. R. W. Stephens *Life Freeman* (1895) I. 8 In a long life of pedagoguery. **1803** A. WILSON in *Poems & Lit. Prose* (1876) I. 103. The same routine of *pedagoguing matters. **1830** *Blackw. Mag.* XXVII. 482 A climax of *pedagoguish vanity. *a* **1878** MOZLEY *Lect.* i. (1883) 15 Those narrow and pedagoguish tactics of law. . . .

pedagogy (ˈpɛdəgɒdʒɪ, -gəʊdʒɪ, -gɒgɪ). Also 6–7 peda-, pædagogie, 7- pædagogy. [a. F. *pédagogie* (Calvin 16th c.), ad. Gr. παιδαγωγία office of a παιδαγωγός: see PEDAGOGUE. So mod.Ger. *pädagogie.*]

1. The function, profession, or practice of a pedagogue; the work or occupation of teaching; the art or science of teaching, pedagogics.

1623 COCKERAM II, Skoole-masters-ship, *pedagogie*. **1659** HEYLIN *Certamen Epist.* 334 Prince Charles . . was committed to the Pedagogy of M. Thomas Murrey, a Scot by Nation. **1691** WOOD *Ath. Oxon.* I. 219 He continued, notwithstanding in his beloved Faculty of Pedagogy. **1858** BUSHNELL *Nat. & Supernat.* xii. (1864) 379 With disquisitions, theories, philosophies, pedagogies, schemes of reformation. **1990** G. C. BRODRICK *Mem. & Impr.* 12 An excellent old-fashioned teacher blissfully ignorant of 'pædagogy'.

2. *fig.* Instruction, discipline, training; a means or system of introductory training. (In 17th c. frequently used of the ancient Jewish dispensation, in reference to *Gal.* iii. 24: cf. PEDAGOGUE I b.)

1583 STUBBES *Anat. Abus.* I. (1879) 37 He would that this their meane and base attyre should be as a rule, or pedagogie, vnto vs. **1614** RALEIGH *Hist. World* II. iv. §5 The law of Moses . . was . . ordained to last untill the time of the Pædagogie of Gods people, or introduction to Christ, should be expired. *a* **1703** BURKITT *On. N.T., Acts* x. 2 Proselytes of the covenant, that is, such Gentiles as submitted themselves to . . the whole Mosaical pædagogy.

3. A place of instruction; a school or college. (Also *fig.*) *Obs.* exc. *Hist.*

c **1625** DONNE *Serm. Ps. xxxii.* I, 2 S. Paul was in a higher Pedagogy, and another manner of University . . caught up into the third Heavens, . .

and there he learnt much. **1783** W. F. MARTYN *Georg. Mag.* II. 151 An incredible number of colleges, gymnasia, pedagogies. **1895** H. RASHDALL *Univ. Eur. Mid. Ages* II. II. 609 The poorest students could not afford the cost of residence in a Pædagogy. *Ibid.* 611 The Proctors should go to the Colleges or Pædagogies of the offenders.

pedant ('pɛdənt), *sb.* (*a.*) Also 7 pædant. [a. F. *pédant* (1566 in Hatz.-Darm.) or its source It. *pedante* teacher, schoolmaster, pedant.

The origin of the It. is uncertain. The first element is app. the same as in *peda-gogue,* etc.; and it has been suggested that *pedante* was contracted from a med.L. *pædagōgānt-em,* pr. pple. of *pædagōgāre* to act as pedagogue, to teach (Du Cange); but evidence is wanting.]

†1. A schoolmaster, teacher, or tutor (= PEDAGOGUE 2, but often without implication of contempt; in quot. 1662 = PEDAGOGUE I). *Obs.*

1588 SHAKS. *L.L.L.* III. i. 179, I that haue beene . . A domineering pedant ore the Boy. **1599** B. JONSON *Cynthia's Rev.* II. i, Hee loues to haue a fencer, a pedant, and a musician, seene in his lodgings a mornings. **1601** SHAKS. *Twel. N.* III. ii. 80 Like a Pedant that keepes a Schoole i'th Church. **1654** H. L'ESTRANGE *Chas. I* (1655) 145 From a Countrey Pedant, he became . . a Peer of the Realm. **1662** J. BARGRAVE *Pope Alex. VII* (1867) 48 He kept a small school in Rome, which he left to serve Cardinal Maffeo Barberino, to wait upon his nephews as a pedant . . , conducting them every day to school to the Roman College and bringing them back again. *a* **1704** T. BROWN *Eng. Sat.* Wks. 1730 I. 27 Oldham ow'd . . nothing to his birth, but little to the precepts of pedants.

2. A person who overrates book-learning or technical knowledge, or displays it unduly or unseasonably; one who has mere learning untempered by practical judgement and knowledge of affairs; one who lays excessive stress upon trifling details of knowledge or upon strict adherence to formal rules; sometimes, one who is possessed by a theory and insists on applying it in all cases without discrimination, a doctrinaire.

1596 NASHE *Saffron Walden* 43 O, tis a precious apothegmaticall Pedant, who will finde matter inough to dilate a whole daye of the first inuention of *Fy, fa, fum.* **1663** BUTLER *Hud.* I. i. 94 A Babylonish dialect, Which learned Pedants much affect. **1711** ADDISON *Spect.* No. 105 ¶4 A Man who has been brought up among Books, and is able to talk of nothing else, is . . what we call a Pedant. But, methinks, we should enlarge the Title, and give it to every one that does not know how to think out of his Profession and particular way of Life. **1812** MISS MITFORD in L'Estrange *Life* (1870) I. vi. 172, I mean your learned young ladies—pedants in petticoats. **1874** GREEN *Short Hist.* viii. §2. 465 He [Jas. I] had the temper of a pedant; . . a pedant's love of theories, and a pedant's inability to bring his theories into any relation with actual facts.

3. *attrib.* or as *adj.* That is, or has the character of, a pedant; of or pertaining to a pedant; pedantic.

1616 R. C. *Times Whistle* VI. 2505 Each pedant Tutour. **1670** DRYDEN *2nd Pt. Conq. Granada* III. ii, It points to pedant colleges, and cells. **1703** ROWE *Fair Penit.* v. i, The pomp of words, and pedant dissertations. **1845** CARLYLE *Cromwell* (1871) IV. 71 Respectable Pedant persons. **1875** L. MORRIS *Evensong* cliii, The pure thought smirched and fouled, or buried in pedant lore.

4. *Comb.*

1611 COTGR., *Pedantesque,* pedanticall, inkhornizing, pedant-like. **1884** SYMONDS *Shaks. Predec.* vii. 263 The honours of that pedant-rid Parnassus.

Hence ′**pedantess,** a female pedant; ′**pedanthood,** the condition or character of a pedant.

1784 R. BAGE *Barham Downs* I. 75 Unfeeling pedantess, says I . . thou art no wife for me. **1843** CARLYLE in *Last Words of T. C.* (1892) 217 Hard isolated Pedanthood.

pedantry (′pɛdəntrɪ). Also 7 pedanterie, -ery. [ad. It. *pedanteria* (used by Sidney), f. *pedante;* or its F. repr. *pédanterie* (Pasquier, 1560 in Hatz.-Darm.): see PEDANT and -ERY, -RY.]

1. The character, habit of mind, or mode of proceeding, characteristic of a pedant; mere learning without judgement or discrimination; conceit or unseasonable display of learning or technical knowledge.

1612 DONNE *Progr. Soul* ii. 291. When wilt thou shake off this pedantery Of being taught by sense and fantasie? **1646** SIR T. BROWNE *Pseud. Ep.* I. vi. 24 A practise that savours much of Pedantery. **1710** STEELE *Tatler* No. 224 ¶7 Pedantry proceeds from much Reading and little Understanding. **1766** FORDYCE *Serm. Yng. Wom.* (1767) I. vii. 298 That men are frighted at Female pedantry is very certain. **1802–25** SYD. SMITH *Ess.* (ed. Beeton) 95 Pedantry is an ostentatious obtrusion of knowledge, in which those who hear us cannot sympathise. **1841** D'ISRAELI *Amen. Lit.* (1867) 100 The pedantry of mixing Greek and Latin terms in the vernacular language is ridiculed by Rabelais.

b. with *pl.* An instance of this: a piece of pedantry, a pedantic form, expression, etc.

1581 SIDNEY *Apol. Poetrie* (Arb.) 19 Skill of gouernment, was but a Pedanteria in comparison. **1656** BLOUNT *Glossogr., Pedanteries,* pedantick humors, phrase affectings, Inkhorn terms. *Br.* **1778** WARTON *Hist.*

Eng. Poetry xxv. II. 133 The narrow pedantries of monastic erudition. **1864** BURTON *Scot Abr.* I. i. 19 A series of feudal pedantries.

2. Undue insistence on forms or details; slavish adherence to rule, theory, or precedent, in connexion with a particular profession or practice.

[**1724** SWIFT *Drapier's Lett.* v, The pedantry of a drapier in the terms of his own trade.] **1845** S. AUSTIN *Ranke's Hist. Ref.* III. 124 Even Erasmus, spite of the favour he enjoyed at court, found no mercy from monkish pedantry. **1883** P. BARRY *Dockyard Econ.* 119 He who slavishly adheres to rule displays pedantry at every turn. *a* **1869** VISCT. STRANGFORD *Sel. Writ.* I, 92 Pedantry, we take it, signifies undue stress laid on insignificant detail, and over-valuation of petty accuracy. **1902** FAIRBAIRN *Philos. Chr. Relig.* II. ii. 410 To require that every element in a figurative word be found again in the reality it denotes, is not exegesis but pedantry.

†**pe'danty.** *Obs. rare*–¹. [ad. It. type **pedante* from *pedare* to foot it (Florio).] '? Running footman' (Latham).

1606 WARNER *Alb. Eng.* XIV. xci. 369 For most, like Iehu, hurrie with Pedanties two or three.

pedanty: see PEDANTE *Obs.*

Part Two

Early Articulations of Pedagogy

The new is not found in what is said, but in the event of its return.
—Michael Foucault, *The Order of Things*

With increasing frequency, and with potentially profound consequences for future educational practices in U.S. colleges and universities, radical thinkers from different disciplines are systematically addressing issues of knowledge formation and reception (cf. Giroux 1988; Goleman 1995; Ferguson 1988; Spivak 1987, 1993; Bové 1990; Morton and Zavarzadeh 1991; Landy 1991; Knecht 1992; Gore 1993; Gallop 1982, 1995; Flannery, 1995). Some of them explicitly focus on undergraduate (but also on high-school and, less frequently, graduate) teaching as a site that can make visible the consequences of how those issues are theorized. Several make a point of naming as "pedagogy" (rather than as "education," or "teaching," or "instruction") classroom practices that deliberately subvert teachers' and students' excessive reliance on the transmission and reproduction of knowledge. But even those who deploy this term in a deliberately valorizing fashion do not necessarily make clear whether their use of the term marks a *re-vision* of past conceptualizations of pedagogy (which would acknowledge that pedagogy has a past) and why, or a *new* theoretical and overtly political conceptualization of it. Thus as they provide a much needed and cogent critique of the kinds of learning possible in institutional settings, some nevertheless betray a peculiar forgetfulness toward the fact that, in the past, comparable[1] issues of knowledge formation and reception had been addressed and articulated and that, also in that past, *this* kind of intellectual investigation *was* called *pedagogy.*[2] As I suggest in "Introduction: Chronicle of a Search," current valorizations of pedagogy cannot ipso facto undo the power of those negative constructions of it that are responsible for its ancillary and contested status in the U.S. Academy.[3] The processes that led to the formation of these constructions need to be exposed and understood to prevent uncritical replications of them. But as long as this part of pedagogy's past is kept invisible, that past cannot document the specific theoretical and institutional reasons that toward the end of the nineteenth century contributed to the tradition of academics' opposition to pedagogy—an opposition forged in the name of

59

the alleged incompatibility of liberal and useful (practical and professional) knowledge (Borrowman 1956; Conant 1963; and documents in this part). And as long as we cannot gain access to texts that record the specific terms in which, in the past, this incompatibility was conceived and sustained, we cannot in the present ask of this tradition the same kind of critical and skeptical questions that current theories of knowledge formation and reception have taught us to ask of any potentially oppressive and devaluing tradition.

In order to reclaim a version of pedagogy's past that can neither be ignored nor easily dismissed, I have deliberately looked for documents that *call into question* what I consider two of its most resilient and dysfunctional constructions: (a) pedagogy as a teacher's mechanical application (hence, for some, "pedantic" and "pedestrian"—see part one) of someone else's theories;[4] (b) pedagogy as the automatic, or the natural extension of a teacher's knowledge of "subject matter."[5] As they focus on the teacher, both constructions obfuscate the role of the learner in the teaching/learning process. Although seemingly very different from one another in terms of the intellectual endowments they assign teachers (one produces "pedants," the other "scholars"), both constructions ultimately dismiss pedagogy, the first by rendering it intellectually uninteresting, the second, intellectually unnecessary.[6]

To argue that the responsibility for the existence and the persistence of these constructions rests solely with pedagogy's critics would be facile. The fact is that texts by early advocates of pedagogy suggest that they might have unwittingly participated in forming and disseminating them. To understand how and why this happened might be one of the most sobering lessons we can learn from pedagogy's past.

The documents I collect in this section include excerpts from records on the establishment of normal schools, minutes from NEA meetings, U.S. government reports on education, and speeches and addresses by legislators and educators. Two themes run through these seemingly disparate documents and invite reflection: (a) a disenabling contradiction between the great expectations placed (by themselves and others) on early theorists and practitioners of pedagogy, and the scarcity of the intellectual and monetary capital necessary to train teachers who could meet those expectations;[7] (b) the belief that acknowledging the importance of, and granting intellectual status to, the profession of teaching would not only solve educational problems but positively influence the entire nation.

At the present, at a time when pedagogy is increasingly invoked as the means to foster a teacher's critical understanding of different cultures, at a moment, that is, when pedagogy is called upon again to perform the humanistic and sociopolitical function that early proponents of pedagogy had claimed was within its province, we are, I believe, ideally positioned to hear and to learn from the stories of both hopes and disappointments, of successes and defeats, of intellectual honesty and compromise that constitute pedagogy's richly textured past.[8]

The establishment of public normal schools in the United States (mainly in the northeast) in the first half of the nineteenth century was hailed by proponents and supporters of pedagogy as a sign of the intellectual maturity of a country that acknowledged the political, economic, and cultural need to provide for and to support the professionalization of primary and secondary school teachers. As Henry Barnard, who carefully chronicled the emergence of these institutions, pointed out, the efficacy of free common schools, which Americans had established following the Prussian example, depended on the availability of teachers who could meet the tremendous challenge of educating a population of students who varied considerably in terms of age, class, and ethnicity. (The issue of race began to be discussed only after the Civil War, and more in the southern and eastern states. See "Intermezzo." See also Barnard 1851, 36.)[9]

However, as several historians of education recognize, and as proponents and teachers of normal schools were to acknowledge, the mere establishment of these institutions could neither automatically nor extensively promote the projected high standards for and cultural appreciation of teaching and of the teaching of teaching. Educating teachers in the fundamental knowledge and practices of their profession was, simply, not generally thought to be important.[10] (See Cremin 1988; Borrowman 1956, 1971; Beck 1980.) Documents from the time suggest several complex and inextricably connected reasons for such apathy toward or overt opposition to the education of teachers. An often cited reason is a strain of anti-intellectualism in the American public.[11] Another reason, one that can be gleaned out of accounts of legislative, economic, and institutional battles fought in the name of education, was that, more often than not, debates turned educational issues into expedient political games (Stowe 1838), thus diverting attention from and failing to educate the public about what was really important about teaching and the teaching of teaching. But the reason that is cited, with most consistency, as a determining factor in the precarious status of teaching is that teaching did not constitute a profitable occupation for ambitious young *men,* most of whom took it into consideration only as a temporary stage in their "progress" toward their real occupation (see, for example, Barnard's "Connecticut," below, but also Mayo's "The Training of the Teacher in the South" in "Intermezzo").

Though confronted with widespread skepticism about the feasibility and worth of their project, proponents of normal schools continued to trust that the status of teaching, and the public's support for it, would improve when and if the intellectual and professional preparation of teachers was improved (Barnard 1851, 14–15, 40). Their arguments were logical and sensible: a teacher's *good performance* and *commitment* to teaching (40) would educate the public as to the intricacies, responsibilities, and moral, cultural, and intellectual effects of "good teaching." An educated public, in turn, would encourage their offspring to elect teaching as a profitable and worthy profession and would support channelling money into the establishment, sustenance, and improvement of such needed institutions. (But see Samuel Hall's acrid remarks in *Lectures on School-Keeping*, below, about the priorities of some of his students' parents.) The seductiveness of the argument's cause-effect structure might have prevented some early educators from fully appreciating the intricacies of the educational problem they confronted and might have blinded them to the condescension and violence inherent in their plans for widespread literacy.

In spite of wishful projections and several promising beginnings, *the teaching of teaching* failed to evolve into a discipline that could represent itself and would be widely and consistently recognized as theoretically rigorous and sophisticated. Ideological, economic, and institutional circumstances were to exert tremendous pressure on the conceptualization and enactment of pedagogy as the interconnectedness of theory and practice. Under that pressure, pedagogy was reduced to practice, as such, to the handmaid of theory. This prevented pedagogy from attaining and sustaining the power and the prestige that, on the one hand, would have justified and subsidized a teacher's continuous, in-depth philosophical investigation of how one knows and learns to know, and on the other hand, would have granted authority and plausibility to the requirement that anybody involved in the formation and dissemination of knowledge, *at any level,* should be intellectually capable of and committed to engaging in this investigation. (The *reduction* to theory divorced from practice, a later phenomenon, as we see in part three, had equally deleterious consequences.)

The earliest argument for what should constitute the preparation of a teacher, however, consistently *insisted on the necessity* to provide teachers with the theoretical knowledge (science) necessary to guide and control their practice (art). In other words, the theory *and* the practice of teaching were seen neither as interchangeable (as dictionary definitions of pedagogy as "the theory *or* practice of teaching" record and prescribe) nor as hierarchically related (as the view of pedagogy as merely the implementation and application of theory implies), but as two different though inextricably and dialectically connected ways of knowing.[12]

The first book on education ever printed in the United States, Samuel R. Hall's *Lectures on School-Keeping* (1829), offers an early strong formulation of pedagogy. Considering the particularly inauspicious circumstances that motivated it, the book—its humble title notwithstanding—is a remarkably sophisticated theoretical account of Hall's reflections on his teaching of teachers, on conducting school, and on the appropriate curriculum for common schools and for future teachers of common school students. *Lectures on School-Keeping* grew out of his experience as the principal and teacher of the first normal school in this country (the Columbian School, later incorporated as Concord Academy).

At a time when instruction was "the hit and miss method of poorly trained teachers" ("Introduction," *Lectures*, 13), Hall had the advantage of having been raised in a context and in a family that had the inclination and the material means to value intellectual learning and that taught him to value and pursue it.[13] Like that of most early better-educated teachers, Hall's formal education was religious; quite uncharacteristically, however, he never let his teacher's role be subsumed by his preacher's role. The professional and intellectual distance he was able to establish between preaching and teaching made it possible for him to have a lucid sense of his work's worth, and more importantly, to exact from others the appreciation—intellectual and monetary—that it deserved.[14]

When in 1828, as a result of the favorable impression he had made as a preacher and as a teacher during his work in that area, he was offered a position as minister in Concord, Vermont, he accepted that position on condition that he would be helped to establish a center for the teaching of prospective teachers. The terms of the contract he set up are quite interesting. Not only was his teaching granted the remuneration he demanded; he also succeeded in having a written clause in the contract specifying that "during the terms of the school" his duties as minister would be considerably lightened (see excerpt).[15]

Within Hall's conceptualization of pedagogy, a teacher is not only *one who knows*,[16] but above all *one who knows how and why he or she knows,* one who learns to develop the reflexive knowledge necessary to teach others to produce their own knowledge. Of the necessary prerequisites for a schoolmaster to teach arithmetic, he wrote, for example:

> A thorough knowledge of Arithmetic is also indispensable to the schoolmaster. I do not mean that smattering of science, which so often passess for a knowledge of it; but a thorough acquaintance with its principles. To be able, by the aid of rules and manuscripts, to solve the question given, is very far from being the knowledge necessary. No one is properly qualified in this branch of science, until

able, from his own knowledge of its principles, to originate rules, even if they were not given in his book. He should be able to tell the "why and wherefore" in every operation, else is not prepared to teach. (1929, 70)[17]

Though Hall's practice as a teacher was guided by and shot through with his religious beliefs, those beliefs, as his comments here demonstrate, did not lead him to conceptualize teaching as essentially a matter of inspiration and divine intervention, as others did.

Not only does Hall's text mark the beginnings of pedagogy in this country; it marks it as an autochthonous phenomenon. There is no evidence that Hall has been influenced by Prussian models or German theorists' and philosophers' writings on pedagogy (a term he did not use), though his training in theology and his voracious and precocious reading habits clearly must have shaped his ability to reflect, to infer, and to theorize. (This is not to say, as some argue, that exposure to and readings of theology, philosophy, etc., are ipso facto sufficient to turn one into a theologian, philosopher, etc., nor that that knowledge, as vast as it can be, makes one ipso facto a productive teacher of those subjects.)

Hall's awareness of the educational needs of his time is remarkable, but even more remarkable is that he was not unique in sensing them. Hall came to articulate his theory of teaching simultaneously with, though independently of, other early proponents of teacher education. In 1825 there appeared in print (as pamphlets or newspaper articles) Thomas H. Gallaudet's "Plan of a Seminary for the Education of Instructors of Youth," James G. Carter's "Essays on Popular Education, Containing a Particular Examination of the Schools of Massachusetts, and an Outline of the Institution for the Education of Teachers," and Walter R. Johnson's "Observations on the Improvement of Seminaries of Learning." Also in 1825, Governor Clinton of New York commended to the consideration of the legislature "the education of competent teachers," and in 1826 he called for the establishment of a teacher's seminary (Barnard 1851). In the same year, at Amherst College's annual meeting of the board of trustees, the faculty recommended to annex to the college a new department for systematic instruction in the "noble, but strangely neglected" science of education. This is how the argument was framed:

> No respectable College would think itself organized, without a department of Natural Philosophy, and another of Chemistry—nor without Professors of Rhetoric and the Languages. And yet, how few who enjoy these advantages in College, expect ever to be practical Chemists, or Philosophers, or Critics. How then can the most distinguished and useful literary institutions in the land, go on from year to year without a single instructer devoted to the science of education,

when three fourths of their sons expect to be teachers, in one form or another themselves, and when the primary schools, academies and higher institutions of learning, require twice, or thrice as many thousands to supply them, as are wanted for all the learned professions together? Every third or fourth man we meet, is, or has been a school-master; but who among a thousand of the best qualified, was ever regularly instructed himself in the science and art of teaching, for a single quarter? ("Amherst College Report," 17)

Very few teachers in the 1820s, and afterward, had the necessary exposure to knowledge and understanding that would make it possible for them, in Hall's words, "to originate rules" from their knowledge of a science's principles. In spite of this, Hall and several of his contemporaries and immediate successors did not opt for just providing teachers with those rules.

Among other early articulations of pedagogy in this country, those by Calvin Stowe, David Page, and Baynard R. Hall deserve special attention.

Stowe's "Normal Schools and Teachers' Seminaries" (1838) is a detailed and rigorously mapped out plan for the establishment of normal schools, the conceptualization of the theory and practice of teaching they ought to disseminate, and their appropriate curriculum.

Stowe modelled his plan on the Prussian institutions that he spent considerable time examining. What makes this document so interesting to read is the consideration it dramatically forces on us of the particular conditions that framed it. Stowe insists, for example, that normal school students should be at least sixteen when received in a teachers' seminary. His insistence confronts us with the realization that fourteen- and fifteen-year-old individuals, themselves barely educated, were commonly entrusted with educating others. (The situation was to be replicated in the 1880s when the first normal schools for African Americans were established.) And this realization confers special resonance to the insistence by contemporary and later theorists of education that a teacher's knowledge should *exceed*—in terms of breadth and methods—the specific subject matter he or she is supposed to teach.

Though conceptualized specifically to address the theory and practice of teaching in the emerging normal schools, Stowe's lucid distinction between the study of a topic for the purpose of applying it to practical use, and study for the purpose of teaching it, is particularly relevant today, when even in research universities, teaching is being resurrected as the proper thing to do, though not necessarily as an opportunity to engage in reflexive praxis. For Stowe the difference between the two ways of studying results from two different "processes," two different ways of learning and of knowing, only one of which is geared toward making it possible for others to become autonomous learners.

Stowe uses "tact" to describe the orator's "sense" of how to dispose the parts of his subject "in the order best calculated for effect." His use of this category and his explanation of how it works can help expose the shortcomings of subsequent deployments of this term or category to characterize "good teaching" (see part three). Tact, he argues, is a function of mental processes (hence neither divinely inspired nor osmotically acquired through exposure to the "right" culture) by which the orator achieves the calculated effect *as if by instinct*. In other words, tact is *not* instinctive, neither is it natural: it is the result of appropriately cultivated and educated processes. An orator's processes

> are generally so rapid, so evanescent, that it may be impossible for him to recall them so as to describe them to another; and it is this very rapidity of intellectual movement, which gives him success as an orator, that renders it the more difficult for him to succeed as a teacher. . . . The teacher must stop to observe and analyze each movement of the mind itself, as it advances on every topic; but men of genius for execution, and of great practical skill, who never teach, are generally too impatient to make this minute analysis, and often, indeed, form such habits as at length to become incapable of it. (Stowe 1838; see excerpt, below)

The reflexivity that Stowe poses as the sine qua non of good teaching is difficult to learn and even more difficult to teach: it is threatening to engage in, since it may expose errors of logic in one's habitual thinking patterns and may reveal biases and presuppositions in need of revision; and above all, because it is so time-consuming, it is almost impossible for it to be practiced in educational contexts geared toward rapid transmission and reception of knowledge. Yet it is this reflexivity that keeps theory and practice critically and self-reflexively interconnected. That historically pedagogy has been alternatively and repeatedly "elevated" to *theory* or "reduced" to *practice* (but from my perspective either option is a reduction) can be construed as an implicit but dramatic demonstration of its fundamental complexity. Indeed, I would suggest that the reasons for pedagogy's various simplifications and reductions might be found in pedagogy's complexity, rather than in its inadequacy as a discipline.

Compared with Hall's and Stowe's articulations of pedagogy, David Page's *Theory and Practice of Teaching; or, The Motives and Methods of Good School-Keeping* stands out as an odd, at times contradictory, mixture of theoretical insights and mystical visions. Page insists that aptness to teach

> like aptness to do anything else, is usually an acquired power, based on a correct knowledge of what it is to be done, and some accurate estimate of the fitness of the means for the end. If there are exceptions to this, they are very uncommon; and the safer way, therefore, for the majority of teachers, is, to study carefully

the rationale of their processes, and to rely rather upon sound and philosophical principles in their teaching, than upon a very doubtful intuition. (1847, 105)

In other words, Page posits as a teacher's prerequisite the ability to reflect on, so as to study, the rationale of one's processes, and the willingness and ability to remember the difficulties one encountered in the pursuit of learning (for a similar argument, see Salvatori, "Towards a Hermeneutics of Difficulty"). If and how one can teach others to develop that ability, however, Page does not make consistently clear to his contemporary and later audience. Occasionally, the development of that ability seems to be dependent on a moral or religious inclination, one that ultimately sets up learning as strongly dependent on faith.

Though Page is aware of and stresses the "proverbial [low] compensation" of teachers, and its consequences for the status and power of teaching, he opens up heavenly vistas and promises ultraterrestrial rewards for "the faithful, self-denying, patient teacher" that dignifies his profession. Though he exposes the inadequacy of "sermons and homilies" and (anticipating Paulo Freire) the "pouring-in process" for which he would like to substitute the "drawing-out process," he often ends up being sermonic, homiletic, and didactic. In spite of his subtle insights, in spite of his awareness that teaching needed to develop from a mostly haphazard practice into a thoughtfully reasoned theory and into a powerful science, in spite of his attempts to move in that direction, he ultimately undercuts the effectiveness of his work by making his theory and science of teaching so contingent on faith.

In his editor's preface to the 1885 edition of *Theory and Practice of Teaching*, William H. Payne describes the main traits of David Page's character as follows:

> industry, perseverance, decision, energy, great executive ability, ready tact, and conscientious adherence to what he regarded as duty. But no language can describe the fascination of his manner, the attraction of his presence, his skill in what he was accustomed to call the drawing-out process, or his tact in making all his knowledge available. . . . He possessed, beyond most men, the happy talent of always saying the right thing at the right time. (1885, 18)

For Calvin Stowe tact works *as if by instinct.* For Page, as pointed out in the quotation above, tact seems to have been *the happy talent of always saying the right thing at the right time,* a talent that no language can fully describe, no theory can account for. There is a most substantial difference between the potential effectiveness of these two men's conceptualizations of pedagogy. Within one, tact is a matter of careful, rigorous instruction; within the other, a matter of instruction *assisted* by something mysterious, spiritual. What looms within Page's conceptualization are the questionable consequences of a compensatory excessive reliance on the mysterious when both teachers and students are inadequate to the task of describing and reflecting on their processes of knowing. The terms in which Payne describes Page's work point this out. Payne writes, encomiastically,

> Far more than any other book of its kind, it has set before the young teacher, in a clear and attractive manner, the problem of the school, and at the same time has enlisted the feelings as a motive power in attaining the ends thus pointed out. This treatment embodies the highest philosophy; for to know the end is almost to know the way, and to feel a strong impulse to reach the end, is finally to find the way. (5–6)

As we see in part three, this comment is representative of the conceptualization of pedagogy that William Payne himself, reputed to have been the first *university* professor of pedagogy in the United States, contributed to disseminate in the 1880s. Without detracting from Page's accomplishments, without denying the impetus that feelings and impulses can give one's teaching, I want nevertheless to point out the inherent danger of suggesting to inexperienced teachers that to know the end is to know the way. Even if it could be demonstrated that this axiom is valid for *experienced* teachers, the kind of learning that it fosters still needs to be problematized. For teachers and for teachers of teachers to rely on this axiom can be counterproductive, if not unethical, since this reliance may minimize a teacher's and a learner's reflexive investigation of the steps that one takes to finally get to know the end and the way to that end. Dismissive evaluations of teaching must perforce obfuscate the importance and the difficulty of attaining these two kinds of knowing.

As my interested reading of these early texts suggests, early conceptualizations of pedagogy posit (some, indeed, more problematically than others) a kind of reflexivity, intellectual scrutiny, and movement inward as ways of sustaining the inextricability of theory and practice. The fact that such reflexivity could neither be articulated nor always effectively taught and disseminated cannot always be traced to some kind of flaw in pedagogy's theoretical construction. Therefore, we might need to consider the possibility that pedagogy's failures might be actually signs of its exigency—an exigency that laws of supply and demand ruled in excess of teachers' intellectual aptness to attend to it, and consequently in need of mediation and simplification. The translation of Rosenkranz's *Pedagogics as a System* by Anna Brackett, and William Torrey Harris's subsequent popularization of that translation, is a representative case.

Anna Brackett, who in 1863 had been appointed principal of the St. Louis

Normal School in St. Louis, Missouri (she was the first female normal school principal in the United States), published her translation of Rosenkranz's text, in three consecutive installments, in the *Journal of Speculative Philosophy*. Her fluency in German philosophy, and in the German language necessary and suited to formulate Rosenkranz's arguments, made it possible for his text to be made available in this country at a time of need. (Her story is one I plan to return to and record.) In 1886, William Torrey Harris, founding editor of the *Journal of Speculative Philosophy*, reissued Brackett's translation as the first volume of the Appleton Series on Education, of which he was also the editor. His decision to inaugurate the series with that volume was clearly meant to call attention to that text and its subject matter. Interestingly, however, he deemed it necessary to name that subject matter "education" rather than "pedagogy," and to make Brackett's translation more accessible by means of summaries and paraphrases (see the introduction and part three for the significance of this name change). That decision acknowledged that the audience for which the book was intended needed assistance in understanding it—a view that historical accounts of the preparation of teachers at the time seemed to confirm. Whether or not that need was presumed or widespread is, ironically, immaterial. The fact is that Harris's gesture can be seen as an emblematic assessment of a teacher's inability to gain unmediated access to theory. The industry of textbooks, at its worst, contributed to simultaneously producing and reproducing this construction of teachers.

Though produced for contexts other than the normal schools, I have included in this section exerpts from texts by Emma Willard (1819), Almira H. Lincoln Phelps (1833), Caleb Atwater (1841), and William Fowle (1873) as documentation of a widespread commitment to education in this country. Addressed, respectively, to legislators (Willard), students and teachers of female seminaries (Phelps), teachers and students of teachers' institutes (Fowle), and "parents, guardians and instructers [sic] of youth" (Atwater), these texts, and others they may lead to, can provide, I believe, important materials to investigate the nature of and possible determining factors for the establishment and longevity of so many alternative institutions for the preparation of teachers. Although these institutions fulfilled, admirably in many cases, a much needed educational function, these documents force us to consider the consequences of the assumption that teacher preparation needed neither special nor protracted attention. Moreover, these documents can serve to uncover certain moves and themes in the writings of early and passionate advocates of education that, I contend, might have unwittingly led them to defining a teacher's moral and intellectual endowments and concomitant responsibilities in terms so exceptional that they could neither be realistically attained nor advantageously sustained. Let me try to be more specific.

In "A Plan for Improving Female Education," Emma Willard calls for the establishment of female seminaries to improve "one half of society, and that half, which barbarous and despotic nations have ever degraded." Strategically invoking the power mothers are assumed to have in shaping the moral and intellectual character of their progeny, Willard deftly exposes as untenable the assumption that "mothers" are naturally (i.e., biologically) fit to "rear the human plant to its perfection." This is how she argues the case for "female education":

> How important a power is given by this charge! yet, little do too many of my sex know how, either to appreciate or to improve it. Unprovided with the means of acquiring that knowledge, which flows liberally to the other sex—having our time of education devoted to frivolous requirements, how should we understand the nature of the mind, so as to be aware of the importance of those early impressions, which we make upon the minds of our children?—or how should we be able to form enlarged and correct views, either of the character, to which we ought to mould them, or of the means most proper to form them aright?
> (1819, 6)

Setting aside, for the moment, Willard's identification of womanhood with motherhood, and her possible class bias, I want to suggest that, having defined in no uncertain terms the tremendous importance of mothers as teachers, and having skillfully deployed that very point to urge for the categorical necessity of providing them with an education appropriate to that task, she sets up for them standards that are impossible to uphold.

> It is the duty of a government, to do all in its power to promote the present and the future prosperity of the nation, over which it is placed. *This prosperity will depend on the character of its citizens. The characters of these will be formed by their mothers;* and it is through the mothers, that the government can control the characters of its future citizens, to form them such as will ensure their country's prosperity. If this is the case, then it is the duty of our present legislators to begin now, to form the characters of the next generation, by controlling that of the females, who are to be their mothers, while it is yet with them a season of improvement. (16, emphasis added)

Far from slighting Emma Willard's achievement and her contributions to other female educators who were equally aware of the need to demystify women's "natural" propensity to be teachers, I would like to make visible the untenable position that Willard found herself immured in,[18] as did other early educators. Consider, for example, Caleb Atwater's claim that "there are, and certainly must be, some great and capital defects in all our systems of education in the entire nation, otherwise, there could not exist among us, everywhere, so much vice and crime" (1841, 33). Atwater identified as the problem the "awful error to cultivate the *mind* and neglect the *heart*" (33). (The opposition that Atwater, and many others, perceived between heart and mind offers an interesting perspective from which to investigate and to complicate the charges of anti-intellectualism frequently levied against the U. S. public.) To remedy such "great and capital defect" in the educational system, he proposed an approach to teaching that requires that teachers be models of Christian perfection: "But we return to the professional teachers of youth, and say, that for them and their pupils to copy after, in their manners, morals, principles, precepts, and examples, we propose to them, the Great Teacher of mankind, Jesus, their friend and Saviour." (63)

Consider, also, the demands that Rev. Baynard Hall's conceptualization of pedagogy makes. In *Teaching, a Science; The Teacher, an Artist* (1848), he invokes art, tact, and instinct as crucial categories. However, as if aware and weary of their potential ephemerality and their imperviousness to being taught, he bridles them with incredible demands:

> Teaching is a science; and the teacher, reducing its principles to practice, is an artist. . . . The true teacher is an artist—a former—a creator. . . . The teacher, as an artist, possesses intellectual and moral qualifications that must class him with the best, and show that his office or profession ranks among the highest in dignity and importance. The teacher must be, among other things, a philosopher, a judge, a ruler, a parent, a preacher; and he must be, also, learned and scientific. (18, 19, 21)

It seems to me that as they tried to persuade the public and the legislature of how important and complex was the "noble, but strangely neglected" discipline of education, early educators, undoubtedly in good faith, assigned teachers extraordinary, in fact superhuman, qualities and functions—qualities and functions to which teachers, in those and subsequent times, could not possibly measure up (cf. Hofstadter 1963, n. 6).

Of all the texts I have read, the one that offers the most encomiastic but emblematically ambiguous articulation of a teacher's mission and its commensurate rewards is William B. Fowle's *The Teacher's Institute; or, Familiar Hints to Young Teachers* (1873). It is with this text that I want to conclude this section. Here is a lengthy excerpt from it:

> The faithful teacher, on every plan, has much to do and much to endure. He must be contented to labor and be ill-rewarded; he must be willing to see his pupils increase while he decreases; and even to see the world, whose movement he has accelerated, leaving him behind. No matter;—the school of life last not long, and its best rewards are reserved till school is over.

> When Jupiter offered the prize of immortality to him who was most useful to mankind, the court of Olympus was crowded with competitors. The warrior boasted of his patriotism, but Jupiter thundered;—the rich man boasted of his munificence, and Jupiter showed him a widow's mite;—the pontiff held up the keys of heaven, and Jupiter pushed the doors wide open;—the painter boasted of his power to give life to inanimate canvass, and Jupiter breathed aloud in derision;—the sculptor boasted of making goods that contended with the Immortals for human homage; Jupiter frowned;—the orator boasted of his power to sway a nation with his voice, and Jupiter marshalled the obedient hosts of heaven with a nod;—the poet spoke of his power to move even the gods by praise; Jupiter blushed;—the musician claimed to practice the only human science that had been transported to heaven; Jupiter hesitated,—when, seeing a venerable man looking with intense interest upon the group of competitors, but presenting no claim,—"What art thou?" said the benignant monarch. "Only a spectator," said the gray-headed sage; "all these were once my pupils." "Crown the faithful *teacher* with immortality, and make room for him at my right hand!" (258)

Since I embarked on this project, I have wanted to be able to cite a myth, a tale of origins, that would grant pedagogy if not the status of a goddess at least that of a muse—ideally, a muse who would combine the powers of Clio (history) and Mnemosyne (memory).[19]

When I got to the very last page of William B. Fowle's text, I was elated, at first, finally to read a story—albeit apocryphal—that crowns a (male) teacher with immortality and places him at the right hand of Jupiter for having been "most useful to mankind." But before I even got to the end of that last page, I realized, with some dismay, that there unfolded, in front of me, yet another problematic construction of teachers, and teaching's status and function. How exactly and why has the teacher in Fowle's account been "most useful to mankind"? Is the grey-headed sage crowned for choosing *not* to compete? For being wiser (how so?) or knowing more (what?) than his former students who, their status notwithstanding, do not obviously earn Jupiter's esteem? (If so, is his being crowned nuanced with the ominous hues of a Dantesque *contrappasso* punishment? Is he, in other words, even in his glory, condemned to be forever a "spectator" of his pupils' shortcomings?) And why does "the faithful teacher, on every plan, [have] much to do and much to endure?"and "be contented to labor and be ill-rewarded"? and wait for "the school of life['s] best rewards" to be bestowed "till school is over"? Given its position in Fowle's text—the last paragraph—the story seems to have been offered as an apodictic apotheosis: if so, however, the story glorifies and perpetuates the habit, since time immemorial, of placing impossible demands upon teachers who for their labors can nevertheless only expect extraterrestrial, or indefinitely deferred, rewards.[20]

Documents

The documents in part two trace pedagogy's past back to the normal schools, the institutions established to provide appropriate preparation for much-needed teachers of common schools. In order to reclaim a version of pedagogy's past that can neither be ignored nor easily dismissed, I have deliberately looked for, located, and reproduced documents that *call into question* what I consider two of its most resilient and dysfunctional constructions: (a) pedagogy as a teacher's mechanical (hence, for some, "pedantic" and "pedestrian"—see part one) application of someone else's theories; (b) pedagogy as the obvious, or the natural extension of a teacher's knowledge of "subject matter." Insofar as this search has uncovered texts by early advocates of pedagogy that, I argue, unwittingly participated in forming and disseminating these dysfunctional constructions, I have tried to give them adequate representation.

Readers of these documents should notice that not all theorists and legislators refer to the theory and practice of teaching as "pedagogy." Some call it "education" and make a point of distinguishing it from "instruction." The appearance of the term *pedagogy* in these texts may be taken to signal the influence of German scholarship on the subject, much sought after by American educators (many of whom traveled to Germany to study pedagogy) because of its well-established philosophical tradition. In the historical period covered by this section (1820s through 1870s) both *education* and *pedagogy* were valorizing terms: in other words, they were not yet used to mark the disciplinary hierarchy that, in the last two decades of the nineteenth century, began to restrict pedagogy to "practice" and consequently to marginalize it as a discipline and subject of study unworthy of university status. Although I would not claim that meanings can ever be stable and precisely agreed upon, I think it might be productive to consider, and to hypothesize reasons for, the peculiar confusion and lack of shared understanding that marks the use of terms and concepts at the center of the teaching profession.

From: Emma Hart Willard, *A Plan for Improving Female Education* (1819)

EMMA HART WILLARD (1787–1870) was born in Berlin, Connecticut. Her education began at home, at the Hart fireside, where her family gathered to discuss the best books available and political, religious, and moral issues. She attended the district school and Berlin Academy. She taught in Berlin (later Westfield, Massachusetts), and from 1807 to 1809 she took full charge of the Female Academy in Middlebury, Vermont. In 1809 she married John Willard, a physician and politician, and gave up her position. When her husband's nephew, a student at Middlebury College, moved in with them, she became interested in the subjects of study young men were exposed to (mathematics and philosophy). She studied them on her own and decided to teach them to young girls, confident that they would be able to master them without losing their health, refinement, or charm.

In 1814, when there were no high schools for girls and no college in the world would admit women, she opened in her own home a school for young ladies, the Middlebury Female Seminary. In 1818 she sent to Gov. DeWitt Clinton of New York *An Address to the Public: Particularly to the Members of the Legislature of New York, Proposing a Plan for Improving Female Education.* This ambitious document, published the following year, was well received by DeWitt and other legislators; however, ridiculed by many others, it did not achieve the desired results. Having moved to Waterford, New York, she established Waterford Academy, and in 1821 she opened Troy Female Seminary thanks in part to local citizens who provided her with a building. Now known as the Emma Willard School, the Troy Seminary was looked upon as a model of education for women in the United States and in Europe.

ADDRESS, &C.

The object of this Address, is to convince the public, that a reform, with respect to female education, is necessary; that it cannot be effected by individual exertion, but that it requires the aid of the legislature; and further, by shewing the justice, the policy, and the magnanimity of such an undertaking, to persuade the body to endow a seminary for females, as the commencement of such reformation.

The idea of a college for males will naturally be associated with that of a seminary, instituted and endowed by the public; and the absurdity of sending ladies to college, may, at first thought, strike every one to whom this subject shall be proposed. I therefore hasten to observe, that the seminary here recommended, will be as different from those appropriated to the other sex, as the female character and duties are from the male. . . .

That the improvement of female education will be considered by our enlightened citizens as a subject of importance, the liberality with which they part with their property to educate their daughters, is a sufficient evidence. . . .

If the improvement of the American female character, and that alone, could be effected by public liberality, employed in giving better means of instruction; such improvement of one half of society, and that half, which barbarous and despotic nations have ever degraded, would of itself be an object, worthy of the most liberal government on earth; but if the female character be raised, it must inevitably raise that of the other sex: and thus does the plan proposed, offer, as the object of legislative bounty, to elevate the whole character of the community.

As evidence that this statement does not exaggerate the female influence in society, our sex need but be considered, in the single relation of mothers. In this character, we have the charge of the whole mass of individuals, who are to compose the succeeding generation; during that period of youth, when the pliant mind takes any direction, to which it is steadily guided by a forming hand. How important a power is given by this charge! yet, little do too many of my sex know how, either to appreciate or improve it. Unprovided with the means of acquiring that knowledge, which flows liberally to the other sex—having our time of education devoted to frivolous acquirements, how should we understand the nature of the mind, so as to be aware of the importance of those early impressions, which we make upon the minds of our children?—or how should we be able to form enlarged and correct views, either of the character, to which we ought to mould them, or of the means most proper to form them aright?

Considered in this point of view, were the interests of male education alone to be consulted, that of females becomes of sufficient importance to engage the public attention. Would we rear the human plant to its perfection, we must first fertilize the soil which produces it. If it acquires its first bent and texture upon a barren plain, it will avail comparatively little, should it be afterwards transplanted to a garden. . . .

DEFECTS IN THE PRESENT MODE OF FEMALE EDUCATION, AND THEIR CAUSES.

Civilized nations have long since been convinced that education, as it respects males, will not, like trade, regulate itself; and hence, they have made it a prime object to provide that sex with everything requisite to facilitate their progress in learning: but female education has been left to the mercy of private adventurers; and the consequence has been to our sex, the same, as it would have been to the other, had legislatures left their accommodations, and means of instruction, to chance also.

Education cannot prosper in any community, unless, from the ordinary motives which actuate the human mind, the best and most cultivated talents of the community, can be brought into exercise in that way. Male education flourishes, because, from the guardian care of legislatures, the presidencies and professorships of our colleges are some of the highest objects to which the eye of ambition is directed. Not so with female institutions. Preceptresses of these, are dependent on their pupils for support, and are consequently liable to become the victims of their caprice. In such a situation, it is not more desirable to be a preceptress, than it would be, to be a parent, invested with the care of children, and responsible for their behavior, but yet, depending on them for subsistence, and destitute of power to enforce their obedience.

Feminine delicacy requires, that girls should be educated chiefly by their own sex. This is apparent from considerations, that regard their health and conveniences, the propriety of their dress and manners, and their domestic accomplishments.

Boarding schools, therefore, whatever may be their defects, furnish the best mode of education provided for females. . . .

Thus the writer has endeavored to point out the defects of the present mode of female education; chiefly in order to show, that the great cause of these defects consists in a state of things, in which legislatures, undervaluing the importance of women in society, neglect to provide for their education and suffer it to become the sport of adventurers of fortune, who may be both ignorant and vicious. . . .

It is the duty of a government, to do all in its power to promote the present and future prosperity of the nation, over which it is placed. This prosperity will depend on the character of its citizens. The characters of these will be formed by their mothers; and it is through the mothers, that the government can control the characters of its future citizens, to form them such as will ensure their country's prosperity. If this is the case, then it is the duty of our

present legislators to begin now, to form the characters of the next generation, by controling that of the females, who are to be their mothers, while it
is yet with them a season of improvement.

But should the conclusion be almost admitted, that our sex too are the
legitimate children of the legislature; and that it is their duty to afford us a
share of their parental bounty; the phantom of a college-learned lady, would
be ready to rise up, and destroy every good resolution, which the admission
of this truth would naturally produce in our favour.

To shew that it is not a masculine education which is here recommended,
and to afford a definite view of the manner in which a female institution
might possess the respectability, permanency, and uniformity of operation
of those appropriated to males; and yet differ from them, so as to be adapted
to that difference of character and duties, to which the softer sex should be
formed, is the object of the following imperfect

SKETCH OF A FEMALE SEMINARY.

From considering the deficiencies in boarding schools, much may be
learned, with regard to what would be needed, for the prosperity and usefulness of a public seminary for females.

I. There would be needed a building, with commodious rooms for lodging
and recitation, apartments for the reception of apparatus, and for the accommodation of the domestic department.

II. A library, containing books on the various subjects in which the pupils
were to receive instruction; musical instruments, some good paintings, to
form the taste and serve as models for the execution of those who were to be
instructed in that art; maps, globes, and a small collection of philosophical
apparatus.

III. A judicious board of trust, competent and desirous to promote its
interests, would in a female, as in a male literary institution, be the corner
stone of its prosperity. . . .

IV. Suitable instruction. This article may be subdivided under four heads.

1. Religious and Moral.
2. Literary.
3. Domestic.
4. Ornamental.

1. Religious and Moral. A regular attention to religious duties
would, of course be required of the pupils by the laws of the institution.
The trustees would be careful to appoint no instructors, who would not
teach religion and morality, both by their example, and by leading the

minds of the pupils to perceive, that these constitute the true end of all education. It would be desirable, that the young ladies should spend a part of their Sabbaths in hearing discourses relative to the peculiar duties of the sex. The evidences of Christianity, and moral philosophy, would constitute a part of their studies.

2. Literary Instruction. To make an exact enumeration of the branches of literature, which might be taught, would be impossible, unless the time of the pupils' continuance at the seminary, and the requisites for entrance, were previously fixed. Such an enumeration would be tedious, nor do I conceive that it would be at all promotive of my object. The difficulty complained of, is not, that we are at a loss what sciences we ought to learn, but that we have not proper advantages to learn any. Many writers have given us excellent advice with regard to what we should be taught, but no legislature has provided us the means of instruction. Not however, to pass lightly over this fundamental part of education, I will mention one or two of the less obvious branches of science, which, I conceive should engage the youthful attention of my sex.

It is highly important, that females should be conversant with those studies, which will lead them to understand the operations of the human mind. The chief use to which the philosophy of the mind can be applied, is to regulate education by its rules. The ductile mind of the child is intrusted to the mother: and she ought to have every possible assistance, in acquiring a knowledge of this noble material, on which it is her business to operate, that she may best understand how to mould it to its most excellent form.

Natural philosophy has not often been taught to our sex. Yet why should we be kept in ignorance of the great machinery of nature, and left to the vulgar notion, that nothing is curious but what deviates from her common course? If mothers were acquainted with this science, they would communicate very many of its principles to their children in early youth. From the bursting of an egg buried in the fire, I have heard an intelligent mother, lead her prattling inquirer, to understand the cause of the earthquake. But how often does the mother, from ignorance on this subject, give her child the most erroneous and contracted views of the causes of natural phenomena; views, which, though he may afterwards learn to be false, are yet, from the laws of association, ever ready to return, unless the active powers of the mind are continually upon the alert to keep them out. A knowledge of natural philosophy is calculated to heighten the moral taste, by bringing to view the majesty and beauty of order and design; and to enliven piety, by enabling the mind more clearly to perceive, throughout the manifold works of God, that wisdom, in which he hath made them all.

In some of the sciences proper for our sex, the books, written for the other, would need alteration; because, in some they presuppose more knowledge than female pupils would possess; in others, they have parts not particularly interesting to our sex, and omit subjects immediately relating to their pursuits. There would likewise be needed, for a female seminary, some works, which I believe are no where extant, such as a systematic treatise on housewifery.

3. Domestic Instruction should be considered important in a female seminary. It is the duty of our sex to regulate the internal concerns of every family; and unless they be properly qualified to discharge this duty, whatever may be their literary or ornamental attainments, they cannot be expected to make either good wives, good mothers, or good mistresses of families: and if they are none of these, they must be bad members of society; for it is by promoting or destroying the comfort and prosperity of their own families, that females serve or injure the community. . . .

BENEFITS OF FEMALE SEMINARIES.

. . . Let us now proceed to inquire, what benefits would result from the establishment of female seminaries.

They would constitute a grade of public education, superior to any yet known in the history of our sex; and through them, the lower grades of female instruction might be controlled. The influence of public seminaries, over these, would operate in two ways; first, by requiring certain qualifications for entrance; and secondly, by furnishing instructresses, initiated in their modes of teaching, and imbued with their maxims.

Female seminaries might be expected to have important and happy effects, on common schools in general; and in the manner of operating on these, would probably place the business of teaching children, in hands now nearly useless to society; and take it from those, whose services the state wants in many other ways.

That nature designed for our sex the care of children, she had made manifest, by mental, as well as physical indications. She has given us, in a greater degree than men, the gentle arts of insinuation, to soften their minds, and fit them to receive impressions; a greater quickness of invention to vary modes of teaching to different dispositions; and more patience to make repeated efforts. There are many females of ability, to whom the business of instructing children is highly acceptable, and, who would devote all their faculties to their occupation. They would have no higher pecuniary object to engage their attention, and their reputation as instructors they would consider as important; whereas; whenever able and enterprizing men, engage in this business, they consider it, merely as a temporary employment, to further some other object, to the attainment of which, their best thoughts and calculations are all directed. If then women were properly fitted by instruction, they would be likely to teach children better than the other sex; they could afford to do it cheaper; and those men who would otherwise be engaged in this employment, might be at liberty to add to the wealth of the nation, by any of those thousand occupations, from which women are necessarily debarred.

But the females, who taught children, would have been themselves instructed either immediately or indirectly by the seminaries. Hence through these, the government might exercise an intimate, and most benificial control over common schools. Any one, who has turned his attention to this subject, must be aware, that there is great room for improvement in these, both as to the modes of teaching, and the things taught; and what method could be devised so likely to effect this improvement, as to prepare by instruction, a class of individuals, whose interest, leisure, and natural talents, would combine to make them pursue it with ardour. Such a class of individuals would be raised up, by female seminaries. And therefore they would be likely to have highly important and happy effects on common schools.

From: James Gordon Carter, *Essays Upon Popular Education with an Outline of an Institution for the Education of Teachers* (1826)

JAMES GORDON CARTER (1795–1849) was born in Leominister, Massachusetts. He attended Groton Academy and Harvard College while teaching district schools and lecturing on the history of Masonry. Graduated from Harvard with honors in 1820, he began in 1821 his efforts in behalf of public education. His 1826 *Essays Upon Popular Education* were widely and favorably discussed. In 1827 he tried but failed to convince the legislature to support a project for the realization of normal schools. In 1830, Carter helped to found the American Institute of Instruction. Elected to the U.S. legislature, he served in the House and in the Senate and, as chairman of the committee on education, he played an influential role in the growth of common schools, in spreading a Pestalozzian approach to teaching (see *Meyers Grosses Konversations Lexicon,* 1943, in this collection), and in the establishment of normal schools.

It was necessary, however, to dwell at some length upon a few of the moral and political advantages of a correct system of education; and it was necessary to point out, somewhat in detail, the defects and abuses of our schools, in order to show that a reform was required,—*a thorough and radical reform.* But I am not visionary enough to suppose for a moment, that a change involving such important interests and consequences,—a change requiring such bold innovations upon established usages, as a new organization of our system of public instruction, however desirable it may be in itself, can be affected suddenly. I know that it cannot. It is a sound maxim, that reforms on all moral and religious subjects are slow and progressive. Political changes, too, unless they are affected by violence and revolution, are also slow. And there is no reason to suppose, that a reform in the organization of our schools, or in the principles of government and instruction adopted in them, is an exception to the general rule. But I am persuaded, that some changes and improvements in our schools are most necessary; and I trust they have been proved to be so. In order, therefore to complete the design, which I proposed to myself to accomplish in these essays, it only remains, to sketch in a very concise manner, how and where, as it seems to me, we

81

should begin a reformation; the future being left to take care of itself. There will, no doubt, be opportunities to pursue the subject more at length, hereafter.

In this view of the general subject of popular education, all that immediately concerns us, is reduced to a very small compass. Two objects embrace the whole. First, to provide competent teachers; and second, to secure to the public their employment as such. Indeed, the latter of these objects is so entirely subsequent to the former, that we may fairly say, that we have, at present, to attend to but one single object, and that is, to provide competent teachers.

The character of the schools, and of course their political, moral, and religious influence upon the community, depend, almost solely, upon the character of the teachers. Their influence is strong or weak, just in proportion as the instructers are skilful or ignorant—energetic or feeble; it is in this direction or that direction, just as they are imbued with one or another principle. So that whatever is done to elevate the character of teachers, elevates, at the same time, and in the same degree, the character of the schools which they teach, and enlarges and strengthens their influence upon the community. And whatever is done or suffered to lower the character of the teachers, must sink, at the same time and in the same degree, the character of the schools, and destroy or pervert their influence upon society. Many other considerations must be taken into account in organizing a perfect and an energetic system of public instruction. These are some of them; a generous appropriation of money to the purpose, a proper classification of scholars, an efficient and independent tribunal to ensure competency in teachers and to overlook, examine, and report to the public whether their duties have been faithfully performed, and lastly, good books. But all of these objects though highly important, are subsequent in their nature to the preparation of teachers. And no one of them can be attempted with a reasonable expectation of accomplishing it to the greatest advantage, till good teachers are provided and ready for the work.

It will do but little good, for example, for the legislature of the State to make large appropriations directly for the support of schools, till a judicious expenditure of them can be ensured. And in order to this, we must have skilful teachers at hand. It will do but little good to class the children till we have instructers properly prepared to take charge of the classes. It will do absolutely no good to constitute an independent tribunal to decide on the qualifications of teachers, while they have not had the opportunities necessary for coming up to the proper standard. And it will do no good to overlook and report upon their success, when we know beforehand, that they have not the means of success. It would be beginning wrong, too, to build houses and to tell your young and inexperienced instructers to teach this or to teach that subject; however desirable a knowledge of such subjects might be, while it is obvious that they cannot know how properly, to teach any subject. The *science of teaching,* for it must be made a science, is first, in the order of nature, to be inculcated. And it is to this point that the public attention must first be turned, to affect any essential improvement.

And here let me remark upon a distinction in the qualifications of teachers, which has never been practically made; though it seems astonishing that it has so long escaped notice. I allude to the distinction between the possession of knowledge, and the ability to communicate it to other minds. When we are looking for a teacher, we inquire how much he *knows,* not how much he can *communicate;* as if the latter qualification were of no consequence to us. Now it seems to me, that parents and children, to say the least, are as much interested in the latter qualification of their instructer as in the former.

Though a teacher cannot communicate more knowledge than he possesses; yet he may possess much, and still be able to impart but little. . . .

One great object in the education of teachers which it is so desirable on every account to attain, is, to establish an intelligible language of communication between the instructer and his pupil, and enable the former to open his head and his heart, and infuse into the other, some of the thoughts and feelings, which lie hid there. *Instructers and pupils do not understand each other.* They do not speak the same language. They may use the same words; but this can hardly be called the same language, while they attach to them such very different meanings. We must either, by some magic or supernatural power, bring children, at once, to comprehend all our abstract and difficult terms; or our teachers must unlearn themselves, and come down to the comprehension of children. One of these alternatives is only difficult, while the other is impossible.

The direct, careful preparation of instructers for the profession of teaching must surmount this difficulty; and I doubt if there be any other way, in which it can be surmounted. When instructers understand their profession; that is, in a word, when they understand the philosophy of the infant mind, what powers are earliest developed, and what studies are best adapted to their developement; then it will be time to lay out and subdivide their work into an energetic system of public instruction. Till this step towards a reform, which is preliminary in its very nature, be taken, every other measure must be adopted in the dark; and, therefore, be liable to fail utterly of its intended result. Houses and funds and books are all, indeed, important; but they are only the means of enabling the minds of the teachers to act upon the minds of the pupils. And they must, inevitably, fail of their happiest effects, till the minds of the teachers have been prepared to act upon those of their pupils to the greatest advantage.

If, then, the first step towards a reform in our system of popular education be the scientific preparation of teachers for the free schools; our next inquiry becomes, how can we soonest and most perfectly achieve an object on every account so desirable? The ready and obvious answer is, establish an institution for the very purpose. To my mind, this seems to be the only measure, which will ensure to the public the attainment of the object. . . .

An institution for the education of teachers, as has been before intimated, would form a part, and a very important part of the free school system. It would be, moreover, precisely that portion of the system, which should be under the direction of the State whether the others are or not. Because we should thus secure at once, an uniform, intelligent and independent tribunal for decisions on the qualifications of teachers. Because we should thus relieve the clergy of an invidious task, and ensure to the public competent teachers, if such could be found or prepared. An institution for this purpose would become by its influence on society, and particularly on the young, an engine to sway the public sentiment, the public morals, and the public religion, more powerful than any other in the possession of government. It should, therefore, be responsible immediately to them. And they should, carefully, overlook it; and prevent its being perverted to other purposes, directly or indirectly, than those for which it is designed. It should be emphatically the State's institution. . . .

The next question, mentioned above, as arising in the progress of this discussion, was, what would be the leading features of an institution for the education of teachers. If the institution were to be founded by the State, upon a large scale, the following parts would seem to be obviously essential. 1. An appropriate library with a philosophical apparatus. 2. A Principal and assistant Professors in the different departments. 3. A school for children of different ages, embracing both those desiring a general education, and those designed particularly for teachers. 4. A Board of Commissioners, or an enlightened body of men representing the interests and the wishes of the public.

From: Samuel Read Hall, *Lectures on School-Keeping* (1829)

SAMUEL READ HALL (1795–1877) was born in Croydon, New Hampshire. Although his father's death and the loss of his property prevented him from attending college, the education he received as a child, and the course of classical studies he took at Kimball Union Academy (Meriden, New Hampshire), drew him to study and to propose solutions for the educational problems of the country. In 1823, he established a training school for teachers at Concord, Vermont, which in November 1829 was incorporated as Concord Academy. Although many educators at the time were discussing the need for such schools, Hall is reputed to have taken the first practical step by the opening of his normal school. The *Lectures* are a record of his extraordinary work there. He was one of the founders of the American Institute of Instruction, the oldest educational association in America, organized in Boston in 1830. He was also principal of Phillips Academy at Andover, Massachusetts, Holmes Plymouth (New Hampshire) Academy, and the Craftsbury (Vermont) Academy.

LECTURE 1.

Young Gentlemen,

I am induced by various considerations to address you in the following course of Lectures. You expect soon to assume the responsibilities and care of the district schools, in which your services may be needed. It is, therefore, highly important, that a portion of your time *now* should be devoted to the subject which is about to occupy your whole attention. Indeed, all the progress you may be able to make in *science* will not be a sufficient preparation for the work before you. Without some knowledge of the *nature of your business,* how can you be qualified to engage in it? Without having made the "*science of teaching*" a study, how can you be better prepared for success in it, than you would be to succeed in law or medicine, without having studied either? It is true, that many have engaged in teaching school, without having gained any knowledge of the nature of their work, save what they had acquired in the schools which they attended while children. But that others have pursued a course inconsistent and unreasonable, is no reason why you should imitate their bad example, and thus render your labours useless, or even injurious, to the children placed under your care. A moment's attention to the subject, is, it would seem to me, sufficient to show, that no one ought to assume the office of teacher, without having endeavoured first to obtain some correct views of the subject; of the obstacles in his way—the manner in which they may be overcome—the labour he is to perform—and the most probable means of benefiting, in the highest degree, his youthful charge. . . .

There is generally no lack of conviction, that *education* is important. Very few are found, even among the ignorant, who are slow to acknowledge, that learning is necessary to enjoyment and usefulness. Among the well edu-cated, no one remark is more frequently heard, than that a good education is necessary for every citizen in a land of civil and religious freedom. But it is equally obvious to me, that while the importance of education is generally acknowledged, the immense value of common schools is not realized. When it is recollected, that from these minor fountains of knowledge, and from these only, the great mass of the community receive all their instruction in science, the marked indifference to their character and usefulness which so often appears, is truly astonishing. "Most of our legislators, our judges and governors have commenced their preparation for the high stations they have filled in society, by drinking at these simple springs of knowledge. We see the magic influence of our schools, in the habits of industry, sobriety and order which prevail in the community; in the cheerful obedience yielded to the laws, and in the acts of charity and benevolence, which are every day multiplied around us. Rarely have we seen a native of our state, paying his life to her violated laws," if his early years were spent in the schools of our land. These are facts known and generally acknowledged. But still, with many, there is a criminal indifference to the character and usefulness of common schools. . . .

The indifference complained of, and which is so perceptible after all the legislating there has been on the subject, is yet great; and requires only to be mentioned to be condemned by the reflecting and judicious. It may have its origin in habit, in ignorance, and in want of reflection.

Habit effects a part. The parent who never visits the school which his children attend, will perhaps hardly give as a reason, that he never saw his father within the walls of a school room, though it is very possible this may be a chief reason. Still, if interrogated on the subject, he will probably say he lacks time, or does not feel competent to judge of the character of the school, &c. The fact, however, may be, that he has, from his very youth, formed a habit of considering the school a subject of far less consequence than it is. He has imperceptibly imbibed the sentiments of his own parents, and as they appeared but little interested in the character of the schools which they maintained, so the habit has come down to him. It may also have been induced from others. We are strongly inclined to go with the multitude whether right or wrong. When the greater part of parents are indifferent to the character of the school, this feeling is very naturally extended to those who at first might have felt some solicitude on the subject. Thus habits of indifference have extended from family to family, from neighborhood to neighborhood and from district to district. The effect becomes permanent, and year after year continues or increases it. But other circumstances have an influence in producing these lamentable effects. It is very apparent that the value of primary schools is not duly considered. A large proportion of parents very seldom sit down to reflect on the influence which their own actions will have on the general happiness of the country, or the influence to be exerted by themselves on the character, usefulness and enjoyment of their children. Few realize as they ought, that their indifference to these subjects is a sin against their country's welfare, their own, and that of their families. They see not the connexion between the institutions in which the character of their children is moulded, and the future welfare of their children. . . .

LECTURE 2.

I have in a preceding lecture adverted to the fact, that there is a delinquency on the part of many parents, in considering the value and importance of primary schools. This is owing to various causes, and has the effect to render schools far less useful than they otherwise might be. In connexion with the former remarks, I shall now advert to several other causes which have had an influence to prevent the usefulness of our schools.

1. There is a backwardness on the part of many parents to furnish the necessary apparatus. It is not known or not realized, that a few dollars expended in obtaining some very cheap apparatus, would probably add very greatly to the usefulness of the institutions at which their children are placed, to obtain the first rudiments of knowledge. . . .

5. A very prominent reason, why common schools are not more useful, is the imperfect qualifications of instructors.* I shall, in another lecture,

*A writer in the Journal of Education, No. 65, p. 163, uses the following language:—
"The ultimate and fruitful source of all these evils is found in the rejection of correct principles in the science of education. The artizan adopts with eagerness any new principle in mechanics; men of the highest attainments and skill in every department of professional life, are alone employed and liberally rewarded; and a long course of study is thought necessary in every science. Not so in this science which is to lay the foundation of every other. Every stripling who has passed four years within the walls of a college, every dissatis-

dwell on the requisite qualifications of persons employed in the important business of teaching, and shall here advert to the character of different classes who resort to this employment. A portion of those who engage in teaching are such as have received no instruction, except what they derive from common schools. Having pursued the studies usual in the school, and having become so far advanced as to derive but little benefit from attending longer, they are desirous of teaching. The employment is a little more respectable, in their estimation, than manual labour, and they inquire for, and usually find, a backward school. If sufficient success attend their first engagement, to enable them to keep the school the specified time, it is usual for them to continue the employment. Such may perhaps have studied the branches required by law, but have not a thorough knowledge of any. They have ''gone through'' arithmetic, while probably scarcely a rule is understood. Scarcely one in a thousand of this class, have been found able to explain the principles on which the simple rules are founded. Of English grammar, their knowledge is equally superficial. The nature of language,—''the philosophy of grammar''—has claimed as little attention as the most abstruse branches of physics. The more common rules of syntax they may be able to apply, but other parts of grammar have been almost, or entirely neglected. Other branches may have been attended to in the same superficial manner. Now, how is it possible for such an instructer to benefit a school extensively, while there is so great a deficiency in his own qualifications? There may be found some exceptions to the truth of these statements, but so far as my acquaintance has extended, these are very few.

Another class of teachers are those, who, in addition to the benefits of the district school, have resorted to an academy for a single season. Some, after attending but a few weeks, and others, after a few months, engage in the capacity of instructers. In this class there is a diversity. Some are instrumental in raising the character of their schools, while others do more hurt than good. Yet all lack instruction in those things which regard the business of teaching.

There is another class who engage in teaching for a season, for the sake of pecuniary compensation. They are preparing for college, or are members of college, when they are from twelve to sixteen years of age, and while they

fied clerk, who has not ability enough to manage the trifling concerns of a retail shop, every young farmer who obtains in the winter a short vacation from the toils of summer,—in short, every person who is conscious of his imbecility in other business, esteems himself fully competent to train the ignorance and weakness of infancy, into all the virtue and power and wisdom of maturer years—to form a creature, the frailest and feeblest that heaven has made, into the intelligent and fearless sovereign of the whole animated creation, the interpreter and adorer, and almost the representative of Divinity.''

are paying exclusive attention to classical studies. The knowledge, which they have been able to gain of common school studies, is limited; and when they wish to be employed as teachers, they find themselves greatly deficient. They have perhaps fine talents, and are esteemed as young gentlemen of high promise. But their qualifications for instructing a district school with success, are not better than those who were included in the class before mentioned, and they are perhaps even inferior. . . .

6. Another reason why the standard of education in common schools, has not been more elevated, is to be found in the unwillingness, on the part of school districts, to make adequate compensation to teachers of approved talents and qualifications. How else does it happen, at a time when the merchant is overstocked with clerks, and the professions of law and medicine are thronged with students, there is such a lamentable deficiency in the number of those who have the inclination and ability to engage in the business of instruction? Is it not to be ascribed to the more liberal encouragement offered to other employments, compared with the compensation of school teachers? Institutions for the formation of teachers are desirable: but the education of teachers would be unavailing unless the districts could appreciate the importance of affording such compensation as would command their services. There could be no other guarantee, that those who were educated for the purpose, would engage in the business of teaching. . . . The business of education should be committed to the best talents in the country; and it is vain to expect the choicest fruits, without paying the market price. The monthly wages of the teachers of district schools, are frequently one third less, than the amount paid to experienced clerks and journeymen mechanics in the same vicinity. In consequence of this state of things, many of the schools are taught by those who resort to the employment as a temporary expedient, to help them in acquiring some other profession. These persons are without experience, and can have little excitement to establish a character in a business to which they have resorted as a temporary employment. . . . When suitable compensation is allowed for the services of teachers, we may expect that there will be a great improvement in the character of those employed, and consequently, in the usefulness of district schools.

LECTURE 11.

In the preceding Lectures, I have remarked on the studies usually required in district schools. But I am not satisfied that these should be the only subjects introduced into these important institutions. In this lecture, I shall speak of some other branches which ought to be pursued, and remark on improving all the opportunities which may occasionally be offered of making salutary impressions on the minds of scholars. Among the subjects that should receive attention beside those already mentioned, *Composition* is pre-eminent. "That which gives to any branch of study its greatest value, is its practical utility." If this sentiment be just, Composition should never be neglected. Every one who can write, has occasion to compose letters of business or friendship, and in some way or other, to express his thoughts on paper more or less frequently. To neglect, while acquiring an education for common business, some things which are as important as others which receive *particular* attention is not the dictate of reason. But this consideration is not the only evidence that this subject claims attention.—Arranging our ideas in sentences, and combining those sentences so as to express a continued train of thought, is one of the best means of making the knowledge, which we gain, practical. Perhaps hardly any exercise is a better discipline of the mind than the writing of Composition. It is the application of knowledge to the business of life. Without such application, much that is acquired will soon be lost, and if not lost, of what value can it be to its possessor? Of what use to the farmer were all the theory that might be obtained, if he never applied his knowledge to his business?

When Composition is neglected in district schools, it becomes a very burdensome exercise to such as may afterwards attend a higher school or an academy. Many have I seen weep, because this was then made a requisition for the first time. "I was never called upon to write before, and now it seems to me that I cannot," has been said to me by many. "I wish I had been required to write when I attended the district school, and now it would not be such a task."

The following directions may be of service to you on this subject.

1. Labour to impress the minds of the school with a sense of its great importance. This may be done by representing the many situations in which they would highly value the art of expressing their thoughts on paper—the interest they will feel in being able to compose a letter to a friend in handsome style—the inconvenience they must often suffer, if they neglect this study until obliged to write and expose their ignorance, or have to make application to others to do that, which they ought to be able to do for themselves. All this may be impressed upon their minds by means of familiar illustrations.

2. It has been found profitable to commence with young scholars, by giving them a number of words, and requiring them to write a sentence, in which one or more should be used. The first words may be nouns, the next adjectives—the next pronouns, &c. Give the child a slip of paper with the directions and words, as for instance, the following—Write sentences, and

use one of the following words in each. Man, gold, stars, indemnity, gravitation, lines, eagerness, play, home, garden. Compositions should afterwards embrace a variety of other single words or of words compounded.

The object of this course is to make the task easy—to have the invention of the scholar brought into vigorous exercise—and to have him excited to learn the exact meaning of words. It is conceived that by such a mode all these objects are gained, in a more or less important degree.

3. When the scholars are sufficiently exercised in this kind of composition, it may be useful to read a story to them, and then let them relate as much of it as they can in their own words. This enables them to see the importance of paying close attention to what they hear, and of fixing the most prominent ideas, so as to treasure them up. But as they will not be likely to retain any full sentence, it leads them to the exercise of arranging ideas in sentences, nearly as much as writing an original composition. They will not suffer from not knowing what to write, and will probably be amused and pleased with the exercise.

4. Subjects may afterwards be given them on which to write. These should be those with which they are familiar, or may become so by reading.

It is always better to *give* subjects than to let the pupil *select* for himself; for he will often choose without judgment, and is frequently unable to decide on any one, till he has become exceedingly confused. He will often select the hardest subjects thinking them the easiest. Of this kind, are such as the following: friendship, love, hope, spring, summer, autumn, winter, youth, &c.

In selecting subjects it is very important they should be such as will benefit the scholars in a moral point of view, or in supplying rules and precepts for the transactions of life. If a young person can be excited to a proper course of reflection on the influence which different habits will have upon his happiness and usefulness, he will be much more likely to form correct ones, than he would without such reflections. It is therefore of very great importance to lead the young to such reflections as shall be of the greatest benefit in the formation of correct habits. Such questions as the following, when given, as subjects of composition, have been found very useful. What four things ought the young to seek first, in order to promote their happiness? What six habits may I form while young, that will secure to me the greatest personal enjoyment, and respectability? By the formation of what five habits can I do the most good to my fellow-creatures? By what five habits can I most injure society? Describe the character of such persons or families as you would wish for your neighbours. Must the drunkard be an unhappy man? If so, why? Do you believe the thief, liar, &c. can be happy? if not, why?

Questions on subjects of this character may be multiplied and varied according to the judgment of the teacher, and may be rendered easier or harder according to the ability of the class. The scholars thus, not only derive satisfaction from the easy accomplishment of their tasks, but are excited to reflect, and to make up their opinions on subjects very important to them, while forming habits and characters for life.

5. Recommend to your pupils to correspond with each other by letters—to ask each other questions to be answered in writing, and also to write down their own reflections for their own private use.

The effect of this course will unquestionably be salutary. They will not only be excited to a cultivation of the social affections, but will undoubtedly be much advanced in the art of composition. This knowledge, however, will not long be retained without practice. Practice, in the way recommended, will be likely to cause them to examine rules, and to correct as far as they can, their own compositions. Every thing, which has a tendency to call forth their own powers of mind, is important and will be productive of good.

After composition, or in connexion with it, it is highly important that you should lead the scholars to become interested in the subject of moral philosophy. It may not indeed be practicable in some, perhaps a majority of schools, to introduce the regular study of this branch, but you may make your scholars acquainted with some of its important principles. You may teach them to examine the reasons of moral distinctions. You may teach them to examine the character of the things they approve, and of those they disapprove;—why some things please and others displease them. They may be taught that in *all* there is implanted a moral sentiment, and this has a material influence on human happiness. You may inform them what feelings and what actions are virtuous and what are vicious by referring them to the great rule of duty as presented in the law of God.

It is important for every one to have some acquaintance with some of the *first principles* of Natural Philosophy and Chemistry. With the *results* of these principles every one is daily acquainted. But of the principles which produce these results multitudes are totally ignorant.

LECTURE 13. TO FEMALE INSTRUCTERS.

Young Ladies,

In the preceding lectures addressed to young men, many of the directions are equally applicable to yourselves. The qualifications natural and acquired, which it is important for *them* to possess, are not stated higher than those to be expected from *you*. The mode of governing and teaching recommended to gentlemen, should be nearly the same with a teacher of either sex. The subject of gaining the confidence of a school, so as to be able to exert the influence necessary to the benefit of the scholars, and the importance of adopting such a course in the general management of a school, as shall promote the convenience of the teacher and success of the pupils, should claim much of your attention. But still there are some points, in the proper management of the schools which you will instruct, that require variation of manner, and some directions may be given to you, which could not be given properly in the lectures you have already heard. I shall, therefore, address you separately in a concluding lecture.

It will devolve on you to lay the foundation, on which all that succeed you are to build. You are to give direction to the pliant twig, the first bias to the infant intellect. Your station is one of great responsibility. You have it in your power either to promote the welfare of the little group around you, or to do them the greatest injury. Next to mothers, the character of children will depend on you. If you are judicious and faithful, you may be benefactors to the community,—if you are negligent of duty, or misjudge on important points, the best of parents, and the best of teachers can never repair the mischief, you may do to the infant charge committed to your trust.

You have it in your power to create in the minds of the children a taste for the school—for its exercises and amusements; and from you they may derive such an aversion to these pursuits as will not be overcome by the labours of your successors in many years. But these subjects will claim attention in their order, and I need only advert to them here.

The first remarks I shall make, will regard the youngest children, placed under your care. These are usually from three to seven years old, though sometimes younger. The first object at which you should aim, is *to please them*—to make the school as pleasant to them as possible. In order to do this, you must consider what they are, and how their attention can be excited; how they are pleased, and in what manner they may, most easily be governed. . . .

2. I would recommend *to spend a part of each day in questioning the children on the meaning of words.* This may be done by giving a word and requiring them to tell its opposite. . . .

3. The next direction I wish to give you is, *Keep the children fully occupied.* This is important for children of every age. In order to attain this object with the youngest, you will be obliged to employ the assistance of some of the older pupils, while you are attending to the other exercises of the school. . . .

4. I should be glad to avoid the following remarks, on the subject of *neatness,* did I not believe they are *sometimes* needed. I have not always

observed that attention to it, which is important. Children should always be led to associate order, comfort, neatness and regularity, with the school which they attended. This cannot be, where the floor is left covered with leaves and litter, from week to week; and where there is no effort to make use of the means at hand for ornamenting the room with evergreens, &c. Every school-room should have as many attractions for the young as possible. Every degree of negligence on the subject of neatness, must have a bad effect on the school, and should be carefully avoided.

5. Another part of your duty will be to teach the children propriety of conduct. The remark is often made to an unmannerly child, ''You must go to school to learn manners.'' But with what propriety is it made, when so little attention is generally given to the subject in schools? Still it is important, and should receive attention. Children should be instructed how to go into a room, and how to speak, when they have entered. They should be told what is proper when leaving the house of a neighbour, or when spoken to by persons in the street, or addressed by a visitant at home. Propriety of address and manners should be inculcated, in regard to every situation in which they may be placed. Every species of rudeness and clownishness should be carefully corrected, lest it grow to a habit when they become older. If children are early taught to treat each other with politeness, the habit will be likely to show itself in their treatment of every body else. The truly polite person will never say or do that unnecessarily, which will make any one around him unhappy. Every mode of speaking or allusion to things which will injure the feelings of others is therefore to be discountenanced and reproved. All vulgar joking, blackguarding, or desire to accuse others of things of which they are not guilty, must be considered as the opposite of politeness and good manners. It is the duty of the teacher to keep a watchful eye on every thing connected with this subject.

To conclude: Let it be your endeavour, and spare no pains, to make the children fond of their studies, and desirous of doing right. Strive to have them early accustomed to vigorous mental exertion, and to do right, whether at home or abroad, at school, or at play. Go daily to Him, for guidance and direction, at whose tribunal you must account for the manner you teach the youthful charge entrusted to your care. His assistance alone will enable you to succeed in your efforts to do them good. His approbation and that of your own conscience, will be an abundant reward for every exertion you can make, to promote the best interest of those who look to you for guidance and instruction.

From: Almira Hart Lincoln Phelps, *Lectures to Young Ladies: Comprising Outlines and Applications of the Different Branches of Female Education for the Use of Female Schools, and Private Libraries* (1833)

ALMIRA HART LINCOLN PHELPS (1793–1884) was born in Berlin, Connecticut. Like her famous sister, Emma Willard, she was raised in a lively intellectual environment and decided quite early to become an educator. In 1816, she accepted charge of an academy at Sandy Hill, New York. Married in 1817 to Samuel Lincoln, a Hartford newspaper editor, she was widowed in 1823. Left with two young children to raise and in financial strictures, she went back to teaching, joining her sister at the Troy Female Seminary (New York). In 1831, she married John Phelps, a lawyer and politician, widowed father of one of her students at the seminary.

Almira Phelps's contributions to female education were especially in the fields of chemistry, geology, and natural philosophy. Her *Familiar Lectures on Botany* (1829), a textbook based on inductive, objective teaching, went in less than ten years into nine editions, selling 275,000 copies by 1872. A popular writer of textbooks, she combined poetry, history, and moral observations with science, to make of science an exercise in personal, intellectual, and philosophical growth. *Lectures to Young Ladies* (1833) documents her faith in the ability of women to study difficult subjects. She shared this faith with her sister Emma Willard. But like her sister, although she was such a strong and effective proponent of educational equality for women, she actively opposed women's suffrage; in fact, she went as far as joining the Woman's Anti-Suffrage Associations for Washington, D.C.

In 1841, she became the principal of Patapsco Female Institute at Ellicott's Mills, Maryland, where she offered collegiate quality courses to prepare young women to become homemakers and teachers. Her goal was to turn out "good women rather than fine ladies" and to take "away from females their helplessness."

Her science textbooks led to her election, in 1859, as the second woman member of the American Association for the Advancement of Science, following in the footsteps of Maria Mitchell.

95

LECTURE 4.
PRIVATE AND PUBLIC EDUCATION.—PUBLIC SCHOOLS.

Much has been said and written on the most proper mode of conducting female education;—some have contended that girls should be brought up under the watchful eye of maternal care; while others have considered the emulation which springs up where there is rivalship, to be important, if not necessary, to the full development of the mental powers. Whether a young lady remains with her mother during the period allotted for her education, or whether she goes abroad, the character of the latter will depend much upon that of the former. The daughter's ideas of dress, of expense, of what qualities are to be most respected and valued in others, and her religious impressions, all will, in some degree have taken, their color from this earliest guide.

It would seem that of all others, a mother was the most proper person to superintend the education of a young female. The maternal watch is vigilant and active: none else can feel the deep and anxious solicitude which marks a mother's care; and yet this very anxiety, by becoming too intense, may be injurious to the child. The quick imagination of the parent seizes upon the most trifling indications of future character, and she is alternately agonized with fear or delighted with hope. These strong emotions are not favorable to a steady and even course of education; for as one or the other feeling prevails, there is danger of trifling actions becoming the subjects of inadequate blame or praise.

It would seem as if in the shade of domestic life, and under the care of a wise mother, a young female would blossom into maturity, lovely and intelligent and fitted for the discharge of the various duties, which may hereafter devolve upon her. This idea has been a favorite one with the poet and novelist, who have delighted in painting their heroines as combining all the simplicity of infancy itself, with the most court-like and elegant manners; as entirely ignorant of the world, and yet knowing all of it that is valuable; as amiable and docile, without ever having suffered restraint; as generous and disinterested, and yet knowing only to be indulged and caressed. Now this is all absurd; reasoning *a priori,* we should say that to know the world, one must have intercourse with it, and facts show that a young girl always kept at home, is awkward and constrained in her manners, often selfish and un-amiable in her disposition, and ignorant of the customs of society. Her mother may have moved in the most refined circles, be intimately acquainted with the forms and customs of polite intercourse; she may have been faithful in imparting this knowledge, but mere rules in this case are of as little use, as it would be for a pupil to study the theory of drawing and music, without practice. Selfishness, pride and conceit are also fostered in the mind of one accustomed to feel herself the great centre of attraction, and to consider every one around her as subservient to her pleasure.

With respect to literary improvement, it may be thought that the quiet of domestic life is peculiarly favorable. We will suppose the mother herself to be entirely competent to instruct in all necessary branches of female education. Is it certain that she will have the requisite time for superintending her daughter's education, and conducting it on those systematic principles which will ensure a suitable attention to each department of knowledge? The mother, however competent she may be to the task, however anxious to devote herself to her daughter's improvement, has many other claims upon her than those of maternal duty. As a wife she must share in the cares and anxieties of her husband;—as the mistress of a family she must direct its internal concerns, and this alone might render it difficult for her to give that individual attention to literary subjects, which is necessary in an instructer. Society too has its claims; and her time is always liable to be taken up with a friendly visit, a ceremonious call, or an appeal to charity: these interruptions break in upon the regularity of the prescribed systematic division of time, and the pupil feeling it very uncertain that her lesson will, if learned, be heard, relaxes her diligence and acquires a habit of idleness and procrastination. We have said nothing of the claims that younger children may have upon the mother's care, or of various other indispensable duties; but enough has been observed to show, how very difficult it must be for the most intelligent and energetic woman, charged with a variety of cares, to bestow that time and attention upon a daughter's education which is necessary for the successful cultivation of the youthful mind.

I have seen the attempt made by an energetic and judicious woman, whose pecuniary circumstances being somewhat embarrassed, and who, entertaining no very favorable opinion of public schools, resolved to educate her daughter. I had known this lady in her youth, and seen her the admiration and pride of society; I did not not see her again until her eldest daughter was about sixteen. How great was my astonishment, to behold in this daughter, an awkward, ignorant girl, with less polish of manners and less information than is ordinarily possessed by children of ten years of age. All who know anything of instructing, are aware of the time and patience which is requisite, even for teaching a child its letters: add to this, reading, spelling, writing, geography, grammar, arithmetic, and so on, to the higher branches of education, and it will not appear strange that the lady just mentioned with an extensive circle of acquaintance, and several younger children, should have failed in her attempt to educate her daughter. Seeing at length the impossibility of success answerable to her wishes, she placed her daughter abroad at a public school; but the confirmed irregularity of her habits was unfavorable to improvement, and rendered irksome the systematic rules to which she was subjected. She felt, too, the need of those indulgences which home afforded, and which had greatly tended to render her intellect dull and torpid. From these circumstances, rather than any natural inferiority of mind, her improvement was not creditable either to herself, or to those under whose care she was placed.

But may not parents provide private teachers for their children, and thus keep them under their own observation? Doubtless this is more practicable where the expense can be afforded, than for parents themselves to give regular instruction. Young persons thus educated may, with a faithful instructer, make tolerable proficiency in literature; but there is great danger of their becoming selfish and haughty, when all around seem to live for them. Educated under the paternal roof, they can have little idea of a world in which their interests will clash with those of others, and where forbearance and self-denial will be continually needed. Parents may faithfully warn their children of these things; they may tell them that the world will present a scene very different from that in which their least complaint receives attention, and their slightest unhappiness meets with sympathy; but the habit of being served and indulged, becomes so strong, that when in after years the scene is reversed, and the petted child is called upon to sacrifice her own ease and comfort for that of others, she finds the task difficult and discouraging, and either shrinks from the performance of known duties, or becomes unhappy in the discharge of them.

We see then, that however beautiful in theory it may be to educate girls at home, it is not easy in practice. The mother herself who sets out with the resolution to persevere in teaching her child, or in superintending her education, will at length feel that there are difficulties and evils growing out of her excessive anxiety: she will see that by close and constant contact with her child, and a habit of minute attention, she is prevented from seeing the outline of her character, and forming and executing those general rules to which subordinate ones should be subservient.

I have heard mothers who had been in the practice of instructing youth, say that they found more difficulty in governing and managing one or two of their own children, than they had done in controlling and instructing a large school. This may be easily accounted for; an instructer has, or ought to have, her mind free from other cares than those connected with her profession; if conscientious, she feels a sufficient degree of interest in the progress and character of her pupils to induce her to make every possible exertion, but she does not suffer that excessive solicitude which often impedes the mother's progress. Physicians frequently profess an unwillingness to prescribe for their own families, on the ground that too great anxiety influences their judgment;—in all cases requiring the full exercise of the reasoning powers, it is important that the mind should, as little as possible, be influenced by the emotions.

Parents are often deceived in the characters of their children. We have at this place frequent opportunities of witnessing this. Sometimes one who brings to the Seminary a bold and conceited girl, (excuse me if the terms seem harsh) says, 'My daughter is excessively diffident, and needs to be brought forward and encouraged.' At another time, a child of dull intellect is committed to our care as a remarkable genius, who is capable of comprehending the most abstruse sciences. One who can scarcely raise the eight notes of the gamut is frequently considered as possessing great talents for music; another has learned to daub paper with water colors, and her parents wish that her fine taste in drawing may be cultivated, although the poor girl may not have sufficient correctness of eye to make a horizontal or perpendicular line. These mistakes are far from being confined to ignorant parents; parental blindness often falls upon those, who in other respects are wise and enlightened.

We have, in the preceding remarks, considered private education in its most favorable aspect, not taking into account the numerous cases in which the mother is inadequate to the task of instructing, from her own defective education, or from feebleness of constitution. Many young females being early deprived of a mother's care, the father may be compelled to send his daughters abroad for education. It seems, then, that there is a necessity for female schools; and yet, strange as the fact may appear, no provision for such an object has ever been made, by the guardians of the public welfare. Napoleon indeed established the school of St. Denis, for educating the daughters of his legion of honor; but this was conducted on an imperfect plan, and very limited in its operation.

The founder of this institution was early impressed with the importance of female education. Her views on this subject are expressed in a small volume published about the year 1818, and called 'Plan of a Female Seminary, by Emma Willard.' The author sketched the plan of a Female Seminary, to be founded and endowed by public munificence. She urged the claims of the daughters of the republic, to share, in some small degree with the sons, in those privileges for mental improvement which were so abundantly bestowed upon the latter. After pleading the justice of the claim and the expediency of granting it, as proved by a variety of important considerations, she thus remarks of female education in reference to national character and glory:—'Ages have rolled away, barbarians have trodden the weaker sex beneath their feet, tyrants have robbed us of the present light of heaven and fain would take its future. Nations, calling themselves polite, have made us the fancied idols of a ridiculous worship, and we have repaid them with ruin for their folly. But where is that wise and heroic country, which has considered that our rights are sacred, though we cannot defend them? that, though a weaker, we are an essential part of the body politic, whose corruption or improvement must affect the whole? and which, having thus considered, has sought to give us by education, that rank in the scale of being, to which our importance entitles us. History shows not that country. It shows many, whose legislatures have sought to improve their various vegetable productions, and their breeds of useful brutes; but none, whose public councils have made it an object of their deliberations, to improve the character of their women. Yet though history lifts not her finger to such an one, anticipation does. She points to a nation, which, having thrown off the shackles of authority and precedent, shrinks not from schemes of improvement, because other nations have never attempted them; but which, in its pride of independence, would rather lead than follow, in the march of human improvement; a nation, wise and magnanimous to plan, enterprising to undertake, and rich in resources to execute.'

The late Governor Clinton entered warmly into the views of Mrs. Willard: he encouraged her to petition the legislature of New York, and in a message to that body, publicly expressed his own opinions with respect to the justice of the claim. The novelty of the petition caused considerable sensation, and gave rise to much discussion, both in the House and abroad. The more enlightened members seemed, generally, in favor of considering females as the legitimate children of the state, and making some provision for their intellectual improvement. There were those, however, who gravely asserted in the public council of the state, that 'learning was of little use to women, as it would tend to lead them from their own sphere of domestic duties, and thus prove injurious to the interests of society.' The bill for an endowment of a Female Seminary, after having received a favorable report from the committee, to whom it was referred, was defeated through the influence of those, who without attempting to deny the right which was claimed, thought it should be waived on the ground of the evils which might result, from enlightening the minds of those, who were destined to a limited and subordinate sphere.

It is upon a similar mode of reasoning that the slave-holding States found their objections to the instruction of those degraded beings, who are entailed upon them, a curse which they would gladly shake off. As respects the slave, this reasoning is undoubtedly correct; let the black population of the south be taught that they in fact possess the greater physical power; let their minds be opened to the truths of man's equality by nature, and of the unjust tenure by which they are kept in bondage; let them have the means of communicating with each other from distant places, thus enabling them to act in concert; let all this be done, and the fair regions of the south would soon present one universal scene of blood and carnage. While we deplore a necessity founded on the principle of self-defence, which holds in darkness so great a portion of human intellect, we cannot admit that such a necessity does, in the present state of things, exist.

But let the question come fairly before those who object to female improvement on grounds, which if not similar, are certainly analogous. Neither the *right* of holding slaves or keeping them in ignorance is now claimed; it is wholly a matter of *expediency.* The rights which the stronger sex possess of keeping the weaker in a state of intellectual bondage and darkness is no less questionable. Let it then be considered on the ground of expediency. What would be the state of society, if females were generally taught the laws of the material and mental world, the nature of right and obligation, their own duties, and their high responsibilities as moral and intellectual beings? Would such knowledge be likely to cause them to forsake the path of duty, and to seek a sphere of action, which, from knowing the constitution of society, and especially the nature of their own obligations, they perceive does not belong to them? There is an absurdity in such suppositions; and if a Mary Wolstoncraft, or a Frances Wright, have thrown aside that delicacy which is the crowning ornament of the female character, if they have urged the rights of their sex to share in public offices and in the command of armies;—if they have demanded that they shall be permitted to leave the sacred hearth, the domestic altar, and all the delights and duties of home, to mingle in political commotions or the din of arms, they have but expressed the overflowings of their own restless spirits, their own unnatural and depraved ambition. *They* are not to be considered as the deputed representatives of our sex; they have thrown off the female character, and deserve no longer to be recognized as women; they are monsters, a kind of *lusus naturæ,* who have amused the world to the great injury of that sex whom they have pretended to defend.

But let us look to such women as Hannah More, Maria Edgeworth, Mrs. Hemans; and, in our own country, many others equally distinguished in the walks of literature;—are such disorganizers of society, pedantic, unfeminine, neglectful of duty in their various domestic relations? Are they not generally equally distinguished in private life for their amiable and domestic qualities, and for a faithful discharge of their relative duties, as in public for their high intellectual powers?

My dear pupils, may the whole tenor of your own lives be a constant refutation of the degrading assertion, that '*woman must be ignorant in order to be useful.*' On you the attention of many is fixed, and your future conduct, will be hereafter referred to as proving or disproving the problem, '*Is it for the good of society that women shall receive a liberal and enlarged course of education?*'

From: Calvin Ellis Stowe, "Normal Schools and Teachers' Seminaries" (1838)

CALVIN ELLIS STOWE (1802–1886) was born in Natick, Massachusetts. He studied at Gorham Academy (Gorham, Maine), Bowdoin College, and Andover Theological Seminary. In 1831 he became professor of Greek at Dartmouth College, and in 1833 he was called to the chair of biblical literature in Lane Theological Seminary, Cincinnati, Ohio. Two years after his first wife died, he married Harriet Elizabeth Beecher. Without abandoning his interest in biblical literature, Stowe became involved in improving the common schools and was responsible for the establishment of the College of Teachers in Cincinnati. In 1836 the state of Ohio appointed him commissioner to investigate the public school systems of Europe, especially of Prussia. When he returned, in 1837, he published his famous *Report on Elementary Instruction in Europe,* a copy of which the legislature put into every school district of the state. The report was reprinted by the legislatures of Massachusetts, Pennsylvania, Michigan, and other states, in *Common Schools and Teachers' Seminaries* (1839), and in E. W. Knight, *Reports on European Education by John Griscom, Victor Cousin, Calvin E. Stowe.* His description of the kind of knowing that teachers need to develop to be teachers (in this excerpt) comes from Henry Barnard's *Normal Schools and Other Institutions,* and remains one of the most sophisticated conceptualizations of pedagogy by early educators.

The following remarks were originally prepared and delivered as an Address before the College of Professional Teachers in Cincinnati and Columbus, Ohio. They were first published in the American Biblical Repository for July, 1839, and in the same year republished in Boston by Marsh, Capen, Lyon and Webb, in a little volume, with the author's *"Report on Elementary Public Instruction in Europe, which was made to the General Assembly of Ohio, in December, 1837."*

> "Ich versprach Gott: Ich will jedes preussische Bauerkind für ein Wesen ansehen, das mich bei Gott verkeagen kann, wenn ich ihm nicht die beste Menschen-und-Christen-Bildung schaffe, die ich ihm zu schaffen vermag."

''I promised God, that I would look upon every Prussian peasant child
as a being who could complain of me before God, if I did not provide for
him the best education, as a man and a Christian, which it was possible
for me to provide.''

     —Dinter's Letter to Baron Von Altenstein.

When the benevolent Franke turned his attention to the subject of popular
education in the city of Hamburgh, late in the seventeenth century, he soon
found that children could not be well taught without good teachers, and that but
few good teachers could be found unless they were regularly trained for the
profession. Impressed with this conviction, he bent all his energies toward the
establishment of a teachers' Seminary, in which he finally succeeded, at Halle,
in Prussia, about the year 1704; and from this first institution of the kind in
Europe, well qualified teachers were soon spread over all the north of Germany,
who prepared the way for the great revolution in public instruction, which has
since been so happily accomplished under the auspices of Frederick William
III and his praiseworthy coadjutors. Every enlightened man, who, since the
time of Franke, has in earnest turned his attention to the same subject, has been
brought to the same result; and the recent movements in France, in Scotland; in
Massachusetts, Connecticut, New York, Ohio, and other States in the American
Union, all attest the very great difficulty, if not entire impossibility, of carrying
out an efficient system of public instruction without seminaries expressly designed for the preparation of teachers.

Having devoted some attention to this subject and having spent considerable time in examining institutions of the kind already established in Europe,
I propose in this paper to exhibit the result of my investigations. . . . I propose what I think ought to be aimed at, and what, I doubt not, will ultimately
be attained, if the spirit which is now awake on the subject be not suffered
again to sleep.

The sum of what I propose is contained in the six following propositions,
namely:

I. The interests of popular education in each State demand the establishment, at the seat of government, and under the patronage of the legislature,
of a NORMAL SCHOOL,† that is, a *Teachers' Seminary and Model-school,* for
the instruction and practice of teachers in the science of education and the
art of teaching.

II. Pupils should not be received into the Teachers' Seminary under six-

---

†The French adjective *normal* is derived from the Latin noun *norma,* which signifies a
carpenter's square, a *rule,* a *pattern,* a *model;* and the very general use of this term to
designate institutions for the preparation of teachers, leads us at once to the idea of a *model-
school for practice,* as an essential part of a *Teacher's Seminary.*

teen years of age, nor until they are well versed in all the branches usually taught in common schools.

III. The model-school should comprise the various classes of children usually admitted to the common schools, and should be subject to the same general discipline and course of study.

IV. The course of instruction in the Teachers' Seminary should include three years, and the pupils be divided into three classes, accordingly.

V. The senior classes in the Teachers' Seminary should be employed, under the immediate instruction of their professors, as instructors in the model-school.

VI. The course of instruction in the Teachers' Seminary should comprise lectures and recitations on the following topics, together with such others as further observation and experience may show to be necessary:

1. A thorough, scientific, and demonstrative study of all the branches to be taught in the common schools, with directions at every step as to the best method of inculcating each lesson upon children of different dispositions and capacities, and various intellectual habits.

2. The philosophy of mind, particularly in reference to its susceptibility of receiving impressions from mind.

3. The peculiarities of intellectual and moral development in children, as modified by sex, parental character, wealth or poverty, city or country, family government, indulgent or severe, fickle or steady, &c., &c.

4. The science of education in general, and full illustrations of the difference between education and mere instruction.

5. The art of teaching.

6. The art of governing children, with special reference to imparting and keeping alive a feeling of love for children.

7. History of education, including an accurate outline of the educational systems of different ages and nations, the circumstances which gave rise to them, the principles on which they were founded, the ends which they aimed to accomplish, their successes and failures, their permanency and changes, how far they influenced individual and national character, how far any of them might have originated in premeditated plan on the part of their founders, whether they secured the intelligence, virtue, and happiness of the people, or otherwise, with the causes, &c.

8. The rules of health, and the laws of physical development.

9. Dignity and importance of the teacher's office.

10. Special religious obligations of teachers in respect to benevolent devotedness to the intellectual and moral welfare of society, habits of entire self-control, purity of mind, elevation of character, &c.

11. The influence which the school should exert on civilization and the progress of society.

12. The elements of Latin, together with the German, French, and Spanish languages.

On each of the topics above enumerated, I shall attempt to offer such remarks as may be necessary to their more full development and illustration; and then state the argument in favor of, and answer the objections which may be urged against, the establishment of such an institution as is here contemplated.

To begin with the first proposition.

I. The interests of popular education in each state demand the establishment, at the seat of government, and under the patronage of the legislature, of a Normal School, that is, a Teachers' Seminary and model-school, for the instruction and practice of teachers in the science of education and the art of teaching.

If there be necessity for such an institution, there can be little doubt that the legislature should patronize and sustain it. . . .

Colleges and institutions for the higher branches of classical learning, have seldom flourished in this country under legislative patronage; because the people at large, not perceiving that these institutions are directly beneficial to them, allow their legislators to give them only a hesitating, reluctant and insufficient support. . . . But an institution of the kind here contemplated, the people at large will feel to be for their immediate benefit. It is to qualify teachers for the instruction of their own children; and among the people throughout most of the free States, there is an appreciation of the advantages and necessity of good common-school instruction, which makes them willing to incur heavy sacrifices for the sake of securing it. They will, therefore, cheerfully sustain their legislators in any measure which is seen to be essential to the improvement and perfection of the common-school system; and that the establishment of a Normal School is essential to this, I expect to prove in the course of this discussion. . . .

II. Pupils should not be received into the Teachers' Seminary under sixteen years of age, nor until they are well versed in all the branches usually taught in the common schools.

The age at which the pupils leave the common school is the proper age for entering the Teachers' Seminary, and the latter should begin just where the former closes. This is young enough; for few persons have their judgments sufficiently matured, or their feelings under sufficient control, to engage in school-teaching by themselves, before they are twenty years old. It is not the design of the Teachers' Seminary to go through the common routine of the common-school course, but a thorough grounding in this is to be assumed as the foundation on which to erect the structure of the teachers' education.

III. The model-school should comprise the various classes of children usually admitted to the common schools, and should be subject to the same general discipline and course of study.

The model-school, as its name imports, is to be a model of what the common school ought to be; and it must be, therefore, composed of like materials, and subject to similar rules. The model-school, in fact, should be the common school of the place in which the Teachers' Seminary is situated; it should aim to keep in advance of every other school in the State, and every other school in the State should aim to keep up with that. It is a model for the constant inspection of the pupils in the teachers' department, a practical illustration of the lessons they receive from their professors; the proof-stone by which they are to test the utility of the abstract principles they imbibe, and on which they are to exercise and improve their gifts of teaching. Indeed, as School-counselor Dinter told a nobleman of East-Prussia, to set up a Teachers' Seminary without a model-school, is like setting up a shoemaker's shop without leather.

IV. The course of instruction in the Teachers' Seminary should include three years, and the pupils be divided into three classes, accordingly.

The course of study, as will be seen by inspecting it in the following pages, cannot well be completed in less time than this; this has been found short enough for professional study in the other professions, which is generally commenced at a maturer age, and after the pupil has had the advantage of an academical or collegiate course; and if it is allowed that five or seven years are not too much to be spent in acquiring the trade of a blacksmith, a carpenter, or any of the common indispensable handcrafts, surely three years will not be deemed too much for the difficult and most important art of teaching.

V. The senior class in the Teachers' Seminary should be employed, under the immediate inspection of their professors, as instructors in the model-school.

The model-school is intended to be not only an illustration of the principles inculcated theoretically in the seminary, but is calculated also as a school for practice, in which the seminary pupils may learn, by actual experiment, the practical bearing of the principles which they have studied. After two years of theoretical study, the pupils are well qualified to commence this practical course, under the immediate inspection of their professors; and the model-school being under the inspection of such teachers, it is obvious that its pupils can suffer no loss, but must be great gainers by the arrangement.

This is a part of the system for training teachers which cannot be dispensed with, and any considerable hope of success retained. To attempt to train practical teachers without it, would be like attempting to train sailors by keeping boys upon Bowditch's Navigator, without ever suffering them to go on board a ship, or handle a ropeyarn. One must begin to teach, before he can begin to be a teacher; and it is infinitely better, both for himself and his pupils, that he should make this beginning under the eye of an experienced teacher, who can give him directions and point out his errors, than that he should blunder on alone, at the risk of ruining multitudes of pupils, before he can learn to teach by the slow process of unaided experience.

VI. Course of instruction in the Teachers' Seminary.

1. A thorough, scientific, and demonstrative study of all branches to be taught in the common schools, with directions, at every step, as to the best method of inculcating each lesson on children of different dispositions and capacities, and various intellectual habits.

It is necessary here to give a general outline of a course of study for the common schools of this country. The pupils usually in attendance are between the ages of six and sixteen, and I would arrange them in three divisions, as follows:

FIRST DIVISION, including the youngest children, and those least advanced, generally between the ages of six and nine.

Topics of Instruction.—1. Familiar conversational teaching, in respect to objects which fall daily under their notice, and in respect to their moral and social duties, designed to awaken their powers of observation and expression, and to cultivate their moral feelings.

2. Elements of reading.

3. Elements of writing.

4. Elements of numbers.

5. Exercises of the voice and ear—singing by rote.

6. Select readings in the Pentateuch, Psalms, and Gospels.

SECOND DIVISION, including those more advanced, and generally between the ages of nine and twelve.

Topics of Instruction.—1. Exercise in reading.

2. Exercises in writing.

3. Arithmetic.

4. Elements of geography, and geography of the United States.

5. History of the United States.

6. Moral and religious instruction in select Bible narratives, parables, and proverbs.

7. Elements of music, and singing by rote.

8. English grammar and parsing.

THIRD DIVISION, most advanced, and generally between the ages of twelve and sixteen.

Topics of Instruction.—1. Exercises in reading and elocution.

2. Calligraphy, stenography, and linear drawing.

3. Algebra, geometry, and trigonometry, with their application to civil engineering, surveying, &c.

4. English composition, forms of business, and book-keeping.

5. General geography, or knowledge of the earth and of mankind.

6. General history.

7. Constitution of the United States, and of the several States.

8. Elements of the natural sciences, including their application to the arts of life, such as agriculture, manufacturers, &c.

9. Moral instruction in the connected Bible, history, and life and discourses of Christ, the religious observation of Nature, and history of Christianity.

10. Science and art of vocal and instrumental music.

Thorough instruction on all these topics I suppose to be essential to a complete common-school education; and though it may be many years before our schools come up to this standard, yet I think nothing short of this should satisfy us; and, as fast as possible, we should be laboring to train teachers capable of giving instruction in all these branches. When this standard for the common school has been attained, then, before the pupil is prepared to enter on the three years' course of study proposed in the Teachers' Seminary, he must have studied all the topics above enumerated, as they ought to be studied in the common schools.

The study of a topic, however, for the purpose of applying it to practical use, is not always the same thing as studying it for the purpose of teaching it. The processes are often quite different. A man may study music till he can perform admirably himself, and yet possess very little skill in teaching others; and it is well known that the most successful orators are not unfrequently the very worst teachers of elocution. The process of learning for practical purposes is mostly that of combination or synthesis; but the process of learning for the purpose of teaching is one of continued and minute analysis, not only of the subject itself, but of all the movements and turnings of the *feelers* of the mind, the little *antennae* by which it seizes and retains its hold of the several parts of a topic. Till a man can minutely dissect, not only the subject itself, but also the intellectual machinery by which it is worked up, he cannot be very successful as a teacher. The orator analyzes his subject, and disposes its several parts in the order best calculated for effect; but the mental processes by which he does this, which constitute the tact that enables him to judge right, as if by instinct, are generally so rapid, so evanescent, that it may be impossible for him to recall them so as to describe them to another; and it is this very rapidity of intellectual movement, which gives him success as an orator, that renders it the more difficult for him to succeed as a teacher. The musician would perform very poorly, who should stop to recognize each volition that moves the muscles which regulate the movement of his fingers on the organkeys; but he who would teach others to perform gracefully and rapidly, must give attention to points minute as these. The teacher must stop to observe and analyze each movement of the mind itself, as it advances on every topic; but men of genius for execution, and of great practical skill, who never teach, are generally too impatient to make this minute analysis, and often, indeed, form such habits as at length to become incapable of it. . . .

The teacher, also, must review the branches of instruction above enumerated with reference to their scientific connections, and a thorough demonstration of them, which, though not always necessary in respect to their practical application to the actual business of life, is absolutely essential to that ready command which a teacher must have over them in order to put them into the minds of others.

Nor is this all. There is a great variety of methods for inculcating the same truth; and the diversities of mind are quite as numerous as the varieties of method. One mind can be best approached by one method, and another mind by another; and in respect to the teacher, one of the richest treasures of experience is a knowledge of the adaptation of the different methods to different minds. These rich treasures of experience can be preserved, and classified, and imparted in the Teachers' Seminary. If the teacher never studies his profession, he learns this part of his duties only by the slow and wasteful process of experimenting on mind, and thus, in all probability, ruins many before he learns how to deal with them. Could we ascertain how many minds have been lost to the world in consequence of the injudicious measures of inexperienced and incompetent teachers; if we could exhibit, in a statistical table, the number of souls which must be used up in qualifying a teacher for his profession, by intrusting him with its active duties without previous study, we could prove incontrovertibly that it is great want of economy, that it is a most prodigious waste, to attempt to carry on a system of schools without making provision for the education of teachers.

2. The philosophy of mind, particularly in reference to its susceptibility of receiving impressions from mind. . . .

3. The peculiarities of intellectual and moral development in children, as

modified by sex, parental character, wealth or poverty, city or country, family government, indulgent or severe, fickle or steady, &c. . . .

Many other circumstances give rise to diversities no less important. It is the business of the Teachers' Seminary to arrange and classify these modifying influences, and give to the pupil the advantages of an anticipated experience in respect to his method of proceeding in regard to them. No one will imagine that the teacher is to let his pupils see that he recognizes such differences among them; he should be wise enough to keep his own counsel, and deal with each individual in such manner as the peculiar circumstances of each may render most productive of good.

4. The science of education in general, and full illustration of the difference between education and mere instruction.

Science, in the modern acceptation of the term, is a philosophical classification and arrangement of all the facts which are observed in respect to any subject, and an investigation from these facts of the principles which regulate their occurrence. Education affords its facts, and they are as numerous and as deeply interesting as the facts of any other science; these facts are susceptible of as philosophical a classification and arrangement as the facts of chemistry or astronomy; and the principles which regulate their occurrence are as appropriate and profitable a subject of investigation as the principles of botany or zoology, or of politics or morals. I know it has been said by some that education is not a science, and cannot be reduced to scientific principles; but they who talk thus either make use of words without attaching to them any definite meaning, or they confound the idea of education with that of the mere art of teaching. Even in this sense the statement is altogether erroneous, as will be shown under the next head.

The teacher should be acquainted with these facts, with their classification, their arrangement and principles, before he enters on the duties of his profession; or he is like the surgeon who would operate on the human body before he has studied anatomy, or the attorney who would commence practice before he has made himself acquainted with the first principles of law.

It is a common error to confound education with mere instruction; an error so common, indeed, that many writers on the subject use the words as nearly, if not entirely, synonymous. Instruction, however, comprehends but a very small part of the general idea of education. Education includes all the extraneous influences which combine to the formation of intellectual and moral character; while instruction is limited to that which is directly communicated from one mind to another. *"Education* and *instruction* (says Hooker) are the means, the one by *use,* the other by *precept,* to make our natural faculty of reason both the better and the sooner to judge rightly between truth and error, good and evil.'' A man may become well *educated,* though but poorly *instructed,* as was the case with Pascal and Franklin, and many others equally illustrious; but if a man is well *instructed,* he cannot, without some great fault of his own, fail to acquire a good *education. Instruction* is mostly the work of others; *education* depends mainly on the use which we ourselves make of the circumstances by which we are surrounded. The mischiefs of defective *instruction* may often be repaired by our own subsequent efforts; but a gap left down in the line of our *education* is not so easily put up, after the opporunity has once passed by.

5. The art of teaching.

The *art* of teaching, it is true, is not a *science,* and cannot be learned by theoretic study alone, without practice. The *model-school* is appropriately the place for the acquisition of this art by actual practice; but, like all the rational arts, it rests on scientific principles. The theoretical instruction, therefore, in this branch, will be limited mainly to a development of the principles on which it is founded; while the application of those principles will be illustrated, and the art of teaching acquired, by instructing in the model-school under the care of the professors, and subject to their direction, and remarks. The professor assigns to the pupil his class in the model-school, he observes his manner of teaching, and notices its excellences and defects; and after the class is dismissed, and the student is with him alone, or in company only with his fellow-students, he commends what he did well, shows him how he might have made the imperfect better, and the erroneous correct, pointing out, as he proceeds, the application of theoretic principles to practice, that the lessons in the model-school may be really an illustration of all that has been taught in the Teachers' Seminary.

6. The art of governing children, with special reference to the imparting and keeping alive of a feeling of love for children. . . .

7. History of education, including an accurate outline of the educational systems of different ages and nations; the circumstances which gave rise to them; the principles on which they were founded; the ends which they aimed to accomplish; their successes and failures, their permanency and changes; how far they influenced individual and national character; how far any of them might have originated in premeditated plan on the part of their founders; whether they secured the intelligence, virtue, and happiness of the people, or otherwise, with the causes, &c.

To insure success in any pursuit, the experience of our predecessors is justly considered a valuable, and generally an indispensable aid. . . . In every science and every art we recognize the value of its appropriate history; and there is not a single circumstance that gives value to such history, which does not apply, in all its force, to the history of education. Yet, strange to say, the history of education is entirely neglected among us; there is not a work devoted to the subject in the English language; and very few, indeed, which contain even notices or hints to guide one's inquiries on this deeply interesting theme. . . .

8. The rules of health and the laws of physical development. . . .

9. Dignity and importance of the teacher's office.

Self-respect, and a consciousness of doing well, are essential to comfort and success in any honorable calling; especially in one subject to so many external depressions, one so little esteemed and so poorly rewarded by the world at large, as that of the teacher. No station of so great importance has probably ever been so slightly estimated.

From: Caleb Atwater, *Essay on Education* (1841)

CALEB ATWATER (1778–1867) was born in North Adams, Massachusetts. He graduated from Williams College in 1804 with a master's degree and moved to New York City, where he kept a school for young women while studying theology and becoming a Presbyterian minister. Active in the legislature, he was chairman of a committee on school lands and carried on a vigorous campaign for public schools. One of the intellectual and social pioneers of the middle west, Atwater was appointed by President Jackson (May 1829) one of three commissioners to treat with the Winnebago and other Indians in the vicinity of Prairie du Chien, Wisconsin. The treaties, promptly concluded and ratified by the Senate, became the subject of an account he wrote two years later, which was subsequently collected in *The Writings of Caleb Atwater*. In 1838 he published *A History of the State of Ohio*, the first published history of this state. In 1841 appeared *An Essay on Education*, characterized by C. L. Martzolff (*Ohio Archeological and Historical Quarterly*, July 1905) as "the best thing he ever wrote" and a treatise which "makes good pedagogical reading even at this time."

MENTAL EDUCATION

This should be various, interesting and valuable; such as will invigorate and enlarge the mind, and strengthen the memory. It should store the memory with good precepts, apt illustrations and striking allusions. It should expand and elevate the sense of duty, refine and purify all the affections of our nature. We should study knowledge, not so much for the sake of remembering it, as for the sake of applying all the principles necessarily involved in it. We should not only treasure up a great many useful facts, but having developed them fully in all their relations, they should enter into the very structure of our minds, and become a part of the mind itself. These facts, thus treasured up, would enhance the faculty of thinking, improve the discipline of the intellectual powers, and enlarge the mind itself. Thus educated, every man and woman in our country might not have the opportunity, the time and the means of becoming very learned, but they might have real wisdom and skill, and no inconsiderable share of intellectual power. A profusion of learning, without order or method, may hang loosely about a person, like the drapery thrown over a marble statue: but give us a mind which is master of its knowledge; that enters into its very essence, and forms a part of the mind itself. Education should be such, that it should be not a mere mirror, reflecting its own image, but a crucible, that melts down, decomposes and forms anew all its materials into other beautiful and useful forms. . . .

Having taken this broad, though comprehensive view of education, we now proceed to point out some few though awful defects as we believe, in our system of education, mental and moral, now, and for many years past, quite too prevalent in our country—our whole country. But although there are many and great defects in our mental education, yet the greatest and most appalling defect has been, and is now, in our setting a higher value on mental than on moral instruction. The cultivation of the moral faculties has been neglected more than the mental faculties. . . .

DEFECTS IN OUR MORAL EDUCATION, AS A PEOPLE

There are, and certainly must be, some great and capital defects in all our systems of education in this entire nation, otherwise, there could not exist among us, every where, so much vice and crime. These vices and crimes produce a vast amount of physical, mental and moral evil and misery. Some of these defects originated in commonly received opinions, and have been handed down to us through ages past, and not a few of them have grown up among us within a few years. But, the greatest and the most prominent defect in our system, is the universal preference of *mental* over *moral* excellence. Nothing is more common than a belief, that early wickedness shows talent and genius; whereas, docility, gentleness, affection for parents, brothers, sisters and friends show stupidity. Generally speaking, the very reverse is true—witness George Washington. How often do we see worthless men teaching youth to swear, to drink spirits, and learn them other vicious practices? Where depravity is permitted to take root, in early life, reformation is all that can be hoped for; and how seldom does reformation, in that case, appear, except, like a ghastly spectre, it approaches the miserable, ruined wretch on his death-bed? It is an awful error to cultivate the *mind,* and neglect the *heart.* It would seem as if not a few of our wealthiest men in the nation wished to so educate their sons, that they may become the mere sport of their passions; and their daughters, so that they may resemble the meteor, flash, shine, sparkle, glitter and glare, for a moment, and then vanish from our sight, and be forgotten forever. Look all over the Union, and behold the immense wreck of mind, of health, of happiness and of all the moral affections, and then tell us, whether the thousands and tens of thousands of wretched, ruined human beings whom we see, have not been awfully and shamefully neglected in their early education, by their parents, teachers or guardians. . . .

Oh! what parent would not prefer to be poor, and struggle along through life, to give his children a plain, sound, good, common education, and rear them up in the fear of God, and have children that would eventually become honest, industrious, plain, useful citizens, than to give them great riches, and afford them great opportunities of becoming learned professional men, and thereby run the great and awful risk of their becoming dissipated, vicious and worthless creatures? Look all over the nation, and see who are the very first men, in every prominent station in society; (except political stations)—in mechanical skill, in mercantile pursuits, in agricultural wealth, in learning, in civil, naval or military stations. Those men, so high, so rich, so learned, so respected, caressed and honored now, were once poor boys, mostly, and have seen the time, and can remember the day, when they neither had, nor knew where they could procure, even one dollar. . . .

Generally speaking, we may safely affirm that our men, most distinguished for wealth, honor, fame, skill, learning, wisdom, and success in any calling, belonged either to parents who were poor, and so were driven to straits, and they struggled hard, to educate their children in the best way they could, teaching them to be industrious and skillful in their business; to be honest, faithful and kind to their fellow-men; and, above all, to fear God and keep his commandments: or such distinguished and prosperous men were once orphans, without any father to educate them, though belonging to pious widows. Of such men, it may be said, that their temperance, industry, honesty, fair dealing, attention to their business, promptness, kindness and respect for their fellow-citizens, their strict integrity in all their dealings, their careful observance of all the duties which they owed to themselves, their friends and their God, procured them confidence, friends and patronage. Whatever they attempted to do, whether they aimed at the pinnacles of wealth, learning, fame, or honor, ascending step by step, they finally placed themselves on the very summit of all their wishes. . . . Why is it that the sons of rich men so often come to ruin, whereas, poor men's sons so frequently succeed in the world? Is it not owing, mostly, to the preference of the rich for mental cultivation to the moral culture demanded by God, as well as by reason and true wisdom? And why do such men persist in such a course, regardless of the certain and the awful consequences of such a treasonable abuse of their high and holy trust of educating their offspring in the fear of God?

Parents should govern their children, and teach them to govern themselves. . . . The want of good, strict parental government, we fear, is one of
the great defects in education, at this time. To the reading of good books,
and the keeping of good, virtuous company, and good instruction from parents, should be added the good *example* of the parents themselves. Precept
without example is many times useless. During a life of more than sixty
years, spent mostly in public life, and among the crowd, consisting of all
sorts of people, from the most savage and ignorant and barbarous people in
North America, up to the very first in learning, science and literature: from
the poorest to the most wealthy—from the worst to the best in all the land, I
can say, that I have never known even one young man go to ruin, except it
was owing to the conduct of his parents, guardians or instructors. . . .

FEMALE EDUCATION

The treatment and education of females, in this country, compared with the
treatment and education which they receive in any other country, form a
most striking contrast. This subject, so important in itself, as it affects not
only our females, but our whole community, demands our serious consideration. We are aware of the fact, that much has been written on this subject,
especially of late years. Some writers, more particularly female authors,
have said many excellent things, touching this matter; but, we are equally
well aware, that nearly all that has appeared in novels, or in silly periodicals;
written, or conducted, mostly by frivolous young men, are utterly unworthy
of women; and injurious, and even disgraceful to our country. Having said
thus, we leave to themselves such self-conceited and frivolous authors, and
their readers and admirers.

In all countries, except in this Union, whether in Europe or America, the
females labor out of doors in the open air. They drive or hold the plow, and
sometimes draw it, beside an ass or a mule, (as in Italy). They rake hay, they
use the hoe, the axe and the saw; they sow and reap the grain; and, in fact,
perform all sorts of labor on the farm. They make long journies on business,
and carry it on in their houses, shops, and store-rooms. At court, they are
politicians. Forty years since, the farmers' wives and daughters labored on
the farm, in parts of New York, Pennsylvania, and in all the settlements
where Germans or Irish people dwelt in considerable numbers. The arrival
of the New Englanders among them, banished the females from the fields to
their houses and fire-sides. The change was beneficial to both sexes; but,
from one extreme, how prone are we to vibrate to the other! Are our females
to be either kitchen-maids, without a particle of information, except it belong to mere labor of body, without any mental cultivation?

A FASHIONABLE FEMALE EDUCATION

If they are taught any thing more, shall it be only, how to play on the harp, the guitar, and the piano-forte, to draw figures on paper or cloth, with a painter's brush or a needle? To dance a waltz; walk gracefully on their toes; make a handsome courtesy; keep an album; sing a fashionable song; wear a corset-board, false curls and artificial flowers; hold a silly conversation on nothing; leer and look languishing; and,—act the fool?

We have banished the former state of things, as to the treatment of females, and we now anxiously desire to see driven out of our land, the present frivolous practices which we have named. They are a disgrace to this enlightened age.

The main objects of educating females are precisely the same with those of educating the other sex—to develop all their powers and faculties, and, to prepare them for happiness and usefulness. We take it for granted, because we know it is in fact so, that females are as capable of attaining all sorts of knowledge as the other sex. Indeed they learn more easily, and at an earlier age, than the other sex. They are more easily governed and more plastic. We have already hinted at a fashionable female education. We now proceed to state what we wish our females to learn. In addition to the common branches of education, such as reading, writing, English grammar and arithmetic; we wish to see superadded, geography, chemistry, botany, vocal music, astronomy, algebra, rhetoric, mineralogy, geology, mechanics, natural and moral philosophy, geometry, and all the branches of the higher mathematics; civil and ecclesiastical history, biography; including more especially, the lives of great, good and distinguished women. By raising the character of woman, Christianity has already done a great deal for her, and itself. We wish to see it do more still, for her education, especially in our own country. . . .

As we admit of no difference, in the capacities of the two sexes for attaining knowledge, so we know of no difference in the modes of conveying it to their minds. . . .

INSTRUCTORS

. . . As to THE QUALIFICATIONS OF TEACHERS, we desire them to possess an intellect, strong, vigorous, prompt, and inquisitive,—a temper open, generous, cheerful, noble, forgiving, condescending and kind; full of tenderness, and alive to every social feeling, ardent, and at the same time enterprising and persevering. They should love their employment and be fond of children. They should be industrious, active, vigilant, and easy of access. They should always be ready to enter into all the little incidents of a child's life, so as to turn them all into lessons of wisdom. They should maintain a strictly impartial government over their pupils, and never permit any of their scholars to tyrannize over their fellow-pupils. Teachers should govern their own spirits on all occasions. The very first step towards governing others is to govern ourselves. This remark applies to all who command men. Those great and mighty men, who have commanded armies and navies which have achieved victories, great, splendid, and glorious, were cool, collected, and calm in danger, and in the battle. Without possessing this self-government, no one is fit to teach a school, govern a family, or pass through life in any station with reputation, honor, or usefulness. Their literary and scientific acquirements cannot be too good nor too great to fit them to teach even the youngest child. To teach any one of our common schools, the teacher should be a good reader, one who could spell and pronounce correctly, every word in our language, write every sort of hand in use, understand book-keeping, English grammar, arithmetic, geography, history, especially of our own country, and be well acquainted with our constitution and the institutions resting on its provisions as a foundation. All these things should be entirely familiar to the teacher, so that he or she perfectly understands them. In addition to all which knowledge, there should be a faculty of conveying all their information to their pupils, so that they may entirely and perfectly understand and fully comprehend all the ideas belonging to the several branches of learning which they teach. We have seen teachers who appeared to know more than they could well teach others. We do know some teachers, however, who possess the faculty of conveying knowledge in so clear and perfect a manner, that we have sometimes feared that their scholars would rely too much on the teacher's instruction, at recitation, and so would neglect to study their lessons as thoroughly as they ought to do. Such instructors, as those whom we have last referred to, being confined mostly, in this state, to Cincinnati, we need say no more on that failing, if it be one. There is more danger to be apprehended, perhaps, in this state, of young men being employed as teachers, while they are studying some profession themselves; and, of their studying their *own lesson* and neglecting to teach their scholars theirs! For parents to spend their money in educating the young men who travel over the land teaching school, to collect the means of educating themselves, and studying, instead of teaching, is neither just nor profitable to those who are thus imposed on by such young men. Every teacher should understand vocal music well, and be able to teach that branch of learning. Every school should be opened with the Lord's prayer, every scholar standing on his feet and audibly repeating it. This being done, the teacher should point to his gamut-board, sounding every note, backwards and forwards, every scholar accompanying the teacher with his or her clear voice until the instructor points to the notes of some full tune, which being sung by the notes correctly, it may then be sung by the words set to it, while every little eye in the school-room sparkles with delight, and every little voice is heard clearly joining in the song.

In his or her manners, every teacher of any school should be, if a man, a perfect gentleman—if a woman, a perfect lady. Children always catch the manners of their parents, their teachers, and their associates; more especially all their singularities, rudeness, and every thing vicious or bad. Hence, we see the absolute necessity of employing only persons of good manners, good principles, and pure morals, as instructors and companions of children and youth. So apparent are these truths to all persons of reflection and observation, that we need only mention them in order to gain the assent of all well-informed parents and guardians. But, however apparent these truths are, we feel it our duty to add, that teachers of youth can only *teach* what they themselves thoroughly *understand* and *know;* and what they love and are imbued with; how then, can a rough boor of a man, or a coarse virago of a woman, teach gentleness of manners, mildness, kindness, benevolence of disposition, respect for superiors, condescension to inferiors, and politeness to equals? How can a vicious man, or woman, teach virtue? Example is better than precept, and, unless they accompany each other, we should doubt the success of the latter, where the former was wanting.

Thousands have been everlastingly ruined by being placed under the instruction of unprincipled teachers. A drunkard, a gambler, a profane swearer, a sabbath-breaker, an infidel, and a dishonest man, should never undertake to instruct children or youth; even to teach them their letters, much less any profession, art, or trade. Such wicked men will have enough to answer for, when called on to account for the destruction of their own souls, without superadding to their guilt, the ruin of the souls of others, who were placed under their care and superintendence. How often are orphans apprenticed to men, for the purpose of learning some trade, whose education and morals are shamefully neglected? The laws of the land may never reach such delinquents, but their punishment is sure, and not very distant. There is an Eye that sees all their sins, and a Hand that will reach them and punish them. The orphan's tears, sighs, and groans, under the oppression of cruel and unfeeling masters and mistresses, are all numbered, seen, heard, and every one of them is taken down in a book, which will be opened to read to the guilty, before an assembled universe.

But we return to the professional teachers of youth, and say, that for them and their pupils to copy after, in their manners, morals, principles, precepts, and examples, we propose to them, the Great Teacher of mankind, Jesus, their friend and Saviour.

"A New Jersey Teacher's Contract" (1841). In Sol Cohen, *Education in the United States: A Documentary History,* vol. 3 (1977).

Joseph Thompson hereby agrees to teach a common English day school for the term of thirteen weeks of five days in each week (or an equivalent) in the Center schoolhouse, being District No. 8, of Bridgewater, to which is attached a part of Readington Township. He will give instruction to all the youth of the district that may be placed under his care in some or all of the following branches, as their capacities may reach, viz: Orthography, reading, writing, arithmetic, English grammar, geography, history, composition, and bookkeeping by single entry. And we, the trustees of said school, do hereby agree to furnish said teacher with fuel and all necessaries for the comfort and convenience of said school, and at the expiration of the term pay to him or his order in compensation for his services the sum of sixty-five dollars. The said teacher shall have the privilege of instructing his own children in said school and not be required to pay any proportional part of the above sum. All pupils which do not belong in the district and attend this school to learn any of the above-named branches, one half of their schooling shall belong to the teacher, and the other half to go into the funds of the school. The excess of charge for higher branches (if any are taught) shall belong exclusively to the teacher. If circumstances should occur to render it necessary to discontinue the school before the expiration of the term, a majority of the trustees or the teacher may discontinue, and he receive pay for the time then taught.

In witness whereof the parties have to these presents interchangeably set their hands this thirtieth day of October, in the year of our Lord 1841.

JOSEPH THOMPSON,
Teacher.

ABRAHAM A. AMERMAN,
PETER Q. BROKAW,
ABRAHAM AMERMAN,
Trustees.

121

From: David Perkins Page, *Theory and Practice of Teaching; or, The Motives and Methods of Good School-Keeping* (1847)

DAVID PERKINS PAGE (1810–1848) was born in Epping, New Hampshire. He began to teach at sixteen, after attending Hampton Academy for a few months. At nineteen, he opened a private school in Newburyport. He began with five pupils, but before the end of the term there were more applicants than he could accommodate. From 1831 to 1843, he was associate principal in the Newburyport High School, in charge of the English Department. In 1844, when a normal school was established at Albany, New York, Page was appointed principal of it on the recommendation of Horace Mann and other eminent educators. In spite of tremendous opposition to the project, in spite of the fact that by the time the school was to open it was yet unfinished, Page overcame every obstacle, and by 1847 the school was no longer considered an experiment. Page is reputed to have had a singular aptitude for teaching. Very much an autodidact, he acquired considerable knowledge of Latin and Greek, mathematics, natural sciences, and chemistry, in addition to history and literature. He was well liked as a teacher and respected as a speaker on educational matters. His only published book, *Theory and Practice of Teaching,* was considered an invaluable guide for inexperienced teachers.

If we arrange these three conceptions of fitness for teaching in the order of their historical sequence, they will stand as follows:

1. Scholarship.
2. Scholarship and Method.
3. Scholarship, Method, and Science.

In which stratum of thought are we living today? In all three. The first is represented in the laws regulating the granting of licenses to teach; the second, speaking generally, in normal schools; and the third, in universities where the study of education has been made a part of the curriculum. . . . In this country, the professional instruction of teachers in universities is of recent date, and consists chiefly in communicating the cardinal doctrines of education and teaching, on the hypothesis that students who have been liberally trained will be able, on the occasion of experience, to draw a rational art of teaching out of a science of teaching. The current of the educational thought of today may be interpreted as follows: True fitness for teaching, so far as it can be gained from instruction, consists first of all in a liberal scholarship, then in a knowledge of the best methods of doing the work of the school, and of the principles that underlie these methods. Many, perhaps the most, of those who are to teach for a long time to come, will fall short of these attainments; but this is a reasonable ideal toward which all should aspire. . . .

Those who are beginning the study of education should be reminded that the field of inquiry is a vast one, and that if they would attain the highest professional standing, they must pursue this subject in its three main phases—the practical, the scientific, and the historical. If the time for preparation is short, a beginning should be made in becoming acquainted with the best current methods of organizing, governing, and instructing a school. Then should follow a study of the science of education, to the end that the teacher may interpret the lessons of daily experience, and thus be helped to grow into higher and higher degrees of competence; and, finally, for giving breadth of view, for taking full advantage of all past experience and experiments, and for gaining that inspiration which comes from retracing the long line of an illustrious professional ancestry, there should be a study of the history of education.

All who propose to teach need to recollect that the very basis of fitness for teaching, so far as it can be gained from study, is a broad and accurate scholarship. To be a teacher, one must first of all be a scholar. So much stress is now placed on method, and the theory of teaching, that there is great danger of forgetting the supreme importance of scholarship and culture. For these there is no substitute; and any scheme of professional study that is pursued at the expense of scholarship and culture, is essentially bad. To be open-minded, magnanimous, and manly; to have a love for the scholarly vocation, and a wide and easy range of intellectual vision, are of infinitely greater worth to the teacher than any authorized set of technical rules and principles. Well would it be for both teachers and taught, if all who read this book were to be inspired by Plato's ideal of the cultured man: "A lover, not of a part of wisdom, but of the whole; who has a taste for every sort of knowledge and is curious to learn, and is never satisfied; who has magnificence of mind, and is the spectator of all time and all existence; who is harmoniously constituted; of a well-proportioned and gracious mind, whose own nature will move spontaneously towards the true being of every thing; who has a good memory, and is quick to learn, noble, gracious, the friend of truth, justice, courage, temperance." . . .

IT is the object of the following remarks feebly to illustrate the extent of the teacher's responsibility. It must all along be borne in mind that he is not *alone* responsible for the results of education. The parent has an overwhelming responsibility, which he can never part with or transfer to another while he holds the relation of parent.

But the teacher is responsible in a very high degree. An important interest is committed to his charge whenever a human being is placed under his guidance. By taking the position of the teacher, all the responsibility of the relation is voluntarily assumed; and he is fearfully responsible, not only for what he *does,* but also for what he neglects to do. And it is a responsibility from which he can not escape. . . .

I. *The teacher is in a degree responsible for the* BODILY HEALTH *of the child.* It is well established that the foundation of many serious diseases is laid in the school-room. These diseases come sometimes from a neglect of exercise; sometimes from too long confinement in one position, or upon one study; sometimes from over-excitement and over-study; sometimes from breathing bad air; sometimes from being kept too warm or too cold. . . .

The growing prevalence of myopia among school children should excite the watchful care of all teachers. Specialists have observed that cases of near-sight rapidly increase from the primary grades upward; and so common has this defect of the eye become, that it is now called a "school disease". The causes acting within the school-room to induce this malformation of the eye are the following: Insufficient light, causing the pupil to bring the book too near the eye; a stooping posture of the body, inducing congestion of the membranes of the eye; typography that is "trying to the eye". . . .

II. *The teacher is mainly responsible for the* INTELLECTUAL GROWTH *of the child.* This may be referred chiefly to the following heads:—

1. *The order of study.* There is a natural order in the education of the child. The teacher should know this. If he presents the subjects out of this order, he is responsible for the injury. In general, the *elements* should be taught first. Those simple branches which the child first comprehends, should first be presented. *Reading,* of course, must be one of the first. . . . Whether the pupil is merely learning words, or is really gaining ideas, may be tested in a very simple and effective way: *Require him to express the thought of the paragraph in his own words.* If he can do this accurately, it is certain that he has comprehended the thought; for he is able to separate it from the form of words employed by the author, and to embody it in a different form. This *translation of thought* should form an essential part of every reading exercise; expressive reading will then be a very simple thing. Reading proper, or the gaining of thought from the printed page, should be distinguished from elocution, or the *expression* of thought. A rule for good teaching is, first make sure that the thought has been gained, then attend to its proper expression.

Next to Reading and its inseparable companions—*Spelling* and *Defining*—I am inclined to recommend the study of *Mental Arithmetic*. . . .

RIGHT VIEWS OF EDUCATION

The conclusions of the honest and intelligent inquirer after the truth in this matter, will be something like the following:—That education (from *e* and *duco,* to lead forth) is development; that it is not instruction merely— knowledge, facts, rules—communicated by the teacher, but it is discipline, it is a waking up of the mind, a growth of the mind,—growth by a healthy assimilation of wholesome ailment. It is an inspiring of the mind with a thirst for knowledge, growth, enlargement,—and then a disciplining of its powers so far that it can go on to educate itself. It is the arousing of the child's mind to think, without thinking for it; it is the awakening of its powers to observe, to remember, to reflect, to combine. It is not a cultivation of the memory to the neglect of every thing else; but it is a calling forth of all the faculties into harmonious action. If to possess facts simply is education, then an encyclopedia is better educated than a man.

It should be remarked that though knowledge is not education, yet there will be no education without knowledge. Knowledge is ever an incident of true education. No man can be properly educated without the acquisition of knowledge; the mistake is in considering knowledge the *end* when it is either the *incident* or the *means* of education. The discipline of the mind, then, is the great thing in intellectual training; and the question is not, how much have I acquired?—but, how have my powers been strengthened in the act of acquisition?

Nor should the intellectual be earlier cultivated than the moral powers of the mind. The love of moral truth should be as early addressed as the love of knowledge. The conscience should be early exercised in judging of the character of the pupil's own acts, and every opportunity afforded to strengthen it by legitimate use. Nor should the powers of the mind be earlier cultivated than those of the body. . . .

I have dwelt thus fully on this subject, because it is so obvious that egregious mistakes are made in education. How many there are who are called "good scholars" in our schools, of whom we hear nothing after they go forth into the world. Their good scholarship consists in that which gives them no impulse to go on to greater attainments by themselves. Their learning is either that of *reception*—as the sponge takes in water—or that of mere memory. Their education is not discipline; it kindles none of those desires which nothing but further progress can satisfy; it imparts none of that self- reliance which nothing but impossibilities can ever subdue. While these are pointed out by their teachers as the ornaments of their schools, there are others, known as the heavy, dull, "poor scholars", in no way distinguished but by their stupidity,—of whom no hopes are entertained, because of them nothing is expected,—who in after-life fairly outstrip their fellows and strangely astonish their teachers. Almost every teacher of fifteen years' experience has noticed this. Now, why is it so? There must have been somehow in such cases a gross misjudgment of character. Either those pupils who promised so much by their quickness, were educated wrong, and perhaps educated too much, while their teachers unwittingly and unintentionally educated their less distinguished companions far more judiciously; or else, nature in such cases must be said to have been playing such odd pranks that legitimate causes could not produce their legitimate effects. We must charge nature as being extremely capricious, or we must allege that the teachers entirely misunderstood their work. . . .

It is the object of the following paragraphs to point out some of these encouragements; for, having in the preceding pages required very much at his hands, I feel that it is but just that he should be invited to look at the brighter side of the picture, so that when he is ready to sink under the responsibilities of his position, or to yield to the obstacles that oppose his progress, he may have something to animate his soul, and to nerve him anew for the noble conflict. . . .

THE REWARDS OF THE TEACHER

In view of what has been said, let the teacher cease to repine at his hard lot. Let him cast an occasional glance at the bright prospect before him. He deserves, to be sure, a higher pecuniary reward than he receives; and he should never cease to press this truth upon the community, till talent in teaching is as well compensated as talent in any other calling. But whether he gains this or not, let him dwell upon the privileges and rewards to be found in the calling itself, and take fresh encouragement.

The apostle Paul exhibited great wisdom when he said, *"I magnify mine office."* If the foregoing views respecting the importance of the teacher's calling are correct, he may safely follow the apostle's example. This is not, however, to be done merely by boastful words. No man can elevate himself, or magnify his office in public estimation, by indulging in empty declamation, or by passing inflated resolutions. He must *feel* the dignity of his profession, and show that he feels it by unremitted exertions to attain to the highest excellence of which he is capable,—animated, in the midst of his toil, chiefly by the great moral recompense which every faithful teacher may hope to receive.

Let every teacher, then, study to improve himself intellectually and morally; let him strive to advance in the art of teaching; let him watch the growth of mind under his culture and take the encouragement which that affords; let him consider the usefulness he may effect, and the circumstances which make his calling honorable; let him prize the gratitude of his pupils, and of their parents and friends; and above all, let him value the approval of Heaven, and set a proper estimate upon the rewards which another world will unfold to him,—and thus be encouraged to toil on in faithfulness and in hope,—till, having finished his course, and being gathered to the home of the righteous, he shall meet multitudes instructed by his wise precept, and profited by his pure example, who "shall rise up and call him blessed."

From: Baynard Rush Hall, *Teaching, a Science; The Teacher, an Artist* (1848)

BAYNARD RUSH HALL (1798–1863) was born in Philadelphia, Pennsylvania. His father, a surgeon, died when he was only three years old. A small legacy from a maternal uncle and his work as a printer enabled him to obtain a liberal education. He graduated from Union College in 1820 and from Princeton Theological Seminary in 1823. He lived his life as a Presbyterian clergyman and an educator. In 1824 he became the first principal of a state seminary in Bloomington, Indiana. From 1828 to 1831 he was elected professor of ancient languages, after the seminary received a college charter. From Indiana he went to Bedford, Pennsylvania, where he opened an academy in which he taught for seven years, while preaching in the Presbyterian Church. He did the same in Bordentown, New Jersey, and in Poughkeepsie and Newburgh, New York. Besides the book I have excerpted here, he was the author of such diverse books as *Latin Grammar* (1828); *Something for Everybody* (1846), a collection of homilies; *The New Purchase; or, Seven and a Half Years in the Far West* (1843), which he published under the pen name, Robert Carlton; and *Frank Freeman's Barber Shop: A Tale* (1852).

That persons more or less incompetent and unworthy, may be found in every department of teaching, from the meanest hedge-school to the noblest university, is true. It is also true that many crowd into the humbler walks of the profession, because they can do nothing else; some, too, out of indolence, supposing a few shillings can be there picked up without bodily labor; some from worse motives. But medicine has its quacks, law its pettifoggers, divinity its fanatics, and teaching has its pedagogues. Such fungi and poisonous accretions, black and fœtid, are not, however, the stately tree itself to which they adhere. They may, indeed, for a while conceal the tree; but when they are scraped away and removed, the beauteous symmetry of the columnar trunk appears.

Be it remembered—weeds spring and flourish only in suitable and neglected soil. In a truly enlightened, liberal, benevolent, discriminating community, quackery could not live! "Like people, like priest," applies to teachers as well as to parsons; and "The poor pay, and the poor preach," are comrades in teaching as in divinity. When a society retails hackneyed jests and worn witticisms at the expense of an honorable profession, they are either too deplorably ignorant to know good teachers exist, or too miserly to pay their just price. The latter is more common—the former not infrequent.

But while blur and blotch deface the profession, and more especially in the inferior grades, it is happily true, that in those grades are many men of noblest genius and talent. Men are there who, after a severe and laborious apprenticeship, shall one day stand forth pillars and columns of matchless excellence and grandeur. Let them bide their time. Their light may now be small, but it is true and certain; and at length it shall burn a sun in the moral and intellectual firmament. Be assured that they "shall reap if they faint not."

Concentrating all that has been advanced, and allowing the whole to rest upon the balance, the profession of teaching, both as a science and an art, must, in importance, grandeur and dignity, weigh, with equal poise, against any other profession in the opposite scale, while it will easily outweigh many, either separate or united. It challanges the trial.

Behold, too, the school-books of a mere practical age. Surely "of *making* books there is no end!" They are, indeed, *made,* not *written!* Booksellers, if they would take the time, need not pay for the jobs; but by the division of labor, much and every way, is gained. Systems and books are truly—productive! Happy era! two boys may trade the same jacket between them, till each shall gain five dollars! The same book-stuff may be hashed and cooked in a dozen different ways:—pictures now at the top of a page, and questions at the bottom!—then, pictures and questions reversed!—then, pictures in the middle, surrounded by a frame of crabbed-looking questions in small type! Wonderful variety!—it furnishes *little* and big potatoes to-day, and to-morrow, *big* and little potatoes!

We contend, that to impart knowledge is not the chief, nor most important part of true education. It is, in fact, no part of discipline. Without discipline, knowledge is almost useless; not infrequently a folly and injury. Mere knowledge "puffeth up." Rarely is it ever increased beyond the meagre details of elementary books. The mind untrained, endless misapplications of knowledge lead to losses and constant derision. The "knowledges," as they may be called, are innumerable; but rigorous discipline requires few books, and, after all the loud cry in favor of cheapness, it requires less price, and, if not a less, at least a definite time.

We are ready, now, to say what the end of education should be, and what it always has been with the wise. It is to teach an art. It is to create or form thinkers. The end of education is, the Power or Art of Thinking. By this art is meant, *a state of the soul or mind in which it is fitter for all and for more uses than in its natural state.* Like other arts, this may be taught and learned; and, like them, it depends partly on rules and principles derived from masters, and partly on its own exertions and practice. When the power approximates perfection, the soul begins to see intuitively, and the pupil has what is termed *presence of mind.*

When perfect, this art renders the mind calm, thoughtful, discriminating, prompt, energetic. It helps to see and weigh the absolute and relative importance of every subject within our scope; to follow truth in what is new, and reject error in what is old. The soul, in possession of itself, hastens not to conclusions; it sees the end from the beginning; it counts the cost. We learn not to be amazed at the mighty achievements of human skill, ingenuity, perseverance: we scarcely are surprised. We praise and blame, not as schemes are successful and unsuccessful, but according to their intrinsic character at the hour of formation. . . .

In our intercourse, this art becomes *tact.* This keeps us attentive to the minutest actions. To the discerning, a man of disciplined mind may be known by the way in which he walks, stands, sits, eats—by the way he takes up or lays down a book, opens or shuts a door, manages an umbrella, stirs a fire! The art promotes politeness, order, decency, reverence, good will; in short, ''whatsoever is lovely and of good report.'' . . .

The art of thinking is not for the poor, nor the rich; not for the mechanic, nor the farmer; not for the clergyman, nor the layman; it is for all. It may, in some degree, be taught to all. True education is not to constitute the pupil a *practical* artist of any kind—a doer; it does not make one immediately even a scholar. Education, while elementary, is to fit the pupil by training his mental powers for the subsequent instruction of masters in law, medicine, divinity, merchandise, politics, eloquence, poetry, painting, engineering, farming—in everything intrinsically worthy of being styled an art, trade, science, profession. . . .

This valuable art can be learned. But the way is long and difficult; not, perhaps, more so than the way through ''the knowledges:'' and yet well worth double the toil and expense of the popular method, if the intrinsic excellence and practical advantages of the art are appreciated. The mind must be long exercised in severe and rigorous studies.

The teacher, as an artist, possesses intellectual and moral qualifications that must class him with the best, and show that his office or profession ranks among the highest in dignity and importance. The teacher must be, among other things, a philosopher, a judge, a ruler, a parent, a preacher; and he must be, also, learned and scientific. He must have power over himself.

He must be conversant with men as well as books. He must be disinterested. He must possess an ardent love of learning, and must delight in his creations, as specimens of an approximation to the beau ideal. And this spirit, and this enthusiasm, make him press onward through difficulties and discourage-ments, and over obstacles and impediments, unwearied, towards the attain-ment of his end, unmoved by the carpings of the envious, the insolence of the rich and covetous, the revilings of the slanderous, the prejudices of the ignorant, the baseness of the fraudulent, the anger of the revengeful, the ingratitude of the thankless and the vile!

From: Henry Barnard, "Introduction," "Connecticut," and "Topics for Discussion and Composition on the Theory and Practice of Education," in *Normal Schools and Other Institutions, Agencies, and Means for the Professional Education of Teachers* (1851)

HENRY BARNARD (1811–1900) was born in Hartford, Connecticut. He shares with Horace Mann the distinction of stimulating and directing the revival of popular education in this country. He graduated from college in 1830, studied in the Yale Law School (1833–1834), was admitted to the bar the following year, and became active in politics. His main interest was education. He founded the *Connecticut Common School Journal* and the *American Journal of Education* (which appeared at irregular intervals between 1855 and 1882), edited documents and papers associated with the founding of normal schools, which he strongly supported, helped establish the Rhode Island Institute of Instruction, and relentlessly tried to educate the public on the necessity to give teachers appropriate preparation for their profession. He held many influential positions: he was chancellor of the University of Wisconsin (1858–1860), president of St. John's College (Annapolis, Maryland, 1866–1867), and became the first U.S. commissioner of education. A deeply religious man, he had utmost faith in the perfectibility of human nature and believed that the sole hope of a righteous, peaceful, and prosperous world lay in an educated democracy.

INTRODUCTION

The Normal Schools already established in this country are, it is believed, doing much good, and realizing the promises of those who have been active in getting them up; but as compared with European Institutions of the same kind, and the demands for professional training in all our schools, they labor under many disadvantages.

1. Pupils are admitted without adequate preparatory attainments, and without sufficient test of their "aptness to teach."

2. A majority of the pupils do not remain a sufficient length of time, to acquire that knowledge of subjects and methods, and especially that intellectual power and enlightenment, which are essential to the highest success in the profession.

3. There are no endowments to reduce the expense of a prolonged residence to a class of poor but promising pupils.

4. They are not provided with a sufficient number of teachers for the number of pupils admitted.

5. From the want of a well-defined and limited purpose in each institution, they are aiming to accomplish too much—more for every class of pupils,—those with, and those without previous experience,—the young, and the more advanced,—those intended for country and unclassified schools, and those intended for the highest grade of city and town schools,—than can be well done for either class of pupils.

Further experience will make these deficiencies more apparent, not to those who have the immediate charge of these institutions, for they are already painfully conscious of them, but to the people, legislatures, and liberally-disposed men, who must apply the remedies by increased appropriations to existing, and the establishment of additional schools.

The following is a list of the Normal Schools already established, with the location and date of the establishment of each school.

TABLE OF NORMAL SCHOOLS IN AMERICA.

State and Location	Number	Date When First Established
MASSACHUSETTS	3	
West Newton	—	1839
Bridgewater	—	1839
Westfield	—	1839
NEW YORK	1	
Albany	—	1845
PENNSYLVANIA	1	
Philadelphia	—	1848
CONNECTICUT	1	
New Britain	—	1849
MICHIGAN	1	
Ypsilanti	—	1850
BRITISH PROVINCES	2	
Toronto, for Upper Canada	—	1846
St. John's, for New Brunswick	—	1848

CONNECTICUT.

The earliest mention of the establishment of a Seminary for Teachers in Connecticut, was made by Mr. William Russell,* in August 1823, in a pamphlet, entitled *Suggestions on Education:*

*Mr. Russell was at that date a teacher in the New Township Academy, New Haven. He afterward removed to Boston, where he engaged earnestly in the work of educational

"The common schools for children, are, in not a few instances, conducted by individuals who do not possess one of the qualifications of an instructor; and, in very many cases, there is barely knowledge enough 'to keep the teacher at a decent distance from his scholars.' An excellent suggestion was lately made on a branch of this subject, by a writer in a periodical publication. His proposal was, that a seminary should be founded, for the teachers of district schools; that a course of study should be prescribed to persons who are desirous of obtaining the situation of teachers in such schools; and that no individual should be accepted as an instructor, who had not received a license, or degree, from the proposed institution. The effects of such an improvement in education seem almost incalculable. The information, the intelligence, and the refinement, which might thus be diffused among the body of the people, would increase the prosperity, elevate the character, and promote the happiness of the nation to a degree perhaps unequalled in the world."

In the first number of the Connecticut Observer, published in Hartford, Conn., January 4, 1825, Rev. Thomas H. Gallaudett, then Principal of the American Asylum for the Education of the Deaf and Dumb, commenced a series of Essays, with the signature of "A Father," on a *Plan of a Seminary for the Education of Instructors of Youth*. These essays attracted much attention in Connecticut, and other parts of New England, and were collected and published in a pamphlet of 40 pages, in Boston, in the same year. Selections from the same were re-published in the newspapers, and the plan was presented and discussed in the educational conventions which assembled in Hartford, in 1828 and in 1830. The following is the substance of the plan:

"Suppose, Mr. Editor, an Institution, call it by what name you please, should be established somewhere in New England, for the training up of young men for the profession of instructors of youth in the common branches of English education. Suppose such an institution should be so well endowed, by the liberality of the public, or of individuals, as to have two or three professors, men of talents and habits adapted to the pursuit, who should devote their lives to the object of the 'Theory and Practice of the Education of Youth,' and who should prepare and deliver, and print, if you and they please, a course of lectures on the subject.

Let the Institution be furnished with a *library,* which should contain all the works, theoretical and practical, in all languages, which can be obtained on the subject of education, and also with all the apparatus that modern ingenuity has devised for this purpose; such as maps, charts, globes, orreries, &c. &c.

Let there be connected with the Institution a school smaller or larger,

improvement. In 1826 he became editor of the Journal of Education, the first periodical devoted exclusively to the subject, published in the English language. Mr. Russell is now Principal of the Normal Institute at Merrimack, New Hampshire.

as circumstances might dictate, of indigent children and youth, and *especially of foreign youth whom we are rearing for future benevolent efforts,* in which the theories of the professors might be reduced to practice, and from which daily experience would derive a thousand useful instructions.

To such an Institution let young men resort, of piety, of talents, of industry, and of adaptedness to the business of the instructors of youth, and who would expect to *devote their lives* to so important an occupation. Let them attend a regular course of lectures on the subject of education; read the best works; take their turns in the instruction of the *experimental school,* and after thus becoming qualified for their office, leave the Institution with a suitable certificate or diploma, recommending them to the confidence of the public.''

In 1838, an *"Act to provide for the better supervision of Common Schools,"* creating a Board of Commissioners, with a Secretary, who was ''to devote his whole time to ascertain the condition, increase the interest, and promote the usefulness of common schools,'' was passed by the Legislature. In a speech made by the chairman of the Committee that reported the bill, in the House of Representatives, (Henry Barnard, of Hartford) the following remarks were made in reference to this particular subject:

''This measure, if adopted and sustained by the Legislature and the people for ten years, must result in making some legislative provision for the better education, and special training of teachers for their delicate and difficult labors. Every man who received his early education in the district schools of Connecticut, must be conscious, and most of us must exhibit in our own mental habits, and in the transactions of ordinary business, the evidence of the defective instruction to which we were subjected in these schools. And no one can spend a half hour in the best common school in his neighborhood, without seeing, both in the arrangements, instruction, and discipline of the teacher, the want, not only of knowledge on his part, but particularly of a practical ability to make what he does know available. He has never studied and practiced his art, the almost creative art of teaching, under an experienced master, and probably has never seen, much less spent any considerable portion of time visiting, any better schools than the one in which he was imperfectly taught—in which he *said his lessons,* as the business is significantly described in a phrase in common use.

The first step will be to get at the fact, and if it is as I suppose, that our teachers are not qualified, and that there is now no adequate provision made in our Academies and higher seminaries for the right qualification of teachers of district schools, then let the fact be made known to the Legislature and the people, by reports, by the press, and by popular addresses,—the only ways in which the Board can act, on either the Legislature or the schools;—and in time, sooner or later, we shall have the seminaries, and the teachers, unless the laws which have heretofore governed the progress of society, and of education in particular, shall cease to operate. It is idle to expect good schools until we have good teachers, and the people will rest satisfied with such teachers as they have, until their attention is directed to the subject, and until we can demonstrate the necessity of employing better, and show how they can be made better, by proper training in classes or seminaries established for this specific purpose. With better teachers will come better compensation and more permanent employment. The people pay now quite enough for the article they get. It is dear at even the miserably low price at which so much of it can be purchased. Let us have light on the whole subject of teachers,— their qualifications, preparation, compensation and supervision, for on these points there is a strange degree of indifference, not to say ignorance, on the part both of individuals, and of the public generally.''

During the year following the establishment of the Board, the Secretary, (Mr. Barnard) published in the Connecticut Common School Journal a number of articles, original and selected, in which the professional education of teachers was discussed, and the history of Normal Schools in Prussia, Holland, and France presented. In the course of the four years in which the Journal was published, the Essays of Mr. Gallaudet, the Report of Prof. Stowe on Normal Schools and Teachers' Seminaries, all that portion of Prof. Bache's Report on Education in Europe, devoted to an account of particular institutions for the education of teachers, and many other documents and articles on the same subject, were spread before the people of this state. Of several numbers of the Journal devoted to these publications, more than ten thousand copies were circulated.

In the First Annual Report of the Secretary of the Board of Commissioners of Common Schools, submitted to the General Assembly, in May, 1839, the establishment ''of at least one seminary for teachers,'' is urged in the following manner:

"As there are some who still regard it as an experiment, it can be at first for the training of female teachers for the common schools. Such an institution, with a suitable principal and assistants, and especially a model school connected with it, in which theory could be carried into practice, and an example given of what a district school ought to be, would, by actual results, give an impulse to the cause of popular education, and the procuring of good teachers, that could be given in no other way. The time of continuance at such an institution could be longer or shorter according to circumstances. Even a short continuance at it would often be of vast benefit. It would furnish an illustration of better methods of instruction and government than 'the district school as it is' can give, which is the only model a large majority of our teachers are now familiar with. The expense to those attending, need not be great, if such a seminary were moderately endowed from the public treasury, and the contributions of towns and public spirited individuals. To secure this most desirable co-operation, the state appropriation might be made on condition that an equal or greater amount be raised from other sources. Once established, it would speedily draw to it numbers of our young women, to improve the qualifications they already possess for teaching, and give the experience and skill which are necessary. If wisely managed, it would give credentials to none but the best of teachers.

They will command good wages. Those employing them would expect to give such wages. For the object in applying to this source would be to get teachers of superior qualifications at an enhanced price. The supply would create a demand. The demand would in turn secure a greater supply of well-educated teachers for the primary schools. Through them, better methods of teaching, by which an increased amount of instruction, and that of a more practical character, would be disseminated through a large number of districts. The good done would thus not be confined to the comparative few who should pursue the studies of the seminary, or acquire skill and experience in the model school. Each would carry out the same methods. Enterprising teachers, too, who had not enjoyed the same opportunity for improvement, would strive to excel those who had; and thus a wholesome spirit of emulation would be provoked among teachers.

One such seminary, with the model school annexed, or rather forming an essential part of the institution, where the best methods of school government, and all the numerous and complicated processes of teaching, developing, and guiding the human mind, and cultivating the moral nature, could be taught and illustrated, would be the safest and least expensive way of testing the practicability of introducing others, both for males and females, into every county of the state, as a part of our common school system.''

This document was referred to a ''Joint Select Committee on Common Schools,'' of the two Houses of the General Assembly, to whom the following *"Report and Resolution respecting the Education of Teachers,"* was submitted, May, 1839:

''The Joint Select Committee on Common Schools, to whom was referred the Report of the Board of Commissioners of Common Schools, together with the Report of their Secretary, have had the same under consideration, and beg leave to report in part, that in their estimation, the main deficiency in the common schools of the State, is an inadequate supply of well-qualified teachers, and that to supply this deficiency, and thereby improve the quality, and increase the amount of instruction communicated in these schools, which must forever remain the principal reliance of a vast majority of parents for the education of their children, the experience of other states and countries demonstrates the necessity of making some legislative provision for the education of teachers. With this view, and to secure the co-operation of counties, towns and individuals who may be more directly benefitted by this appropriation, or who may choose to unite with the State in elevating the character of the common schools in the mode attempted, the Committee recommend the passage of the accompanying resolution. All of which is respectfully submitted,

By order of the Committee,
John A. Rockwell, *Chairman.*

Resolved, That the Comptroller of public accounts is hereby authorized to draw an order on the Treasurer, in favor of the Board of Commissioners of Common Schools, for the sum of $5000, or such portions thereof as they may request, to be paid out of any money not otherwise appropriated; provided said Board shall certify that an amount equal to that applied for, has been placed at their disposal; both sums to be expended under the direction of said Board in promoting and securing the qualifications in teachers for the common schools of Connecticut.''

The resolution called forth a full expression of opinion in the House of Representatives, and was finally passed in that body without a dissenting voice. . . .

TOPICS FOR DISCUSSION AND COMPOSITION ON THE THEORY AND PRACTICE OF EDUCATION.

1. The daily preparation which the teacher should bring to the school-room.

2. The circumstances which make a teacher happy in school.

3. The requisites of success in teaching.

4. Causes of failure in teaching.

5. The course to be pursued in organizing a school.

6. The order of exercises or programme of recitations.

7. The policy of promulgating a code of rules for the government of a school.

8. The keeping of registers of attendance and progress.

9. The duties of the teacher to the parents of the children and to school-officers.

10. The opening and closing exercises of a school.

11. Moral and religious instruction and influence generally.

12. The best use of the Bible or Testament in school.

13. Modes of promoting a love of truth, honesty, benevolence, and other virtues among children.

14. Modes of promoting obedience to parents, respectful demeanor to elders, and general submission to authority.

15. Modes of securing cleanliness of person and neatness of dress, re-

spect for the school-room, courtesy of tone and language to companions, and gentleness of manners.

16. Modes of preserving the school-house and appurtenances from injury and defacement.

17. Length and frequency of recess.

18. The games, and modes of exercise and recreation to be encouraged during the recess, and at intermission.

19. Modes of preventing tardiness, and securing the regular attendance of children at school.

20. Causes by which the health and constitution of children at school are impaired, and the best ways of counteracting the same.

21. The government of a school generally.

22. The use and abuse of corporal punishment.

23. The establishment of the teacher's authority in the school.

24. Manner of treating stubborn and refractory children, and the policy of dismissing the same from school.

25. Prizes and rewards.

26. The use and abuse of emulation.

27. Modes of interesting and bringing forward dull, or backward scholars.

28. Modes of preventing whispering, and communication between scholars in school.

29. Manner of conducting recitations generally; and how to prevent or detect imperfect lessons.

30. Methods of teaching, with illustrations of each, viz:
    a. Monitorial.
    b. Individual.
    c. Simultaneous.
    d. Mixed.
    e. Interrogative.
    f. Explanative.
    g. Elliptical.
    h. Synthetical.
    i. Analytical.

31. Modes of having all the children of a school (composed as most District schools are, of children of all ages, and in a great variety of studies,) at all times something to do, and a motive for doing it.

32. Methods of teaching the several studies usually introduced into public schools—such as—
    a. The use, and nature, and formation of numbers.

    b. Mental Arithmetic.

    c. Written Arithmetic.

    d. Spelling.

    e. Reading.

    f. Grammar—including conversation, composition, analysis of sentences, parsing, &c.

    g. Geography—including map-drawing, use of outline maps, atlas, globes, &c.

    h. Drawing—with special reference to the employment of young children, and as preliminary to penmanship.

    i. Penmanship.

    j. Vocal music.

    k. Physiology—so far at least as the health of children and teacher in the school-room is concerned.

33. The apparatus and means of visible illustration, necessary for the schools of different grades.

34. The development and cultivation of observation, attention, memory, association, conception, imagination, &c.

35. Modes of inspiring scholars with enthusiasm in study, and cultivating habits of self-reliance.

36. Modes of cultivating the power and habit of attention and study.

37. Anecdotes of occurrences in the school, brought forward with a view to form right principles of moral training and intellectual development.

38. Lessons, on real objects, and the practical pursuits of life.

39. Topics and times for introducing oral instruction, and the use of lectures generally.

40. Manner of imparting collateral and incidental knowledge.

41. The formation of museums and collections of plants, minerals, &c.

42. Exchange of specimens of penmanship, map and other drawings, minerals, plants, &c., between the different schools of a town, or of different towns.

43. School examinations generally.

44. How far committees should conduct the examination.

45. Mode of conducting an examination by written questions and answers.

46. School celebrations, and excursions of the school, or a portion of the scholars, to objects of interest in the neighborhood.

47. Length and frequency of vacations.

48. Books and periodicals on education, schools and school systems.

49. Principles to be regarded in the construction of a school-house for schools of different grades.

50. Principles on which text-books in the several elementary studies should be composed.

51. The use of printed questions in text-books.

52. The private studies of a teacher.

53. The visiting of each other's schools.

54. The peculiar difficulties and encouragements of each teacher, in respect to school-house, attendance, supply of books, apparatus, parental interest and co-operation, support by committees, &c, &c.

55. The practicability of organizing an association of the mothers and females generally of a district or town, to visit schools, or of their doing so without any special organization.

56. Plan for the organization, course of instruction, and management generally of a Teachers Institute.

57. Advantages of an Association or Conference of the Teachers of a Town or State, and the best plan of organizing and conducting the same.

58. Plan of a Normal School or Seminary, for the training of Teachers for Common or Public Schools.

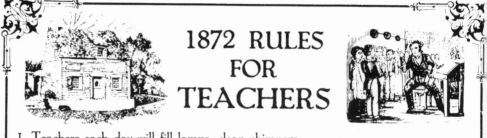

1872 RULES FOR TEACHERS

1. Teachers each day will fill lamps, clean chimneys.

2. Each teacher will bring a bucket of water and a scuttle of coal for the day's session.

3. Make your pens carefully. You may whittle nibs to the individual taste of the pupils.

4. Men teachers may take one evening each week for courting purposes, or two evenings a week if they go to church regularly.

5. After ten hours in school, the teachers may spend the remaining time reading the Bible or other good books.

6. Women teachers who marry or engage in unseemly conduct will be dismissed.

7. Every teacher should lay aside from each day pay a goodly sum of his earnings for his benefit during his declining years so that he will not become a burden on society.

8. Any teacher who smokes, uses liquor in any form, frequents pool or public halls, or gets shaved in a barber shop will give good reason to suspect his worth, intention, integrity and honesty.

9. The teacher who performs his labor faithfully and without fault for five years will be given an increase of twenty-five cents per week in his pay, providing the Board of Education approves.

OLDEST WOODEN SCHOOLHOUSE
St. Augustine, Florida

From: *Pedagogics as a System* (1872–1874) by Karl Rosenkranz;
Anna Callender Brackett, translator

ANNA CALLENDER BRACKETT (1836–1911) was educated at both private and
public schools in Boston, at Mr. Abbott's noted academy for girls, and at the
state normal school at Framingham, Massachusetts, where she later served for
two years as assistant principal. In 1860 she became vice principal of a normal
school in Charleston, South Carolina, and then principal of the normal school
at St. Louis—the first woman to head a normal school in the United States.
Like Emma Willard and Almira Phelps, she made the education of American
girls her major interest. *The Education of American Girls* (1874) and *Woman and
the Higher Education* (1893) are records of the high respect she had for woman's mental vigor. She was greatly influenced by the German philosopher Karl
Rosenkranz, Doctor of Theology and Professor of Philosophy at the University
of Königsberg, whose work she read and studied in the original language, and
she translated *Pedagogics as a System* once for the *Journal of Speculative Philosophy* (1872–1874), and again, in simpler prose and in its entirety, for the International Educational Series edited by William Torrey Harris (1886).

PEDAGOGICS AS A SYSTEM.

[Inquiries from teachers in different sections of the country as to the sources
of information on the subject of Teaching as a Science have led me to believe
that a translation of Rosenkranz's Pedagogics may be widely acceptable and
useful. It is very certain that too much of our teaching is simply empirical,
and as Germany has, more than any other country, endeavored to found it
upon universal truths, it is to that country that we must at present look for a
remedy for this empiricism.

Based as this is upon the profoundest system of German Philosophy, no
more suggestive treatise on Education can perhaps be found. In his third
part, as will be readily seen, Rosenkranz follows the classification of National ideas given in Hegel's Philosophy of History. The word "Pedagogics," though it has unfortunately acquired a somewhat unpleasant meaning
in English—thanks to the writers who have made the word "pedagogue" so
odious—deserves to be redeemed for future use. I have, therefore, retained
it in the translation.

In order that the reader may see the general scope of the work, I append
in tabular form the table of contents, giving however, under the first and

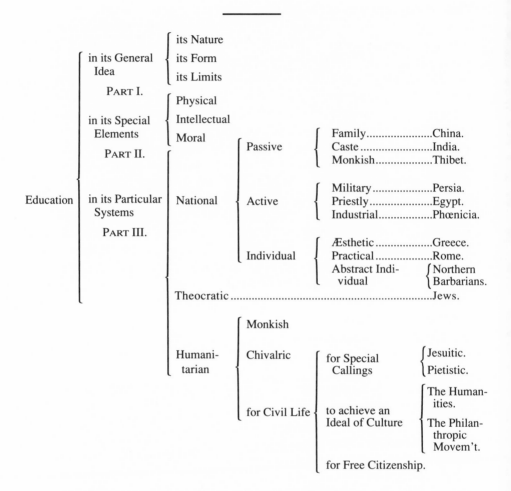

A N A L Y S I S .

second parts, only the main divisions. The minor heads can, of course, as they appear in the translation, be easily located.—*Tr.*]

INTRODUCTION.

§1. The science of Pedagogics cannot be derived from a simple principle with such exactness as Logic and Ethics. It is rather a mixed science which has its presuppositions in many others. In this respect it resembles Medicine, with which it has this also in common, that it must make a distinction between a sound and an unhealthy system of education, and must devise means to prevent or to cure the latter. It may therefore have, like Medicine, the three departments of Physiology, Pathology, and Therapeutics.

§2. Since Pedagogics is capable of no such exact definitions of its principle and no such logical deduction as other sciences, the treatises written upon it abound more in shallowness than any other literature. Short-sightedness and arrogance find in it a most congenial atmosphere, and criticism and declamatory bombast flourish in perfection as nowhere else. The literature of religious tracts might be considered to rival that of Pedagogics in its superficiality and assurance, if it did not for the most part seem itself to belong, through its ascetic nature, to Pedagogics. But teachers as persons should be treated in their weaknesses and failures with the utmost consideration, because they are most of them sincere in contributing their mite for the improvement of education, and all their pedagogic practice inclines them towards administering reproof and giving advice.

§3. The charlatanism of educational literature is also fostered by the fact that teaching has become one of the most profitable employments, and the competition in it tends to increase self-glorification. . . .

§4. In the system of the sciences, Pedagogics belongs to the Philosophy of Spirit,—and in this, to the department of Practical Philosophy, the problem of which is the comprehension of the necessity of freedom; for education is the conscious working of one will on another so as to produce itself in it according to a determinate aim. . . .

§5. Much confusion also arises from the fact that many do not clearly enough draw the distinction between Pedagogics as a science and Pedagogics as an art. As a science it busies itself with developing *a priori* the idea of Education in the universality and necessity of that idea, but as an art it is the concrete individualizing of this abstract idea in any given case. And in any such given case, the peculiarities of the person who is to be educated and all the previously existing circumstances necessitate a modification of the universal aims and ends, which modification cannot be provided for beforehand, but must rather test the ready tact of the educator who knows how to make the existing conditions fulfil his desired end. It is exactly in doing this that the educator may show himself inventive and creative, and that pedagogic talent can distinguish itself. The word "art" is here used in the same way as it is used when we say, the art of war, the art of government, &c.; and rightly, for we are talking about the possibility of the realization of the idea.

—The educator must adapt himself to the pupil, but not to such a degree as to imply that the pupil is incapable of change, and he must also be sure that the pupil shall learn through his experience the independence of the object studied, which remains uninfluenced by his variable personal moods, and the adaptation of the teacher's part must never compromise this independence.

§6. If conditions which are local, temporal, and individual, are fixed as constant rules, and carried beyond their proper limits, are systematized as a valuable formalistic code, unavoidable error arises. The formulæ of teaching are admirable material for the science, but are not the science itself.

§7. Pedagogics as a science must (1) unfold the general idea of Education; (2) must exhibit the particular phases into which the general work of Education divides itself, and (3) must describe the particular standpoint upon which the general idea realizes itself, or should become real in its special processes at any particular time. . . .

§9. The second division unfolds the subject of the physical, intellectual and practical culture of the human race, and constitutes the main part of all books on Pedagogy. Here arises the greatest difficulty as to the limitations, partly because of the undefined nature of the ideas, partly because of the degree of amplification which the details demand. Here is the field of the widest possible differences. . . .

§10. The third division distinguishes between the different standpoints which are possible in the working out of the conception of Education in its special elements, and which therefore produce different systems of Education wherein the general and the particular are individualized in a special manner. In every system the general tendencies of the idea of education, and the difference between the physical, intellectual and practical culture of man, must be formally recognized, and will appear. The How is decided by the standpoint which reduces that formalism to a special system. Thus it becomes possible to discover the essential contents of the history of Pedagogics from its idea, since this can furnish not an indefinite but a certain number of Pedagogic systems. . . .

§11. The last system must be that of the present, and since this is certainly on one side the result of all the past, while on the other seized in its possibilities it is determined by the Future, the business of Pedagogics cannot pause till it reaches its ideal of the general and special determinations, so that looked at in this way the Science of Pedagogics at its end returns to its beginning. The first and second divisions already contain the idea of the system necessary for the Present.

First Part.
The General Idea of Education.

§12. The idea of Pedagogics in general must distinguish,

(1) The nature of Education in general;

(2) Its form;

(3) Its limits.

I. The Nature of Education.

§13. The nature of Education is determined by the nature of mind—that it can develop whatever it really is only by its own activity. Mind is in itself free; but if it does not actualize this possibility, it is in no true sense free, either for itself or for another. Education is the influencing of man by man, and it has for its end to lead him to actualize himself through his own efforts. The attainment of perfect manhood as the actualization of the Freedom necessary to mind constitutes the nature of Education in general. . . .

§15. The idea of Education may be more or less comprehensive. We use it in the widest sense when we speak of the Education of the race, for we understand by this expression the connection which the acts and situations of different nations have to each other, as different steps towards self-conscious freedom. In this the world-spirit is the teacher.

§16. In a more restricted sense we mean by Education the shaping of the individual life by the forces of nature, the rhythmical movement of national customs, and the might of destiny in which each one finds limits set to his arbitrary will. These often mould him into a man without his knowledge. . . .

§17. In the narrowest sense, which however is the usual one, we mean by Education the influence which one mind exerts on another in order to cultivate the latter in some understood and methodical way, either generally or with reference to some special aim. The educator must, therefore, be relatively finished in his own education, and the pupil must possess unlimited confidence in him. If authority be wanting on the one side, or respect and obedience on the other, this ethical basis of development must fail, and it demands in the very highest degree, talent, knowledge, skill, and prudence. . . .

§18. The general problem of Education is the development of the theoretical and practical reason in the individual. If we say that to educate one means to fashion him into morality, we do not make our definition sufficiently comprehensive, because we say nothing of intelligence, and thus confound education and ethics. A man is not merely a human being, but as a reasonable being he is a peculiar individual, and different from all others of the race. . . .

§19. Education must lead the pupil by an interconnected series of efforts previously foreseen and arranged by the teacher to a definite end; but the particular form which this shall take must be determined by the peculiar character of the pupil's mind and the situation in which he is found. Hasty and inconsiderate work may accomplish much, but only *systematic* work can advance and fashion him in conformity with his nature, and the former does not belong to education, for this includes in itself the idea of an end, and that of the technical means for its attainment.

§20. But as culture comes to mean more and more, there becomes necessary a division of the business of teaching among different persons, with reference to capabilities and knowledge, because as the arts and sciences are continually increasing in number, one can become learned in any one branch only by devoting himself exclusively to it, and hence becoming one-sided. A difficulty hence arises which is also one for the pupil, of preserving, in spite of this unavoidable one-sidedness, the unity and wholeness which are necessary to humanity. . . .

§21. As it becomes necessary to divide the work of teaching, a difference between general and special schools arises also, from the needs of growing culture. The former present in different compass all the sciences and arts which are included in the term "general education," and which were classified by the Greeks under the general name of Encyclopædia. The latter are known as special schools, suited to particular needs or talents.

—As those who live in the country are relatively isolated, it is often necessary, or at least desirable, that one man should be trained equally on many different sides. The poor tutor is required not only to instruct in all the sciences, he must also speak French and be able to play the piano. . . .

The Form of Education.

§23. The general form of Education is determined by the nature of the mind, that it really is nothing but what it makes itself to be. The mind is (1) immediate (or potential), but (2) it must estrange itself from itself as it were, so that it may place itself over against itself as a special object of attention; (3) this estrangement is finally removed through a further acquaintance with the object—it feels itself at home in that on which it looks, and returns again enriched to the form of immediateness. That which at first appeared to be another than itself is now seen to be itself. Education cannot create; it can only help to develop to reality the previously existent possibility; it can only help to bring forth to light the hidden life.

§24. All culture, whatever may be its special purport, must pass through these two stages—of estrangement, and its removal. Culture must hold fast to the distinction between the subject and the object considered immediately, though it has again to absorb this distinction into itself, in order that the union of the two may be more complete and lasting. The subject recognizes then all the more certainly that what at first appeared to it as a foreign existence, belongs to it as its own property, and that it holds it as its own all the more by means of culture.

—Plato, as is known, calls the feeling with which knowledge must begin, wonder; but this can serve as a beginning only, for wonder itself can only express the tension between the subject and the object at their first encounter—a tension which would be impossible if they were not in themselves identical. . . .

§25. This activity of the mind in allowing itself to be absorbed, and consciously so, in an object with the purpose of making it his own, or of producing it, is *Work*. But when the mind gives itself up to its objects as chance may present them or through arbitrariness, careless as to whether they have any result, such activity is *Play*. Work is laid out for the pupil by his teacher by authority, but in his play he is left to himself.

§26. Thus work and play must be sharply distinguished from each other. . . .

§27. Work should never be treated as if it were play, nor play as if it were work. In general, the arts, the sciences, and productions, stand in this relation to each other: the accumulation of stores of knowledge is the recreation of the mind which is engaged in independent creation, and the practice of arts fills the same office to those whose work is to collect knowledge.

§28. Education seeks to transform every particular condition so that it shall no longer seem strange to the mind or in any wise foreign to its own nature. This identity of consciousness, and the special character of anything done or endured by it, we call Habit [habitual conduct or behavior]. It conditions formally all progress; for that which is not yet become habit, but which we perform with design and an exercise of our will, is not yet a part of ourselves.

§20. As to Habit, we have to say next that it is at first indifferent as to what it relates. . . .

The aim of Education must be to arouse in the pupil this spiritual and ethical sensitiveness which does not recognize anything as *merely* indifferent, but rather knows how to seize in everything, even in the seemingly small, its universal human significance. But in relation to the highest problems he must learn that what concerns his own immediate personality is entirely indifferent.

§30. Habit lays aside its indifference to an external action through reflection on the advantage or disadvantage of the same. . . . A habit which is advantageous for one man in one case may be disadvantageous for another man, or even for the same man, under different circumstances. Education must, therefore, accustom the youth to judge as to the expediency or inexpediency of any action in its relation to the essential vocation of his life, so that he shall avoid that which does not promote its success.

§31. But the *absolute* distinction of habit is the moral distinction between the good and the bad. . . .

§32. As relates to form, habit may be either passive or active. The passive is that which teaches us to bear the vicissitudes of nature as well as of history with such composure that we shall hold our ground against them, being always equal to ourselves, and that we shall not allow our power of acting to be paralyzed through any mutations of fortune. *Passive habit* is not to be confounded with obtuseness in receiving impressions, a blank abstraction from the affair in hand which at bottom is found to be nothing more than a selfishness which desires to be left undisturbed; it is simply composure of mind in view of changes over which we have no control. . . .

—Active habit [or behavior] is found realized in a wide range of activity which appears in manifold forms, such as skill, dexterity, readiness of information, &c. It is a steeling of the internal for action upon the external, as the Passive is a steeling of the internal against the influences of the external.

§33. Habit is the general form which instruction takes. For since it reduces a condition or an activity within ourselves to an instinctive use and wont, it is necessary for any thorough instruction. But as, according to its content, it may be either proper or improper, advantageous or disadvantageous, good or bad, and according to its form may be the assimilation of the external by the internal, or the impress of the internal upon the external, Education must procure for the pupil the power of being able to free himself from one habit and to adopt another. Through his freedom he must be able not only to renounce any habit formed, but to form a new one; and he must so govern his system of habits that it shall exhibit a constant progress of development into greater freedom. We must discipline ourselves, as a means toward the ever-changing realization of the Good in us, constantly to form and to break habits. . . .

§34. Education comprehends also the reciprocal action of the opposites, authority and obedience, rationality and individuality, work and play, habit and spontaneity. If we imagine that these can be reconciled by rules, it will be in vain that we try to restrain the youth in these relations. But a failure in education in this particular is very possible through the freedom of the pupil, through special circumstances, or through the errors of the educator himself. And for this very reason any theory of Education must take into account in the beginning this negative possibility. It must consider beforehand the dangers which threaten the pupil in all possible ways even before they surround him, and fortify him against them. Intentionally to expose him to temptation in order to prove his strength, is devilish; and, on the other hand, to guard him against the chance of dangerous temptation, to wrap him in cotton (as

the proverb says), is womanish, ridiculous, fruitless, and much more dangerous; for temptation comes not alone from without, but quite as often from
within, and secret inclination seeks and creates for itself the opportunity for
its gratification, often perhaps an unnatural one. The truly preventive activity
consists not in an abstract seclusion from the world, all of whose elements
are innate in each individual, but in the activity of knowledge and discipline,
modified according to age and culture. . . .

§35. If there should appear in the youth any decided moral deformity
which is opposed to the ideal of his education, the instructor must at once
make inquiry as to the history of its origin, because the negative and the
positive are very closely connected in his being, so that what appears to be
negligence, rudeness, immorality, foolishness, or oddity, may arise from
some real needs of the youth which in their development have only taken a
wrong direction.

§36. If it should appear on such examination that the negative action was
only a product of wilful ignorance, of caprice, or of arbitrariness on the part
of the youth, then this calls for a simple prohibition on the part of the educator, no reason being assigned. His authority must be sufficient to the pupil
without any reason. Only when this has happened more than once, and the
youth is old enough to understand, should the prohibition, together with the
reason therefor, be given. . . .

§38. Only when all other efforts have failed, is punishment, which is the
real negation of the error, the transgression, or the vice, justifiable. Punishment inflicts intentionally pain on the pupil, and its object is, by means of
this sensation, to bring him to reason, a result which neither our simple
prohibition, our explanation, nor our threat of punishment, has been able to
reach. But the punishment, as such, must not refer to the subjective totality
of the youth, or his disposition in general, but only to the act which, as result,
is a manifestation of the disposition. It acts mediately on the disposition, but
leaves the inner being untouched directly; and this is not only demanded by
justice, but on account of the sophistry that is inherent in human nature,
which desires to assign to a deed many motives, it is even necessary.

§39. Punishment as an educational means is nevertheless essentially corrective, since, by leading the youth to a proper estimation of his fault and a
positive change in his behavior, it seeks to improve him. At the same time
it stands as a sad indication of the insufficiency of the means previously
used. . . .

§40. Punishment as a negation of a negation, considered as an educational means, cannot be determined *a priori,* but must always be modified
by the peculiarities of the individual offender and by the peculiar circum-

stances. Its administration calls for the exercise of the ingenuity and tact of the educator. . . .

—There are two widely differing views with regard to the limits of Education. One lays great stress on the weakness of the pupil and the power of the teacher. According to this view, Education has for its province the entire formation of the youth. The despotism of this view often manifests itself where large numbers are to be educated together, and with very undesirable results, because it assumes that the individual pupil is only a specimen of the whole, as if the school were a great factory where each piece of goods is to be stamped exactly like all the rest. Individuality is reduced by the tyranny of such despotism to one uniform level till all originality is destroyed, as in cloisters, barracks, and orphan asylums, where only one individual seems to exist. There is a kind of Pedagogy also which fancies that one can thrust into or out of the individual pupil what one will. This may be called a superstitious belief in the power of Education.—The opposite extreme disbelieves this, and advances the policy which lets alone and does nothing, urging that individuality is unconquerable, and that often the most careful and far-sighted education fails of reaching its aim in so far as it is opposed to the nature of the youth, and that this individuality has made of no avail all efforts toward the obtaining of any end which was opposed to it. This representation of the fruitlessness of all pedagogical efforts engenders an indifference towards it which would leave, as a result, only a sort of vegetation of individuality growing at hap-hazard. . . .

§48. (2) *The Objective limit of Education* lies in the means which can be appropriated for it. That the talent for a certain culture shall be present is certainly the first thing; but the cultivation of this talent is the second, and no less necessary. But how much cultivation can be given to it extensively and intensively depends upon the means used, and these again are conditioned by the material resources of the family to which each one belongs. The greater and more valuable the means of culture which are found in a family are, the greater is the immediate advantage which the culture of each one has at the start. With regard to many of the arts and sciences this limit of education is of great significance. But the means alone are of no avail. The finest educational apparatus will produce no fruit where corresponding talent is wanting, while on the other hand talent often accomplishes incredible feats with very limited means, and, if the way is only once open, makes of itself a centre of attraction which draws to itself with magnetic power the necessary means. The moral culture of each one is however, fortunately from its very nature, out of the reach of such dependence.

SECOND PART: THE SPECIAL ELEMENTS OF EDUCATION

Second Division: Intellectual Education

Second Chapter: The Logical Presupposition or Method

... Pedagogics can be in nothing more specious than in its method, and it is here that charlatanism can most readily intrude itself. Every little change, every inadequate modification, is proclaimed aloud as a new or an improved method; and even the most foolish and superficial changes find at once their imitators, who themselves conceal their insolence behind some frivolous differences, and, with laughable conceit, hail themselves as inventors.—

Third Chapter: Instruction.

108. All instruction acts upon the supposition that there is an inequality between present knowledge and power and that knowledge and power which are not yet attained. To the pupil belong the first, to the teacher the second. Education is the act which gradually cancels the original inequality of teacher and pupil, in that it converts what was at first the property of the former into the property of the latter, and this by means of his own activity.

1. The Subjects of Instruction.

109. The pupil is the apprentice, the teacher the master, whether in the practice of any craft or art, or in the exposition of any systematic knowledge. The pupil passes from the state of the apprentice to that of the master through that of the journeyman. The apprentice has to appropriate to himself the elements; journeymanship begins as he, by means of their possession, becomes independent; the master combines with his technical skill the freedom of production. His authority over his pupil consists only in his knowledge and power. If he has not these, no external support, no trick of false appearances which he may put on, will serve to create it for him.

110. These stages—(1) apprenticeship, (2) journeymanship, (3) mastership—are fixed limitations in the didactic process; they are relative only in the concrete. The standard of special excellence varies with the different grades of culture, and must be varied that it may have any historical value. The master is complete only in relation to the journeyman and apprentice; to them he is superior. But on the other hand, in relation to the infinity of the problems of his art or science, he is by no means complete; to himself he must always appear as one who begins ever anew, one who is ever striving, one whom a new problem ever rises from every achieved result. He cannot discharge himself from work, he must never desire to rest on his laurels. He is the truest master whose finished performances only force him on to never-resting progress. ...

The Act of Learning.

115. In the process of education the interaction between pupil and teacher must be so managed that the exposition by the teacher shall excite in the pupil the impulse to reproduction. The teacher must not treat his exposition as if it were a work of art which is its own end and aim, but he must always bear in mind the need of the pupil. The artistic exposition, as such, will, by its completeness, produce admiration; but the didactic, on the contrary, will, through its perfect adaption, call out the imitative instinct, the power of new creation.

—From this consideration we may not justify the frequent statement that is made, that teachers who have really an elegant diction do not really accomplish so much as others who resemble in their statements not so much a canal flowing smoothly between straight banks, as a river which works its foaming way over rocks and between ever-winding banks. The pupil perceives that the first is considering himself when he speaks so finely, perhaps not without some self-appreciation; and that the second, in the repetitions and the sentences which are never finished, is concerning himself solely with *him.* The pupil feels that not want of facility or awkwardness, but the earnest eagerness of the *teacher,* is the principal thing, and that this latter uses rhetoric only as a means.—

From: William Bentley Fowle, *The Teacher's Institute; or, Familiar Hints to Young Teachers* (1873)

WILLIAM BENTLEY FOWLE (1795–1865) was born in Boston, Massachusetts. His father was a man of considerable literary attainment; his mother was the sister of William Bentley. William attended school at three, and became so adept at memorizing texts that at ten he was awarded the Franklin Medal for proficiency in grammar. At thirteen he discovered the shortcomings of memorization (he did not know what it meant to conjugate verbs) and began to hate grammar, whose method of teaching, as an adult, he decided to reform. In 1821 he was called upon to organize and teach a school of two hundred children. He employed the monitorial system, a system that, by using more advanced pupils to teach the more backward, was meant some-how to lessen the problem of a lack of adequately prepared teachers that so affected common schools. In 1823 he established the Female Monitorial School, equipped with scientific apparatus adequate to illustrate the subjects taught. He compiled and published more than fifty textbooks during his life. He edited and published the *Common School Journal* (1848–1852), taking it over from its founder, Horace Mann, and was one of Mann's most able assis-tants in the Teachers' Institute. He is remembered for his vehement denunci-ation of slavery.

BLACKBOARDS.

In this volume, no set lesson on the use of blackboards is given, because the whole volume, from beginning to end, is a practical lesson on the use of this indispensable part of school apparatus. . . .

PREFACE.

Since the revival of education in Massachusetts, and, I may justly say, in the United States, in consequence of the establishment of our Board of Education, several valuable treatises on the important subject of Public Instruction have been published, and each in its way has done good service to the great cause; but still, it seems to me, there is room for the little volume which, perhaps, with more zeal than discretion, I am about to "cast upon the waters."

When I was invited by the Secretary of the Board of Education to take part in the instruction to be given at the Teachers' Institutes, which he proposed to hold in different parts of the State, I was not aware that my notions of the matter and manner of teaching were so different from those which prevailed. When, however, at the Institutes, some of the lessons which I had given at least a quarter of a century ago were viewed as novelties, and listened to with attention as unexpected as it was gratifying, I readily yielded to the repeated suggestion that it might aid the cause of education to publish such of my hints as could be written out, however inferior they must necessarily be to the living lessons that I had given in person.

Those lessons were all given without any book, and usually without any notes; but this volume contains, I believe, a faithful sketch of them, with three of the many lectures that I delivered, and such additional remarks as occurred to me while the work was in progress. It makes no claim to be a complete treatise on education, for I had neither time nor inclination to attempt so high a task. It is no compilation, however, but a familiar record of my own experience, written in the midst of business, and with the printer at my heels,—two disadvantages which those only can fully appreciate who have been so incautious as to try a similar experiment.

Teachers' Institutes are assemblies of teachers, convened for the purpose of receiving and imparting instruction in regard to the art of teaching. They are, in fact, temporary Normal Schools, although, of course, conducted with less system and less preparation. The duty of calling them devolved upon the Secretary of the Board of Education, and he was present several days at each of the ten that were held in the autumns of 1845 and 1846, of which duty an interesting report is given in his Ninth Annual Report to the Board. The exercises consisted mainly of lessons given by some experienced teacher; of mutual instruction by the members of the Institute; of free discussions, in which the citizens, especially school-committeemen, often took part; and of lectures by gentlemen who had paid attention to the progress of public education in the State. Of course, as far as possible, teachers and lecturers on all systems, and on all educational subjects, were invited to teach and lecture, that the young teachers might see and hear all that was abroad, and be able to carry home many inventions that they would never, perhaps, have wrought out in their almost isolated districts. I spent a longer time than any other teacher at these Institutes, and probably said and did more than any other. I must, of course, have said many things about which there is a difference of opinion in this community, for I am accustomed to speak what I think, without asking whether the thought is popular or not. It is my duty, therefore, to declare, that neither the Board of Education, who honored me by the invitation, nor their Secretary, is accountable for any sentiments I uttered at the Institutes, and much less for any thing I have written in this volume. The truth of the matter is, that, until it was published, neither the Board nor its Secretary had any knowledge of the contents of this book, nor even of my intention to publish it.

After the child is acquainted with the alphabet and the elementary sounds, the question arises, "How must he be taught to read?" This is a question of some moment, and one, at first sight, might be excused for thinking it a difficult matter to answer it. I am inclined, however, to think that, with proper management, it is a very easy matter to make children read well. I should lay it down, however, as a prerequisite, essential to success, that *the teacher of reading should be a good reader himself.*

It has often been objected to this position, that children have been taught to read well by instructors who were very indifferent readers. That children have learned to read under such teachers I am willing to admit, because the fact is evident; but that they have been taught by their masters, I do not admit, for *I consider it impossible for any person to teach well what he does not understand.* If a child has sometimes learned to read or write, or cipher or sing, under an incompetent instructor, it has been, not *because* of the teacher, but *in spite* of him, and the question is, not how much has he learned, but how much more would he have learned had the instructor been fully prepared to teach him.

Before the child reads, some attention should be paid to his position. For a general rule, he should rest on the left foot, which should be a little turned out, and the right heel should be about opposite the middle of the left foot, and two or three inches from it; a position not unlike that which the dancing-masters call their second position. The book, unless very heavy, should be held in the left hand, opposite the chest, and never so high as to conceal the chin of the reader.

The reader should also be placed at a good distance from the teacher, for it is desirable that he should read so as to be heard across a common school-room, and few children will do this, if placed near the teacher, for they naturally calculate to make those whom they address hear them, and few children read aloud, if reading in a low voice is sufficient to make the teacher hear. If possible, the class should always stand while reading, and so stand that the teacher can see the entire person of every one, that he may watch their positions. At one of the Teacher's Institutes, I required every teacher to stand on a platform in full view of the others. It evidently cost many of them a great effort, and more than half of them had never been so exposed before. One young female, who had taught several summers, faltered at the first word she uttered, then trembled, dropped her book to her side, and burst into tears. She then made for her seat, but I stopped her, and encouraged her not to yield, but to do as she would advise a pupil to do in similar circumstances. She rallied, resolved, and in a minute or two read without further trouble. When called on in turn again, she came forward, and read with a sort of satisfaction at the victory she had obtained over herself. But, some children have weak voices, and cannot read so loud as their fellows. The teacher must, therefore, be careful to favor such voices, and, while he endeavors gradually to strengthen them, he must not rudely break or injure them by requiring too great an effort at first.

I am persuaded that nothing but the incompetency of teachers has led to the preparation of various series of reading books, intended, as far as possible, to help the pupil to learn independently of the master. Perhaps these books are doing a good work by calling the attention of the teacher to what he would otherwise neglect, but my experience satisfies me that, if the teacher knows how to read, those aids in which many school books abound, are worse than useless, because positively injurious.

The competent teacher needs but two rules by which to be guided in teaching his pupils to read. He must make them understand what is to be read, and then require them to read naturally. To expect a child to read what he does not understand is unreasonable, and yet nothing is more common. Until very lately, teachers were generally accustomed to pay no attention to the explanation of such pieces as are found in School Readers, and turned their attention almost entirely to the pauses and the pronunciation; important points, to be sure, but by no means the life-giving elements of good reading. . . .

The teacher should consult all the practical works on the art of reading, but, as far as my observation goes, it is idle to put marks and rules and directions, whether by words or characters, into books intended to be read by children, for plain reason that they seldom or never use them. The chief reading-book, when I was at school, was Scott's Lessons, and this was furnished with from fifty to a hundred pages of what were called Lessons in Elocution; but I never was required to read a word of them, and they were never explained to me, yet they cumbered the book, and increased its price one quarter at least. I am told by teachers that the same is the case with more modern books. . . .

Much has been said of the matter contained in school reading books, and a great mistake, I think, prevails on this subject. The imperfect way in which reading has been taught, in so far as little or no attempt has been made to explain the text, has led many teachers and school committees to suppose that the selections were above the comprehension of children; but I have never seen such a selection, and do not believe that any such exists.

Another mistake is made by those who suppose that a book is unfit for use because it has been in use so long. This objection, in my opinion, will lie only against such books as are brought down to the capacity of children, so that they need no study, no explanation. It seems to me that books which are to be read more than once should be so constructed that at every successive reading the master may have something new to explain, and the pupil something new to learn; and, as the old book is new to new classes, and can be more effectually taught the better it can be read and explained by the teacher, the older the book the better, if it was a good one at first. It is a favorite notion of some excellent friends of education that the reading lessons in our common schools should be mainly selected with a view to the imparting of useful knowledge, and the inculcation of virtuous sentiments. To a certain degree this plan may be adopted, but in every case in which it has been fully carried out, it has failed. We have had Peace Readers, Temperance Readers, Agricultural Readers, Scientific Readers, Religious Readers, &c., &c., and these one-idea books have contained much that is valuable; but they have always failed to make *good* readers, in the highest sense of the term *good.* Reading is an *art,* a glorious art, which can no more be learned or taught from humdrum books of science or from moral essays, than English composition can be learned by the perusal of Murray's Grammar.

In Massachusetts and New York, the legislature has provided a large supply of useful reading in the school libraries, which have been established in the districts. The books thus provided are no doubt intended to furnish the knowledge which no school Reader, made or to be made, can supply to any considerable degree, while they enable the class books to be more fully adapted to teach something more of reading than the mere pronunciation of words, and the dull monotony, which are about all that the reading of a scientific tract requires. Books of useful knowledge should be read, but not at school. The few minutes devoted each day to reading, if spent only upon the most suitable books, will hardly suffice to make good readers; and it is with reading, as with spelling, if the necessary knowledge and practice are not obtained at school, there is but little chance of their ever being obtained afterward. I think I have never known a good reader who was contented to teach from such books; and if good readers with poor tools can effect but little, what can be expected when both the teacher and the tools are bad? . . .

ENGLISH GRAMMAR.

If any one branch taught in our common schools is very badly taught, that branch is English grammar. Whatever may be the textbook used, the object undoubtedly ought to be, to teach the child to speak and write correctly and with ease; and, if the teacher is competent, this object may be attained with any of the popular textbooks, or even without any of them.

Unfortunately, however, the number of district school teachers who are skilful in the use of language is very small, although many are acquainted with the technics of grammar, and can analyze sentences made by others with tolerable facility. To such, and to all teachers, let me say, that their time will be better spent if they begin earlier to teach the *use* of language, leaving the grammar to come in, as it originally came, after the language has been formed.

To enable the teacher to do this, he must begin early with the child, and make every exercise bear upon this. In my remarks on reading and orthography, I have shown how a beginning may be made, and I shall endeavor not to repeat what I have said.

I should begin to teach English grammar, then, when I begin to teach the English language; that is, when I begin to teach reading, spelling and talking. The mischief has been, that children have been allowed to read without intelligence, to spell without any application of the words, and to talk without care, although they talk before they read, or spell, or write; and being allowed to talk badly, the chief object of teaching technical grammar afterwards is, to undo what has been previously done, but what should have been avoided. If parents only felt the importance of speaking correctly, and even elegantly, in the presence of their children; if they paid a hundredth part as much attention to language as they do to dress and external appearance, we should hear little of grammar, except as it affords directions for foreigners who wish to learn our idioms, and have not time to do so by practice in writing and speaking it. . . .

But the most popular grammars used in the United States abound in difficulties, and, by perplexing the teachers and disgusting the pupils, they fail to aid either in the great work of using their mother tongue with facility and effect. Something is fundamentally wrong. All teachers and all pupils feel this, and yet no reform that has been proposed reaches the difficulty, or, in any considerable degree, obviates it. Will the reader bear with me while, at some length, I point out what I consider to be the evil, and endeavor to propose an adequate remedy for it.

The first school that I undertook to teach was to be conducted on the monitorial plan, and the monitors, as usual, formed the highest class, and were under my special instruction. The first time that I endeavored to give them a lesson in English grammar, I found that they all applied to the dictionary to ascertain to what part of speech a word belonged. As the same word, in different circumstances, might belong to different classes of words, and the pupils seemed never to have exercised their ingenuity in attempting to class words by the use that was made of them in the sentence, I directed all dictionaries to be banished, and the definitions of the various parts of speech to be thoroughly learned before the next lesson. When the time arrived, I selected a sentence from the reading book, and I shall never forget it. It was, "David smote Goliah." "Well," said I to the first pupil, "what part of speech is David?" "A noun, sir." "What is a noun?" "A substantive or noun is the name of any thing that exists, or of which we have any notion." "Is David, in this sentence, the name of any thing that exists?" "No, sir; David died long ago." "Is it the name of any thing of which you have any notion?" "Yes, sir; I have some notion of him as a very small man, and a king." As the object was only to ascertain the part of speech, I asked the next pupil what part of speech *smote* was. "A preposition, sir." "A preposition!" said I, with astonishment, "pray what is a preposition?" "Prepositions serve to connect words with one another and to show the relation between them." "Very well," said I, with all the importance of a teacher who felt it his duty to expose the ignorance of his pupil, "what words does *smote* connect?" "David and Goliah, sir, for there is nothing else to connect them." "Yes," said I, somewhat flurried, "but what relation does it show between them?" "Not a very friendly one, I should think, sir," said the pupil. I was struck with the truth of the answers, and had the honesty to say, "You are right, miss, or the definition in your book is wrong."

This incident shook my faith in the perfection of Murray's Grammar; and the long course of study which followed, resulted in the settled conviction that *Murray's* Grammar is far from being synonymous with *English* grammar, and that any time spent in teaching it is worse than thrown away.

From: *The Philosophy of Education,* by Karl Rosenkranz (1886);
William Torrey Harris, editor, Anna C. Brackett, translator

WILLIAM TORREY HARRIS (1835–1909) was born in North Killingly, Connecticut. He received his education in Providence, Rhode Island, and at various academies, including Phillips Academy in Andover, Massachusetts. He attended Yale College for two and a half years but did not complete his studies there. He taught in the St. Louis public schools, and from 1867 to 1880 was superintendent of them. He was particularly interested in the German philosopher Georg W. F. Hegel, about whom he wrote several books. In 1889 he was appointed U.S. commissioner of education, exerting a strong influence as he served in that position until 1906. He edited Appleton's International Education Series, was assistant editor of *Johnson's Cyclopaedia,* founded and edited the *Journal of Speculative Philosophy* (1867–1893), and was editor in chief of *Webster's International Dictionary* (1900). He was the founder of the Philosophical Society of St. Louis, and member of the National Education Association (life director and president, 1875), the National Association of School Superintendents (president, 1873), and the American Social Science Association, and he represented the Bureau of Education at the International Congress of Education in Belgium (1880) and Italy (1889).

EDITOR'S PREFACE.

This work was translated originally for *The Journal of Speculative Philosophy,* appearing in volumes vi, vii, and viii of that periodical (1872–'73–'74). It was intended for the use of philosophical students—who, in general, admire precise technical terms—and the terse German of the original was rendered by equally terse English. An edition of two thousand copies was reprinted in a separate volume. Demands for the work continuing after the first edition was exhausted, it was determined to publish a new one. For this purpose a revision has been made of the translation with a view to better adapt it to the needs of readers not skilled in philosophy. Where it has been thought necessary, phrases, or even entire sentences, have been used to convey the sense of a single word of the original. Typographical errors that had crept into the first edition, through careless proof-reading, have been carefully corrected. It may be safely claimed that no obscurity remains except such as is due to the philosophic depth and generality of the treatment. In

162

this respect the translation is now more intelligible than the original. In addition to these helps, a somewhat elaborate commentary on the whole work has been undertaken by the editor, who has also prefixed to it a full analysis of the text and commentary.

It is believed that the book as it now appears will meet a want that is widely felt for a thorough-going Philosophy of Education. There are many useful and valuable works on ''The Theory and Practice of Teaching,'' but no work that entirely satisfies the description of a genuine Philosophy of Education. To earn this title, such a work must not only be systematic, but it must bring all its details to the test of the highest principle of philosophy. This principle is the acknowledged principle of Christian civilization, and, as such, Rosenkranz makes it the foundation of his theory of education, and demonstrates its validity by an appeal to psychology on the one hand and to the history of civilization on the other.

This work, on its appearance, made an epoch in the treatment of educational theory in Germany. It brought to bear on this subject the broadest philosophy of modern times, and furnished a standard by which the value of the ideas severally discussed by radicals and conservatives could be ascertained. It found the truth lying partly on the territory of the established order and partly on the territory of the reformers—Ratich, Comenius, Rousseau, Pestalozzi, and their followers. It showed what was valid in the idea that had come to be established in the current system of education, and also exposed the weakness that had drawn the attack of the reformers.

Its Author.—Johann Karl Friedrich Rosenkranz was born at Magdeburg, April 23, 1805. He took up his residence in Berlin in 1824, distinguishing himself as a disciple, first of Schleiermacher, and afterward of Hegel. In 1833 he became Professor of Philosophy at Königsberg, and occupied for forty-six years, until his death in 1879, the chair held for twenty-four years by the celebrated Herbart, and for thirty-four years by the still more celebrated Kant. He wrote extensive works on philosophy and literature, and published the present work in 1848 under the title of *Paedagogik als System.*

Points of Great Value.—Special attention is called to the deep significance of the principle of self-estrangement *(Selbst-Entfremdung)* as lying at the foundation of the Philosophy of Education (p. 27). It furnishes a key to many problems discussed by the educational reformers from Comenius to Herbert Spencer. Since man's true nature is not found in him already realized at birth, but has to be developed by his activity, his true nature is his ideal, which he may actualize by education. Hence the deep significance of this process. Man must estrange himself from his first or animal nature, and assimilate himself to his second or ideal nature, by habit. At first all things that belong to culture are strange and foreign to his ways of living and think-ing. Education begins when he puts aside what is familiar and customary with him, and puts on the new and strange—that is to say, begins his "self-estrangement." The nature of such important matters as work and play (p. 28) and habit (§§ 29–34) becomes evident from this insight.

The distinction of corrective and retributive punishment (§§ 38–45) is of great value practically in deciding upon the kind of punishment to use in an American school where pupils have a precocious sense of honor.

The part of this work devoted to educational psychology (§§ 82–102) is believed to possess great interest for the thoughtful teacher, as tracing the outlines of the only true science of the mind. The phases most worthy of the educator's attention are certainly those that relate to the development of the intellectual and moral powers; it is their *development* rather than their mere *existence* that the practical teacher wishes to know about. This treatise is commended to the notice of those who have hitherto been unable to find a satisfactory psychological basis for their educational theories. They are invited to ponder what is said about attention (p. 73); how the lower faculties grow into higher faculties, and how the higher faculties re-enforce the lower (pp. 75, 76); the function of the imagination in forming general types and in leading to abstract ideas (pp. 84–87).

The methods of treating the three grades of capacity—the blockhead, the mediocre talent, and the genius—are especially suggestive to the teacher (p. 109).

The subject of morality is treated with great care, and all will admire what is said on the inadmissibility of vacations in moral obedience (p. 153), as well as what is said (p. 147) on the subject of urbanity (politeness with a dash of irony), as the flower of social culture.

Rosenkranz very properly makes religious education the last and highest form of the particular elements of education. In no place may one find deeper insights in regard to the proper culture in religion in an age abound-ing in unbelief and skeptical influences. His distinction of three stages of theoretical culture in religion—(a) pious feeling, (b) enjoyment of religious symbols, (c) interest in the dogmas as such—to which he adds the three practical stages of (a) self-consecration, (b) performance of church ceremon-ies, (c) the attainment of a pious trust in the divine government of the world—these distinctions are thorough-going. What he says (p. 167) on the dangers of unduly hastening the child from the stages of religious feeling to religious thought and reflection, or, on the other hand, of unduly repressing religious reflection in those who have begun to ask questions and suggest doubts, is very instructive to religious teachers, whether in the Sabbath-school or in the family. So, too, is the distinction (p. 170) drawn between the provinces of morality and religion.

The entire third part of the work is taken up with a history of education, based on the philosophy of history. It is rather an outline of the history of human culture than a special history of schools or of pedagogics. As such, it is highly valuable, not only for the teacher or parent, but also for all who desire to see in a condensed form the essential outcome of human history. . . .

CHAPTER 8. INTELLECTUAL EDUCATION *(continued).*

(B.) THE LOGICAL PRESUPPOSITION, OR THE METHOD.

§103. The logical presupposition of instruction is the order in which the subject-matter develops for the consciousness. The subject, the consciousness of the pupil, and the activity of the instructor, interpenetrate each other in instruction, and constitute in actuality one whole.

[Instruction presupposes a certain logical order of development in its theme. In arithmetic, for example, fractions must not be studied before simple addition. Political geography should be studied after mathematical and physical geography; grammar, after reading and writing; general history after the history of one's own country.

The three elements which instruction combines are: (1) the subject to be taught; (2) the consciousness of the pupil; (3) the insight and labor of the teacher.]

§104. (1) First of all, the subject which is to be learned has a specific determinateness which demands in its exposition a certain fixed order of sequence. However arbitrary we may be, the subject has a certain determination of its own which no mistreatment can wholly crush out, and this inherent immortal rationality is the general foundation of instruction.

To illustrate: however one may handle a language in teaching it, he can not change the words in it, or the inflections of the declensions and conjugations. And the same restriction is laid upon our inclinations in the different divisions of natural history in the theorems of arithmetic, geometry, etc. The theorem of Pascal remains still the same theorem wherever it is set forth.

[The subject has a nature of its own which requires it to be studied in a certain definite order. Whatever modifications are made in the subject to adapt it to the immature mind of the pupil, this essential nature of the subject must not be changed.

As regards the "logical presupposition" above spoken of, it is clear enough that all subjects to be taught possess logical relations of dependence of one part on another and of the parts on the whole. There must be therefore a certain order of exposition of the subject: the dependent parts must be shown in their dependence, otherwise the subject will not be taught properly. We can not teach the zones or parallels and meridians unless we have previously taught the spherical form of the earth.]

Intermezzo

Intermezzo: Serie di componimenti [poetici] che segna il passaggio tra
esperienze di ispirazione diversa. [Series of (poetic) compositions marking
the movement between experiences of different inspirations.]
—DeVoto e Oli, *Dizionario della Lingua Italiana*

B efore considering how pedagogy gained entrance into the Academy, it might be useful to pause and take a look at some of the issues that normal school professors of pedagogy were discussing in the last two decades of the nineteenth century—a time when their institutions were facing extremely complex theoretical, practical, economic, and political problems connected with their expansion and diversification and the post–Civil War educational needs they were called upon to meet.

In this period, normal school circles were not the only contexts within which pedagogy was being discussed. By then, a few U.S. universities (see part three), following the example of other nations (see, for instance, Compayré's entry on *pedagogy* in *La Grande Encyclopédie,* excerpted in part one; see also *Education Report, 1888–1889,* 275–78, 283, 295–99, 306, not in this volume), had acknowledged pedagogy as a field of study and a discipline worthy of university status. Such an acknowledgment was by no means widespread or uncontested. Most university professors were openly critical of pedagogy, which they identified with the teaching of teaching as practiced within normal schools. In some institutions, that criticism became a justification for establishing university chairs and departments of pedagogy so as to give pedagogy, it was argued, the intellectual booster normal schools could not provide for it. In other institutions, that criticism was instead deployed to oppose granting pedagogy university status.

The excerpts in this section mark and call attention to "the movement between experiences (of pedagogy) of different inspirations" (DeVoto e Oli 1971). It is important to consider what happened to pedagogy—how did it arrive? and how did it have to be constructed?—when it migrated from the normal schools (part two) to the university milieu (part three). Because these and other related questions are often (conveniently) ignored, they forestall much needed radical interrogations of facile dismissals of pedagogy.

167

George Gary Bush's "The Education of the Freedmen" (from *History of Education in Florida*, 1889, in this collection), provides useful information about the education of the freedmen in Florida. Bush tells how "colored people [from] the Northern States" became involved in the education of former slaves by means of such agencies as the African Civilization Society and the Home Missionary Society of the African Methodist Episcopal Church, and the work of other northern societies, foremost among which was the New York branch of the American Freedmen's Union Commission. By the close of 1865, Bush points out, African-American slaves "who had acquired a little learning in their bondage, and were anxious to elevate the condition of their race" (24), taught in about half of the colored schools. Between 1866 and 1867, because of an act of the legislature that apparently put Florida ahead of all other southern states in the education of the freedmen (see excerpt), "the number of colored schools rapidly increased. The freedmen, in many instances, erected school-houses at their own expense, and heartily seconded the action of the Legislature" (24). Enthusiasm for teaching and goodwill, however, were not sufficient to provide adequate instruction. It was not until 1878 that, after many slow improvements, "the colored people expressed themselves satisfied that justice had been done them" (25). According to Bush, those improvements were to be attributed to the provision of teachers' institutes and normal schools. (This document also provides important information on school statistics from 1840 to the 1880s, and on the differences among various centers for the preparation of teachers.)

Eliphalet Oram Lyte's essay on the state normal schools of the United States, which he wrote at the request of the commissioner of education, focuses on the difference between academies, colleges, and normal schools. Contrary to those who considered elementary education easy and unimportant, Lyte identifies the issue of elementary education as "one of the most important problems with which a free people must deal." To prepare teachers for that task, he argues, is a question "that should be of vital importance to all thoughtful citizens" (1904, 1104), and a responsibility that normal schools, because of their "peculiar" function, are eminently fit to fulfill.

> The academy and the college aim to teach their students the various branches of knowledge, the normal school aims to teach its students *not only* the branches of knowledge, but also the processes by which the learning mind acquires knowledge and the resultant of these processes. These objects and aims distinguish normal schools from other institutions of learning and determine the courses of study in them and the methods by which the studies must be taught. . . . the

function of normal schools is peculiar, and . . . its responsibilities are greater than those of other educational institutions. (1104, emphasis added)

In terms strongly reminiscent of Calvin Stowe's (see part two), Lyte's construction of pedagogy demands that teachers not only know how to teach the various branches of knowledge, but also how the learning mind acquires that knowledge. The intellectual preparation normal school teachers need to meet their responsibilities, in his view, is not more limited but more complex than the intellectual preparation of academy and college teachers.

Like the two reports above, for which it was a source, J. P. Gordy's *Rise and Growth of the Normal-School Idea in the United States* (1891) is attentive to the differences between the nature and the function of normal schools and their theories of pedagogy, and those of other institutions of higher learning. More than those reports, however, Gordy's *Rise and Growth* provides valuable insights into the theoretical rationales and the institutional maneuvers that led to the establishment of university chairs and departments of pedagogy.

The excerpts from the 1888 and 1889 *NEA Proceedings* suggest the kind of professional issues most likely to be discussed at the time by normal school professors, principals, and superintendents. Some of the questions most persistently posed at these professional meetings were: Should normal schools emulate the work of other institutions of higher learning or should they focus on the professional preparation of teachers? Do (and should) urban normal schools differ from rural ones; those in the north from those in the south; those in the east from those in the west; normal schools for white students from normal schools for "colored" students? What constitutes "academic professional" preparation; how does it differ from "scholarly professional" preparation? What constitutes a normal school curriculum? Which "science" ought pedagogy to rely on? Ought pedagogy to be eminently theoretical or practical?

These questions suggest the gamut of issues that normal schools had to confront when they came to be defined as either professional, industrial, vocational, or liberal. Considering the *NEA Proceedings'* questions in light of the reports I have cited, one might conclude that forty years after their inception it was not yet clear what normal schools were about and in which direction they were going. But although, undoubtedly, it is possible to suggest that these questions signal NEA participants' anxiety and confusion about the mission of normal schools, it is also possible to suggest that they demonstrate their commitment to assess the consequences of normal schools' increasing differentiation of purpose.

Most striking, among these excerpts, are those that give a sense of how the role and responsibility of normal schools in the education of African American teachers and students were being framed and discussed. In terms of the need for and the difficulty of promptly providing adequately prepared teachers to fulfill the educational demands of the African American population, educators involved in establishing and theorizing the structure of normal schools for African American citizens in the late 1880s and the 1890s were confronted with issues and difficulties very similar to those that had confronted the founders of early normal schools. I do not mean, by this comparison, to minimize or to gloss over the specific and particular circumstances of this phase of African American education. I want to point out instead what most of these discussions return to, over and over again: the *problems* and the *promises* of teacher preparation; the tremendous demands that are placed upon teachers in moments of need; the need, the temptation, and the tendency to simplify pedagogy by reducing it to either theory or practice; the tendency to disregard past experiences; the reasons and prejudices inflecting various positions (consider, for example, how J. S. Steele's perspective on African Americans' intelligence might have influenced his position on what the work of normal schools should have been). The return to these issues, I suggest, could most profitably function as a way of understanding, though not of condoning, past simplifications of educational practices, and could stimulate commentaries on the difficulty, yet the necessity, of nurturing rather than weakening the *nexus* between theory and practice so as to prevent pedagogy from becoming either essentially theoretical or essentially practical.

An imposing figure emerges, although *in absentia* (in the excerpts I provide he is referred to by two of the speakers), from one of these documents: Booker T. Washington, principal of the Tuskegee (technical) Normal School, Alabama (see Steele 1889). Washington's support of the professional ideal and W. E. B. Du Bois's well-known opposition to it in the name of an academic scholarly ideal could provide an important lens through which to reexamine which conditions seem to call for and to justify that opposition. (How does Steele's support of the professional ideal stand in comparison with Booker T. Washington's?)

Current pressures on our profession are daunting; but so were those confronting nineteenth-century theorists of pedagogy. It is my hope, and belief, that making their texts more immediately available might help current proponents of pedagogy in composition programs, in departments of English, as well as in schools of education and in other disciplines to understand and to guard against the kinds of theoretical simplifications, unreasonable expec-

tations, misplaced trust, and institutional and political uncritical and unreflex-
ive decisions that in the past led to pedagogy's etiolation.

To ignore that outcome, or to begin anew as if pedagogy had no history
we can read and learn from, be it even in negative terms, sets up an unpro-
ductive pattern of unnecessary and perhaps damaging repetitions.

As we listen, in the next section, to the stories of pedagogy told by and
circulated among its university proponents and critics, it might be worth rec-
ollecting the stories of pedagogy that the excerpts in this Intermezzo suggest.

Documents

In *The Cheese and the Worms: The Cosmos of a Sixteenth-Century Miller,* Carlo Ginzburg writes:

> In the past historians could be accused of wanting to know only about "the great deeds of kings," but today this is certainly no longer true. More and more they are turning toward what their predecessors passed over in silence, discarded, or simply ignored. "Who built Thebes of the seven gates?" Bertolt Brecht's "literate worker" was already asking. The sources tell us nothing about the anonymous masons, but the question retains all its significance. (Ginzburg, "Preface to the Italian edition," xiii)

The authors of the documents I collect in this section are not anonymous, at least not in the way Ginzburg's miller is. Yet their texts call attention to significant silences. In most cases, these authors' deeds have not been recorded for posterity within the pages of major biographical encyclopedias, possibly because their deeds were limited to papers delivered at professional gatherings (the NEA, in this case). (Notice, however, how even these documents reveal significant omissions: who is the black man placed at the head of the "Florida Normal and Industrial College" in 1886? See Bush, "The Education of the Freedmen.")

Not to underline differences in status, I decided not to provide biographical information for any of them. My corrective gesture, of course, can be seen not only as reinscribing prior silences, but also making "anonymous" figures that were not. On the other hand, it might call attention, as it is intended, to the various ways—fortuitous, deliberate, innocent, overdetermined, condescending, or well-intentioned—by which, in our scholarship, we grant agency to, or take it away from, protagonists of history.

The documents come mainly from two sources: government reports on normal schools, the *NEA Proceedings* on topics specifically connected with normal schools. Their authors provide engrossing narratives of the rise and growth of these institutions, as well as dramatic records of the problems resulting from normal schools' increasing differentiation into professional, industrial, vocational, and liberal educational sites. These "anonymous" voices offer valuable opportunities to call into question the reasons for, and to resist, the easy dismissal of normal school professors of pedagogy, and of their work, that some of the texts in part three starkly document.

172

From: George Gary Bush, "The Education of the Freedmen,"
History of Education in Florida (1889)

A mong the first agencies employed in the effort to educate the freedmen
were two which were under the control of colored people in the Northern States, and were known as the African Civilization Society, and the
Home Missionary Society of the African M. E. Church. These societies established schools at different points in the Southern States, a few of which
were opened in Florida, and were of much value in laying the foundation for
the education of the colored race. Other northern societies had their representatives here, the New York branch of the American Freedmen's Union
Commission being foremost. Through these different agencies about half of
the colored schools of this period were sustained. Nearly as many more were
taught by freed persons who had acquired a little learning in their bondage,
and were anxious to elevate the condition of their race. In all, some thirty
colored schools were in successful operation at the close of 1865. In January,
1866, a bill was introduced into the Legislature providing for the education
of the children of the freedmen, and levying a tax of one dollar each upon
"all male persons of color between the ages of 21 and 45" years, and a
tuition fee of fifty cents a month to be collected from each pupil. As soon as
this became a law, a commissioner was appointed by the Governor with
authority to organize colored schools, and enlist in his work the cooperation
of all good citizens. This officer was everywhere welcomed and aided by the
planters of the State; and during the first year he organized twenty day
schools and thirty night schools. The latter were intended specially for
adults, who often formed weird groups as they studied their books around
the changing and uncertain light of the pine fire. There were enrolled in
these schools 2,726 pupils, and, in addition, as many as 2,000 were thought
to be receiving private instruction. In this movement for the education of the
freedmen Florida is believed to have taken precedence of all the other Southern States.

During 1866 and 1867 the number of colored schools rapidly increased.
The freedmen, in many instances, erected school-houses at their own expense, and heartily seconded the action of the Legislature. And just at this
point the Freedmen's Bureau proved itself the efficient friend and ally of the
colored people. This it did, principally, by aiding in the promotion of

"school societies," whose object was to acquire by gift or purchase the perfect title to eligible lots of ground for school purposes. Each of these lots, not less than an acre in extent, was to be vested in a board of trustees. The Bureau also supplied lumber and other materials necessary to the construction of school buildings. This work was ably seconded by many landed proprietors, who furnished school lots and otherwise rendered moral and material support. But this prosperity was soon checked by reason of the "hard times," and the unsettled political condition of the State which followed after the War. For the four years from 1865 to 1869 the largest number of schools was seventy-one and the largest number of teachers was sixty-four. Of the teachers one-half were white. The average number of pupils in attendance was thought to be about 2,000. The studies were "the alphabet, easy reading, advanced reading, writing, geography, arithmetic, and higher branches." The cost of these schools was reported to be, for 1867, $21,000, and for 1868, $19,200, of which amounts $600 were contributed each year by the freedmen. At a later period we find the Freedmen's Bureau rendering aid by paying a rental of ten dollars each on seventy-five school-houses, which were scattered through nine counties. In reality this money was devoted to the payment of teachers' salaries.

In the common school law of 1869 no reference is made to the complexion of the children for whom it was framed, and henceforth it became the business of the State to see that equal school privileges were accorded to the two races. That progress among the colored people was for many years slow is evident from the annual school reports. The teachers employed were largely men and women of their own race, who, having had very inadequate opportunities for education, often brought the schools into disrepute. But, as the years passed, one improvement followed another, until, as early as 1878, the Superintendent reports that the colored people expressed themselves satisfied that justice had been done them. Today their children are taught in separate schools, but they have the same help from the school funds, the same supervision, and are subject to the same regulations as those of the white race. Teachers' institutes and normal schools have been provided for both, but it is yet too soon to expect that in general the qualifications of the colored man will compare favorably with those of the white man. As the former is still the teacher of the colored children, these must to a certain extent suffer loss. It is to be hoped, however, and from the superior advantages now offered to colored teachers it is fair to conjecture, that this inequality will ere long be remedied.

Secondary Colored Schools—Lincoln Academy at Tallahassee and Union Academy at Gainesville were the first schools established with the view of furnishing instruction to colored youth in advanced studies. Some time after their organization an appeal was made to the agent of the Peabody Fund to contribute to their support. This was granted, and at first $300 was given annually to each academy, but on the condition that it should be used principally for the training of teachers. After 1879 the amount was increased to $400, and this, or the former sum, continued to be donated for many years. In 1881 Lincoln Academy had an efficient corps of teachers, consisting of a principal and four assistants, with two hundred and fifty pupils, and the school year extended through nine months.

The Legislature of 1886 ordered the establishment of a normal college for colored youth. This was opened in Tallahassee in 1887. Its history will be given in connection with the normal college for whites. Probably the best equipped colored school in Florida is the public school in Jacksonville. In addition to its regular work an industrial department has been recently added. This was brought about as follows: During 1887, through the earnest efforts of the State Superintendent, seconded by the county board of Duval County and the colored people of the City of Jacksonville, the necessary steps were taken to secure from the agent of the Slater Fund an annual appropriation of $1,000 to be used for the teaching of the industrial arts. Through the commendable enterprise of the colored people a suitable building was speedily erected on the grounds of the graded school above referred to, and this was opened for instruction in October a year ago. "Eight sets of woodworking tools were procured, work benches built, and everything in readiness. A teacher was employed, a white man, a practical architect and draughtsman, and mechanic and builder, and of excellent character and qualification. Instruction in the nature and use of the various tools, and in the working of wood was commenced for the boys on the first floor; and the girls were taken to the second floor, where needle-work, cutting, darning, and other needful work of the kind are taught, and where it is designed that cooking, laundry work, and other things qualifying the good housewife shall be taught." Two hours each day, so appointed as not to interfere with his studies in the school, are spent in this way by each pupil, and the results have already been most satisfactory. This, it is hoped, will be but the beginning of the adoption of industrial training in the schools of the State.

*Cookman Institute—A normal and biblical school for colored students.—*This Institute was founded and is sustained by the Freedmen's Aid Society of the Methodist Episcopal Church. Its mission is set forth in the following language: "The public schools need a better class of teachers, and the pulpits a more intelligent ministry. . . . Cookman Institute supplies a great want of many of the colored people whose future largely depends upon our efforts. We have enlarged our plans to meet the demand and hope to fill each teachers' positions and pulpits with more efficient workmen.'' The president of the school says: "Our graduates honor themselves in their success in life, and show what education will do for the people when extended courses of study are pursued. The lawyer, the doctor, the minister, comes to be a man of power when he avails himself of such facilities for study."

The school, which is open to both sexes, was founded in 1872, in Jacksonville, and had as its object the education and elevation of the needy and neglected masses among the freed people. Since its founding it has made a great advance in the quality of the instruction given and in its courses of study. The growth of its material interests has been no less pleasing. Beginning in a "little old church," it finds itself today in a commodious brick building, free of debt, which is capable of accommodating 50 boarders and 150 day pupils. The school year continues through nearly seven months, viz, from the second week in October to the close of April. The number of pupils in attendance during the year 1886–87 in the academic and normal departments was 167. The courses of study seem well adapted to the needs of the pupils. There is a thorough course in English, a course in history, and a four years' course in the following branches: in mathematics, ending with the sixth book in geometry; in Latin, in which the most advanced authors read are Cicero and Virgil; and in descriptive and physical geography, to which later are to be added the primary principles of botany, geology, mineralogy, and natural history. Besides these studies there are in the curriculum political economy, pedagogy, mental science, philosophy, and rhetoric. The necessary expenses for tuition and board are very small, and none who have an ambition to obtain an education ought to feel debarred on this account. The president, Rev. S. B. Darnell, has been at the head of the Institute during the whole of its history, and deserves much credit for his wise management of its affairs. There are seven others associated with him in the board on instruction.

A college for colored youth has also been established, by the Baptist Missionary Society of the North, at Live Oak, in Savannah County, which is said to be doing good work. Besides its aim to furnish a literary education, it insists that its students shall pursue an industrial course of study.

The Congregational Church has interested itself in a like work, and has established near Lake City the "Florida Normal and Industrial College." This school was opened in 1886, and a colored man placed at its head.

From: A. J. Steele, ''Normal-School Work Among the Colored People'' (1889)

The question which I am here to discuss was originally assigned to Principal B. T. Washington of the Tuskegee Normal School, Alabama. On account of domestic bereavement and ill-health very late in the season, I understand, Mr. Washington found that he could not perform the task assigned him, and so notified the President of this Department.

On the 5th of the present month, at the earnest solicitation of those interested in this department, and this particular discussion, I consented, in a moment of indiscretion, to undertake the presentation of this important topic. Under these circumstances, it is with no slight feeling of reluctance that I have set out upon the discharge of this duty, with so little time at my command, and with no opportunity to gather the evidence requisite to my purpose.

As was originally planned, it would have been more fitting that this paper should have been presented by a colored man, who should speak from his more intimate knowledge of his own race—their situation, aspirations, and needs—with a degree and kind of assurance and authority that I cannot claim. My own excuse or motive for attempting the treatment of this subject in this presence, must be my anxiety to have discussed here one of the interests of an important cause—a cause that has for the past quarter of a century enlisted the sympathy and the cooperation of the benevolent and philanthropic of our entire land, and with which it has been my happiness and honor to be connected for the past twenty years. I would fain hope that our discussion today may in the future bear fruit in the stimulation and encouragement of a wise and successful system of professional training for those who are in the immediate future to be the teachers of the colored race in this country, and mayhap, to some extent, of the greater body of that race in the Dark Continent. So far as I know, the history of education—or of the world, for that matter—does not anywhere present a question so remarkable, or a situation so fraught with consequences of good or ill to mankind, as is found in the great question of the education and training of the colored people of the United States. The phase of that question to which I particularly invite your attention is a most vital one, namely the training of the teacher of that race.

Rev. Dr. Haygood, in his comprehensive and excellent article on "The South and the School Problem," in the July number of *Harper's Monthly*, tells us in so many words, "Of true normal-school work there has not been much in the South outside the splendid work done in the best of the higher institutions for the negro." And again: That in these same institutions, while perhaps "five out of the hundred were pursuing the higher branches of the college course, the ninety-five in every hundred were learning just what they should have been learning—they were fitting themselves to be intelligent men and women, and to teach in the public schools for their people." Taken separately and in their proper connections in the article in question, these statements give no wrong impression; but taken *out* of their connection and placed side by side, as I have purposely done, they would lead us to the conclusion that a large amount of true normal-school work had been done for the colored people in the South—which is not the case, any more than it is the impression that Dr. Haygood would convey. On the contrary, the writer might truthfully have said, "Of true normal-school work, tried by any correct standard, there *has not been* much in the South," dropping the modifying clause that is liable to mislead. The pupils in the schools referred to have doubtless been well taught in the branches usually included in a fair English course of study; and this process has required all their time and energy, as well as that of their teachers.

Thus far in the normal work undertaken for the colored student, it is my experience that there is found but little time for anything but the tolerably fair mastery of the academic studies of the normal course, to say nothing of special professional training or true practice work. The very necessities of our work limit us in this direction. These limitations are broadening from year to year; and it may be truthfully said, *wherever* normal-school work has been attempted, similar limitations from somewhat similar causes have had to be overcome by patient labor—as I am confident they will be overcome in the colored normal schools.

According to statistics as given in the report of the commissioner of Education for 1886–7, there exists a colored school population of 2,222,611, with 1,118,556 of this number enrolled and in school attendance, taught by 15,815 teachers. The same report for 1883–4, which gives the latest official figures that I can find on the subject, gives the number of colored normal schools as 56, with an enrollment of upward of ten thousand pupils. Dr. Haygood, whom I have already quoted, tells us that there are in the South, in 1889, 150 schools able to prepare colored men and women to teach in the common schools.

As has been intimated, to call these schools in any true sense normal schools, would be sometimes like a libel on normal-school methods. In many cases their chief ambition is to do secondary or real college work; and, on the other hand, to do grammar or even primary-school work, absorbs all their time and strength, leaving but slight margin or opportunity for really proper normal training, even if the other conditions of the situation admitted of such work.

It is no part of my task on this platform, to argue the general question of the value or desirability of normal training. Happily that constitutes one of the settled questions in the minds of educators generally, and in most countries special normal instruction is provided in proportion to the state of progress and efficiency of the schools.

There are, however, special reasons in the peculiar circumstances, antecedents and situation of the colored people of the South, that furnish abundant food for thought and the excuse for this discussion. . . .

Reference has been made to the difficulties that are usually met in the establishment and upbuilding of normal methods of instruction anywhere it is undertaken. In the colored schools of the South these difficulties are much greater than are usually met with elsewhere.

No one without experience in teaching those deprived of such benefits can realize how great is the momentum which centuries of intelligence [*sic*] and freedom give the mind of the learner, or how unconscious is the acquisition of the great bulk of knowledge which goes to make up the Caucasian mind of the nineteenth century. This momentum the colored student very generally lacks. He has by his school efforts not only to master the usual subjects, but he must also, as best he can, get along without that substratum of general intelligence which is to the majority of the free white students the natural inheritance, or the unconscious acquisition of observation and experience of life in the home, in society, and in the business circle all of which are practically inaccessible to the colored learner, who usually comes to the school from communities and homes where the range of thought and experience is exceedingly limited. This could not well be otherwise with any race scarcely a generation removed from bondage, and since their freedom excluded by custom and prejudice almost as completely as in the days of slavery from association with those of superior privileges and opportunities, by which, almost more than any other means, the horizon of thought and knowledge, and life itself, is widened. . . .

Leaving for the time the class of mind, its limitations and difficulties with which our question has to do, I would direct your attention to the environment into which this work of normal instruction is to be transplanted, as it were, the atmosphere whence it must draw its support.

When it is remembered that the professional training of teachers, as the work is understood in the most advanced schools of the country, is of but recent growth and none too thoroughly comprehended where most successfully practiced, shall we wonder at the failure to appreciate its advantages where two decades measure the life of the school system, and where King Solomon and the hickory rod are held up as embodying the highest authority for the school-room and the end of argument with the teacher. Any treatment less heroic than this is looked upon with distrust and suspicion, as weak and inefficient. . . .

I notice yet another serious difficulty in the way of the successful professional instruction of colored teachers at the South. It lies in the great preponderance of rural or country schools, which are of necessity of low grade, paying low wages, and offering but small inducements even to those to whom few other avenues of labor and influence are open. In New York or Wisconsin, both of which States may justly boast of the popularity and efficiency of their normal schools—take away the incentive to professional training furnished by the positions paying fair salaries in the city and village graded and high schools, and I venture that the normal schools would straightway languish for want of students in the advanced classes and professional work.

In passing it may well be remarked that this excess of ungraded country schools, in which nearly all the colored children are to have their school training, may and doubtless does indicate an adaptation of normal training to suit the conditions of the schools in which the most of the work is to be done—with the hope of advancing the standard of the training as the conditions of the work make it practicable.

Allow me to summarize. These untoward conditions and peculiar circumstances to which I have tried to direct your attention, have up to the present time restrained and hampered in even the few schools where true normal-school work has been attempted, and whatever any particular institution may claim to have accomplished, or faithfully have tried to do, I am quite certain that to no great extent has the spirit of true normal training obtained a foothold or an influence even in the best of the higher institutions of the negro to which Dr. Haygood refers. The constant absorbing aim of the college and so-called university is toward the higher education, the college idea; and with the normal schools, institutes, and high schools even, in the rare cases where there has been any just comprehension of true normal methods, the more pressing necessities of our work, other interests that have demanded our attention, and the generally untoward circumstances, have kept professional training in the back-ground.

Thus much for the past and present condition of normal-school work among the colored people. What of the future? How shall the agencies be introduced or the influences be set in operation to remedy this state of things? . . .

Shall the circle of schools that have already done so much for the colored people, that have done the pioneer work amid all these difficulties, now that some advancement has been made, some vantage-ground been gained—shall they, in view of future advances made imperative and certain by the past, be found unequal to future demands, and give place to other agencies better adapted to this work, and with other aims and predilections?

Whoever may be destined to enter this door of opportunity, it is a great and inspiring one. To train the teacher is to shape the school and determine its work very largely, and this means everything to a race that must look for so much from the public school as must the negro of this country.

For one, I fully believe these schools are equal to the emergency. No such circle of schools has ever before existed in this land. They are absolutely unique in their position, influence, and control. They are worthy of study. They do not correspond to the academy of the Northern States, and they differ yet more from the private school or seminary of the South. They are not like the public school in any section, nor are they in any way or sense in competition, and much less in any antagonism to them, as is the case with the ordinary church or parish school of whatever denomination. They are in vital connection and closest sympathy with the common schools. They have thus far done the most that has been done to furnish teachers for the colored schools, and there seems to be no reason why they may not take now a step in advance, and that step in the direction of special professional training for those who go from them, expecting to teach for a longer or shorter time.

From: Albert Salisbury, "Discussion" (1889)

It is a matter of regret that Prof. Washington was unable to perform the part allotted to him on this occasion. Aside from the value of his own experience with the problem before us, it would have been of great interest to see how he, a representative colored man, would have approached this topic; what phases of it have impressed themselves most deeply upon his attention, and what practical courses of action he is prepared to urge or suggest. But since we are denied this, a satisfactory compensation is found in the fact that his place has been filled by one who has had so long and fruitful a connection with normal-school work among the colored people.

The lateness of his appointment to this task, however, enforces upon me a somewhat more independent treatment of the subject before us than would otherwise have been appropriate or desirable.

The question of normal-school work among the colored people is not only a question of what has been, but also of what shall be. It is, moreover, only one element of the general problem of normal-school work for all the people. Especially in the consideration of ultimate aims it is to be maintained, and never forgotten, that the negro is a *man,* neither less nor more. The great laws of human nature lying at the bottom of all true pedagogy and all social science, are the same with him as with other men. There is no "colored" psychology or pedagogics.

And yet no one can well deny that the negro has his psychological peculiarities, qualities incident to his present stage of race-development, and qualities resultant from his recent and present environment; and these must all be duly regarded in all that is done for him or with him. How, then, shall the American negro receive such a psychological and pedagogical study as he deserves? Who will make it? Who is qualified to do it? Certainly not those who have no contact with him, and as certainly not those who have no consideration for him or faith in him.

Looking back over the history of the past quarter-century, one can hardly resist the temptation to speculate as to what ideally should have been done with these freed people educationally. What an opportunity was here! Millions of children who had never been spoiled by false educational methods— virgin soil, so to speak, for the educational reformer! What a field for the

182

"new education"—so little to be undone! Had we possessed at that juncture a few thousand Pestalozzis, what might not have been accomplished!

Whence were all the needed teachers to come? If all could have been foreseen and understood, what an achievement it would have been for our national government at once to have established a hundred well-equipped normal schools for the thorough, practical training of colored teachers. Ought not such a preparation, logically, to have been made for the great expansion of primary instruction which was inevitably to ensue? But the nation could not see, and did not understand—does not yet understand, in fact, with all the light which the passing years have thrown. . . .

It requires no supernatural insight to discover the reasons why the South did not undertake this task. They have often been set forth with more or less completeness. Poverty was the first reason. The white people, after the war, were scarcely able to provide an education for their own children. They did not believe the negro capable of education, nor deserving of it; and if it were to be given him, they felt no inclination nor obligation to the task. But what I wish to emphasize in this connection is the fact that the South at that time had no experience of or interest in pedagogical questions. It sent sons to college, it is true—to the best colleges; but it scarcely knew that such a thing as normal schools had an existence. Teaching was hardly counted as a reputable calling; and "methods," as a pedagogical term, was blissfully unfamiliar.

Under such conditions, whence was to come the help of the freedmen's children? . . .

There was one grand resource, one fountain of supply which opened wide and has not yet wholly closed. Christian philanthropy, working through the church organizations of the North, sent forth a great corps of devoted teachers, inadequate in numbers, deficient in pedagogical training often; yet I do not hesitate to say in this presence that no more self-sacrificing, single-hearted, ill-paid, and sorely misunderstood army of workers ever walked before the Lord than these missionary teachers of the colored schools. I speak from close observation and direct personal acquaintance with them and their works in every Southern State.

From the purely pedagogical point of view, this work has often been crude and uncritical, though often, also, it has been equal to the best that can anywhere be found. It has been much modified by religious considerations, inseparable from the origin of the work and its support; and classical prepossessions have often unduly and unfortunately interfered with more needful and practical forms of education. Yet the fact remains, and a most interesting and valuable fact it is, that chiefly through the Northern missionary associations has the conception of normal schools, of the systematic and scientific preparation of teachers for their distinctive work, been brought within the knowledge and experience of the colored people.

I should much regret to seem unfair or unappreciative in this connection; but it is my clear conviction—and I have some opportunities for forming an intelligent opinion—that normal-school work, in any strict or justifiable use of that term, is still scarcely to be found among these people, except where founded and directed by the benevolent organizations already mentioned.

In these later years, the South is passing through an experience not unfamiliar at the North. The name "Normal" attached to a school has been found a useful advertisement, a good "card;" and so it is being flaunted by schools having no right to the title—schools whose managers are as hopelessly ignorant of what constitutes a true normal school as they are of the principles of pedagogical science. The temptation is strong to quote from the prospectus of one of these pseudo-normal schools; but I forbear.

A number of so-called normal schools for colored people have now been established by State authority, but I make bold to say that none of them are normal schools in the proper sense. They are not, perhaps, afflicted with the charlatanism to which I have just alluded; but they are simply high schools, and not very high at that. Prospective teachers are instructed there in the subject-matter of the several studies; but nothing is given, or practically nothing, of the science of education; nothing, or next to nothing, of methods of teaching; and nothing of practice-teaching in training departments. No teacher within my ken so much needs something beyond mere instruction in the text-books as the colored teacher of the South. No teacher so much needs a thorough and common-sense induction into the methods and practice of elementary instruction; and no teacher gets less of it.

This condition should not continue. The future is big with promise, and large in its demands. At the North and the South, for black and white, there is need for great struggle and effort to establish and diffuse truer ideals, and sounder methods of education. But nowhere is there need of more thoughtful study and persevering effort than in the future shaping of normal-school work among the colored people. This work should be marked by both progressiveness and conservatism—progressiveness in fearlessly cutting loose from hide-bound traditions and prejudices, and conservatism in avoiding all that is fanciful and sentimental. Gush and platitude are equally fatal; and open-eyed, open-hearted common-sense is the safest guide.

From: A. D. Mayo, ''The Training of the Teacher in the South'' (1889)

I count it a privilege that I can deal with the topic assigned me as a practical question, on which a somewhat unusual opportunity for observation of school-work in the South enables me, possibly, to offer a few useful suggestions. And I am favored by the fact that an interesting department of this theme—the training of the colored teacher—has already been treated by a gentleman who has no superior among the younger men of his race in the administration of the class of schools in which the teachers of a million colored children and youth are to be educated within the coming twenty years. The absolute necessity of a general, systematic course of training for the teacher is now conceded by all who regard instruction what it really is, the fundamental profession underlying all others. I am not called here to plead before this array of the foremost professional ability of the nation in behalf of such a common-place proposition, but to indicate, in as few and simple words as possible, what seems to me the best angle of approach upon a field so vast and so sparsely occupied in a majority of the Southern States.

In nine of the sixteen States we used to call the South, we find established what is known elsewhere as the State Normal School. Five of these, Maryland, West Virginia, Missouri, Texas, and Tennessee, have already developed this agency to a recognized power in the teaching force of the State. In Virginia, Florida, and Louisiana, separate institutions for the training of white teachers have been established within a few years, with fair prospects of success. Alabama has a special system of subsidizing academical schools, for both races, for this purpose. Other States have established a professorship of pedagogy in their State University; made normal instruction one department in an institution, like the Mississippi Normal and Industrial College for Girls; aided a city training school to receive additional pupils, as in South Carolina; or, like several States, contributed to one of the colleges, of the Northern missionary type, for colored youth, the means for training teachers. The summer institute, in several cases aided by the Peabody Education Fund, is now well under way in all these States. Perhaps half a dozen city training schools, of the Oswego pattern, and an increasing number of classes in city graded schools, are working on the same line. In every Southern State the necessity of normal instruction is persistently urged by its superior teachers and acknowledged by the educational public, which, for the past twenty years, has shouldered the prodigious labor of establishing the American common school through this vast realm.

But, so far, the result has only been a suggestion of what must be done, and the revelation of a mighty need. When we consider that Massachusetts, the first American commonwealth to establish a State normal school, after fifty years, does not yet draw one-half her ten thousand common-school teachers from the graduates of her score of State and city normals, we should not be surprised that the first twenty years of common-school work in the South finds even the educational public of all these States just wakening to the overwhelming necessity of the expert in the school-room. . . .

The great civil war cast upon the public of eleven of these commonwealths a large number of able men and women, qualified for the work of the higher education. From Gen. Robert Lee, down, a large number of eminent military men were summoned to the office of president and professor in the collegiate and secondary schools—revived or newly established in the years after 1865. Whatever difference of opinion may prevail concerning the "Southern brigadier in Congress," all competent observers bear testimony to the splendid service of "the brigadier" in the school-room. No class of Southern gentlemen have done so much in the educational revival of the past twenty years as these men; who hung up the sword to wield the professor's "pointer" and retired from the well-fought field of arms to maneuver, on the blackboard, the columns of symbolic signs that prophesy the coming civilization of a continent.

Multitudes of excellent women, often of the highest personal and social distinction, have been called to the management of the corresponding class of schools for girls. I have met the wives and daughters, "sisters, cousins and aunts" of numbers of men of national fame in these positions; and the services of this devoted and able body of people, during the years of preparation for the present arrangement of the educational new South, can hardly be overrated.

A similar work has been done by the admirable men and women from the North and the Canadas who have come southward to manage the higher schools, in which twenty thousand colored youth are now being trained for the educational leadership of their people. And, worthy of all honor, should be remembered a considerable body of white teachers of Southern birth and training, who, in their larger cities—Charleston, Baltimore, New Orleans, Richmond—have worked in the common school for the colored folk, and, with various degrees of ability and success, but with almost uniform goodwill and devotion, have toiled among the foundations of the new civilization for the freedmen.

But this vast work of the past twenty years in building the Southern common school, has only been the overture to the inspiring drama of a whole people for the first time invited to enter the open school-house door. Even now, after what every well-informed observer must regard the most notable educational achievement of modern times—the establishment of the people's common school in these sixteen great American States—the work is only on the threshold. The bottom fact about education in the South is, that while the higher and secondary instruction is better organized, both in quantity and quality, than even before, (although large numbers of good families are unable to avail themselves of its opportunities,) yet little more than half of our Southern children of the actual school age, from six to fourteen, are now in average attendance upon any school four months in the year. . . .

In the last twenty-five years a new generation of young men and women has appeared, from which this material for teachers is to be gathered. For years to come many thousands of the best girls in all these States will enter upon the work of teaching. The great opportunities for profitable industry by young women, in the finer manufactures and similar employments, in the North, have not been largely opened in these Southern States. The superior young white boys of the South are swept out of the school-room by the big broom of the rising industrial spirit, and it will be hard, for a generation to come, to secure enough of these to fill the higher positions of instruction and school supervision. A large number of superior colored men will find in teaching the best opportunities now offered for high usefulness to their race.

But, more and more, the South will be compelled to depend on its young women of the better sort of families, where education has been a tradition, for its working force of teachers in common and academical schools. I am constantly reminded, as I go about this country, of the condition of affairs in New England in my own youth, when the daughter of the parson, the doctor, the lawyer, the governor—almost every girl who aspired to consideration in society—was, for a time, a teacher in the common school of the village or rural district. And, with no desire to bring down upon myself the charge I have now and then encountered, of "drawing a long bow" in my talks about Southern educational affairs, I repeat that no country has to-day more valuable material for the best teaching force than is found in the young men who are determined and the larger number of young women who are inclined to enter the Southern school-room.

Of course, the first conditions of success for these young people must be had in a preparation of good schooling that will send them to their profession with an outfit of reliable knowledge. *"You never can teach what you don't know''* should be written over the teachers' desk in the plantation primary and the university. But this obvious fact is now and then turned inside out by the assertion that professional instruction in pedagogy can well afford to wait till this general culture is obtained. But, pray, how are the youth of the South to acquire this accurate and ample knowledge, until the teachers are prepared to furnish it? . . .

All effort in the practical training of the Southern teacher must recognize and adapt itself to the present conditions. Thirty years ago, the social lever in the South pried over the plantation; to-day the fulcrum is the town. What in common Southern parlance is called ''the city,'' including city and village in the North, has now become the center of influence, where all new enterprises originate, and especially whence the rising educational influence of the country goes forth. An increasing number of these communities, of a population of one thousand and upwards, are now establishing the graded public school for both races. In the State of Texas one hundred and thirty; in each of the sixteen Southern States a considerable number of these towns have this arrangement for the schooling of their youth. I have never known a failure in such an attempt when the superintendent or leading teacher has been competent and has been permitted to have his or her reasonable way. Many towns have failed from placing at the head of the enterprise a superintendent who had neither knowledge of nor sympathy with the organization or methods of instruction in a modern graded school. Of course half a dozen quarrelsome families of local influence can wreck this, as any worthy enterprise; but the majority of such attempts succeed reasonably well, and often achieve a success that makes the establishment of the graded school the beginning of a new era for the community. In such case the success is largely due to the persistent work of an accomplished superintendent in training his teachers. . . .

Many of these superintendents have established a class in pedagogics, in the upper division of the school, where several young people, generally girls, for a year are instructed in the best methods of elementary school work, with some opportunity for observation and practice in all the grades. Thus, without a formal normal school, which the community is not prepared to support, the work of training the superior youth in the upper class for teaching goes on. . . .

Here is the vital point of departure for the uplifting of the teaching force of the rural district adjacent to this place. In a few years, a considerable number of the brightest girls, especially from the surrounding country, pass through the higher grades of the school, are instructed by the superintendent, and go home and take up the good work of improving the local schools.

They can better afford to teach, for the small wages paid to county instructors, than others, and often bring to the improvement of the masses the social influence and personal culture so valuable in this work. There is no good reason why every considerable town in the South, in connection with its graded schools, should not build up a department for the training of teachers for the adjoining country, and in no other way that I perceive can this reform so well be inaugurated.

The academies of the South, one of which is found in almost every town, and sometimes in a little hamlet in the open country, should cooperate with this work. . . .

There is no good reason for the jealousy now and then manifested between this class of institutions and the graded schools of the larger towns. . . .

And a most valuable factor in this improvement will be the establishment of a genuine department of pedagogics. Every academy in these sixteen States should at once make arrangements for such a department, under the charge of an expert in elementary methods of instruction. . . .

Several of the colleges and universities of the South for white, and a number for colored, students have already established a chair of normal instruction, and, whenever the incumbent has been competent and able to hold his own against reactionary influences in the faculty of the institution, the experiment has been a success. It would seem a queer anomaly that a faculty of educated men, devoted to good learning, should look down with undisguised contempt or indifference on a man of equal scholarship, consecrated to the most important of all professions—the art of instruction. It would be a great lift in all American colleges should every graduate be required, during his course, to read and be examined in a good history of philosophy and a history of pedagogy. . . .

One of the most vexatious hindrances in the common-school work is the attitude of a considerable body of college professors towards the teacher in the elementary school, an attitude that reacts on the higher education. It is from lack of suitable preparation in the country district and town graded schools that the material for college work is still so crude and unsatisfactory in the South, compelling learned professors to "make bricks without straw" in the effort to instruct a class of youth in the higher education who never have learned how to study or to handle their own minds. When the college and university life of the South has been adjusted to the needs of the people, making a vital connection with both the academical and common school, and recognizing the absolute need of training the young men who are to go forth often to the superintendence of graded schools, this lamentable waste of educational power will be avoided.

From: "Report of the 'Chicago Committee' on Methods of
Instruction, and Courses of Study in Normal Schools (1889);
Thomas J. Gray, chairman

The committee appointed two years ago at the meeting of the National Educational Association, in Chicago, to continue the inquiry into the question of the courses of study and methods of instruction pursued in the normal schools of the United States, begs leave to submit the following report:

It should be remarked that the geographical relation of the committee has made any conference impossible. The chairman prepared the circulars and submitted them to the other members, who approved them. Later, a couple of letters were sent to the New England members asking for suggestions, that brought forth no fruit. Beyond this the chairman was obliged to assume the entire responsibility.

The present report was intended, as I understood the instructions of this body to imply, rather as a completion of the line of thought in the report for 1887, than as the opening of new fields of inquiry. In view of the miscellaneous results to the inquiries sent out two years ago, it was thought wiser to confine the present circulars to normal and training schools supported in whole or in part by public taxation. It was believed that a better understanding of the problem could be thus gained; a clearer definition of terms, and information secured based upon a more nearly common use of them.

The results fully confirm this judgment. While the report does not cover all of the points upon which information is needed, nor exhaust many questions started by it, *the results may be taken as expressing the average view of the leading normal schools of this country; as in fact an expression of the way in which the problem is now regarded by those who must be acknowledged as most competent to judge.*

The whole number of schools reporting is 49; those answering nearly all of the questions number about 35. These are the leading State schools of the entire country, embracing Maine, Massachusetts, Vermont, Rhode Island, Connecticut, New York, Pennsylvania, Maryland, Alabama, Louisiana, Indiana, Michigan, Wisconsin, Minnesota, Iowa, Nebraska, Illinois, Missouri, Kansas, New Hampshire, California, and New Jersey. In addition to these, eight city training schools sent replies more or less complete.

The following is a copy of the circular sent:

190

NATIONAL EDUCATIONAL ASSOCIATION: A CIRCULAR CONCERNING THE METHODS OF INSTRUCTION IN USE IN THE NORMAL SCHOOLS OF THE UNITED STATES.

With a view of carrying forward the work of the last two years, the committee appointed at the last meeting of the National Educational Association, held in Chicago, July, 1887, were instructed to inquire with greater detail into the methods of instruction and courses of study pursued in the normal schools of the United States.

The work of the past two years has so clearly developed the real character of many educational institutions of the country going by the name of normal schools, that it seems wiser, because of the promise of more substantial results, to confine further inquiry, for the present at least, to those normal schools which are supported in whole or in part by public money, and to colleges and universities having a well-defined department of pedagogy.

As a further contribution, therefore, toward the solution of the problem of the professional training of teachers, replies are respectfully asked to the questions contained in this circular. The hearty and explicit responses hitherto sent show the appreciation of the importance of the work in which the committee is engaged. If this inquiry can be prosecuted by the Association with zeal and intelligence, substantial benefits must accrue to all schools engaged upon this most vital of all educational problems—the training of teachers.

> Thomas J. Gray,
> Albert G. Boyden,
> C. C. Rounds,
> *Committee.*

Please return all replies to the Chairman, St. Cloud, Minn.

[CIRCULAR.—Heading omitted.]

1. Name of the Institution,————. Location,————. Its chief officer, title————, name————. If a chair of pedagogy, the name of the professor also.

2. Upon what branches are candidates for admission to the school examined?

[NOTE.—If a college, please answer this question by giving the name of the class or classes instructed in pedagogy.]

3. State in weeks the time given to each of the following subjects:

[NOTE.—A week will be understood to be one recitation of 45 minutes daily for five days. Please reduce all answers to this standard.]

History of Education,————. Text-book in the hand of the pupil, not reference books,————. Science of Education————, text-book————. Methods of Teaching the Various Branches————, text-book————. Mental Science or Psychology————, text-book————. School Economy ————, text-book————.

[NOTE.—If two or more of these subjects are included in your course under a single name, please do not duplicate your answers. The Committee wish to obtain exact information concerning each subject separately.]

4. Is there a school of children, or as it is commonly called, a Model or Practice School, connected with your school? How many grades does it embrace?

[NOTE.—The term grade will be understood as a year of average public-school work.]

5. Do the students of pedagogy (those in training for teaching) do practice-teaching in the model school?

[NOTE.—The term practice-teaching will be understood to mean *actual instruction of learners,* not the exemplification of educational principles with classmates who are assumed to be children, or the observation of the work of other teachers.]

6. Do these students spend any time in observing the work of other teachers in the model school?

7. How many periods of 45 minutes each are required of the practice-teachers in actual teaching during their course of study as a condition of graduation?

8. How many in observation?

[NOTES.—(1) Observation will be understood to be the work to which a pupil is regularly assigned, and upon which he is to give a subsequent report. (2) If the time called for in 7 and 8 varies with the different students, please give the average required for graduation.]

9. Is the practice-teaching a daily exercise during the time of its continuance?

10. Do you require all practice-teachers to teach for the same length of time?

11. What pedagogical branches are completed before the student is allowed to begin to practice? [See question 3.]

12. Do your practice-teachers recite as students in any branches of their course of study during the days in which they are engaged in practice-teaching? On an average, how many daily?

13. Do your practice-teachers do practice-teaching in any other school than a model or training school?

[NOTE.—If so, please answer questions 4, 5, 6, 7, 8, 9, 10, 11 and 12 as applying to this teaching.]

14. Do your students exemplify their methods of teaching by giving lessons to their classmates who assume to be children? [See note, question 5.]

15. How many such lessons is each student required to give?

16. Is any portion of the time indicated in question 7 included in your reply to question 8? If so, what part?

17. What are the main points upon which you criticise the work done by the practice-teachers?

18. What plan have you for the work of ''observation,'' and how do you get at the results?

19. Do you find the principles of the science of education to be better learned in connection with practice-teaching, or following it, or preceding it, or without it? What would be your ideal arrangement of the order of the pedagogical subjects in question 3?

20. How long a course of pedagogy ought to be required of those having adequate academic preparation to admit them to the profession with the rank of assistants in high schools and higher positions?

21. In your judgment, can a knowledge of a subject from the teaching point of view be acquired by the pupil while he is pursuing it as a learner? Please define ''teaching point of view,'' that is, designate what you understand by a *teacher's* knowledge of a subject.

22. For the purposes of pedagogical training, where, in the course of study in normal schools, should come the consideration of the so-called elementary or instrumental subjects, (reading, writing, geography, grammar, and arithmetic)—before or after the general academic work?

23. Inasmuch as normal schools cannot supply one-tenth of the number of teachers actually needed by the public schools, would it be better for them rather to define their courses in pedagogy to attract to them the men and women of liberal education, who are seeking to enter the profession, or to continue to depend largely upon the country schools to fit their material?

24. Would a conference of normal-school teachers and professors of pedagogy to formulate such a course of study be of service to the cause of education? Is such a thing feasible? Please answer *ad libitum*.

25. What changes would you suggest in the following classification:

PEDAGOGICAL SUBJECTS.—History of Education, Science of Education, School Economy, Mental Science or Psychology, Moral Science, Methods of Teaching applied to the instrumental subjects [see question 22], Practice Teaching.

ACADEMIC SUBJECTS.—All other subjects of the course.

26. What is the average age of your graduating class?

27. What per cent. of your students enrolled in the pedagogical course graduates?

28. What per cent. of your graduates from the pedagogical work are young men?

29. What average length of time do your graduates teach after leaving school?

30. In what year did you graduate your first class?

31. How many students have you enrolled in your classes this year who expect to teach? [Please give answer in figures.]

32. What per cent. of these students are graduates of high schools or colleges?

The Committee will consider it a great favor if you will send any printed matter showing the organization and plans of your school, or of any special work. They will likewise accept in the same spirit any criticisms, suggestions or discussions of any points connected with the important duty they have to discharge. It would seem that the time is ripe for a better definition of the work of training teachers, and a more thorough understanding among those to whom society has committed this labor of love.

Please return this circular to the undersigned, Chairman of the Committee.

Thomas J. Gray, St. Cloud, Minnesota.

The difficulty of reducing a series of answers to a common standard, so as to tell the truth as the authors intended, will be appreciated by every one who has tried to go through the process. One needs that rare gift of "reading between the lines" to fairly interpret the replies to such a list of questions as the circular contains. Where questions cover the same ground as in the circular of 1887, they are to be interpreted as a request for better-defined information.

QUESTION 2, asking for requirements for admission to normal schools, had the following answers: In 22 schools only the common branches are required—the common branches meaning reading, writing, spelling, geography, grammar, and arithmetic. In no case does the entrance examination appear to be a final examination, but one intended to prove to the examiner a fair working ability in those subjects, making it possible to study them more broadly while in the normal school. In Minnesota the questions used by the county superintendents for the second-grade teacher's certificate (there being three grades known in the State—third, second, and first) are, by official sanction of the State Normal School Board, made the minimum requirement. The following sets of questions, taken from the catalogue of the State Normal School at Worcester, Massachusetts, suggest the grade of scholastic knowledge deemed necessary on the part of the beginner in a teachers' training school in the native American home of normal schools:

QUESTIONS USED AT THE ENTRANCE EXAMINATION (WRITTEN PART), FEBRUARY, 1887.

ARITHMETIC.

The examiners wish to see all the figuring. Except in No. 2, decimals are to be carried to two places only.

1. Define the following terms: Draft, exponent, unit, cube root, complex fraction.

2. Add two and three hundred-thousandths, two hundred and four thousandths, forty-three thousand two hundred sixty-one hundred-thousandths, four hundred four thousandths; from the sum subtract 202.84; multiply the remainder by fifty thousand, and divide the product by .012.

3. A can walk around a garden in 9 minutes, B in ten, C in 12, and D in 15. They start together, and walk until they are together again. How long does it take?

4. When the principal, rate, and interest are given, how is the time found?

5. How many yards of carpeting, one yard wide, must be bought to cover a floor 20 ft. long and 16 ft. wide, allowing $1\frac{1}{2}$ yds. for matching the figures?

6. May 1, 1885, Mr. P. A. Brown borrowed one hundred dollars of Mr. S. F. Allen, and gave a note promising to pay the money in three months. Write the note.

7. June 1, 1885, Mr. Allen wanted the money, and went to a bank where the note was discounted at six per cent. How much money did he receive?

8. Solve by proportion: A contractor found that it would take 16 men 6 weeks, working ten hours a day, to do a certain piece of work. He decided to have it done in 8 days of 12 hours each. How many men were hired?

9. Analyze the following: $\frac{3}{4}$ of Charles's money equals $\frac{2}{3}$ of Henry's, and together they have 46 cents. How much has each?

GRAMMAR.

1. Write the principal parts of the following verbs: *Give, come, seek, teach, lay, join, slay.*

2. Write the forms of the personal pronoun of the first person.

3. Write the subjunctive form of the verb *be* in the past tense, in all the persons and numbers.

4. Make a sentence in which the word *that* is a conjunction, and one in which *that* is a relative pronoun.

5. Criticise the expression: "The money belongs to John and I."

6. "The large house might have been painted." Parse "*might have been painted.*"

7. "This house is ours." Parse *ours.*

8. "We hope that you will return soon." What is the grammatical construction of the expression, *that you will return soon,* and what do you call it?

9. Write a sentence containing an adverbial phrase, and draw a line under the phrase.

GEOGRAPHY.

1. Choose one: (a) Draw a map of Massachusetts with its counties and cities. (b) Draw a map of New England, locating five mountains, five rivers, and five cities. (c) Draw a map of South America, locating countries, mountains, and rivers.

2–3. On the map of the United States furnished you, draw five principal railroads or canals, five large cities, and the areas producing cotton, wheat, coal, corn, oil, and sugar.

4–5. On the map of Europe furnished you, write the names of the seas, gulfs, bays, and straits; locate the countries and five cities.

6. Name five large cities, and state the natural advantages of each.

7. Describe briefly how six of the following are obtained: Rubbar, silk, tapioca, petroleum, opium, rice, sugar.

8. Choose one: (a) What is the scale of a map? Illustrate how it may be used. (b) What does a map profile show? (c) What is meant by standard time?

9. Choose one: (a) How wide is the temperate zone? (b) What is the Tropic of Cancer, and why is it located where it is? (c) About where do the sun's rays fall vertically to-day?

UNITED STATES HISTORY.

1. What led (1) to the discovery, and (2) to the settlement of this continent?

2. Tell anything you know about the first permanent settlement in America.

3. What battle decided the fate of the French power in this country?

4. How were Europeans represented in North America about the middle of the 17th century?

5. Tell something about the wars between the early colonists and the Indians.

6. Who was Pontiac? and what did he hope to do?

7. What was the Boston Port Act?

8. What great change was made in the map of the United States between 1840 and 1850?

9. What was the result of the Mexican war?

10. Who owned Louisiana before it came into the possession of the United States?

11. What is the difference between royal, charter, and proprietary colonies? Give an instance of each.

12. Mention the names of some of the leading generals on the Confederate, and on the Union side, in the Civil War.

SPELLING.

1. Narragansett. 2. Nicaragua. 3. Savannah. 4. Rio Janeiro. 5. Sacramento. 6. Shanghai. 7. Leicester. 8. Vertical. 9. Which. 10. Stopped. 11. Singeing. 12. Platform. 13. Whipping. 14. Scholar. 15. Military. 16. Agassiz. 17. Humboldt. 18. Talent. 19. Calendar. 20. Metric System. 21. Soldier. 22. Spirit. 23. Salmon. 24. Repetition. 25. Physiology. 26. Philosophy. 27. Committee. 28. Telegraphy. 29. Responsibility. 30. Arid. 31. The *Annual* Exhibition 32. Of the *Menagerie* at the 33. *Zoological* Garden 34. Will take place *Tuesday* 35. *February* 9th, at *half-past eight o'clock.*

W. T. Harris, "Letter of Transmittal" (1891). From: *Rise and Growth of the Normal-School Idea in the United States,* by J. P. Gordy.

Department of the Interior,
Bureau of Education,
Washington, D.C.,

October 20, 1891.

Sir:

The accompanying circular, entitled the "Rise and Growth of the Normal-School Idea in the United States," is the work of Prof. J. P. Gordy, incumbent of the chair of pedagogy in the Ohio University, at Athens, and for some time editor of an excellent "Journal of Pedagogy."

The task which the author has here set himself is, "to trace the growth and development of the normal idea in the United States." He explains his theme more fully, as follows:

"Probably no two students would agree precisely as to the elements that enter into this development. The greater their disagreement, the more widely, of course, would they differ as to the institutions in which these elements first appeared. As the author conceives it, the first form in which the normal idea appeared in this country was the belief that the teacher needs special preparation, but that this special preparation consists in the simple addition of the study of certain subjects to the training required for the professions or for business, and, in his opinion, the institutions in which this idea was embodied were the New York academies. This erroneous conception, as the author deems it, gave place to the truer idea—that the proper preparation of the teacher requires not only a mastery of the art and science of education, as far as that is possible, but a thorough grounding in the subjects he is to teach—that the knowledge of a subject that suffices for the citizen does not suffice for the teacher. This idea, he conceives, was embodied in the normal schools of Massachusetts in the beginning. But while these schools had a definite conception that there is a science of education, they did not formulate their ideas as to what that science is. The normal school at Oswego, it appears to the author, took a step towards determining that science and making explicit the art that should be based upon it. That institution taught that the only nourishment of the mind is realities, and that the whole work of the teacher consists in bringing the mind into contact with the appropriate realities. But this school left to the uneducated tact of the teacher the decision of the question as to what realities are appropriate. The normal school at Worcester took a decided step in advance in insisting that this tact may be wonderfully quickened by the careful study of children, and in successfully embodying this idea in its method of work. The conception that teachers of higher grades of schools need professional preparation is embodied in college departments of pedagogy, and, therefore, a chapter is devoted to that subject. The conception that the institution which gives teachers thorough preparation should be a school of university grade is embodied in the normal idea, as it was attempted to be realized in the normal school at St. Cloud under the presidency of Mr. Gray. That idea, the author thinks, is true, but the attempt to realize it in an institution which undertakes to prepare teachers for elementary schools, must, in the nature of the case, in his opinion, be a failure. The New York College for the training of teachers is an attempt to embody this true idea without encumbering it with conditions that make its realization impossible. That institution clearly realizes that a school of university grade must require students of a university grade of preparation to avail themselves of its advantages.''

The forgoing sketch will give a general idea of the conclusions reached in the circular, and it will explain the selection of the institutions included. If the reputation and excellence of training schools had been the determining reason for treating of them, some institutions would certainly have had a prominent place that are not mentioned in these pages.

Since this circular was prepared—about 18 months ago—numerous changes have taken place that point in the direction of a wider and more general recognition of the importance of education as a university study. The school of pedagogy in the Clark University, the reorganization of the Albany Normal School, the new departure taken by Harvard in the matter of pedagogy are among the suggestive signs of the times. They indicate, let us hope, that "the time is not far distant when an untrained teacher will be considered a greater absurdity than an untrained doctor or lawyer."

Believing that the distribution of this work will do much to encourage those who look upon the teachers' vocation as a profession, and who labor to provide the means of a thorough preparation therefor, I have caused it to be published as a circular of information of this Bureau.

I have the honor to be, sir, very respectfully,

W. T. Harris,
Commissioner.

Hon. John W. Noble,
Secretary of the Interior.

From: Thomas Gray, "The Normal-School Idea as Embodied in the Normal School at St. Cloud" (1891); From: *Rise and Growth of the Normal School Idea in the United States,* by J. P. Gordy

CONTENTS

	Page
Letter of transmittal	5
Introduction	7
Chapter I.　Beginnings of the normal-school idea in the United States	9
Chapter II.　Training of teachers in the academics of New York up to 1844	26
Chapter III.　The first normal school in America	42
Chapter IV.　The normal school at Oswego	61
Chapter V.　The State normal school at Worcester, Mass	76
Chapter VI.　The normal school idea as embodied in the normal school at St. Cloud	90
Chapter VII.　Chairs of pedagogy	98
Chapter VIII.　The New York college for the training of teachers	104
Chapter IX.　The training of teachers in the New York academies under the supervision of the department of public instruction	114
Chapter X.　General survey and summary	120
Subject index	143

CHAPTER 6: THE NORMAL-SCHOOL IDEA AS EMBODIED IN THE NORMAL SCHOOL AT ST. CLOUD. BY PRESIDENT THOMAS G. GRAY.

One can justly criticise only what one has rightly understood.

Fischer.

It is impossible to define the work of an institution in any other manner than to reveal its conception of its problem and purpose. What was it set to do? What means does it employ to accomplish its end?

In the few pages following a brief answer is suggested to these two questions from the point of view which may be said to represent the "normal-school idea" as it is embodied in this institution.

The philosophy of method is the method of philosophy. For the latter is nothing more than the science of knowing and knowledge. The modality of spirit is always in the last analysis the central question of philosophy. Its answer must find its valid ground quite beyond the reach of doubt, otherwise all procedure from it will be halting and uncertain. This ground must be sought in the field of metaphysics. Here alone, in the domain of the science of knowledge itself, can we hope to find a starting point for method. The question is not one of psychology, for the latter science is, as all other sciences are, but data in the science of thought.

This point of view, apparently so self-evident, is one most difficult to attain. The mind becomes so habituated to the external body of fact in the world that the ablest thinker finds it well-nigh impossible to realize for any length of time that the universe for man is the universe we know, the universe as given to us. What it is, if it be at all, or could be, as not known to us, we can form not the slightest conjecture. The knowing mind is quite as large a factor in knowledge as the thing known. We speak of color and form, of species and genera, of truth and error, and quite forget that apart from the knowing mind these very words would cease to exist, with all for which they stand to us.

There can be no doctrine of method that does not undertake to define the mode of knowledge. There is no such thing as method apart from thought. Genera and species have no existence in the vegetable and animal kingdom, and he who becomes a master in botany is not one who learns many individual facts from nature, but he who thinks into unity, under his *a priori* conceptions, the wholly isolated and unrelated facts of the natural world. Nay, rather does the modality of knowledge lie wholly on the spirit side of sensation, not on the matter side.

What is meant by the question, How does the mind know? There have been, from Plato down the line of history, many profound students of this problem. Some of the most powerful intellects of the race have wrought upon it. But only as individuals. In so far as their natural inclinations and surroundings led them to the consideration of what has always been regarded a very abstruse subject, they investigated the question for us and have brought us their results. These are weighty and voluminous and of most rare value.

But it has remained for the present century to see society in its organic capacity set to itself this stupendous problem, and establish an institution whose purpose it is to work out a better solution than the world has hitherto known. This institution is the normal school.

Begun in ignorance of its real mission, still too young to show any final results, it is nevertheless true that this is its purpose, and to this will it rise.

It had to create its faculties, its literature, its atmosphere. It has been met at every state with the conservatism of tradition and pharisaism. The idea resident in the brain of Socrates, of Plato, of Jesus, of Kant, of Bacon, is perennial, nay, immortal; and the normal school is no more subject to dissolution than the conception of the modality of knowledge in the minds of these men. There has no new idea been given the race, except that society, the larger intelligent entity, has now its hold upon it, and the normal school is its externalization.

Some would have us believe that the chair of pedagogy and the normal school are of diverse origin and purpose. Such are shallow observers of the meaning of history. These institutions represent but one idea—chronologically the normal school is the older. But each represents the attempt society is making to answer the same question. So long as institutions do not differ in purpose, their differences in means amount to nothing in the progress of history.

Naturally enough the first attempts upon this problem sought the most empirical facts. The term method, whose meaning inspired the whole movement, was made to stand for an order of evolution or arrangement in the external body of knowledge. This, of necessity, developed into empirical processes, tricks with things, if thereby and therein the soul might be forced or surprised into the act and result of knowing. The body of truth to be taught from pulpit and press, from school desk and at home, was supposed to contain some magic secret of a true order of acquisition, which, when once discovered, would prove an adequate guide to the tyro in teaching, who, though a fool, might not err. This was the dream of Pestalozzi. He declares: "I believe that we must not dream of making progress in the instruction of the people as long as we have not found the forms of instruction which make of the teacher, at least as far as the completion of the elementary studies is concerned, the simple mechanical instrument of a method which owes its results to the nature of its processes, and not to the ability of the one who uses it."

This notion of "logical method," "order of independence," came to be a fetich, and dominated and still dominates, to a degree at least, the normal schools of America.

The newer phase of growth appears in the recognition of the truth that method is an order of thought, not things—it is subjective, not objective. The mind receives to itself as a self-determining entity, or force, the universe, and receives it under the limitations and modes of its own existence. The spirit, infinitely free, goes forth to its own realization, or to the realizing of itself. A house, a hat, a tree, a flower, is the external realization of an idea, human or divine. All soul activity is self activity, and must be the projecting of the self into a world, a cosmos. The spirit can not be passive, inert. The very conception of force precludes this. We can not think of a passive force. If, then, the mind be active, be a force, and a self-determining force at that (a fact necessary to grant and to place beyond the reach of doubt as the first postulate of freedom), it can not, in the nature of the case, be passive. What then, the question returns, is the modality of spirit? This is the sphere of method, this is the significance of the term. We shall never find in the externalizations of ideas the modalities of their expression or acquisition. The science of botany, I would repeat, is not in flowers and stems, roots and leaves. It is in the thinking, knowing mind. The moment the mind passes from the isolated instances of experience in the forms of time and space to the conceptions of unity in a nature of things, the world becomes a reality in us, and we can not dissociate it from ourselves.

If a normal school be true to its mission it must rise to a conception of its purpose and bend its energies to its accomplishment. The first question, therefore, to put to a normal school, or its confrère, the chair of pedagogy, is: "What system of thought or theory of knowledge do you teach?" It will not do to answer "Pestalozzianism," or "Froebelism," for neither of these men ever had anything to be called a theory of knowledge; yet this is the only answer some of the foremost normal schools could give. The chairs of pedagogy are even further behind, for no one in this country has yet produced any considerable contribution to the real problem. They seem to be blindly groping for some solid ground on which to stand. What they and the normal schools must have, and what they will yet attain, is a rational metaphysic, a science of science, a science of knowledge.

It may be further postulated that no advance toward final ground of thought has ever been made from a reliance upon the body of knowledge itself. This is, of course, a mere truism, for knowledge is the result of the knowing process, and therefore the inquiry must be pushed back into the sphere of the soul itself. This is where Plato and Jesus, Bacon, Kant, Fichte, and Hegel placed it, and each, speaking of Jesus merely as an exponent of the modality of knowledge, made some contribution to the great problem. Any other process must result in a mere rearrangement of the parts of the external or objective body of truth, and such is the sole source of the validity of all pedagogical processes based upon the Spencerian school of thinkers. To repeat, sense perception does not contain the content of the term science. We must look to the modes or forms of spirit. If a class is aided by a study of Sully's Psychology it is not because of, but in spite of, his guiding principles. Fortunately no student is ever dependent on his teacher for his *a priori* forms of knowledge; these are his by virtue of his being an intelligent spirit, and by means of, and because of, these he is able to take even from such a guide the elements of an experience and think them into unity in the forms of his own soul. This alone saves every one of us from mental chaos and madness. This suggests the explanation of the oft-noted fact that men in contact with the most diverse in experience yet attain to the stature of cultured, educated manhood.

This resumé of methodology suggests a number of practical laws for the determination of the courses of study and methods of instruction which are to be employed in the training of teachers. Among them may be enumerated:

(1) All the parts of knowledge are or must have been facts in consciousness. One element, therefore, in pedagogical preparation must be the conscious classification of the various facts in all the sciences and departments of learning as data in psychology. That is, a science of knowledge must be made and mastered by the would-be pedagogue. But this implies in the world of thought a task as herculean as that confronting the biologist in the world of life—an infinity of individuals for classification. It is evident, therefore, that the elementary or typical forms of thought must be first determined. Just as in the natural world an oyster studied becomes the type of all its multiplied kind, so a type form may be found in the outgoings of the self-determining spirit. This must lead the student to Kant. To this problem Kant addressed his gigantic energies.

As applied to the particular subject of instruction the principle compels the student to select the characteristic marks or conditioning facts of a subject, those facts without which the science would not be, and under which all details, the instances of an experience, must arrange themselves. This is a crucial test of the student, nor can any teacher without a firm footing in an ultimate theory of knowing make the least approach to any final results. Not mental science and Latin, mental science and arithmetic, mental science and grammar, but mental science in Latin, mental science in arithmetic, mental science in grammar, and all other forms of knowlege,—this must be attained as the view point of teaching.

It is quite needless to add that the study of mental science, as commonly conducted, is almost valueless as an aid to teaching. Handled as if its data were ever doubtful and its conclusions vain imaginations, it is looked upon by the student as a subject quite outside himself, without any real data, and when the text-book is put down his little packages of psychological truths (God save the mark!) are ticketed and labeled and laid carefully away in the archives of memory. Many a man declares that it never occurred to him, as a student, that the mind he was supposed to study was his own; that he was to observe a fact at first hand, and pursue the subject as he would any other science.

(2) It will thus appear that the true order of studies for a course in pedagogical training must be the direct reverse of the academic course. The latter is the order to be followed by the student mind in acquisition, the former is the rearrangement into a science of knowledge of the elements of learning already in possession. However this pedagogical process be related in proximity of time, it must of necessity chronologically and logically follow the academic process. Could normal schools obtain a student body with adequate academic preparation, they could at once devote all of their energies to their real function. But, as was said before, they must create their literature, their faculties, their student body. At present they can hope to show the world what the problem really is; they can not yet present its complete solution.

The course of study must, therefore, recognize as its conditioning law the above principle. The true order of subjects must be: (1) Those that help directly in the formation of a science of knowledge, chiefly metaphysics, psychology, and methodology, including the history of education; that is, the education of history—history regarded as the record of the evolution of ideas, the psychology of the race. (2) Those that look toward intelligent skill in the means of education, as methods; that is, psychology applied to the various activities of the scholar and school, a conscious synthesis of the manifold details in subject, topic, recitation, and organization. This is the true art of education. (3) To the above must be added such subjects as will give the student at least a fair conception of the body of human knowledge as a whole. An effort must be made to fill out the academic conception of subjects; that is, to set a fact in the light of all knowledge. This work should be thrown back upon academic schools, colleges, academies, and high schools, as far as possible, but the normal school faculties must, at present, do more or less of it. It is evident that it should be done before inducting the students into the professional work. If a student must learn arithmetic and chemistry, as an academic student, let him be taught, but do not debase the real work of forming a science of knowledge by making him believe he is getting a sort of magic power, some hocus-pocus by which he will be prepared to teach it. Call the work by its right name. After this work is done, and it is a *sine qua non* take up true pedagogical inquiry in the order above indicated, and then treat of the various subjects from a pedagogical point of view.

(3) It is evident that the so-called elementary subjects, elementary be-

cause they contain the elements of human knowledge, must be the objective ground for all methodology. They form, under ordinary conditions, a sufficiently comprehensive subject-matter for the doctrine of method to cover. At any rate, no start can be made in the science of knowledge that does not first comprehend these subjects. Their consideration from the pedagogical, that is, the normal-school point of view, must come last in the course of study. The inversion of this obvious order has introduced confusion into normal-school work, and brought upon it the contempt of academic schools.

(4) It is also evident that to the department of methodology a model school should be attached—a ground for the operation of experience. "Studies do give forth directions too much at large, except they be bounded in by experience."

(5) Since the normal school is to train teachers in the art of knowing and expressing knowledge, in the art of being, it must, in order to work intelligently, be in possession of the science of knowledge. This fact constitutes it a technical school of university grade, and the highest in a possible series of schools in a system of education, since it assumes to examine into the very grounds of all forms of knowledge, and must thus bring into review the purposes, processes, and results of all other schools. In a word, it is a school of philosophy. It is needless, surely, to interject the remark that this view would not make the normal school a Utopian institution, that it would not place it so far away as to make it of no value to the common-school system. The point of the question turns upon this inquiry: When a pupil enters a normal school what should be his purpose, and what are the means for his realizing it? The normal schools ought and must be able to render some other than the usual answer of academic schools, viz, to make a better scholar, by increasing the sum total of knowledge and mental power. Not to make better scholars, though this, of course, must be an incidental blessing, but to make teachers. Not to make teachers without scholarship, as an occasional lunatic charges upon the schools, but to make teachers out of scholars.

The recognition of the normal school as one of the technical schools of university grade has been of slow growth. With all of Horace Mann's acumen, he apparently did not see that it has this as its true relation in a system of education. Massachusetts, without a State university, was not, in this respect, a fortunate soil in which to plant the normal school. But it must be evident to the most casual observer that a system of education has the following necessary parts and relations:

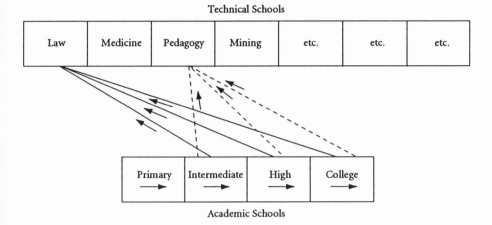

To the child entering the primary school an open way through all the academic schools should appear; beyond these, should be offered the special school needed to convert the accumulated potential energy of an academic course into some form of actual energy needed by society in its organic life. While any technical school is open to a student having the requisite preparation to do its special work, it is plain that the student who has gone through the most extensive course of academic preparation will profit most in the technical course. This fact is already well solved in the schools of law and medicine and business. In these schools, when the student is once entered, the question of academic scholarship is never raised. The geographical location of any technical school can mislead no one as to its logical relation in a system of education.

It must appear that it is highly illogical to place normal and high schools in the same category. They have an entirely diverse purpose. The normal school is not one of primary, secondary, or tertiary grade. It is a technical school.

In the practical solution of the problem of training teachers in the normal school at St. Cloud admits to the lowest class those holding or capable of securing a second grade county certificate. The reason of this is obvious. The State, through the county superintendent, declares the candidate competent to teach, and licenses him for a year. It would be absurd for the State to declare the same person unfitted to enter upon a course of training for teaching in a school the State has established for that special purpose. If he is fit to teach before he comes to the normal school, he ought certainly to be fitted to begin to learn how to teach.

The course of study recognizes the views set forth above. The academic work is placed as far as possible in the first two years, the pedagogical in the last two. Were public opinion but far enough developed this philosophical arrangement would be the real one throughout.

The common branches thus come after the academic work, and after general psychology and methods. This enables the pupil to at least undertake the construction of a science of knowledge. The history of education, regarded as an evolution of thought rather than a chronology of devices, is carried on in conjunction with this work. The practical lessons of experience, as set forth in school economy, are brought to the student as guides to his own conduct, while the whole course is closed with several months of actual daily teaching in the model school, under a superintendence whose chief business it is to interpret for the pupil teacher the philosophy of his work and confirm his skill in the use of means. This pupil teaching thus becomes the real teaching of trained teachers, under the skilled supervision of specialists. The pupil teacher is not a pupil in a class; he is a teacher. He is not assigned to practice for 20 minutes, but teaches the entire school day, until the faculty is satisfied of his efficiency.

It is evident that all supervisory criticism must be helpful and intelligible in proportion as it is the expression of a correct science of knowledge. The formation of every judgment, the smallest fact in knowing or feeling, has its true interpretation from this point alone. In a general way it may be said that the dominant principles of the guiding metaphysic of this institution are those derivable from the science of knowledge as contained in the writings of the men above named, though to formulate such a science would transcend the limits of this outline.

From: J. P. Gordy, "Chairs of Pedagogy," in *Rise and Growth of the Normal-School Idea in the United States* (1891)

There are probably three reasons for the fact that the first institutions founded in this country for the training of teachers were for the teachers of the common schools: (1) There were no schools in which the branches taught in the common schools were taught in the thorough way in which teachers ought to know them; (2) there were very few schools where girls, whose aptitude for teaching primary-school children the New England educational reformers of half a century ago saw very clearly, could get even a good high-school education; (3) these were the schools which European countries had provided for the training of teachers. The organization and courses of study of European normal schools, particularly those of Germany, leave little doubt that the first reason decided the character of their institutions for the training of teachers.

If this is a correct account of the causes that led to the founding of normal schools in this country, it is easy to see why they did not involve, as a logical consequence in the minds of our educators, the establishment of departments of pedagogy in our colleges and universities. If institutions had existed 50 years ago in which intending teachers of elementary schools could have received the thorough instruction in the branches they were preparing to teach, it is safe to say that normal schools would not have been founded. The founders of the first normal school in this country undoubtedly saw that the preparation to teach required not only an ample and accurate knowledge of the subjects to be taught, but a knowledge of the science and art of teaching. But circumstances required them to lay so much stress on the former element that it is not strange that the public generally regarded it as the entire business of the normal school to provide it, and that they themselves came to look upon that as its chief function.

Since then the chief business of normal schools was thought to be to provide instruction in the subjects which intending teachers of elementary schools were preparing to teach, and since institutions already existed for the thorough instruction of those preparing to teach in the higher grades of schools, the perception of the necessity for the establishment of departments of pedagogy in our colleges and universities has not been general, even among educated men. If normal schools had been founded to embody the idea that a knowledge of pedagogy is of the first importance to the teacher, such departments would have been generally established long before this. And the fact that several of such departments have been established in the last 15 years we may regard as a distinct recognition of the fact that scholarship, however ample, is not all that is required of the teacher; that the history and science and art of education are matters which it is of the first importance for him to know.

From 1855 to 1873 the University of Iowa gave elementary normal instruction. In 1873 this professional instruction was modified in form and was transformed into a department of pedagogy, the first permanent department of the kind ever established in an American college.* In 1879 a professorship of pedagogy was established in Michigan University; 2 years later another in the University of Wisconsin; and 3 years later, one in the University of North Carolina, and one in Johns Hopkins University. Since then similar departments have been organized in Ottawa University, Kansas (1885); Indiana University, Cornell, New York, and Ohio University (1886), and the University of the City of New York (1887). Efforts are making to establish such departments in the University of Pennsylvania, the University of the Pacific, Ohio State University, and Vanderbilt University. Some institutions, as Columbia College, N. Y., which have no department of pedagogy, lay special stress on pedagogy in the department of philosophy. These are some of the facts which permit us to hope that a department of pedagogy will soon be recognized as an essential feature of the best colleges and universities in the country.

To give some idea of the kind of work attempted in these departments, I will quote at length from an article in "Didactics in the State University of Iowa" in the March, 1881, number of *Education*. The article was written by Dr. S. N. Fellows, the occupant of the chair of pedagogy in that institution. It is, of course, unnecessary to say that the work in these departments varies greatly in different institutions. I select the University of Iowa simply because the facts at my command enable me to give a somewhat detailed account of it. It should be said, however, that the courses of study in the department in that institution were arranged primarily to meet the wants of its graduates who filled the higher positions in the profession of teaching in the State, particularly superintendencies of schools. The question asked by the Iowa State University was: "What professional qualifications do they (the graduates spoken of above) need?" Dr. Fellows answered the question as follows:

> First. A superintendent needs a knowledge of the means and ends of education, and how to use the former so as to secure the latter. This is

---

*A department of pedagogy was organized in Brown University in 1850, but was discontinued after 5 years.

especially necessary in arranging a course of study, grading and classifying the school, assigning teachers to their respective positions, supplying all the necessary conveniences for work, and in all the management and control of the school.

Secondly. He should be able to guard parents and teachers against the baneful results of incompetent teaching. The opportunity afforded, in schoolrooms where there is no intelligent supervision, for sham and pretense is unequaled. The extent of incompetency will never be known, nor can the evil results in the characters and lives of the pupils be estimated. The superintendent should possess the ability to detect and disclose incompetency in any of its forms, and by wise counsel and influence encourage, inspire, correct, or secure the removal of teachers, as occasion may demand, and thus guard the interests and promote the welfare of all concerned.

Thirdly. He should know how to economize force. The amount of wasted energy in school work is incalculable. Waste may arise from undirected and misdirected effort, too much time given to unimportant matters, a badly arranged course of study, lack of thoroughness, irregularity, want of plan and system, improper physical conditions, lack of enthusiasm, and imperfect discipline. The superintendent should so understand the vital educational forces, their modes and laws of action, that he can overcome these and other forms of friction and waste, and obtain the best results with the least expenditure of energy. To meet these demands well he should possess an acquaintance with the order of development and laws of growth and action of the physical, mental, and moral powers; the relative importance and position of the several branches of study; the principles underlying methods so as to determine the relative value of diverse methods; the relation of physical conditions to health, study, and discipline; the fitness of competing textbooks and all the appliances necessary in the practical work of the schoolroom. Another has said that to be properly furnished for the duties of a superintendent, one needs to possess ''an exhaustive acquaintance with the literature of education, filled at present with the fruits of intense activity of master minds, and the sagacity to actualize all its golden suggestions in the school.'' Such, in brief, are some of the professional qualifications which, added to the ripest scholarship, are demanded for this, perhaps the most important and responsible position in our public-school system.

The nature, extent, relative position, and methods of instruction in didactics in this university have been determined, with the view of fitting as far as practicable, such of our alumni as engage in teaching for the work indicated above.

The following is a syllabus of our course of study, arranged more in its logical than in the chronological order pursued:

Course of Instruction in Didactics.

A. *History of education.*

I. Writers: (1) Bacon, (2) Milton, (3) Locke, (4) Rousseau, (5) Spencer.
II. Practical educators: (1) The Jesuits, (2) Ascham, (3) Sturm,

(4) Raitch, (5) Jacotot, (6) Comenius, (7) Basedow, (8) Pestalozzi, (9) Froebel, (10) Willard, (11) Mann.

B. *National systems of education.*

I. The United States: (1) City systems, (2) State systems, (3) the relation of the Federal Government to education.

II. Other nations: (1) England, (2) France, (3) Germany.

C. *Practical educational topics.*

(1) Illiteracy in the United States. (2) Relative rights of the State and the individual in regard to education. (3) Compulsory education. (4) The high-school question. (5) Industrial education. (6) Moral instruction in schools. (7) The normal-school problem. (8) Higher education of women. (9) Coeducation. (10) The kindergarten. (11) Oral instruction versus textbooks. (12) Gradation of schools. (13) Relation of psychology to didactics. (14) Waste labor in education. (15) Object teaching, its purpose and province. (16) Tenure of office of teachers.

D. *School economy.*

I. School organization: (1) Principles, aims, modes; (2) nature of a graded school; (3) courses of study; (4) reviews, nature, value, frequency; (5) examinations—kinds, frequency; (6) promotions—plans, frequency; (7) records and reports; (8) teachers' meetings; (9) criticisms— advantages, limitations, tendencies, and dangers in the graded system.

II. School management: (1) Employments: (a) Study, (b) recitation, (c) recreation. (2) Government: (a) Objects, (b) forces, (c) principles, (d) methods. (3) Physical conditions: (a) Sites, (b) ventilation, (c) light, (d) temperature, (e) exercise. (4) Moral culture: (a) Conditions, (b) limitations, (c) objects, (d) methods.

III. School supervision: (1) Ends, value, and modes of supervision. (2) The superintendent: (a) His qualifications, (b) duties, (c) his relations to teachers, pupils, parents; discipline, course of study.

E. *Principles of education.*

I. General statement: (1) The educator learns from the study of the child what and how to teach him. (2) It is what the child does that educates him.

II. The being to be educated: (1) Ends of education: (a) To develop all the faculties of the child; (b) to develop them in harmony with one another; (c) to develop them with due regard to (a) their proper order, (b) relative importance, and (c) future employment. (2) Characteristics of faculties: (a) As developed in mature mind; (b) as undeveloped germs in child's mind. (3) Development of faculties: (a) Order of development; (b) periods of development; (c) laws of growth and action. (4) The faculties classified: (a) For purpose of culture; (a^1) As to simultaneous cultivation; (b) as to their mutual relations; (c) with regard to branches taught; (d) with regard to methods of teaching. (5) Motives: (a) Nature and use of motives; (b) motives proper and improper; (c) motives adapted to each period of development. (6) Habits: (a) Nature and strength of habit; (b) kinds—physical, intellectual, moral; (c) forms—active, passive; (d) conditions and laws of growth; (e) habits to be formed in relation to each class of faculties.

III. Matter for exercise of learner's powers: (1) The branches taught: (a) The purpose and province of each; (b) their distinctive characteristics; (c) the order of their study; (d) their adaptation to purposes of culture; (e) their relative importance; (f) demand for increase of number.

IV. Methods of instruction: (1) Importance and utility of method. (2) Principles of method. (3) Tests of methods. (4) Principles of method applied: (a) To each class of faculties; (b) to periods of development; (c) to branches taught.

V. The educator: (1) His functions: (a) To provide suitable materials; (b) to stimulate pupil's activity; (c) to direct and supervise pupil's work; (d) to guide him to the formation of right habits. (2) Qualifications: (a) Personal; (b) scholastic; (c) professional. (3) Motives. (4) Responsibilities.

In this institution didactics is pursued during the senior collegiate year as an elective study.

First. It is a senior study. The knowledge acquired in preceding years contributes to the work in didactics. The collegiate seniors have a discipline and culture that enable them to grasp the principles and philosophy of education with comparative ease. As a historical fact, a large proportion of our own classes have had an experience of at least a year or two in teaching. This being the last year of study before entering permanently upon their chosen life work, they eagerly seize upon every suggestion that will be of practical use in the schoolroom. Besides, they are at the same time pursuing the study of psychology, logic, and moral philosophy, branches related so closely to didactics as to greatly assist in its study.

Secondly. It is an elective study. Only such students as intend to teach are admitted into the class. It would be a serious embarrassment if those desiring only general culture should be admitted. As a result of this provision it requires but little effort to maintain a spirit of zeal and earnest work.

Thirdly. Didactics extends as a daily exercise through the entire school year, and includes about 175 lectures, recitations, and exercises.

The methods of instruction employed are:

First. Recitations from approved text-books, with familiar oral lectures and discussions, in which the members of the class participate.

Second. Lectures by the professor and other members of the faculty.

Third. Wide and careful reading.

Under the first method, including the lectures of the professor in charge, all the subjects are considered that are enumerated in the course of study under the two last general divisions, viz: D, School economy; and E, Principles of education.

About 100 lectures and recitations are devoted to these topics.

There has recently been inaugurated a brief course of lectures by the president of the university and professors of the collegiate department, upon the subjects or branches of instruction pertaining to their respective chairs. The importance, relative positions, distinctive characteristics, and ends aimed at in teaching each branch in public schools are discussed in these lectures.

The ends secured by these lectures are:

(1) A more complete recognition by the university of the need and value of instruction in didactics.

(2) It unites the university more closely with the public schools of the State.

(3) The university becomes a more important factor in State education.

(4) The students in didactics receive the benefit of the experience and observation of the collegiate faculty.

Simultaneous with the above instruction in lectures and recitations, and occupying from one to two days of each week, the class is engaged in careful reading under the direction and supervision of the professors. The subjects thus considered are embraced in the first three general divisions of the course of study, viz: A. History of education; B, National systems of education; and C, Practical educational topics.

To illustrate the method pursued we give in detail the directions and references upon one of the subjects assigned.

Illiteracy in the United States.

Questions to guide in reading.

1. Does illiteracy exist?
2. Where does it exist? (a) Among colored or white population? (b) Among native or foreign population? (c) In manufacturing or agricultural districts? (d) In what States?
3. To what extent in each?
4. Is the ratio of illiteracy to population increasing or diminishing?
5. Relation of illiteracy to labor.
6. Relation of illiteracy to crime.
7. Relation of illiteracy to pauperism.
8. Relation of illiteracy to insanity.
9. Causes of illiteracy.

References.

1. Cyclopedia of Education.
2. Census reports, 1840, 1850, 1860, 1870.
3. Reports of Commissioner of Education for 1870, 1871, 1872, 1877.
4. Report of Massachusetts Board of Education, 1860.
5. Report of Superintendent of Public Instruction, Illinois, 1871–72.

Not only the few hundreds of volumes in the teacher's library but the whole university library is laid under contribution, and by means of the copious indexes provided, students can pursue their investigations beyond the references given. * * * The members of the class read with notebooks and pencils in hand, and the recitation hour of one day in each week is occupied in hearing their reports of progress made, with discussions thereon by the class, and the results are corrected and supplemented by the professor whenever there is need of it. It will be perceived that the above plan of reading is systematic in method, definite in aim, and economizes the time of the student.*

*For a full statement of the work done in the department of pedagogy in Michigan University see appendix to Professor Payne's "Contributions to the Science of Education."

From: "The Relation Between Theory and Practice in the
Training of Teachers" (1903), Faculty of the State Normal
University, Normal, Illinois, in *The Second Year-Book of the
National Society for the Scientific Study of Education*

INTRODUCTION.[1]

The specific problem under discussion.—Ever since normal schools were
called into existence they have had the benefit of adverse criticism. The most
helpful criticisms have always come from the really able and earnest men in
the public schools and the field of higher education, and from the progressive
men in normal-school work.

In a recent address before the National Educational Association, President
Butler of Columbia University said:

> Two generations ago it became patent to the people of this country
> that mere scholarship was not a sufficient preparation for teaching, and
> schools came into existence whose object it was to prepare teachers by a
> study of method. That was a desirable, indeed a necessary, reform, if the
> schools were to increase in efficiency beyond the point they had then
> reached. But I am clear that that movement has now gone too far, and
> that teachers of method have now become enamored of method for meth-
> od's sake. They have forgotten that method is a means and not an end,
> and their fine-spun analysis and long-continued preparation is like plac-
> ing a great, huge vestibule before a very small and insignificant house. It
> makes education wasteful in a very high degree.

Perhaps this is the most general, as well as the most serious, of all the
charges brought against the normal school. It is said to be "top-heavy" in
theory: that its courses present a great body of theory which does not find
concrete embodiment in the normal school itself nor in the actual school
work of normal teachers; it wastes its energies in striking the air.

That such charges have usually been exaggerations there is no question,
but there has always been enough truth in them to keep the schools examining the reasons for their existence and, in the light of clearer understanding,
readjusting themselves to render a maximum of substantial service. Each
individual normal school has been taking form under the pressure of its own
local environment; hence many local varieties have been produced. Today
there is not one, probably, certainly not one of the better schools, that is

1. Committee making the report: President David Felmley, Professor Manfred J.
Holmes, Miss Elizabeth Mavity.

satisfied with itself; and it is believed that comparison and discussion, and a frequent measuring of the normal school as it actually is with what it ought to be will help to promote right development and efficiency.

A specific form of the above criticism is that the theories and methods taught by the various departments are not put into practice by the student when he teaches in the training school. It has been thought that the general criticism can be met by answering this specific form of it. If the normal-school instructor holds himself responsible for understanding just what is needed, and what is practicable, in the public schools; if he remembers that his department exists only for the purpose of contributing to his student's power, resources, and skill in teaching in those schools; and if the student's teaching in the training school measures the value and tests the practicability of the instructor's work, and is its final stage—then he will abandon unpractical theory and be anxious to supervise this final stage of his own work under conditions over which he himself has at least co-operative control. Guided by this thought, more and more normal schools have been getting their training schools and normal departments organized into closer working unity.

Purpose and scope of this paper.—This paper is a report rather than a discussion, and is submitted to the Society for the Scientific Study of Education in response to the invitation to the Society's executive committee, with the hope that it will receive the critical study of really serious students of education, and thereby, through discussion and comparison, promote improvement in this decidedly unsettled problem of educational work. The report aims to show the relation between theory and practice in the training of teachers as that relation exists in the normal school. It does not assume to speak for all normal schools; but simply tries to show how one school is trying to solve the problem of the relation between theory and practice by bringing about a close and effective unity between the instruction in the normal classes and the work in the training school.

From: Levi Seeley, "The Relation of Theory to Practice in the Training of Teachers" (1903), in *The Second Year-Book of the National Society for the Scientific Study of Education*

In discussing this subject it seems to me that we should first agree upon a definition of terms. John Locke says that most of the quarrels that men engage in would never take place if they would stop to ask each other what they mean.

THEORY.

What do we mean by "theory"? There are two views of theory which may be taken, as follows:

1. That which involves a knowledge of the professional subjects necessary to the teacher. These subjects are:

a) History of education, which describes the educational movements of the past; sets forth the lives and teachings of great thinkers who have written educational works or who have been great teachers; outlines the systems and theories of education that have been promulgated; traces the advance of civilization through educational means; gives warning as to the errors of the past; and suggests new fields for future improvement and investigation.

b) Method, which treats of the natural, orderly, and systematic manner of presenting the subject-matter to the mind; or, as Kant puts it, "Method is procedure according to principles." A knowledge of method is essential to the theoretical preparation of the teacher.

c) School management, which considers school discipline, good order, proper habits, correct morals, relation of the school to the community, as well as other matters connected with the internal affairs of the school, such as promotion, classification of the school, the daily schedule of work, school incentives, etc.

d) A knowledge of the *subject-matter,* not only from the culture standpoint, but also concerning its value for the purpose of intellectual discipline. This must embrace a far broader range of material than the specific subjects that one is called upon to teach. The teacher must possess a reserve of knowledge upon which he can draw in case of need.

e) A knowledge of man. This enables the teacher to care for the physical being; it makes him acquainted with the intellectual activities and the laws

218

that govern these activities, that is, with *psychology;* it includes a knowledge of man's moral and religious nature.

f) Philosophy of education, which determines the nature, defines the limits, and states the aim of education.

These subjects set forth the general idea of the theory of education upon which there is an agreement among educators, though they may differ as to details. As there is this general agreement, a discussion of this phase of theory would hardly be profitable. I shall therefore present another view for consideration at this time.

2. This other view of theory is as follows: It contemplates the definite knowledge of each subject of the curriculum, which the pupil-teacher must know before he is ready for practice. It embraces also a knowledge of the order of arrangement of material, of essentials and non-essentials, of the method and order of presentation, of the science and art of teaching. We believe at Trenton that the young pupil-teacher must be grounded in theory in this latter sense before he can successfully practice. Therefore, ten years ago the faculty of the normal school prepared a syllabus of work for all of the subjects of the course of study and for all classes, under the title, "Studies in Plan." This appeared in the *Annual Report* of the school for the year 1893, and awakened widespread interest among educators in many parts of the world. In 1901 this work was revised and presented to the New Jersey Council of Education as Document No. 21, with the title, "A Suggestive Course of Study for Primary, Grammar, and High School Grades."[1]

This document, as its title suggests, attempts to furnish an outline of the material that should be presented in the grades included. In so far as it has succeeded in doing this, it presents a theory upon which the pupil-teachers can base their practice. With such an outline in mind, they have a definite plan by which to present any given subject that they may be called upon to teach. The student has a theory which it is his duty to put into practice. He is thus not left in doubt as to what he is to do. A great deal has been gained when the pupil-teacher is well grounded in theory. Without this the highest success in practice cannot be hoped for.

All of the work involved in the general idea of theory as presented at the outset of this paper cannot be completed before the practice must begin. The subjects enumerated are carried up to the end of the course, while the practice-work must begin a year or a year and a half earlier. But theory according to this second view may be obtained in time to be employed from the beginning of the practice work.

1. Document No. 21 may be had at the Normal School, Trenton, N.J., at a cost of 30 cents.

I shall therefore present for your consideration the outline of work in geography as a type of the theoretical work to be mastered by our student and taught in his practice-work in that subject. As I have already remarked, the document in question, from which this work is taken, includes all of the subjects of the curriculum from the beginning of the primary to the end of the high schools grades. This work will furnish a definite and specific subject for discussion and criticism by the Society.

PRACTICE.

Let us now turn our attention to the question of practice, which I would define as follows: Practice is the systematic training in the actual work of the schoolroom by means of which the novice acquires skill in performing the duties that belong to the teacher, gains confidence in his own ability successfully to perform these duties, and thus verifies the theory previously attained. The work of practice embraces three phases, namely:

1. Observation, in which the student witnesses the work of skilled teachers with pupils. The work thus witnessed must be a model of correct method and good teaching.

2. Instruction by the pupil-teachers themselves of classes of children. This is done under the direction of critic-teachers.

3. Conferences, in which, under the training-teachers, the observation work, the teaching, the lesson-plans, the discipline of the pupil-teachers are discussed, and careful instruction is given to them.

Perhaps a brief description of our organization will assist in making clear the plan of practice-teaching at Trenton and the end sought.

We have a three-years' course, each year being divided into two half-year classes denominated BI and BII, AI and AII, Sen. I and Sen. II. The work of the first year and a half is principally academic, emphasis, however, being laid upon the methods of presenting each subject. Psychology is begun in the AI class and history of education in the AII. Thus the student is gradually introduced to the professional subjects, which increase in number and scope as the course advances, while less stress is laid upon the academic work. Through this means the student becomes grounded in the idea of theory according to the second view presented, namely, that of a knowledge of the material to be taught and the plan of teaching it.[1]

He is now ready to receive the instruction in practice. This begins in the AII class and consists of observation followed by discussion and criticism. The training-teacher takes a whole division of thirty or forty students, gives

1. Illustrated by the work in geography as presented in the foregoing pages.

them preliminary instruction as to what they are to observe, and then goes with them to witness a model class-exercise. At first attention is concentrated upon one or two points—as, for example, how to hold the attention, the correlation of material, plan of the lesson, etc. A period of observation is followed by perhaps two or three days' discussion of the lesson, in which the students are closely questioned as to what they have seen, and their attention is called to what they should have seen.

Gradually more points are added for them to observe, until finally an entire model lesson is included. Then the student is required to discuss the whole lesson without any aid, except that of a general outline which the training-teacher has furnished. This completes the preliminary observation work. The students, however, are taught how to prepare the lesson-plans, which are an important feature of the work which follows. Ten weeks are employed in the foregoing, which, as the exercises are daily, would seem to be sufficient.

The second stage in practice consists in actual teaching by the novice himself. The young student, whose attitude in school has been that of a recipient of instruction, begins to grasp the idea that he has something to give, and to feel an impulse to teach. We may therefore speak of him hereafter as a pupil-teacher. During the last half of the AII class, and the whole of Sen. I, that is, three-quarters of a year, about one-third of the time of the pupil-teacher is employed in practice. Each class is divided into groups of not more than ten, who are assigned specific work. One of the group teaches a class while the others observe. This instruction is carried on in the presence of the grade-teacher, who also is a critic. The training-teacher divides his time among the various classes that are going on simultaneously. The pupil-teacher who is to conduct the lesson must present a written lesson-plan, which is criticised by both the grade- and the training-teacher. Thus every precaution is taken to insure most careful preparation for each lesson before it may be given. This serves not only as a protection to the children in the training-school, but it also instructs the young teacher how to prepare each day's work when he enters upon a permanent position.

The character of the work that the observers have done is readily discovered in the weekly conferences, where the teaching is criticised, and where indifference or inattention on the part of any member of the group will soon appear. The observation by the pupil-teachers assumes a deeper meaning than that of the previous term, for they are held to a closer account, and are, in a sense, participants of each recitation whether conducted by themselves or by a classmate. The observers are required to note the different methods employed, to see where there is originality, to discover the source of power or cause of weakness, to find out the means employed to awaken interest, to consider the matter of discipline, and to measure the work as to its logical arrangement and execution. Besides this general observation of the whole class, each pupil-teacher is encouraged to select some child and watch his progress from day to day—a practical application of the theory of child study.

At the weekly conferences the teaching done by the various pupil-teachers is considered, the other students who have been observers are invited to express themselves with greatest freedom, and all join in the discussion of the work, the training-teacher having the final word. Besides this the young teacher is expected to go to both the grade- and the training-teacher for private criticism. He thus has the advantage of the wisdom and experience of trained and competent critics, who at the same time are sympathetic in their attitude toward him, as well as just.

This work of observing, teaching, discussing, and criticising is continued until the pupil-teachers have satisfied the training-teacher that they have acquired the skill and confidence which have been pointed out as the ends to be reached. Some will succeed sooner than others, but all must continue until the result demanded has been attained, and no one can be passed to the next class or graduated until this has been accomplished.

There still remains the work of the Sen. II, the graduating class. In the meantime the study of theory in the general sense—that of psychology, history of education, school management, philosophy of education, etc.—continues, thus broadening the young novice's view, preparing him better to understand his practice, and introducing him farther into the spirit and modes of thought of the teacher.

We recognize that there remains another phase of practice-teaching to which the young teacher must be introduced. The model school, with its small classes, its full complement of grade teachers who are always present at the lessons, its splendid equipment, its ideal conditions, is quite different from the average school where a position is likely to be secured. Hence we send all of the members of the graduating class out into the state for a month's practice in the public schools. This is the culmination of their practice-work and it brings them into contact with the actual school life upon which they will enter later. Every facility is afforded them by the public-school teachers to gain experience. A final report is made to the normal school as to the character of work done. This has proved an excellent experience to our young men and women. We find that they come back from their four weeks' work with a marked gain in self-confidence and a deeper appreciation of the vocation of teaching. The principals to whom they are sent give them kindly criticism and instruction. Without cordial co-operation from the teachers of the state, a scheme of this kind would fail.

Mutual benefit to both parties also often follows. If a new teacher is needed for the succeeding year the principal has a good opportunity to judge of the merits of the one who practices with him, far better than could be afforded by correspondence or by a conference. On the other hand the pupil-teacher himself is placed on his mettle to prove that he is worthy of an invitation to a position. Thus the month's experiment often results in a satisfactory appointment. Of course four weeks' work is not sufficient to turn the novice into an experienced teacher. But it is at least a beginning under normal conditions such as no practice school can furnish. It therefore offers a kind of training that is seldom provided for in normal schools, a training which I submit is most important and highly practical.

I have thus briefly presented the idea of practice which controls at Trenton. While it is not claimed to be ideal, it will furnish some features for the consideration of the association which may be unique, and which may be studied not without profit. At least this scheme fairly harmonizes the idea of theory and practice as set forth at the beginning of this paper, and in practice our pupil-teachers secure considerable skill and confidence in the teaching and management of a class of children—and these are the ends that we understand should be sought in practice.

From: Eliphalet Oram Lyte, ''The State Normal Schools of the United States'' (1904)

CHAPTER 22.

CONTENTS.

I. Introductory—A normal school defined—Relation to State.

II. Origin of normal schools in the United States—Article in Massachusetts Magazine—Denison Olmsted at Yale College—The movement in Pennsylvania—First city training school in Philadelphia—Prof. Samuel R. Hall, New Hampshire—Rev. James C. Carter, Massachusetts—Dr. Philip Lindsley, Tennessee—Governor Clinton, New York—Governor Lincoln, Massachusetts—Rochester, N. Y.—Washington College, Pennsylvania—Rev. Charles Brooks, Massachusetts—Thomas M. Burrowes, Pennsylvania.

III. The first normal school—Founded at Lexington, Mass.—Governor Edward Everett marks out courses of study—Normal schools at Barre and Bridgewater—Courses of study—Established by public and private funds—First normal school in New York—First normal school in Pennsylvania—First normal schools in other States.

IV. General object—Courses of study—Function of the normal school.

V. Examinations and certificates—Difference in different States—Reciprocity.

VI. Schools of practice—Different names—Observation and practice—Time devoted to practice teaching—Practice work at Worcester, Mass.—Los Angeles—Cedar Falls—Value of practice work, Colonel Parker.

VII. Typical courses of study: New England normal schools—Bridgewater, Mass. Middle States normal schools—Normal College at Albany—Oswego—Millersville—New Jersey State Normal School. Middle West State normal schools—Classes of students—Dekalb, Ill.—Ypsilanti, Mich.—Colorado State Normal School. Southern States normal schools—Two classes of schools—Normal schools for white students, Alabama State Normal College; Peabody Normal College—Normal schools for colored students, Balti-

224

more—Montgomery, Ala.—Hampton Normal and Agricultural Institute—Tuskegee Normal and Industrial Institute. Pacific coast normal schools—Supply of teachers—Los Angeles, Cal.

VIII. Control of State normal schools—General control—California—Colorado — Illinois — Kansas — Maryland — Massachusetts — Minnesota—Missouri—Nebraska—New Jersey—New York—Pennsylvania—Rhode Island—South Dakota—Wisconsin.

IX. Maintenance of State normal schools—Free tuition—Normal-school fund of Wisconsin.

X. City training schools.

XI. Private normal schools.

INTRODUCTORY.

The problem of elementary education is one of the most important problems with which a free people must deal. The most important factor in this problem is the teacher. The schools designed to prepare teachers for the elementary schools of the State present questions of vital interest to all thoughtful citizens. This chapter endeavors to put into convenient form a few of the most important facts concerning the origin and present condition of the schools designated by the laws of the different States of the Union to prepare teachers for the public schools.

A normal school is a school established for the academic and professional preparation of teachers. It is a technical school, differing from academies and colleges in its objects and methods of work. The objects of the academy and college are general culture and the acquisition of knowledge; the object of the normal school is to impart culture, discipline, skill, and learning to its students for a specific and technical purpose, viz, that of fitting them to teach others. The academy and college aim to teach their students the various branches of knowledge; the normal school aims to teach its students not only the branches of knowledge, but also the processes by which the learning mind acquires knowledge and the resultant of these processes. These objects and aims distinguish normal schools from other institutions of learning and determine the courses of study in them and the methods by which the studies must be taught.

The relation of the normal school to the State is close. The State must educate the children within its borders. It must therefore establish and maintain a system of public education. The most important factor of this system is the teacher. The teacher must be educated in institutions provided by the State and under State control, if his work is to be properly done. It is consequently both a duty and a necessity for the State to found and support State normal schools. These views, which are accepted almost universally throughout the civilized world, show that the function of the normal school is peculiar, and that its responsibilities are greater than those of other educational institutions.

The Colorado State Normal School announces the following courses of study:
Outline of Work: Colorado State Normal School.

	Weeks	Periods	Term hours
SOPHOMORE			
(Requisites, 44 term hours.)			
Algebra	36	5	10
Geometry	36	5	10
English	36	4	8
Reading and gymnastics	36	3	6
Physics and biology	36	5	10
Music	36	3	6
JUNIOR			
(Requisites, 40 term hours.)			
Training school:			
1. Observation	36	1	2
2. Seminar	36	$1\frac{1}{2}$	3
3. Arithmetic	36	$1\frac{1}{2}$	3
4. Reading and physical culture	36	2	4
5. Public school art	36	3	6
Psychology	36	3	6
English and literature	36	4	8
Sloyd, domestic economy	36	2	4
Biology	36	2	4
Music	36	2	4
SENIOR			
(Requisites, 40 term hours.)			
1. Practice in teaching	36	5	10
2. Seminar	36	1	2
3. Geography	36	$1\frac{1}{2}$	3
4. History and literature	36	2	4
5. Music	36	2	4
Philosophy and history of education	36	5	10
English and literature	36	3	6
Reading and physical culture	36	$1\frac{1}{2}$	3

ELECTIVES

(Junior, 10 term hours; senior, 10 term hours.)

Electives may be selected from the following subjects or groups. The first numbers following the groups designate the number of recitations per week in each subject; the second designate the term hours.

Group 1:	Latin, German, French, Spanish, English and literature	5	10
Group II:	Anthropology, sociology, history, government	5	10
Group III:	Physiology, psychology, pedagogy	5	10
Group IV:	Physics, chemistry, physiography, biology	5	10
Group V:	Trigonometry, analytical geometry	5	10
Group VI:	Art	5	10
Group VII:	Sloyd, cooking and sewing, library handicraft	5	10
Group VIII:	Reading and physical culture	5	10
Group IX:	Kindergarten	5	10

SOUTHERN NORMAL SCHOOLS FOR WHITE STUDENTS.

There are two classes of southern normal schools: One that is intended for white students, and is modeled, as far as possible, on the best plans, scholastic and professional: and one that is intended for colored students, and in which elementary, academic, and professional training is combined with special industrial instruction. In schools of the first class the problems are much like the problems of the normal schools of other parts of the Union. In the second class the problems are distinctly special and local, and have in mind many more interests and economic needs than simply the preparation of teachers for the ordinary school, as it is the theory that these industrially trained colored normal school graduates have a larger and more important mission than simply the scholastic instruction commonly considered as the province of the elementary school. They are to give a special trend to the industrial activities of the people among whom they labor, and are to become leaders in all progress, intellectual and economic.

The *Alabama State Normal College* was established as a State normal school in 1873, with a four years' course of study. The course in pedagogics proper covers a period of three years. The work of the second year is largely practice work. In the third and fourth years practice and theory are combined. In the second year the aim is to teach pupils to prepare and give lessons as regards matter, method, and manner. The lessons are written, submitted to the teacher for correction, and given to classmates, who endeavor to act the part of the pupils for whom the lesson is intended, and who afterwards present criticisms to be reviewed by the teacher. In the third year the philosophy of methods is discussed.

There are two courses, the advanced and the professional. The advanced, or regular course, occupies four years. The professional course requires but one year, and is intended for teachers of experience and graduates of high schools and colleges who do not wish to take the regular course.

The course of study of the *Louisiana State normal school* covers three years of eight months each, as follows:

First year.—Arithmetic, English grammar and composition, geography, history of United States, physiology and hygiene, penmanship and book-keeping.

Second year.—Advanced arithmetic, algebra, rhetoric, English literature, zoology, botany, general history, psychology, civil government, and history of education.

Third year.—Geometry, English literature, physics, chemistry, psychology, ethics, pedagogy, methods of teaching, school management, and practice teaching in the practice school.

In the practice school, consisting of four primary grades, the usual branches of such grades, including drawing, vocal music, and calisthenics, are taught by the most approved modern methods. These grades are in charge of trained normal graduates and form as indispensable an adjunct to a normal school as is the workshop to a school of practical mechanics or the hospital to a medical college. For an hour each day the members of the senior normal class, divided into groups, are required to give lessons in these grades. This work is not intended to be mere experiment or observation, but bona fide teaching under the direction of trained specialists. Each student teacher is required to prepare the lesson beforehand in all its details, according to a plan devised by the training teacher. At the expiration of the practice hour the members of the senior class again assemble in their class rooms, when their work is subjected to the criticism of their classmates and of their training teacher, who point out errors both in government and in instruction. It is held by the faculty that no young teacher can go through this daily experience for months without acquiring much of that presence of mind, that self-control, that fertility of resources, and that ready knowledge of methods and devices which give the surest guaranty of success, not only in the school room, but in any other field of human endeavor.

The *Peabody Normal College, Nashville, Tenn.*, has occupied a prominent position among the normal schools of the South. It is named for the distinguished philanthropist, George Peabody, who established a large fund to be used for educational purposes in the Southern States. It has been supported by the Peabody fund and the State of Tennessee. The late Dr. J. L. M. Curry, for many years the general agent of the Peabody fund, says of this school:

Giving to all the Southern States the benefit of improved normal instruction widened the college from a local State institution into a college for the South.

And again:

In establishing the college there was no intent to favor Tennessee above other Southern States. The training of teachers for all the Southern States was the object. As the munificence of Mr. Peabody was the stimulus and the means for establishing systems of public schools in the States, so the normal college has pointed the way and aroused the effort for the organizing of the more local but indispensable normal schools.

Normal Schools for Colored Students.

A normal school for colored teachers was opened in Baltimore in 1869. Its income is derived partly from a State appropriation and partly from tuition fees. The instruction given in this school is mainly if not wholly academic.

The State normal school for colored students at Montgomery, Ala., was established in 1874, by the State of Alabama. It was the first and for many years the only school supported by a Southern State for the higher education of the negro. Its board of trustees consists of the governor and State superintendent of education and six prominent citizens of the State. It is strictly a State school, owned and controlled by the State, and receiving no contributions from individuals. While designed primarily for a normal school, it has also industrial departments, in which carpentry, blacksmithing, wagon making, printing, cooking, sewing, and dressmaking are taught. A small appropriation was made by a recent legislature for agricultural science, and quite an interest has been developed, especially among the girls, in kitchen-gardening and floriculture.

The *Hampton Normal and Agricultural Institute* is situated in Elizabeth City County, in Virginia, on the Hampton River, overlooking Hampton Roads. The school, consisting of sixty buildings, stands on a plantation of 185 acres, the site of Hampton Hospital, one of the military hospitals of the civil war. The Hampton Institute was opened in April, 1868, under the auspices of the American Missionary Association, with Gen. S. C. Armstrong in charge. In 1870 it was chartered by a special act of the general assembly of Virginia, and thus became independent of any association or sect. It is not, as is often supposed, a Government or a State school, but is a private corporation controlled by a board of seventeen trustees, representing different denominations, no one of which has majority. Started for the purpose of providing a practical education for the children of the ex-slaves, the school, in 1878, opened its doors to Indian pupils, and has since that time devoted itself chiefly to the development of negro and Indian youth.

The aim of the Hampton Institute was stated in 1870, by its founder, General Armstrong, in the following words:

> To train selected youth who shall go out and teach and lead their people, first by example by getting land and homes; to give them not a dollar that they can earn for themselves; to teach respect for labor; to replace stupid drudgery with skilled hands, and to these ends to build up an industrial system for the sake not only of self-support and intelligent labor but also for the sake of character.

It sustains the following departments: Normal department, domestic art and domestic science departments, agriculture department, business department, Armstrong and Slater Memorial trade school, boys' productive industries, department of domestic work, medical department, military department, and missionary department.

In an article in the Philadelphia Press under date of April 23, 1904, Talcott Williams says of this school:

> In its students to-day it is beginning to reap the fruits of its own labor. Over the twenty years in which I have seen the institute, the advance in the personnel of the attendance is immeasurable. They were once half-grown young men and women physically, dulled by toil and aflame with desire for education. They are to-day students like other students elsewhere, alert, intelligent, full of spirit, and coming here so much better trained that the standard has advanced in a decade nearly two years. Their training leaves them with trades, with model training in the work of teaching and of agriculture and with disciplined characters. The "Hampton man" is coming to be recognized all over the South. The leading missionary in central Africa is a Hampton graduate; so is the leading civil engineer in Liberia. Hampton's Indian graduates are being elected to office in the West in white communities.

The *Tuskegee Normal and Industrial Institute* was established by an act of the legislature of Alabama, passed in 1880, and was opened in a church July 4, 1881. The normal course includes the following branches with others: Algebra, arithmetic, bookkeeping, botany, civil government, drawing, geography, geometry, grammar, history, literature, mental and moral philosophy, music, physiology, physics, political economy, reading, rhetoric, spelling, and theory and practice of teaching. The theory and practice of teaching is one of the eight subjects pursued by the senior class. The industrial department has advanced to a high state of efficiency. It is subdivided into more than twenty-five industries, including the following branches:

Agriculture, brickmaking, carpentry, printing, blacksmithing, tinsmithing, shoemaking, harness making, sewing, laundry and sawmill. Tuition is free. The price of board, including washing, lights, fuel, etc., is $8 per month. Students are given an opportunity to earn $2 or $3 a month, so that with a good outfit of clothing the sum of $50 is sufficient to carry an industrious student through the school year of nine months. The appropriation of $2,000 annually made by the State legislature at first was increased in 1883 to $3,000 annually. The whole State appropriation is used to pay tuition; for all other expenses the school looks to its friends, North and South. This school under the leadership of Booker T. Washington is doing a remarkable work for the colored people of the South. It is a fact that has an important bearing upon the work of the institute that all its officers, teachers, and employees belong to the negro race and that the numerous buildings belonging to the institute have been erected in large part by the students.

Part Three

Pedagogy in the Academy

It is not, as is usually thought, political stances which determine people's stances on things academic, but their positions in the academic field which inform the stances they adopt on political issues in general as well as on academic problems. The margin of autonomy which ultimately devolves to the specifically political sources of the production of opinions then varies according to the degree to which the interests directly associated with their position in the academic field are directly concerned or, in the case of the dominant agents, threatened.

—Pierre Bourdieu, *Homo Academicus*

To treat the science of pedagogy as a matter of secondary concern is fatal, because its value is far from being universally conceded. . . . normal departments and departments of pedagogy should be in charge of men of first rate ability. Until the just claims of the science of pedagogy are universally recognized, it is more than doubtful whether chairs of pedagogy will not do more harm than good when filled by men of ordinary ability, whose feeble and commonplace treatment of their subject fails to show the necessity of such departments.

—J. P. Gordy, *Rise and Growth of the Normal-School Idea*

I AM a teacher and pride myself upon that title. I rather object to being described as "an educator"; the word is new-fangled and suggests, like "pedagogue," someone more interested in how to do it than in doing it, one admirable in the criticism of the work of other people, not quite so successful in his own—when he does any. . . . the glory of our profession is in the process, the art, the very subtle craft of teaching.

—Felix E. Schelling, *Pedagogically Speaking*

The documents in part three chronicle my attempts to reconstruct and understand the debate about pedagogy's nature, and consequently its rights to academic citizenship, that took place in the last two decades of the nineteenth century. The terms of the debate were whether pedagogy could be defined as *art* or *science*—a consequential distinction, as we shall see.

In part two, I call attention to some early pedagogues' reliance on *instinct, tact,* and *inspiration*—educational skills that, they trusted, religion would provide for faithful teachers. Some of the documents in part three, especially

233

excerpts from conceptualizations of pedagogy as art, offer *secular* versions of that *faith*. However, in the 1880s and the 1890s, within the university milieu, the appeal to some version of super-natural and super-rational forces that would assist teachers and learners, whether intentionally or not, seem to have been made less to exalt pedagogy than to assert its superfluousness, at least as an academic discipline. (For a similar argument, although for the teaching of style, see Flannery 1995.) In opposition to this version of pedagogy, another version emerged, pedagogy as science, wherein science was appealed to in order to justify pedagogy's disciplinary status. Within this latter version, the operative terms were not instinct, tact, and inspiration, but rather *habits of attention, methods* (which was to become a highly contested term and concept), theories of *concentration,* and *recitation.*[1]

Although not all educators were unabashedly optimistic about the contributions that science could make to pedagogy (see, for example, Tompkins), the most widely circulated critique of pedagogy was one that derided, and totalized, its move toward science. Felix E. Schelling's invectives against "educators," "pedagogues," and "pedants"—all negative and interchangeable terms for him—are representative of arguments that came to be constructed, especially in the humanities, because of and against the supposed ascendancy of "scientific education": in almost every one of the speeches collected in *Pedagogically Speaking: Essays and Addresses on Topics More or Less Educational* (1929), Schelling, John Welsh Centennial Professor of English at the University of Pennsylvania, cannot refrain from telling the story of how educators and pedagogues had cheapened the *liberal* and *unmercenary* love of knowledge that universities should foster. The documents in this section, as well as those in the previous ones, should make it possible to foreground the theoretical and institutional determinants for Schelling's construction of pedagogy, and to assess the extent to which that construction was, and might still be, representative of English departments' positions, and why.

To retrace this debate is to realize that as either the art or the science version of pedagogy got to be proposed, inevitably, each version called attention to the other, named the other, even as it tried to contest it, thus marking the other as an essential part of its own identity. I am tempted to read this conceptual and linguistic paradox as an implicit commentary on the nexus that pedagogy posits between the art and the science, the practice and the theory of teaching, between the scholarly knowledge of a subject matter and the training in how to teach it. But knowing that the nexus has been (and that, with various justifications, it continues to be) pulled asunder, I nevertheless suggest that we consider the possibility that the reduction of pedagogy's conceptualization to either the science/theory or the art/practice of teaching, and the adoption of either version by both its proponents and critics, might be the result of oppositional stances necessitated by particular circumstances. In other words, to understand pedagogy's contested position within the Academy, we need to consider, as Bourdieu suggests in the first epigraph to this section, the extent to which the political, academic, and theoretical stances adopted by both its proponents and critics were (are) inflected and determined by their positions in the academic field.

Read side by side, over, or through earlier documents, the documents in this last section raise compelling questions about the academy's schismatic constructions of pedagogy. Insofar as these documents suggest that in pedagogy's "academic" past, institutional, programmatic, and theoretical differences have been systematically deployed to inhibit a necessary and penetrating exploration of crucial questions about the teaching of teaching, these documents might contribute to articulating and circulating a much needed cautionary tale.

In the last two decades of the nineteenth century, in some U.S. universities, pedagogy came to be deemed a subject worthy of university status (cf. W. T. Harris 1882; C. H. Judd 1909; Cremin 1961, especially 168ff.). But within less than two decades, professors of pedagogy, who in the beginning had been mostly housed in departments of philosophy and psychology, lost status; in many cases, they became targets of caustic criticism, even of ridicule (see Schelling). Geraldine Jonçich Clifford and James W. Guthrie suggest that such rapid deterioration was to be expected, since in most institutions the "recognition" of pedagogy had been nothing more than an opportunistic move:

> American universities established chairs of pedagogy not in deference to the idea of a science of education nor in imitation of a few German universities which had pioneered chairs in education. It was not to create a discipline of education nor because such noted German intellectuals as Immanuel Kant and Wilhelm Dilthey taught courses on *Paedagogik* in international centers of learning. Rather they launched their initially modest ventures in professional education because it directly served their *own* interests. (1988, 123)[2]

As "a particularly instructive example of university self-interest at work," Clifford and Guthrie cite the not unique case of Harvard University—a case to which I return later.[3]

In contrast to Clifford and Guthrie, Merle Borrowman (1971) constructs a less factious account of pedagogy's entry into the university.[4] He argues that for a brief period, essentially the decade of the 1880s, pedagogy as "the scientific study of education" achieved considerable status and attracted widespread support in the new social science departments of such private universities as Chicago, Clark, and Johns Hopkins, and in such state universities as Michigan and Wisconsin: "scholars and administrators from these universities joined the debates in the meetings and committees of the NEA and encouraged the development of university schools of education" (75). Such felicitous circumstances, however, soon deteriorated. In fact, "once the schools of education were established, scholars from other social sciences and philosophical departments tended to withdraw or to be driven from the study of educational institutions and practices as such" (75).

While Johns Hopkins, Chicago, Clark, and later Stanford continued to support scholarship as the dominant professional method and consequently saw no need for pedagogy, places like Harvard, Teachers' College at Columbia, and the state universities of Michigan, Wisconsin, and California did not present a united front. In these institutions

> sharp divisions occurred between those who perceived themselves as professional scholars and those who took pride in being professional schoolmen. In most of the state universities, some of whose schools of education antedated the emergence of the new research-oriented universities, the professionalism was that of the schoolmen from the beginning; the professors of education were largely recruited from among the successful practitioners. (75)

Clifford and Guthrie, as well as Borrowman, make it possible to conclude that discussions of the identity and the future of pedagogy came to be entangled with pre-existent debates, which prevented a productive interrogation and assessment of it.[5] Generally speaking, participants in the debate seemed to use the occasion or the possibility of pedagogy's entrance into the university to reiterate old positions.[6]

In a 1912 entry for the *Cyclopedia of Education,* E. N. Henderson gave credence to and reinscribed the most commonly adduced reasons for pedagogy's presumed inadequacy as a university field of study: its normal school roots, too weak for the university soil. Here is a part of Henderson's account:

> [Pedagogy] was felt to be essentially a normal school subject, concerned especially with the problem of the elementary school and "rule-of-thumb" methods of teaching the subjects of its curriculum. The specialists of the universities were prone to regard the power to teach as due primarily to knowledge of subject matter. In addition to this they admitted the importance of natural attitude and of experience, but rejected the efficacy of methods. Many ridiculed outright the

pretensions of "pedagogy," and resented its injection into the curriculum of
higher education. . . .

Much of the criticism of pedagogy as a university subject had, doubtedless,
validity, and in consequence it was necessary to modify and expand its content in
order to secure for it a permanent foothold and equality of rank. To mark the
change there grew up a tendency to substitute the word EDUCATION for PEDA-
GOGY as a title for the department and for professorships. Thus the term "pedagogy" has to a considerable extent passed out of vogue. The newer "education"
differs from the older "pedagogy" in two respects. First, it includes far more than
method in teaching and school management; second, it is more scientific.

In Henderson's minihistory of pedagogy, rather than being marked as the
contexts wherein the early articulations and practices of pedagogy took
place, normal schools are practically tainted by their association with pedagogy. And vice versa. One of the reasons adduced for this mutually discredit-
ing association is that pedagogy, as a normal school subject, was *essentially*
concerned with "the problem of elementary school." To make such a claim,
and on such a claim to dismiss both the work of normal schools and the
function of pedagogy, is to be oblivious to the fact that the normal school
student, the subject who was learning how to teach, though very young, had
matriculated from elementary school a few years back. Though at sixteen,
the normal school student was not so much older than the older common
school students, he or she was *not* an elementary school student. Such confusion, caused by collapsing *the teaching of teaching* into *teaching,* makes invisible the very student normal schools had been founded to train: the normal
school student and future common school teacher. This constructed invisibility—one that too often marks the work of proponents as well as of critics of
pedagogy—makes it possible to bypass the most fundamental and demanding
aspect of the teaching of teaching: a teacher's possibility and responsibility to
test and to revise his or her theories of teaching and learning in light of the
understanding of those theories that his or her students, as current learners
and future teachers, make possible.

To mark the fact that pedagogy in the academy had become increasingly
more complex than it had been in normal schools, to call attention to how
the inclusion of theories of psychology, sociology, measurement, and adoles-
cence made it a different field of study, pedagogy was renamed *education.*
(See Emile Durkheim's (1958) differentiation between *education* and *pedagogy.* See also W. T. Harris's introduction to Gabriele Compayré's *History of
Pedagogy* (1971) and the Italian, German and Brazilian dictionary entries on
"pedagogy.") That terminological substitution, I suggest, was simultaneously
a symptom and a cause of a curious and consequential oversight: as university

professors looked away both from normal schools and their "discipline," and avoided scrutinizing the reasons for those institutions' shortcomings, they ended up essentializing rather than historically contextualizing them. One of the paradoxical and unfortunate results of their "oversight" was that they replicated—at a higher level and in disguised form—some of the failures for which they had chastized normal schools (see Albert Bushnell Hart 1883).[7]

But let us listen to some of the voices in the debate.

In *Contributions to the Science of Education* (1886), William Payne attempted to establish "a *rational art* of educating" (emphasis mine), one based on discussion of principles and doctrines rather than on "methods" given or used without a criterion. Implicit in Payne's definition of pedagogy is a critique of what it had been reduced to within the context of normal schools, *and* the promise of an effective remedy.[8] Both in *Contributions* (1886), and in a later text, *The Education of Teachers* (1901), the target of Payne's critique is the "natural" or "inspirational" *art* of educating, an art that in "The Study of Education in the University of Michigan" in *Contributions* he identifies as the "constitutional function" of those institutions—normal schools—from which he intends to disassociate himself:

> In the education of teachers . . . the university and the normal school have independent spheres of activity. . . . so long as both schools remain true to their constitutional function, there can be no valid basis for competition or rivalry.
>
> In what intelligible and respectable sense can a university be said to compete with a secondary school, or a secondary school with a university? An apology might be demanded for dwelling on such truisms, had not some recent events shown that broad distinctions sometimes escape notice. (1886, 339)[9]

If indeed "in the education of teachers . . . the university and the normal school have independent spheres of activity," why did Payne feel he had to invest so much in defining that independence, and to a certain extent, in redimensioning normal schools' function?

Payne's appointment as first Professor of the Science and the Art of Teaching at the University of Michigan was publicly celebrated as a demonstration of that university's progressiveness in acknowledging that "in a society like ours, whose security depends upon educated intelligence, there is no more important function and service than that of teaching the teachers," a work for which Payne was recognized as being "especially fitted" (*Harper's Weekly*, July 26, 1878). However, as intimated by "The Study of Education in the University of Michigan" (see the appendix to *Contributions*), an essay shot through with palpable defensiveness about the reputation of the study of education at the university, that position was difficult to fill. The extent to which that defensiveness inflects his theorization of the difference between pedagogy and education is worth considering.

Payne's denunciation of the mechanical, the empirical, the practical, led him to valorize *exclusively* the theoretical. He chose to teach only theory, leaving it up to his students to turn theory into practice. Paradoxically, implicit in his position are two of the assumptions most consistently invoked to dismiss "the important function and service . . . of teaching the teachers." Insofar as knowledge of theory is knowledge of a subject matter, in fact, his position can be invoked to support the contention that knowledge of subject matter is appropriate and sufficient preparation for teaching it. At the same time, insofar as he reduces pedagogy to that aspect of education that has to do with the classroom practices of common and normal schools but not of university classrooms, his position also can be invoked to confirm the assumption that the teaching of teaching deserves no place in the academy (see Felix Schelling, for example).

In 1891, whether or not in direct rebuttal to Payne, Josiah Royce, a philosopher and professor of philosophy at Harvard University, at the request of Nicholas Murray Butler, wrote an essay titled "Is There a Science of Education?" for the first issue of *Education Review*.[10] Like Payne's, Royce's articulation of education, as he named it, accrues considerable explanatory power when examined and assessed against the specific circumstances within which it was composed.

1891 was the year that Paul Hanus, a professor of pedagogy (such was his title) at the State Normal School of Greeley, Colorado, was appointed by President Charles W. Eliot and the fellows of Harvard College as Assistant Professor of the History and Art of Teaching (note the title's wording). Hanus's appointment marked the establishment of the Department of Education at Harvard University, which was later to develop into that institution's prestigious Graduate School of Education (1920). However, that may not have been the intention of President Eliot, who apparently had engineered Hanus's appointment "to preclude the appearance of a coeducational 'high normal school' in Massachusetts to train college graduates as high school teachers" (Clifford and Guthrie 1988, 131).[11]

In *Adventuring in Education*, an autobiographical account of his "progress" from the normal school to the university culture, Hanus records, with no apparent trace of bitterness, his increasing realization of the pervasive skepticism and contempt that characterized most academics' view of education.[12] About the title he was given, he noted it limited the activities of the department to considering the *art of teaching*, thus *leaving out* the more fundamental and the broader problems of education (the science of teaching).

Hanus was quite aware that most college and university professors of that day objected to the elevation of education to university status; but he was confident enough in his beliefs to discern that what they really objected to were *their own* constructions of it. What they chose to think was that education

> consisted *of necessity* of instruction in methods of teaching; and most of them did not believe that such instruction had any value. The dictum, "Teachers are born, not made," was both implicit and explicit in their consideration of the subject. They ignored the fact that "born" teachers do not happen more frequently than "born" lawyers or doctors or college professors or members of any profession, and that, human beings being what they are and the choice of the profession being free to all, men and women of every profession must develop by training what native ability they have for the work they elect to do. (1937, 111)

At Harvard, among the proponents of the "art" view of pedagogy were such illustrious and influential colleagues of Hanus as Josiah Royce and William James. During the hiring process and at least the first few years Hanus spent at Harvard, both were entrusted by President Eliot with the responsibility to define education *for* their younger colleague.[13] Hanus never openly criticized them, neither did it occur to him to speculate why James and Royce defined education in those terms.[14]

In order to foreground and to disrupt the tradition of pedagogy that James's and Royce's view on the subject can be said to have institutionalized, and because the hold of that tradition rests on *not asking radical questions* about its theoretical base and its intellectual and practical implications, it is important to formulate and to engage some of the questions that Hanus, given the precariousness and powerlessness of his position vis-à-vis Eliot, could or would not raise. In "Is There a Science of Education?" (1891) Royce affirmed his desire to "strengthen the interest of teachers in the theoretical aspects of their profession" (102). But by valorizing the natural, the instinctive, the artistic knowledge of a teacher, he helped to disseminate that conception of education that invalidates both the need for and the possibility of the theoretical. In his definition of education, Royce relied entirely on Wilhelm Dilthey's argument, which rejected not so much the feasibility of *a* science of education, as the feasibility of *a specific science of education* based on the assumption of the universality of human nature and an agreed-upon determination of the end of education as the highest moral perfection of the child. As valid arguments against *the* science of education, Royce deployed Dilthey's insistence on the variability of human nature and on the impossibility to reach an agreement in regard to a moral system that would define the end of education.

Though Royce's conceptualization of education as an art was marked by reflexivity and complex theoretical understanding, the debate about education (pedagogy) in the academy, or what's remembered of it, was cast in such reductive terms that his advocacy for the theorization of a fruitful dialectical relationship between art and science got to be ignored. Royce *did* recognize that teachers needed "scientific training for the calling" because their instinct, if unchastened by science, could lead them to blind self-confidence. However, his participation in the debate seems mostly to have been reduced to a few catch phrases, phrases that irrevocably position him on the art side of the debate: "True pedagogy is an art"; "There is no 'science of education' "; "The divine skill of the born teacher's instincts." In truth, his objection to *a* science of education was qualified in the following terms: "There is no 'science of education' that will not need constant and vast adaptation to the needs of this teacher or of that, constant modification in the presence of the live pupil, constant supplementing by *the divine skill of the born teacher's instincts*" (1891, 22, emphasis added). But although Royce's objection to education as a science was qualified, part of that qualification is itself in need of questioning. What becomes of instruction in a system like Royce's, which sets up the difference between a good and no-so-good teacher in terms of the amount of "divine intervention"?

If Royce was heard, William James had an even larger audience, both inside and outside the university. His book, *Talks to Teachers on Psychology; and to Students on Some of Life's Ideals,* is a collection of public lectures he had been asked to give to Cambridge teachers by the Harvard corporation. In *Talks to Teachers* he powerfully contributed to advancing the view of education as an art among future normal school teachers and their teachers, directly, and among university teachers, indirectly.

As he addressed the teachers who were his immediate audience, he carefully and repeatedly left no doubt—and rightly so—about the fact that psychology did not "contain" pedagogical formulas:

> I say . . . that you make a great, a very great mistake, if you think that psychology, being the science of the mind's laws, is something from which you can deduce definite programmes and schemes and methods of instruction for immediate classroom use. Psychology is a science, and teaching is an art; and sciences never generate art directly out of themselves. An intermediate inventive mind must make the application, by using its originality. (1899, 7–8)

James's didactic tone here covers over a number of assumptions that beg to be questioned. Why should one expect to deduce from psychology (or any other science) "*definite* programmes and schemes and methods of instruction for *immediate* classroom use"? What does this assumption reveal about what James believed to be teachers' educational needs? The documents in part two remind us of times when normal schools, under pressure to produce enough teachers to meet the demands of common schools, constructed teachers' needs and teacher preparation as "something definite and of immediate use." These documents also suggest how under that pressure the "something definite and of immediate use" gets to be further simplified into sets of tips, or rules that are meaningless apart from the theories in which they are grounded. Some textbooks for normal school students produced and published around the time of James's lectures also record simplified conceptualizations of pedagogy (see Putnam 1895; White 1886 and 1901). But these simplifications should not be read as an index of normal school students' constitutional intellectual inferiority nor of pedagogy's deficiency. These simplifications might instead be more profitably read, for example, as warnings against the consequences for education of the intellectual shortcuts made by educators at times when the demand for teachers exceeds their supply. That and why the history of teacher training should have endlessly reinscribed, rather than adequately attended to, this move toward simplification are issues that deserve inquiry.

Given the fact that within James's philosophical system, "teaching" could not be taught, something was needed to justify teaching and the professional preparation of teachers that he had been entrusted with. Not surprisingly, that something was an "additional endowment" that no theory or method could foster. For Royce, and for many pedagogues before him, the additional endowment came from divine intervention. James constructs a secular version of it.

A science only lays down lines within which the rules of the art must fall, laws which the follower of the art must not transgress; but what particular thing he shall positively do within those lines is left exclusively to his own *genius*. . . . To know psychology . . . is absolutely no guarantee that we shall be good teachers. To advance to that result, we must have an additional endowment altogether; a happy *tact* and *ingenuity* to tell us what definite things to say and do when the pupil is before us. The science of psychology, and whatever science of general pedagogics may be based on it, are . . . much like the science of war. Nothing is simpler or more definite than the principles of either. In war, all you have to do is to work your enemy into a position from which the natural obstacles prevent him from escaping if he tries to; then to fall on him in numbers superior to his own, at a moment when you have led him to think you far away; and so, with a minimum to exposure of your own troops, to hack his force to pieces, and take

the remainder prisoners. . . . *Divination* and *perception,* not psychological pedagogics or theoretical strategy, are the only helpers here. (8–11; emphasis added)

James's theory of learning, a brilliant investigaton of the faculties of imitation and emulation, interest, repetition, and memory, presupposes a ground-
edness in a cultural milieu where these faculties have been *socially* cultivated
for so long as to *appear* natural "habits" (see Calvin Stowe, in Barnard 1851,
123–50). But what happens outside of such a milieu? What happens when a
student has not yet developed those habits and a teacher has at her or his
disposition insufficient time to cultivate them? At this time, I think, tracking,
grouping, labelling, and categorizing of students and simplified constructions
of the work of teachers "happen." At this time, teaching declares itself as
unteachable.

James used the metaphor of war to expose the intrinsic powerlessness of
the "science of psychology and whatever science of general pedagogics may
be based on it." Significantly, however, his divination/perception theory is
powerless as well, unless the seeds of what makes an individual's act of divination and perception possible are already there.[15]

I am not trying to suggest that William James, as an educator, was insensitive to his students' culture. Or that he was an ineffective teacher. What I am
trying to point out are the potentially exclusionary and elitist consequences
of his theory of teaching.[16]

In *A Stroll with William James,* Jacques Barzun says that in spite of his success as a teacher, James thought of teaching as "an unnatural act" (1983,
277). Barzun writes:

> He observed, as others have done, that every September he would return to
> the classroom in trepidation and with his mind in a blank. Like other born teach-
> ers—persons whose grasp of the subject is matched by an intuitive knowledge
> of the individual minds before them—he doutless felt that teaching is an invasion
> of privacy, a meddling with a stranger's self-development. (277)

What is it that James considered so unnatural about teaching? I think the
answer is obvious: a *born teacher's* attempts to teach others to teach what
he himself could not teach, his grasp of the subject being *intuitive.* And what
is problematic about this theory of teaching? Clearly *not* a teacher's intuition—a much needed and much valued quality. Rather, the problem lies in
an uncritical reliance on intuition to the exclusion of an equally much needed
though less valued reflexivity on how individual minds grasp a concept or a
subject—a reflexivity that Barzun suggests would not only hamper a born
teacher's intuition, and creativity, but would also feel like an invasion of pri-

vacy.[17] The extent to which this can become a self-serving argument is, I think, obvious enough. (See Calvin Stowe on this subject, in part two.)

The "pedagogy as art" argument receives a carefully reasoned rebuttal in Arnold Tompkins's *The Philosophy of Teaching.* Though he writes of his work that it is "restricted to the *application* of philosophic principles to the teaching process" (emphasis added), his conceptualization of *application* does not suggest a teacher's uncritical dependance on methods. From this point of view, Tompkins complicates Payne's critique of methods as well as Royce's and James's critiques of "pedagogy as science."[18]

Whereas Payne moves away from practice and elevates theory as the beginning and the end of a teacher's education, Tompkins suggests returning to practice as the site and the means to test and to exert pressure on theory. Whereas Royce and James argue that teaching is unteachable, Tompkins theorizes "the essential nature and laws of the teaching process" in ways reminiscent of Calvin Stowe's reflexive conceptualization of pedagogy.

No less than Payne's language or Royce's or James's, Tompkins's language relays his position on and evaluation of what the education of teachers had become: "Dignity of work does not depend on what one does, but on being consciously controlled, in the doing, by universal law. The teacher who is conscious only of the individual process before him, is on the lowest possible plane of unskilled labor; he is the slave of recipes and devices" (1894, xi). Not insensitive to the fact that Aristotle, Kant, Hegel, and Spencer might at first "seem remote from the immediate work of the teacher," he stresses nevertheless that such remoteness is not a result of philosophy itself, but of *how* philosophy is taught:

> We harm ourselves and degrade our work in holding philosophy to be of another world; that the philosophy of education is one thing, and the practice of education another thing; that the philosophy of education belongs to the professional philosophizer on great educational problems, rather than to the day-laborer in the vineyard. It is said that philosophy can bake no bread, but that she can secure to us God and immortality. This ought to be sufficient. But she can bake bread, and must do so or miss God and immortality. To secure heaven she must mix with the daily affairs of earth; and while searching out God and immortality, must bring counsel and comfort to the day-laborer in the school-room. (xi–xii)

In Tompkins's system, terms and concepts pivotal to intellectually challenging constructions of pedagogy are recharged with the power that simplified constructions had sapped from them. Science, we are reminded, cannot provide generalizations that exactly fit the concrete case: "The individuals brought into scientific system retain their individuality. . . . In fact, it would not be a science without such differences. In order to have a science, the general fact, or law, must be seen as manifesting itself in diversity of individuals" (ix).

"Divine skill," a "teacher's instinct," and "tact" are invested with greater germinant power and breadth of application when guided and made discernible by a science of education that is simultaneously attentive to general laws and to individual cases (ix). "Knowledge of subject matter" is proposed not as an end in itself but as a means that provides teachers with the flexibility necessary for them to focus intensely on their pupils' thinking of or through the subject matter rather than on their own efforts to recall that subject matter. "The teacher must be conscious of the process of the pupil in knowing the object in the act of producing that process. . . . *The difference is between thinking the object and thinking the process of thinking the object*" (5, emphasis added).

According to Tompkins, philosophy, as the base for such a science of education, has a lot to offer teachers: it can provide them with the means of arduously yet safely navigating between the Scylla of pedantry and the Charybdis of genial improvisation. Teaching, then, is "a conscious process having three elements: (1) consciousness of the mental experience in the act of producing it, (2) of the means of stimulating the experience on the pupil, and (3) of the value, or purpose, of the experience in the unfolding life of the pupil. . . . The subjective process above described is not teaching till its counterpart is realized in the objective process of the recitation" (9).

Recitation is another term or concept that Tompkins's work might help us reclaim, though we might want to call it *discussion*. Tompkins's construction of recitation is organically connected to his theoretical rejection of the mind as a "receptacle" and of learning as "receiving and retaining something foreign to the self" (2). As he writes about what teachers ought to look for as they observe a recitation, he offers teachers of teachers a frame through which they can be attentive to how they teach others to teach:

> The thing noted first in order of time, and first as logical condition, is the external means employed by the teacher; such as directions, questions, statements, illustrations, etc. The second element in time, and in logical relation, is the experience produced; and the last is the Good resulting to the learner. But the process in the mind of the teacher has a reverse order. The good of the child must be first in mind; then, and not before, the experience necessary to that good may be considered; and the experience to be produced necessarily precedes in thought the stimulus to that experience. (9)

Charles McMurry's and Frank McMurry's *The Method of the Recitation* advances yet another view of methods and practical work. In the introductory paragraph of their text, the McMurrys suggest what they perceive to be the reasons for the long-standing dispute about methods among teachers, and offer *their method* as a constructive solution.

It is clear that their work as theorists of pedagogy is to a large extent determined by and in opposition to theories and practices of teaching whose dissemination had apparently led, through progressive simplifications, to widespread skepticism among scholars and teachers of "anything like a definite science of education."[19]

> The very sciences upon which pedagogy claims to be based, psychology and ethics, lie as much in the field of controversy as pedagogy itself. In the midst of this endless variety and function in the theory and practice of teaching, it is not strange that many educated people, even teachers, take a sceptical attitude toward scientific method, and regard each person as a law unto himself.
>
> This tendency to discredit a science of education is indicated by our use of the term method. There is scarcely a more common word in the teaching profession, and it is frequently employed in the plural form, a partial admission not of one and only one right method, but that their number is legion. Also some of the most common watchwords of our profession point in the same direction, "Freedom and originality," "The teacher is born, not made," "Make your own method." (1912, 2)

Setting up a parallel between the condition of philosophy at the time of the sophists and the current condition of pedagogy, Charles and Frank McMurry suggest that an understanding not of strict and blinding rules but of the "ideal method," of the principles and fundamental laws underlying *any* approach to teaching, might reclaim the value and centrality of method for "a work so important and difficult as teaching" (4).

The McMurrys' plan was to make available the *method of the recitation* to teachers and to teachers of teachers. The method, based upon "the inductive-deductive thought movement in acquiring and using knowledge" and first projected by Herbart, grew out of their several years' work in North American classrooms (viii). According to the McMurrys, "most subjects are treated according to one of *three methods;* namely according to the lecture, the textbook, or the developing method" (120).

In order to judge the relative merits of these methods, they set up the following standard of evaluation: "Since teaching consists in fitting new ideas, feelings, etc., to those that are already at hand, or since it consists in dovetailing the new with the old, or adjusting what the teacher has to give to what is already in the child's mind, that method will prove the most worthy which secures this desired adjustment in the highest degree" (128). Lecturing does not offer sufficient opportunities for a teacher to adjust the knowledge she is imparting to what is already present in the pupil's mind: "Lecturing ordinarily consists simply in offering or telling. The instructor regards the mind as a granary or storehouse, and pours into it the desired knowledge. The learner is not the central thought of the teacher, but the latter directs his attention primarily to the knowledge he is imparting" (129). To an even larger extent, the McMurrys make clear, this is true of textbooks. Although in the case of textbooks this fault can be remedied through appropriate methods of discussion, the parameters of that discussion are severely constrained when textbooks, as they do in most cases, contain mainly answers.

The "developing method" is what the McMurrys propose as *the* alternative because it not only privileges questions over answers but expects the student

> to conceive the[se] answers himself; he is systematically required to make discoveries, to judge what might reasonably follow from a given situation, to put two and two together and declare the result. Often, too, he finds it possible to discover the leading questions involved, as well as their answers; he must often state what should be the next question to be considered, and by practice in such thinking he becomes skilled in conceiving both problems and their solutions. . . .
>
> Another valuable feature of the developing method is the fact that it provides for a close sequence of thought. Textbooks ordinarily omit many of the necessary connecting links of thought. (139)

In spite of what they consider the superiority of the developing method, the McMurrys caution against exclusive use of it because: (1) not all knowledge is knowledge that can or need be developed; (2) as a method it is extremely difficult and time consuming, and if inappropriately used could be counterproductive, and (3) books (as storehouses of intellectual treasures) and textbooks need to be "in constant use in the classroom" and "must occupy a prominent place there" (142–43).

One of the valuable insights, or reminders, *The Method of the Recitation* can provide is that a good discussion is neither a natural nor a spontaneous event. It is a method of producing knowledge collectively, a method requiring sophisticated training and knowledge of specific conventions.[20]

> The skill required in conducting it is shown first of all in the value of the questions asked. It is necessary, therefore, for the ambitious teacher to become a careful student of the *art of questioning*. Especially must she consider the purpose of the questions. Ordinarily they aim merely to test the presence of knowledge supposed to be already acquired in the lesson assigned, as map questions in geography. But those necessary in the developing method can not aim primarily to test memory in this way. They must provoke thought first of all. Hence, instead of cathechetical questions, or others that can be fully answered by a yes or no, or by memorized statements in the book, those are to be put which are suggestive

enough to arouse thought and broad enough to call for even a series of thoughts. (163)

In their theorization of the art of questioning, the McMurrys point back to Socrates, but even more, and more productively, forward to Hans-Georg Gadamer and Paulo Freire.

The last text I present in this section is Colonel Francis W. Parker's *Talks on Pedagogics: An Outline of the Theory of Concentration* (1894), a text said to have provided Samual Hall with the "means to readjust [his] pedagogical clock" (quoted in Cremin 1961, 135).

Parker describes his text as "a general exposition of the theory of *concentration*," a theory believed to provide "a rounded educational doctrine for the study and criticism of teachers" (3). The central focus of this study and criticism is the child, the center of the universe, the being within whom the whole universe is concentrated. To understand "the sum of the world," to learn from the child how to foster his or her growth, Parker suggests that educators turn to the sciences:

> I grant that in the past of education attention has been directed too much to dead forms of thought, and for one good reason at last: the sciences are a modern creation of man and have not yet reached the child. Now we have those marvelous subjects presented to us, worked out by great thinkers of the present, and we are to choose whether we will continue the dead formalism that too often leads to pedantry and bigotry, or whether we are to lead the child's soul in that direction which God designed in this creation of the human being. (24)

In Parker's conceptualization of pedagogy, art and science are not irreconcilable. Brought into a reciprocally vitalizing relation, they provide a "concentration" that makes it possible to begin to understand more fully the task of education: "The study of the science of education gives us a higher knowledge of the human body, and a better knowledge of the conditions to be applied. The art of teaching is the scientific, economical, adaptation of conditions for educative effort" (25). Though the theory of concentration inevitably leads Parker toward the Creator, that move does not become a justification for deferring analyses, explanations, and queries of cognitive processes. Take, for example, his theorization of reading:

> The common saying that reading is getting the thought of an author is not *scientifically* correct. Strictly, no one can ever have any thought but his own. . . . *Upon the richness, fulness, and quality of one's own mind depends the action of printed words*. . . . (emphasis added, 162)
>
> If it were true that reading is "getting the thought of an author," then we should have to suppose that the reader has the power to think as the author

thinks, the same power of imagination, the same power of influence, of generalization; in fact, the power to follow the same process of reading.

   Reading is thinking, and thinking depends entirely upon the individual power
of the mind. (190)

Next to observation, reading is for Parker "the greatest means of mental and
moral development" (222). Hence its centrality to school curricula, as long
as it is conceptualized and taught in ways that "arouse educative thought"
(218), which, he suggests, contemporary methods of teaching do not make
possible:

> The study of text differs from common reading in the intensity of those acts of
> the will that hem the flow of consciousness. Now if the child early forms the
> habit of believing that he reads when he pronounces words . . . there is great
> danger that he will never acquire the fixed habit of thinking by means of words.
> He will suppose that the pronunciation of words is reading, and afterwards, in
> studying, he will suppose that learning a lesson means committing words verba-
> tim. This is one of the most terrible evils in all teaching—this habit of pronounc-
> ing and learning words disassociated from the thought. . . .
>
>   One awful product of this isolated word-learning is the pedant, who fancies
> that he knows a great deal because he can recall a great number of pages.
> (218–19)

In "Democracy and Education," the final chapter of *Talks on Pedagogy*,
Parker formulates a powerful critique of several forms of government, and
the methods of teaching necessary to inculcate their ideals.

   Of the method of mystery, historically one of the most effective means to
control the masses, he writes: "The presumption that certain divinely
anointed persons are the favored recipients of revelation, from which the
ignorant masses are rigidly excluded, and that a human soul is not capable of
finding truth for itself, have thus been the effective means of its utter subjec-
tion" (403). The second method he considers is bribery; the third, the
method of class isolation, which is strongly supplemented by class education,
a potent means of keeping society stratified.

> The primitive method that has dominated up to within a few years was to keep
> the masses of people in utter ignorance, controlling them by mystery, force, and
> bribery. But there came a time when the demands for education were too strong
> . . . a movement toward popular education has marked this century and the
> latter part of the eighteenth. But here arose a great difficulty—how to make
> useful subjects, and at the same time prevent them from thinking and reasoning
> for themselves. The most dangerous thing absolute authority can have is a born
> leader in the lower classes. . . . This spectre, which has ever haunted absolute
> power, is the "perturbed spirit" of all centuries, and will not down. The problem

> was to give the people education and keep them from exercising the divine gift of choice, to make them *believe* that they were educated and at the same time to prevent free action of the mind. The problem was effectively solved in the method of *quantity teaching*. (408)

Parker identifies quantity teaching as the method of "text-books, pages, word-cramming and word-recitation; of learning, believing, and confirming. . . . As the method of pedantry; the method that limits the mental horizon, the method that keeps the mind from looking outside of a certain definite circle; the method of implicit belief" (408). He is also critical and suspicious of the method of charity—not of genuine charity, but of that "form of charity that keeps people from helping themselves, lessens self-effort, and creates paupers" (409). To such methods he juxtaposes "the true method . . . of quality teaching," a method based on and fostering mental action, self-effort toward freedom and truth; a method that makes it possible to "present the right conditions for personal choice" (409).

Parker's work makes it possible to construct a compelling critique of what I have called schismatic constructions of pedagogy. The last chapter of his book, with startling clarity, exposes the connections between forms of control in government and forms of control in teaching. To think, as he urges us to do, of (the teaching of) reading as an analogue for (the teaching of) thinking (as Hans-Georg Gadamer has more recently argued) is to effectively expose the elitist, aristocratic features and exclusionary consequences of that version of "pedagogy as art" which fosters approaches to reading and teaching that shroud the making of meaning in mystery or assign the meaning-making function and ability to "certain divinely and anointed persons [who] are the favored recipients of revelation" (403; see also Salvatori 1989). To think of reading as an analogue for thinking is also to expose the deleterious consequences of that version of "pedagogy as science" that, by separating theory from practice, sets up a caste system. Within such a system, theorists of education theorize *for* teachers, and in so doing, they contribute to defining the work of teachers as the mechanical application, the enervated implementation, of sets of "methods" (see Charles De Garmo on what he describes as two diametrically opposed systems of pedagogy). As Henry Giroux would argue, this approach has led to the de-skilling of teachers, a de-skilling that makes his and other radical educators' appeal to reimagine "teachers as [Gramscian] intellectuals" so urgent (1988). While working toward making such a project possible, let's not lose sight of the fact, however, that proponents of pedagogy had already in the past clearly understood, albeit within the theoretical and political limits of their times, both the danger of and the remedy for such de-skilling.

As I look back at the texts I have excerpted, I begin to understand how and why, caught in a vicious circle of problematic theorizations and unsound rationalizations, the radical question of what pedagogy is, what it is good for, whose concern it is, and the kind of understanding of knowledge formation and reception it determines and requires, has been so effectively silenced, or so reduced, as to be conveniently dismissed. Insofar as the documents I have collected confront us with pedagogy's past, with the fact that *pedagogy does have a past,* albeit a contested one, they might caution us against dismissing it altogether, reconstructing it only according to the voices of its critics, or granting it a truncated history. It is my hope that these documents might lead current critics of pedagogy to realize that in their resistance to interrogate their oppositional stance toward it, they risk making themselves complicitous with parties and positions with which they are actually in theoretical and political opposition. It is my hope that they too will take part in a much needed conversation about and reassessment of pedagogy.

Since I embarked on this project, I have been in the company of pedagogues I will never meet, with whom I will never be able to share my appreciation for what they taught me about pedagogy, whom I will never be able to thank for allowing me to connect with their past and for reassuring me that the understanding of pedagogy that got me started is not, after all, so foreign, so ex-centric, so extra-vagant. I have never felt so much at home as I have while in their company, reading their words on crumbling pages or microfilms, searching for their works on dusty library shelves and in little-known archives, waiting for them to come to me through interlibrary loans. It is therefore with sadness and anxiety that I let go of them, as I must, at the end of this initial phase of my project. But it is with longing and excitement that I think of the time, in the immediate future, when I will return to them.

Documents

The documents in part three make it possible to reconstruct the debate about pedagogy's nature, and consequently its right to university citizenship, that took place in the last two decades of the nineteenth century. It is important that we scrutinize not only the terms of the debate—is pedagogy *art* or *science*?—but the theoretical, disciplinary, and institutional determinants for either definition. The distinction was (and is) neither natural, nor innocent. It resulted from specific theoretical presuppositions and led to specific curricular consequences which grant or take away power from pedagogy. One of the consequences of this distinction, for example, was that the construction of pedagogy as eminently practical that had come to be associated with normal schools, and for which normal schools had been vociferously criticized, was reinscribed at the university level. Since the argument was that the university soil would make pedagogy prosper, whose interest was to retain and disseminate such construction? Insofar as this debate, in different reincarnations, continues—uncritically and unreflexively—to circulate in the current university milieu, it is important that we revisit it so as to understand and assess whether present historical and cultural circumstances warrant its redeployment. Given open admission policies, how can we continue to justify definitions of pedagogy as "art" or "inspiration" or "tactful intuition"— definitions that presuppose, quite unproblematically, a homogenous cultural capital that teachers and students can readily access and invest in?

As readers will notice, these documents provide many complicated, competing, and intersecting accounts of how and why pedagogy came to be acknowledged and then soon contested as a discipline and subject of study worthy of university status. There is, for example, the account provided by William Payne, who was appointed by James B. Angell, president of the University of Michigan, as chair of education, the first in the country (1879–1888). Payne, who in this debate represents the "science" position, relegated "pedagogy" qua practice to the sphere of activity of normal schools and argued that university professors of "education" should only be concerned with the teaching of theories. There is the account of Josiah Royce, an influential representative of the "art" position who, flanked by Nicholas Murray Butler (appointed first dean of the faculty of philosophy at Columbia in 1890 and president of Columbia University in 1901), Charles W. Eliot (president of Harvard University), and psychologist William James, forcefully argued against the advisability of constructing "education" as a science. And there is E. N. Henderson's minihistory of pedagogy (*Cyclopedia of Education,* 1912) with its matter-of-fact remarks about the passing out of vogue of the term *pedagogy* as a university subject and its replacement with *education,* a term that was apparently deliberately chosen to mark the modification and expansion of pedagogy's "content in order to secure for it a permanent foothold and equality of rank" in the Academy.

As readers read the excerpts in this section side by side with, over, and through earlier documents, they will notice and begin to assess the consequences of constructions of pedagogy as *either* art *or* science, *either* practice *or* theory. Insofar as these documents suggest that in pedagogy's "academic" past, institutional, programmatic, and theoretical differences have been systematically deployed to inhibit a necessary and penetrating exploration of crucial questions about the teaching of teaching, these documents will, I hope, contribute to articulating a much needed cautionary tale.

From: William T. Harris, "Chairs of Pedagogics" (1882)

REPORT OF COMMITTEE ON CHAIRS OF PEDAGOGICS IN COLLEGES AND UNIVERSITIES

To the National Council of Education:

Your committee beg leave to offer the following report touching the establishment of Chairs of Pedagogy in Colleges and Universities.

They would respectfully represent that while instruction in the history and philosophy of education, —called Pedagogics,—has been given successfully for many years in the Normal Schools established in the several States of this Nation, and a large number of professional teachers have been sent out into the elementary schools of the land from these institutions,—that, on the other hand, the colleges and universities of the country have, with few exceptions, furnished no instruction in these matters.

Your committee would further represent that, as a consequence of this neglect, the teachers who give the secondary and higher education in this country have generally come to their work without professional training and without a philosophical survey of the science and art of education.

Your committee would further represent that the educated directive power of the country, as it is found in its professional men,—the clergy, the lawyers, the physicians,—has by far the greater influence in the control and management of elementary education, as well as of higher education; and that an ignorance of the history and philosophy of education leads to many wasteful experiments and wrong tendencies, and often results in factious opposition to the best interests of the common-school system in the country.

Your committee would refer to the same cause the conflict existing in the system of higher education with regard to the course of study,—between the advocates of a strict adherence to the disciplinary studies—Latin, Greek, and the mathematics on the one hand—and the advocates of the natural sciences, modern languages, literature, and history, on the other hand. The true functions of these branches not being well defined, by reason the fact that there is no profession whose business it is to investigate the question of course of study, it happens that the advocates of information-studies, or "modern"

254

branches, show a tendency to neglect the classic languages and mathematics, and by this fact slight those studies which give the pupil insight into the forms and usages of modern civilization, which show him their genesis in Greek and Roman life, and which give him ability to analyze the manners and customs of his own time and see their presuppositions. It happens, too, that many of our best institutions are led to make modifications tending toward the union of disciplinary and information-studies, but often with quite unsatisfactory results; the information-study being mistaken for an equivalent instead of a supplement to the disciplinary study. Meanwhile, a great number of the higher institutions adhere to a course of study which makes little account of the chief developments, in modern times, in the fields of literature and natural science, and which clings tenaciously to a course of study in Latin, Greek, and mathematics without requiring a proper quota of information-studies with these disciplinary studies. The course of study in such colleges and universities accordingly makes slight account of the studies of common schools in its requirements for admission, and demands special preparatory schools with a narrow course of study; it postpones the conventional studies that furnish information regarding the modern world of nature and man; for example, it postpones English literature and general history and the sciences of nature until after the pupil has spent from eight to twelve years upon such purely disciplinary studies as pure mathematics, and the life and language of the Greeks and Romans. A course of study carried for so long a time in these branches results in a deep estrangement from the practical world of the present, and partially destroys the disciplinary value of those studies by depriving them of application. This lack of harmony between the higher education and the common-school education your committee would refer to the fact that our colleges and universities do not give sufficient attention to the subject of pedagogy, practically and theoretically.

Your committee would suggest that the history and philosophy of education should not occupy the place of a disciplinary study in college, but that it is quite sufficient if the classes of the last two years of the course receive instruction for a few weeks each year in the science and history of education; the object being gained when correct views are inculcated as to the scope and importance of pedagogics, and the students come to see the possibility of overcoming, by means of correct methods, the difficulties that arise in school.

Your committee would therefore express their satisfaction at the recent movement toward the establishment of chairs of pedagogics in colleges and universities, believing that great benefits are likely to result,—first, in improved methods of instruction and discipline in higher education; secondly, in the more intelligent direction of common schools through the influence of professional men appointed on school committees; and thirdly, in a revision of the course of study that will make elementary and higher education two members correlated in one harmonious system.

Your committee see in this study of pedagogy in colleges and universities not only a resulting harmony between elementary and advanced education, but also the clearer definition of the province of the school as one province of education having a special purpose, coordinated with four other forms of education pertaining to, and peculiar to, the four great human institutions: the family, the social community, the state, the church. Without this clear definition of provinces there arises a constant tendency to make one form of education encroach on the province of another, or responsible for its results; and your committee are of the opinion that the study of education as a science and art in our universities will result in a careful consideration of the limits of the course of study and training in the school, and throw light on the educative character of the cardinal institutions of society here named, so as to discover what education, if any, belongs exclusively to any one of them, and cannot be undertaken by the school without wasting its forces in a vain attempt to perform functions that belong to other institutions; perhaps also relieving the school of the odium that attaches to it in some minds, because it does not remove the evils of society, and, besides this, destroying the empty conceit of school managers that the school is the only institution that educates.

Your committee regard these general studies in pedagogy as important to all the students of colleges and universities, inasmuch as American citizenship makes constant demands upon the individual for a knowledge of educational principles in his capacity of parent, or as voter, or public officer in the management of schools. All correct legislation in school matters and all correct administration of schools imply a correct knowledge of the proper scope of the labors of the school, as well as of the proper subordination of primary to advanced schools.

Your committee believe these considerations regarding the general bearing of education and its several instrumentalities to be a legitimate part of the higher education of all young men and young women in this Nation; and that some general instruction in this important matter should be given to all pupils, while more specific education in the practical methods of teaching should be furnished to all who propose to enter the profession of teaching.

Respectfully submitted:

W. T. Harris,
E. C. Hewett,
Members of Committee present

From: Albert Bushnell Hart, "The Teacher as a Professional Expert" (1883)

ALBERT BUSHNELL HART (1854–1943) was born in Clarksville, Pennsylvania. Educated in the Cleveland (Ohio) public schools, he received the A.B. degree from Harvard University (1880) and the Ph.D. degree from the University of Freiburg, Germany (1883). He also studied at the University of Berlin, Germany, and the Ecole des Sciences Politiques in Paris, France. In 1883 he joined the faculty of Harvard as first instructor of American history and was Eaton Professor of the Science of Government (1912–1926). A prolific author, he wrote over a hundred books on local political issues, foreign policy, and history, and was editor of *Theodore Roosevelt Encyclopedia* (1927–1943), *Harvard Advocate* (1879–1880), and *Harvard Graduates Magazine* (1894–1902).

Americans hold not only the belief that the inexperienced man is as good as the expert, but the conviction that he is a great deal better.

For this state of things there are two principal reasons. In the development of a new country men have had to be masters of many trades; and the man who could clear land, break oxen, build a wagon, shoe a horse, repair a roof, keep a tavern, and settle a dispute, not unnaturally felt that he could also invent cotton machinery, make laws and teach school. The division and subdivision of labor must eventually break up this idea that any man can do anything. The other cause is one which tends rather to grow than to diminish; it is hard for Americans to understand that it is possible for men to be politically equal while intellectually unequal. The "practical man" considers himself an unteachable master in his own field, and at the same time a better judge of professional matters than the expert who has spent his life in acquiring technical knowledge. On the other hand, he has the utmost contempt for any application to his pursuits of those generalities founded on long experience which he calls "theory."

That this is the expressed feeling of the mass of Americans is sufficiently shown by examining the status of the recognized "learned professions." The ministry is the oldest of them, and long the most respected; yet laymen consider their knowledge of biblical history and philology so adequate that

257

they try for heresy learned scholars who disagree with them. The profession of law was looked on with suspicion and dislike in colonial times, and owes its present standing chiefly to its great influence over legislation, and to the selection of judges from its ranks. No established profession meets with less real consideration than the medical; a few years ago in the great city of Cleveland the physician with the largest practice was an ignorant German who never showed a diploma and who diagnosed diseases by examining the palms of his patients' hands. The officers of the army and navy have slowly gained a distinct professional status, and engineers and scientific men are somewhat grudgingly admitted into that category.

What is the teacher's place? How far does the public recognize him as one entitled to confidence and consultation, as one learned in a calling of great benefit to the community?

Perhaps we may find the status of teachers more important than we imagine. Let us proceed to consider three points in regard to it: first, how far teachers practice a profession; second, how far they are recognized as experts; and, third, what may be done to improve the profession.

There are three principal marks of a profession: that it should be a permanent calling taken up as a life-work; that it should require special and intellectual training; and that there should be among members a feeling of common interest and some organization. When we attempt to apply these criteria to the teachers there is certainly some doubt whether we form a profession or no. The teacher's calling is well-known to be less permanent than others. For more than a century teaching has been considered in this country, what it could hardly be in any other country, a makeshift for young men who expect to enter law or medicine. Undoubtedly this system of combining self-education with the education of others has made it possible for many young men to climb the difficult lower stairs of other professions. Two presidents of the United States, John Adams and James Garfield, began their career in this fashion. The conditions are now changing; the colleges used to have a system of vacations which permitted its students to teach a part of every year. Perhaps that was as good a way of earning money as waiting at summer hotels or acting as guide at a World's Fair; but the colleges no longer suffer the interruption. More and more young men enter upon teaching with the expectation that they will follow it steadily; and so far forth the profession gains ground. On the other hand, we in America have large bodies of women teachers; and to them no profession has the same permanence as to a man, the "epidemic of matrimony" sometimes makes inroads on the teaching force in every grade. A few months ago the President of the oldest and one of the best women's colleges in America was in a comical state of mingled wrath and amusement because one of his professsors had, a few days before the beginning of the college year, resigned her place, in order to be married.

When we come to technical training, the teachers stand below other professions. Only very recently have there been opportunities in America for a training corresponding to that of the law, medical, or theological student, or of the West Point Cadet. I do not mean to leave out of account the system of Normal Schools which has done so much to disabuse Americans of the idea that any fairly intelligent person is suitable as a teacher. It seems, however, that the Normal Schools at present occupy the same position as the old Medical Schools, which gave diplomas after attendance on two courses of lectures. The Normal Schools have tried to do two things at once, and have done neither of them with complete success; they found it necessary to offer a general course because of the imperfect preliminary education of many students who came to them; and at the same time they have tried practical training; the general course has been on too narrow a basis, and the practical part has been taught too much by lecture and demonstration, and too little by actual practice. Nor do the college courses in pedagogy entirely fill the requirement of higher professional training; they can test the general acquirements of students; they can point out the development of the human mind and suggest the best ways of participating in that development; they can give a wide outlook over previous experiments in education; their great danger is of running into what the Germans call "methodologie." Practical training in teaching seems to me like that in another science which makes the colleges known throughout the Union—the science of football. The good teacher needs strength and quickness of mind; he needs an acquaintance with the rules of the game; above all he needs personal contact with the problems of his calling. It is impossible to educate a teacher without associating him in some way with those who are to be taught, just as it is impossible to make a good football eleven by studying the rules of the game and looking on from the edge of the crowd. A normal school or a college course without actual classes of children is like football practice with a dummy in a gymnasium. The last element of professional training, professional organization and association, has made great advances in the last four years. . . .

The most technical part of the teacher's work is his method of teaching; here again the profession suffers from itself. The general public feels that we use a lot of professional cant; that certain stock phrases are used to cover a plentiful lack of wit. The spirit of a profession may fairly be gauged by its periodicals; the lawyers, the doctors, the ministers discuss the technicalities of their professions in sober, dignified, and literary fashion. It must be confessed that many of the educational periodicals suggest inferior education: they abound in small gossip, in laudatory book notices, in free-and-easy conversational editorials. It would be unfair to hold the publishers wholly responsible for this sort of journals, because they adapt their wares to the markets. It must be the teachers who subscribe for, and support, what might not inappropriately be called the ''trade journals of education.'' One of our present encouragements is the establishment in the United States of several periodicals of the highest order, suitable exchanges for the best journals of other countries.

In which way may the professional status of the teacher be improved? That it is rising is shown in many ways, especially in the better provision for thorough training. In the first place the Normal Schools are improving, in the second place a scientific study of pedagogy is slowly gaining recognition as a part of University instruction, a third method is starting up of which a special advantage is that it may be applied to teachers who have already begun their work. This is the system of training courses established for teachers by colleges and technical schools. The Lowell Institute has for several years provided lecture courses for teachers in connection with the Institute of Technology of Boston; Harvard University is this year offering courses to the Grammar School teachers of the city of Cambridge, which are still more practical because they include laboratory exercises. This is a kind of university extension in which many colleges might be useful, and which many School Boards might well acccept and pay for. In Cambridge so far but three courses have been offered, geometry, physical geography, and experimental physics; the system may perhaps be extended to include the more familiar branches. The probable effect in bringing about a feeling of harmony and mutual interest between the colleges and schools is too evident to require discussion. . . .

Our standing before the community may also be much improved by a less self-satisfied tone. We are engaged in an excellent and honorable calling; we have chosen it because we think it for us the best and the most useful; but teachers are entirely too apt to congratulate each other on the grandeur of their opportunities and the greatness of their sacrifices. We are not highly paid in comparison with our friends and class-mates who began the race with us; we are subject to vexatious uncertainties as to tenure and promotion. But we have three months vacation in the year; we have fixed salaries instead of fees or donation parties; and we are able to arrange much of our own time. We look, and are, a contented body of men and women; let us accept our content.

From: William Harold Payne, *Contributions to the Science of Education* (1886), *The Education of Teachers* (1901)

WILLIAM HAROLD PAYNE (1836–1907) was born in Farmington, New York. He was educated at the Macedon (New York) Academy (1852–1854) and the New York Conference Seminary at Charlottesville (1854). He taught in New York country schools from 1854 to 1856. From 1858 to 1879 he was principal of the Union School at Three Rivers, Michigan, superintendent of the Nile, Michigan, public schools, principal of the Ypsilanti (Michigan) Seminary, and superintendent of schools at Adrian, Michigan. In 1879, under recommendation of President James B. Angell of the University of Michigan, he was appointed chair of education, the first such chair in the country (1879–1888). He was chancellor of the University of Nashville, and president of the Peabody Normal College (later, George Peabody College for Teachers). On the death of Burke A. Hinsdale, he returned to the University of Michigan where he remained until retirement (1904). He was a proponent of compulsory education. He sought increased pay for increased education and qualifications of teachers and conceived of university education for teachers as eminently theoretical. He translated several texts on education from the French, among them Gabriel Compayré's *History of Pedagogy* (1886) and Jean-Jacques Rousseau's *Émile* (1892).

SCIENCE OF EDUCATION

CHAPTER 1. IS THERE A SCIENCE OF PEDAGOGICS?

This question is ambiguous, the two queries involved in it being, (1) Is there a science of pedagogics *in posse?* Or, (2) Is there such a science *in esse?* I shall attempt to answer these queries in the order stated.

I. Is there, from the very constitution of things, a science of human training as distinguished from the art of human training?

1. Presumptively there is; for the established use of the terms *science of education*, *science of pedagogics*, and *science of teaching*, by the leading thinkers of the age, almost necessarily carries with it the implication that the art of human training has its correlated science. At least, the current use of this term by men addicted to habits of exact thinking establishes a very strong probability that such a science exists *potentially*, if not *actuallly*.

261

2. The existence of such a science *in posse* is established beyond question by the doctrine of two orders of knowledge, a higher and a lower, each of which is the complement of the other.

These two orders of knowledge may be called the *speculative* and the *practical*; the *speculative* resulting from the examination of the established constitution of nature of things, and held by the mind as matter for simple contemplation; and the *practical* resulting from the production of effects by the use of means. For example, the attentive examination of a new substance may end in the discovery of certain properties or sets of uniformities in relation or behavior; and as long as this knowledge remains in the mind as matter for mere contemplation, and is not employed in the way of producing results, it is *speculative*. But when the knowledge of these uniformities is employed for direction in the working out of results, it becomes *practical*. The knowledge of astronomy is chiefly of the speculative order; man has but little opportunity to employ the observed uniformities in the production of results. The knowledge of agriculture, on the other hand, is chiefly practical, consisting in mere methods for the attainment of results. The baker's knowledge of his own art is practical; he can perform all its processes, but can explain none of them. On the other hand, the chemist's knowledge of the baker's art is speculative; he can explain all its processes, but can perform none of them. These contrasted phases of knowledge are universal; and, by general consent, the terms science and art have been used to mark this discrimination. Every art thus implies a science; and, in turn, every science implies an art, actual or possible.

A summary answer to the first query is this: By universal consent there is an art of pedagogics, said art consisting in certain processes for the attainment of results. But these processes necessarily imply certain uniformities, and these uniformities, when ascertained and put in order, constitute a science of pedagogics.

II. Is there a science of pedagogics *in esse?* The answer to this question depends somewhat on the definition of science. If science be an orderly and exhaustive deduction of minor truths from a few first principles that are axiomatic, then there is but one science—mathematics; but if the term science be construed in the sense explained above, the number of possible sciences is indeterminate, and the number of actual sciences very large. This conception of science does not require that the enumeration if its first principles shall be complete, or that they be arranged in a strictly logical order, or that the series of deductions shall be complete. Sciences may be incomplete in matter and imperfect in form, and still be sciences in the accepted and legitimate use of this term.

The science of pedagogics stands in the ease last described; it is still incomplete in its matter, all its first principles not having been formulated; and it is imperfect in form, its admitted principles not having been arranged, and deductions from them not having been make with the required completeness and order. Whoever takes an established psychological law and draws from it legitimate deductions that can be employed for guidance in educational work, has made a contribution to the science of pedagogics; and works like Bain's "Education as a Science," and Rosenkranz's "Pedagogics as a System," that discuss, in a comprehensive way, the doctrines of education, are actual treatises on the science of pedagogics.

The answer to the second query, then, briefly stated, is this: A Science of pedagogics exists as an actual fact, but it is still incomplete in matter and imperfect in form. The need of the hour is a systematic rearrangement of the old material, and the addition of omitted principles and their deductions.

Though not strictly belonging to the above inquiry, I add a paragraph on the general nature of educational science from my own point of view.

The material composing a science of pedagogics is logically distributed as follows:

1. The being to be educated is susceptible of three orders of growth: first, physical; second, mental; third, moral. A rational art of education must be based on the laws that regulate these three orders of growth. The science of pedagogics must therefore borrow principles from physiology, psychology and ethics.

2. All instruction presupposes a medium of communication. This medium is language; and the laws of language, as employed in the communication of knowledge, are expounded in the science of logic. The science of pedagogics will therefore borrow other principles from logic.

3. Growth presupposes aliment; and the aliment, in the present case, is represented by the various subjects of human knowledge. A necessary element in the science of pedagogics is a determination of education values; but, as there is not independent science for determining these values, this is an inductive inquiry, falling within the domain of the science of pedagogics itself.

4. In passing from the single child to aggregates of children, there arises the need of the organization of schools and school-systems; and so the science of pedagogics must borrow other material from history, sociology, political science, and legislation.

5. It must be that much valid educational truth is embodied in current methods. The analytical examination of results is therefore a necessary part

of the science of pedagogics; and the truths thus elicited will serve to verify the deductions drawn from assumed principles.

6. Education, in its ideal or formal aspect, aims at the realization of the typical man, and comprises all the agencies that can be brought under human control for the attainment of this end. The principles that are involved in this whole complex process, when systematically arranged, constitute the science if pedagogics. This I believe to be the authorized use of the term by German, France, and Italian writers on education.

7. The term pedagogy should be used to designate the *art* of education, or, rather, so much of this art as falls within the province of the school. This distinction is made by the Italian educator, E. Latino,* and seems to me worthy of being accepted by educational writers.

8. The current use of the term pedagogics (*Fr.* pédagogic; *It.* pedagogica, pedagogia; *Ger.* pädagogik) in French, Italian, and German literature, is a sufficient warrant for the respectability of the term. To affect a dislike for the word on etymological or historical grounds is childish.†

In his "Histoire de la Pédagogie" M. Compayré takes pains to distinguish the term *pedagogy* from the term *education*, using the former in a limited or technical sense, and the latter in a comprehensive or liberal sense.‡

CHAPTER 2. THE SCIENCE OF EDUCATION— ITS NATURE, ITS METHOD, AND SOME OF ITS PROBLEMS

One of the curiosities of current educational history is the fact that English teachers are still discussing the question, *whether there is a science of education.* The cause of this phenomenon is said to be the low state of philosophical studies among the English. This conjecture is confirmed by the fact that in Germany and in Scotland, where philosophy has long been in high repute, this questions is as far above discussion as an axiom in mathematics. It is probable that, in this country, philosophical culture has not yet attained a depth and a breadth that will make the existence of a science of

---

*"Thus pedagogics (*pedagogica*), or the science of education, is connected with pedagogy (*pedagogia*), or the art of education; for science has need of art in order to be useful to life, and to direct the conduct of human affairs; and art has need of science in order to be enlightened and made conscious of its own scope and power."—Emanuele Latino, "Della Pedagogica" (Palermo, 1876), p. 114.

†"Pedagogy is the science of education. The word pedagogue is of Greek origin, and signifies a conductor of children. A pedagogue was a slave charged with the duty of conducting children to school. From this wholly material sense the word has been raised to a nobler sense. To-day a pedagogue is he who directs the young intellectually and morally. Can there be a grander mission!"—Marion, "Leçons de Psychologie Appliquée à l'Éducation" (Paris, 1884), p. 13.

‡See the Introduction to Compayré's "History of Pedagogy" (Boston, 1886).

education a postulate. It is much more probable that when this subject has become of sufficient importance to be talked about, there will be skeptics and disbelievers here, as in England. On this subject, our present intellectual state is the unanimity of the ignorant. There are yet to come the disagreements of the inquiring, to be followed, let us hope, by the unanimity of the wise.

THE EDUCATION OF TEACHERS

The history of normal schools shows that their original purpose was merely to extend the scholarship of those students who intended to become teachers, the theory being that fitness for teaching consisted in the possession of more than the average amount of learning. This had been the conception held by the ancient universities, which were teachers' seminaries, whose students, obliged to teach as a condition of graduation, bound themselves to teach for a specified time after graduation. It is easy to see how this thought would naturally be transferred to the people's schools at the time when the Reformation had made it necessary that every child should be educated. This new movement required the sudden creation of an army of teachers who were to be improvised, so to speak, by selecting the brighter pupils in the schools and giving them a more thorough and a more extended knowledge of subjects.

The next movement in normal instruction might have been anticipated. It would necessarily happen that teachers having good scholarship would sometimes fail, while other teachers, though having poorer scholarship, would meet with surprising success; and it was an easy inference that method was another element in a teacher's professional outfit almost coordinate with scholarship. Pestalozzi was an illustrious example of the fact that a man of very limited learning may nevertheless become a great teacher. He had such sovereign confidence in method as distinguished from scholarship that he believed a textbook constructed according to his method would enable an illiterate man or woman to become a good teacher. His dream was to make education universal. To this end he would make of every home a school, and of every mother a teacher; and to the obvious objection that these mothers were too ignorant to teach, he replied that, armed with his method, ignorance was no bar to home instruction. Jacotot also aimed at universal instruction, and in answer to the objection that it was not possible to supply the requisite number of teachers, owing to the prevailing ignorance, he resorted to his famous paradox: ONE CAN TEACH WHAT HE DOES NOT KNOW.

Following what may be called the Pestalozzian movement in education method became the dominant feature in normal instruction, and scholarship was relegated to a subordinate place.

The next movement might also have been anticipated. The brilliant success of Pestalozzi brought forth a lusty crop of competitors and rivals. As it was by his "method" that Pestalozzi had triumphed, each contestant felt obliged to exploit his own method in order to make a stand against the reigning craze, just as in these latter days each ambitious educator must exploit his fad in order to compete on even terms with his brethren who are exploiting their fads. Method was thus pitted against method, and it could not fail to happen that each innovator would finally be forced to defend his hobby by pleading some doctrine or principle as its basis and final justification. The center of debate has thus been transferred to the field of science where the final stand must be made, and here the contest is waxing warmer and warmer. One educator invokes the name of Spencer, another of Frœbel, and another of Herbart. Each is apparently deaf to the merits of every system of educational philosophy save his own, holding that his prophet has delivered the final message to the world.

It results from this brief historical statement that experience has developed three main factors in the professional education of teachers: scholarship, method and doctrine. Under scholarship is included little more than a thorough knowledge of the subjects included in the ordinary school course. By a sort of forecast it is determined what subjects a student may be called on to teach; these he is made to master with great thoroughness, and with the ever present thought that they are to be the instruments of his calling, and that their chief value lies in their instrumental use. The narrowing effect of this mode of study is still further intensified by the student's preoccupation with method. Much of the working power of his mind is absorbed in the effort to answer the ever recurring question: "How shall I present this subject to my class?" Insistence on technique reaches its culmination in the practice school when the student, in a class not his own, and in the face of perfunctory critics, is made to exemplify the methods that have been prescribed by the teacher in charge of this branch of the professional work. I am far from saying that this question of method is unimportant. My only purpose in this place is to show that under the conditions named the attainment of real scholarship becomes impossible. Perhaps liberal learning is not desirable as a qualification for the teaching office. That may be an open question; but if it be considered a condition essential to high success in the teacher's vocation, it must be secured under different conditions. In the pursuit of liberal learning, or culture proper, the mind must work in an air of freedom, and must be absorbed in the subject itself, and not in the utilities that it may be made to serve. . . .

I shall now venture to speak of scholarship, method and doctrine, or science, in what seems to me to be the sequence of their importance, and shall try to give in outline my conception of the attainments, general and professional, which constitute real fitness for the teaching office.

It is a flagrant misuse of the term scholarship to limit its content to the branches of study included in the ordinary normal school course, or even in a college course. Scholarship includes spirit as well as matter, an attitude of mind and disposition of soul, as well as the knowledge communicated in class rooms. . . . A sense of mastery and power, a free flight of the liberated spirit, an abiding pleasure in intellectual pursuits, a conscious participation by the individual in the moral life of the race, these are some of the marks of the scholarly vocation. The study that does not lead up to these high endowments misses its supreme prerogative. . . .

It is very certain that students who are pursuing their studies under the galling stress of official and officious criticism, and are constrained to ask at each step of their progress, ''what utility can I draw out of this,'' are working under conditions that are hostile to the rise and growth of the scholarly spirit. An atmosphere of freedom should pervade every school. Every course of study, however elementary, should be liberal in its spirit and purpose. Studies should be learned for their own sake, and not with reference to the utilities that they may be made to serve; for ''they teach not their own use, but that is a wisdom without them and above them, won by observation.'' The more perfect the form and manner in which a study is learned, the greater will be its utilities when experience calls for them; and it is no paradox to say that this form and manner will be most perfect when the study is learned without the least reference to its future utilities. A divine admonition warns us against disquieting ourselves concerning the three great wants of the physical life—food, drink and raiment, and directs us first of all to make sure of that which includes them all, the Kingdom of God, that perfect state of soul which is righteousness and peace and joy.

This sharp insistence on the technical and the practical, which I think has wrought such harm in the education of teachers, has resulted from a false conception of the teacher's art, which degrades it into a handicraft or trade with rules as rigid as those of the mason and the carpenter. Teaching is a spiritual act or art in which mind comes into mysterious and quickening contact with mind, soul with soul, heart with heart, life with life. Analogies drawn from our dealings with matter utterly fail us when we come to deal with spirit. We are not dealing with uniform material and fixed dimensions, but with all the variations and diversities of impalpable spirit. The products of our art are not uniform, but multiform, and our processes must needs be so variable that we cannot follow rules, but must be guided by principles. We are not working in that sphere of activity where two times two is four, but where two times two is often ten. In its highest aspect, teaching is a process of provocation, or induction, whereby a free and impressible spirit takes on moral and scholarly qualities by near presence to a soul highly charged with moral and scholarly qualities. What better advice can be given to a teacher than this: ''Become addicted to the scholarly vocation until you are possessed by the scholarly spirit; charge yourself highly with benevolence, and be kindly affectioned towards those whom you would guide and teach; make large investments in yourself, to the end that you may become 'noble and gracious, the friend of truth, justice, courage, temperance' ''?

The studies whose special value lies in the fact that they are catholic, or breadth-giving, are geography, history and literature; hence the teacher who would endow himself with a proper frame or attitude of mind should addict himself in an especial manner to these three subjects. . . .

Education is becoming more and more an ethnic problem; the conception is growing that the supreme aim of living in this world is the perfection of the race; that in an active and real sense all men and women must become educators; and that the main and particular purpose of the higher institutions of learning is to prepare students for the work of elevating and perfecting the race. Perhaps in an unconscious way the universities of the age are now moving towards this larger conception. The chairs of education established in so many of them serve a high purpose for the general student, as well as a special purpose for the student who expects to teach. It will ultimately appear that their largest following will be from students who are in quest of a liberal education. In other words, it can hardly be doubted that the university of the future will be modeled after the conception so happily expressed by Herbert Spencer: "*The subject which involves all other subjects, and therefore the subject in which the education of every one should culminate, is the Theory and Practice of Education.*" . . .

Education is a derived or composite science drawing its matter chiefly from religion, ethics, sociology, psychology and logic. Teaching, for the most part, is an applied psychology and logic, but education derives its inspiration and aim from the other sciences named. . . .

Whether a teacher's methods shall be inspiring and creative, or obstructive and deadening, will depend on whether, to borrow Carlyle's imagery, he is a live coal, or a dead cinder; and it is necessary to be kept in mind that in some way a student must be transformed into a quickening spirit before he can become a real teacher. In a school devoted to the education of teachers there must be a prevalent spirit provocative of high moral aims, devotion to duty and love of the scholarly vocation. This spirit should be so prevalent and so tonic as to form the vital breath of every learner; it should proceed, not from one instructor, but from all; and it should be so effective that it can be felt as a living, vitalizing power wherever students congregate—in chapel, in classrooms, in lecture halls, in art rooms, in library, everywhere. By virtue of this indefinable but real spirit some schools predispose their students to scholarly habits, to sobriety and refinement of manners, to beneficient purposes, to noble ambitions; and this spiritual tuition is infinately better than mere drill, learning, or method, and must certainly accompany them if education is to be a transforming and perfecting power. If the term enthusiasm had not lost its primitive and noble meaning it might suffice it to say that all real teaching must be pervaded by enthusiasm; but it is now better to say that all real teachers must be inspired, in the same sense that biblical teachers and prophets were inspired; that education will fall sadly short of its transforming and creative power unless it is accompanied by a certain noble ardor and elevation of spirit, unless it affects the noble passions and emotions of the learner. Education is shorn of more than half its power when it is addressed to the head to the exclusion of the heart. . . . Education should be progressive, but this progress should be along historical lines. The future should be a logical evolution out of the past and the present. In this domain revolution is treason. To be swayed about by every wind of doctrine is the mark of an unsound mind. To be absorbed in new and doubtful experiments is to betray a sacred trust. Innocent children should be shielded from the experiments of callow teachers who would use them as material for their ''laboratories.'' It is appalling to think that the normal schools of the country should send out into society relays of half educated teachers devoted to the exploitation of fads, and bent on revolution under the name of progress. The policy of such schools should be a progressive conservatism. They should encourage a hearty respect for the past and its legacies, and should at the same time create an aspiration for a better future.

TEACHING A SPIRITUAL, NOT A MECHANICAL, ART

Oftentimes the best instruction is that which is merely suggestive. It commends some theme for reflection, and leaves each mind free to do its own thinking and to come to its own conclusions. This mode of procedure is particularly necessary when mature minds are dealing with those complex and many-sided questions which are connected with practical education. However long and patient our thinking may have been, it is not very probable that any of us have looked through and entirely around even the simplest question involved in the educating art. It is by a division of labor that these problems are finally compassed. Men severally look at the different phases of a complex question, and thus by discussion, comparison and ultimate agreement, there results a composite view of the truth more or less perfect as the thought has been catholic, penetrating and judicial. . . . Can we forget that the highest office ever conferred by heaven on mortals was to be the teacher of men? The essence of real preaching is effective teaching, and we miss the grandeur of the teaching office if we fail to see that the ministry of the schoolroom is as sacred as the ministry of the altar. . . . Perfunctory teaching that begins and ends merely with a didactic lesson falls sterile on the sensitive soul and leaves nothing which makes for righteousness and peace. Good teaching must have much of the persuasive power of oratory. It must kindle enthusiasm, establish motive, fortify the will and inspire the soul to noble acting. . . . It goes without saying that the prime, the fundamental qualification for teaching service of high value is scholarship. It is true that there are some poor teachers who are good scholars, certain moral or mental defects operating to defeat success; but it is certain that no one need hope for permanent and growing success in the teaching profession without the instincts and habits, and some of the attainments, of the real scholar. To secure and retain professional standing, a teacher must earn the confidence and respect of the better educated people in the community in which he lives. The vocation of teaching will not become a recognized profession until in the popular mind the terms "teacher" and "scholar" become synonymous. It is a very significant fact that the "trained" teacher adds little to the repute of the teaching profession, it being understood that "training" at best implies mere technique, or manual dexterity, and carries with it the suspicion of shallow learning; just as elocution, the noble art of vocal expression and interpretation, has fallen into disrepute through the performances of young persons who mistake sound for sense and gesticulation for eloquence. The spirit of the age has set in strongly towards the mechanical, the empirical, the practical. This spirit has become rampant in normal schools. Teachers are no longer to be educated, but "trained;" and this "training" is to be done in "laboratories," where students are encouraged to operate on children. The inevitable but deplorable consequence of this fad is that normal schools have lost the respect of educated men, and it is very commonly taken for granted that a teacher "trained" in these schools is a man or woman of slender scholarship, who expects to succeed by "devices" and "methods." There seems to be but one way to rescue the vocation of teaching from this false position, and this is to return towards the older conception that a teacher must be a gentleman and a scholar. . . . Seeing that education is the architectonic or master art, it should be the most conservative of all the arts; of all human institutions the school should be the one the least addicted to change, the least exposed to innovations. To be conservative is to be neither stationary nor retrogressive, but to be wisely circumspect and cautious while adapting old methods to new needs. It is the school that is piloting the race across the centuries, and its hands should ever be held firmly on the helm, and its eyes steadily fixed on the compass. In such a voyage experiments in navigation are not only perilous, but criminal.

Paul Henry Hanus, "The New Department of Pedagogy at Harvard University" (1891)

PAUL HENRY HANUS (1855–1941) was born in Hermsdorf, Upper Silesia, Prussia. In 1859 he came to the United States with his widowed mother who married an American mining engineer. Hanus attended public and Episcopal schools in Wisconsin, New York, and Colorado, and for three years, Platteville (Wisconsin) Normal School (later the University of Wisconsin—Platteville). He received the B.S. degree (1878) in mathematics and sciences from the University of Wisconsin. He taught mathematics and science (1878–1886) and was principal (1886–1890) in a Denver high school and a lecturer in teachers' institutes in Colorado. In 1890 he became the first professor of pedagogy at Colorado State Normal School (later, University of Northern Colorado) at Greeley. In 1891 Charles W. Eliot invited Hanus to Harvard as professor of pedagogy. Despite widespread doubts about and opposition to pedagogy there, Hanus remained at Harvard until his retirement (1921), establishing courses for credit in education, a separate education department, a cooperative program with Radcliffe College for teacher training, and the Harvard Graduate School of Education (1920). He was the author of many books on different aspects and subjects of education. His autobiography, *Adventuring in Education* (1937), provides useful insights into the biases and oppositions he had to confront as a university professor of pedagogy. He founded the Harvard Teachers Association in 1891, was the founder and president of the New England and the National Society of College Teachers of Education (1909–1910), and studied and supported vocational education.

The establishment of courses for the instruction of teachers at Harvard University is another recognition of the necessity for trained teachers for secondary schools, and for the higher places in the public schools generally. It is not strange that the demand for such teachers has lately become more pronounced, and that the opinions upon which it is based have been urged with greater emphasis. Experience has proved that we have failed to achieve results which could reasonably be expected from the great general interest in education and the money expended upon it. One of the causes of these inadequate achievements is found in the meager professional equipment of teachers and of influential school officers. We lack men whose professional attitude is rational and whose assumption of leadership in education is justified by a knowledge of principles. Men who, in addition to a liberal general training, possess professional culture and insight. We need more men who can and will study their work philosophically; who are fitted to be leaders because they are able to lead.

All higher schools for the training of teachers, and the establishment of departments for such training in the great educational centers, aim directly at developing such ability, so far as training can do it. In the same sense in which we can make men by education, we can make teachers. No training can, of course, make good native poverty of mind and heart. But no one doubts the effect of training upon persons capable of profiting by it. No doubt professional training of itself can never produce a finished artist. But it can and does develop a permanent professional attitude; it develops a thoughtful student of his profession and confirms that far-reaching and general interest in the study of mind and nature, of men and affairs, without which growth is impossible, and the intelligent solution of educational problems either very difficult and haphazard, or quite out of the question. Professional training does this by making the learner distinctly conscious of his needs, his possibilities, and the means he may employ to realize his aspirations.

The study of any art naturally involves the recognition of its principles and processes. The courses offered at Harvard University, in 1891–92, to teachers, and to men who wish to become teachers, thus naturally fall into two groups. One group deals with the history and the theory of teaching, and the other group deals with management, supervision, and organization, and with the methods of teaching the several academic subjects, Greek, Latin, English, German, French, History, Mathematics (Algebra, Geometry, Trigonometry, Elementary Analytical Geometry), Physics, Chemistry, Botany, Zoölogy, Geology, Geography. The instruction in each of these courses is in charge of one or more of the instructors belonging to the corresponding department. Special requirements, designed to aid in securing the best results, are made of students taking these courses. The additional work thus required is especially determined for each course, but consists in general of prescribed attendance upon other college exercises, of conferences, of exercises suggested by the needs of the students, and of the observation of teaching in schools in the vicinity of the University, with reports of such observations. In addition to these courses, Professor William James will give twelve lectures on "Topics in Psychology of Interest to Teachers." All of these courses are "open to men who are graduates of colleges, or scientific schools, or who are otherwise known to be of suitable age and attainments, under the same conditions as those which govern admission to the graduate school.''

It will be noticed that the instruction of teachers at Harvard University differs from that offered elsewhere, among other things, in the extent to which students study methods of teaching the subjects of a high school or academic course of study, and observe, under direction, the actual teaching of those subjects. The same plan will also be followed, so far as possible, in teaching methods of management, supervision, and government. The tendency to mere imitation is controlled by the courses in Psychology and the Theory of Teaching, which enable the student to realize the rational basis of the methods presented. The instruction throughout will be by lectures and discussions, with frequent opportunities for conference and consultation. It is intended to adjust all details in accordance with the needs of students.

From: Josiah Royce, "Is There a Science of Education?" (1891)

JOSIAH ROYCE (1855–1916) was born in Grass Valley, Nevada County, to parents who crossed the continent to California in the gold rush of 1849. The account of their experience was preserved in the diary of Royce's mother, an intellectual and spiritual woman who was responsible for his early religious and secular education. In 1869 Royce entered the Boys' High School in San Francisco, where his parents had moved. The experience was stimulating and prepared him well for college work. In 1871 he matriculated at the recently established University of California at Berkeley, from which he received his bachelor's degree in 1875. He spent the next year in Germany, studying philosophy, and upon his return to the states he was invited by Daniel Coit Gilman (who had been the president of the University of California during Royce's undergraduate days) to be one of the first twenty fellows appointed at the new Johns Hopkins University. He received his Ph.D. from this institution in 1878 and returned to the University of California where he taught English for four years. During this period he reexamined Kant and Hegel and studied such contemporary philosophers as William James, Charles S. Pierce, Shadworth Hodgson, and the psychologists Wundt and Bain. As he taught rhetoric he found an opportunity to introduce logic and wrote the *Primer of Logical Analysis for the Use of Composition Students* (1881). Because he could not teach philosophy at the University of California, he sought to move east. William James provided such an opportunity when, on his leave of absence in 1882–1883, he saw to it that Royce substitute him. Royce remained at Harvard, where he began to teach with considerable hesitation, doubtful of his ability to enter into sufficiently "close relations" with his students. He was appointed assistant professor in 1885 and professor in 1892. Finally, upon the retirement of George Herbert Palmer in 1914, he became Alford Professor of Natural Religion, Moral Philosophy, and Civil Polity.

(1)

This opening number of a new review for the study of educational problems must naturally contain some article of a very general character, wherein the prospects and difficulties of the whole undertaking are discussed. That the editor should have intrusted to me the task of writing such

275

a general survey of problems is not only an act of very kindly courtesy toward myself, but a sign of his own willingness to make the difficulties of the doctrine of education manifest from the outset. For the academic student of philosophy and of human nature loves the problems of his profession too much to regard or to depict them as easy; the university teacher is in general trained to reflect even more than to advise; and, for my own part, I have always felt unwilling to apply so pretentious and comforting a name as "Science" to any exposition of the laborious and problematic art of the educator. Yet if in this article I make doubts and difficulties prominent, as it is my office to do, I hope that before I am done it will be clear that my aim is as positive as my method is at times negative. A fragmentary, but still not wholly unsuggestive, program of investigations, such as may profitably be pursued by students of the art of education, an indication of certain significant needs of modern pedagogy, a warning against overhasty generalization, and still an encouragement to every loving observer of children to study the science of psychology without neglecting the intricacies of daily life, and to use wisely his own warm experience, rather than to trust to the mere letter of pedagogical dogmas—such are some of the things that I should like to furnish in my article. I have to make a number of critical and negative observations. I do not want to dishearten, rather do I long to strengthen the interest of teachers in the theoretical aspects of their profession.

A natural text for an essay upon the question of our title is just at present furnished by a widely known and much-discussed paper, read before the Academy of Sciences at Berlin, in July, 1888, and published in the proceedings of that body.[1] The author, Wilhelm Dilthey, Professor of Philosophy in the University of Berlin, is known as a many-sided and cautious student, especially of the more historical and humane aspects of philosophy. His excursion into the field of pedagogy is marked by all his usual caution and learning. His question is essentially our present one: "The Possibility of an universally valid Pedagogical Science." His beginning is negative and critical in tone; his statement of the limitations of the "universally valid doctrine of pedagogy" is highly noteworthy; his skepticism is keen; and yet the outcome of his whole article is, after all, hopeful, and even inspiring. I cannot do better than to begin by summarizing his views. I wish that I could hope to supplement them by anything that approached their knowledge of the subject, and their constructive power.

Dilthey begins by observing that all the prominent pedagogical systems,

---

1. W. Dilthey, *Ueber die Möglichkeit einer allgemeingültigen pädagogischen Wissenschaft,* Sitzungsberichte der Berliner Akademie der Wissenschaften, 1888, pp. 807–832.

such as those of Herbart, Schleiermacher, Spencer, Bain, Beneke, Waitz, agree in one respect, that they pretend "to define the end of education, the value of the various branches of study, and the methods of instruction, in an universally valid fashion, and consequently for wholly different times and peoples." And this pretense, says Dilthey, at the very outset of his argument,—this pretense is precisely parallel to that of the old-fashioned theories of the state,—theories which, disregarding history and the varieties of circumstance, undertook to fix for all humanity the absolute forms of political life; and, in consequence, drove men to a revolt against the whole historical social order. This sort of theorizing belonged to the seventeenth and eighteenth centuries, culminated in the French Revolution, and has been replaced in our day by the historical method in political science,—a method which ignores the theoretical "Constitutions" of the *doctrinaires*, and which knows that political organizations are far too vital in their individual traits to be subject to any abstract formulation of the details of the "universally valid" social order. Now pedagogy, as embodied in such "systems" as have just been mentioned, represents precisely this old fashion of theorizing. Pedagogy arose in the seventeenth century, developed farther in the eighteenth, with the "naturalistic" theories, assumed a "natural" universality of aim and method as present, under all human conditions, for the educator, and so became the "comrade of natural theology, of the philosophy of law, and of abstract political economy." "Elsewhere," continues Dilthey, "the historical school has replaced naturalism"; pedagogy alone has, in this respect, refused to progress. As a fact, however, human nature cannot be adequately described through any abstractly universal formulation of its traits. Human nature, as a product of evolution, differs from nation to nation, from century to century. Nor is even an abstractly universal formulation of the ethical end of life a useful undertaking. "No moral system has ever yet been able to win universal recognition" (p. 808). The ends of life can only be defined with constant reference to the vital and growing motives and impulses of concrete humanity; and as the latter change so do the ends themselves, with the ethical systems that embody them. Hence the educator cannot hope to have defined for him, with abstract universality, either the material upon which he must always work,—namely, human nature,—nor the end toward which he must always aim,—namely, the highest moral perfection of his pupil. Both these matters are modified for him by the course of evolution, and by the actual social environment.

And yet, with all this necessary limitation, does there not remain a field for pedagogical science? Yes, answers Dilthey, in case, not the abstract description of human nature, and of the ends of living, but the truly psychological study of the typical forms of human evolution is pursued in the fashion which the historical and biological investigations of modern times have rendered possible. There are a few general laws that hold, not so much as to the content of human nature, but as to the fashion of its organic growth. These biological laws will turn out to have a practical significance. Human nature, namely, no matter how much it varies, in content or in ideals, is always in the first place a collection of impulses, of instincts, of feelings, and of tendencies (*Gefühle und Triebe*) which, from the outset of life, have a teleological character; that is, a character whereby they are adapted to the preservation of the individual in the environment in which the child is placed. These various reactions of feeling and impulse, however, these natural and teleological "reflexes," of each organism (such, for instance, as the reactions of hunger and of shyness, of curiosity and of friendliness), are at the outset, in the individual child, "not in organic connection with one another." No child begins with organized conduct. Its early impulses are as chaotic in their entirety as they are useful in their individual quality. "Observe the child; his desire for food, his avoidance of bodily injury, his social friendliness, appear all of them as isolated impulses, with no relation to the needs of his life as a whole, with no sense of their relative value. Like sunlight and shadow, one feeling chases another across his countenance" (p. 816). It is thus also with the savage. Usefulness of the single reaction, unteleological disorganization of the entirety of the reactions—such is the law of the early stages of human life. The growth, now, of mental life, "produces by continual adaptation those relations amongst" these elementary impulses, "whereby a teleological and complete unity of the character in the individual and in society" shall ideally come to pass. Such complete unity, to be sure, we none of us ever reach. No culture wins to the service of the organism and of the society the united and final co-operation of all human impulses. We all have our chaotic moments, and our anarchical desires. Nor has any form of civilization attained in its completeness the end of an entire organization of all the original impulses in full and mutual adaptation. Nor yet, again, is an abstractly universal description of just what this unity of human life would be, accessible for us. And yet, thus, after all, is the general problem of education (not, to be sure, its general solution) to be defined for our "science." Not the one common end of life, in its precise content, but the type of human growth, in so far as it is growth, is after this fashion expressed. At the outset of life the human being is a chaos of impulses, each useful in itself, but all relatively independent. From the point of view of the highest ideal of growth, these impulses are to be brought from chaos to such complete order that not only in the individual, but in his relations to society, there shall be no chaos left, and only complete unity of life. And the educator is to do what he can to further such a growth in the child. Could we now describe in definite and material terms the content of this ideal of the perfect unity of character, could we tell what the man, and what the social order, would be like, in which the ideal were thus absolutely realized, then indeed we should have that "universal" theory of society and of education which the eighteenth century dreamed of. As a fact, however, we cannot describe the perfectly organized character because we have never seen it, and are subject in our judgement of what tends toward it to the vicissitudes and the accidents of our age and our nation. Any concrete account and picture of the ideal state that we may attempt will, therefore, have elements of chaos left in it. Any complete plan of education that we may devise will, furthermore, have defects, and only a transient significance. But there remains a sense in which the undertakings of pedagogy will be capable of scientific and general discussion. To the educator we in effect say: "Work against the chaos of impulses, by using the very impulses themselves as the material for good order. In a word, organize." Meanwhile, although the actual content of any attempted organization of life will be "historically determined," and so imperfect and transient, relatively general accounts can be given of processes that *do* increase the orderliness of the child. Such accounts will take the form of "pedagogical rules," whose number Dilthey, of course, leaves indefinite. In short, scientific pedagogy, far from telling the teacher finally and completely just what human nature is, and must be, and just what to do with it, will be limited to pointing out what does, on the whole, tend toward good order and toward the organization of impulses into character. "This is the whole province of pedagogy," as a general science. Its application to the conditions of a particular time, nation, family, and child, will be a matter of art, not of science. And "therefore, no concrete education questions can be solved in terms of an universally valid science." Such questions will always contain elements of uncertainty, will always require the practical skill of the individual educator, and will always receive answers that will vary with time and occasion.

The concluding section of Dilthey's paper is devoted to the mapping out of the province of pedagogy as thus defined. After an historical study of the growth of education, of its social relations, and of the general ways in which the child may be considered as at all plastic to the educator's purposes, scientific pedagogy would study the typical growth of the orderly life of impulse as it is manifested (1) in the games of childhood (universally human devices these for organizing infantile impulses), (2) in the consciously intellectual growth, that is, in the perceptive, attentive, memorizing, and reflective life of childhood and youth, and (3) in the parallel processes of the organization of the will. Rules would here be suggested by the science at every point; yet they would never be rules that the educator could immediately apply, except with constant reference to the conditions of his own nation, age, and child. Universal these rules would be, yet never universal in so far as they were precise guides in the concrete case. Aids they would be, but never substitutes for personal insight. In short, pedagogy, as a "science," would be a good staff and a bad crutch.

II.

So far, in substance, Dilthey. As I summarize his discussion I feel the necessary but disagreeable abstractness of my own form of statement. Brevity such as this must needs do injustice to so finely conceived and thoughtfully elaborated a paper as Dilthey's. In one sense, indeed, Dilthey's essay may be said to contain little novelty. To the philosophical student its conclusion will be in some measure familiar. It is in their application to our present problem that these words are so wholesome. The lesson of the historical as well as of the biological sciences is that when you undertake to discuss the growth of a complex organism you must not expect to deduce all the wealth of the details of this life from your account of the general type of the growth itself. The practical application of this lesson is not far to seek; and yet immature theorizers so often miss this application. Are you to interfere for a purpose with the growing organism, your knowledge of the type will be able to help you, and in so far there will be a possible science to guide your interference. If, then, you are an educator, and have to influence for a moral and social purpose the growth of a child, or of a youth, your knowledge, say of psychology, ought to aid you in your work; and in so far there will be a scientific element in education. Only there is all the while, the other, the more immediately practical side of your undertaking, namely, just the application of your insight into that typical growth as such, to the direction of your dealing with the individual living organism itself with the child, or with the youth. And just here it is the detail that will often concern you more than the type. Just what science abstracts from and ignores, just that you now most need to know. Your own surroundings, say as Frenchman or as American; your position as teacher of the sensitive child that needs tenderness, or of the rugged and sluggish child that needs awakening; your place as defender of this or of that worthy ideal, say of this religious creed, or of that, of this social tradition or of some other; your relation as private tutor to the individual child, or as public teacher to the larger class of many children; your experience of the accidental variations of just your own pupils' lives and destinies—all these things will properly interfere with anything like a truly scientific application of your pedagogical principles. You will degrade science,—not help your children,—if you persist in seeing only the "scientific" aspects of your pedagogy. True pedagogy is an art. A noteworthy German text-book of psychiatry, now on my library shelves, observes that the alienist's art, the care and cure of insanity, is one that "can indeed be learned, but that cannot be taught." And yet this text-book is itself a fine little compendium of the principles of the scientific treatment of the insane. Well, if alienism can be learned but not taught, how much more shall this not be the case with pedagogy! Disease seems indeed endlessly wealthy; nervous patients furnish to the alienist a world of capricious problems. But, nevertheless, the riches of health are greater still than the riches of disease; and the art of the true pedagogue could still less be taught in its entirety than can the art of the alienist. It is abstraction that simplifies; and abstraction is invaluable to science. But he who returns from science to life is a poor pupil if he has not learned the art of forgetting his formulas at the right moment, and of loving the live thing more than the describable type.

All these observations of mine are so far mere commonplaces. I almost repent having written them down. And yet, from one point of view, how necessary they seem to be necessary, alas! not only for the pedants who are continually pretending to have discovered this or that complete and scientific and final "system of pedagogy," whereby alone all children may be saved,—but also for those unreflective lovers of child life who are indeed often so much better than the pedants but who falsely imagine that because science cannot furnish a final "system" for all times, teachers, nations, and pupils, science is therefore worthless for the pedagogue. Both parties in such a controversy as that between these pedants and their unlearned opponents are in the wrong. There is no "science of education" that will not need constant and vast adaptation to the needs of this teacher or of that, constant modification in the presence of the live pupil, constant supplementing by the divine skill of the born teacher's instincts. This being true, there is, indeed, no "science of education" whose formulas will not need at the right moment to be forgotten. Yet, on the other hand, it makes great difference to you whether or not you do possess the science that you can be wise enough at the right moment to forget. Ignorance is one thing; the power voluntarily to ignore is quite another thing. The former is a weakness; the latter a high spiritual power. Universally valid your "system" never can be; therefore hold it not as system. But universally significant your scientific insight may become to you, if you once possess it, and can bear in mind that it is after all abstract, and yet noteworthy as an abstraction. Teachers then do need a scientific training for their calling. Instinct, unchastened by science, is blindly self-confident, and when it goes astray its fall from grace is irreparable; its very innocence then proves its doom. Teachers who know nothing of the reflective aspects of their calling, who do not try to comprehend as well as to love their pupils, who despise science because it cannot take the place of devotion and of instinct, may indeed be successful, and in any case, as I just said, their state, so long as by chance they do not go far astray, is vastly better than the present state of those pedants who have heard of modern science, of nerve-cells, and of apperception, and who forthwith have developed or copied some hundreds of systematic principles of "pedagogical method." The unreflective, I say, if the kindly light of nature leads them amid the encircling gloom of educational problems, are, indeed, so far, better than the pedants, who still think that God means to save his people by numbered or unnumbered paragraphs. But then, the pedants, after all, have been trying to learn, after their own fashion. They have formed a habit of learning. And if they are not already too old with their "science," they may perchance yet learn a little more, namely, that this, too, is vanity unless life supplements it. And whenever the pedants do learn this latter fact, they may take counsel of instinct and then become truly wise. For true wisdom is just reason set aglow by instinct. But the unlearned, on the other hand, are trusting only to the kindly light of nature itself. Therefore, if by chance some will-o'-the-wisp lead them astray, they will soon be finally unable to distinguish true from false, and will perish miserably. Healthy instinct outdoes vainly abstract learning. But imperfect learning can be corrected by more instruction; while untutored instinct, once corrupted, is lost.

To both parties to the controversy, then, to the pedants with their systems and to the unlearned with their instincts, we must offer the same suggestion as to the place of science in education. On the whole, special points of difference aside, I should agree with Dilthey. There is no universally valid science of pedagogy that is capable of any complete formulation, and of direct application to individual pupils and teachers. Nor will there ever be one so long as human nature develops, through cross-breeding in each new generation, individual types that never were there before; so long as history furnishes, in every age, novel social environments, new forms of faith, new ideals, a new industrial organization, and thus new problems for the educator. So long as these things go on, the educator's calling will be an art to whose beauty and complexity no science will be adequate. But, on the other hand, it is in vain that the inadequacy of science is made a sufficient excuse for knowing nothing of it. The more inadequate science is when alone, the more need of using it as a beginning when we set about our task. For the inadequacy of beginnings is always an indication that if we are to go further we ought at least to comprehend these beginnings themselves. Instinct needs science, not as a substitute, but as a partial support. Or, as I said, when you teach, you must know when to forget formulas; but you must have learned them in order to be able to forget them.

Yet enough of these generalities. It remains, in this paper to point out certain portions of modern scientific research that promise to be most useful to the educator, within the limits that have been set in the foregoing to all such usefulness. Of pedagogy as a single and determinate science, I have always had serious suspicions; and the reasons for these I have now sufficiently formulated. That the teacher needs to know all that he can (1) of the subjects that he is to teach, and (2) of certain branches of science that promise to be of service to all teachers in general, whatever their special callings, I have never doubted. I reject the pedagogical system. I believe in the training of teachers. And this training, in so far as theoretical science can be of general service to its ends, I conceive to be determined by two considerations. The first is that the teacher should be, as I may word it, a naturalist, loving and, as far as may be, scientifically comprehending the life of childhood and youth, just as other naturalists try to comprehend the life of other organisms. The second is that the teacher should be a man of rational ideals, knowing what moral and social ends he wants to serve, and why he regards them as worthy. The second consideration, being, with all its importance, the one capable of the briefer treatment here, I shall put next in order. The first consideration will then be summarily dealt with as I close.

(2)

III.

The teacher ought to be a man of ideals. The end of education is ethical. We desire to give the state a loyal subject, and society a worthy fellow-worker. To this end we labor with our pupil. Is it possible, then, to define in any scientific terms the moral ideal? Is it useful for the teacher to have studied ethics? To this question Dilthey has already responded, in his skeptical fashion, that, doubtless for good reason, "no moral system has yet won universal assent." Upon this side of pedagogy he lays small stress. The universal type of organization seems to be formulated by him in biological rather than in ethical terms. The child is to be made an harmonious living organism. The ends of life in the abstract cannot be universally defined. There are some who would regard Dilthey's skepticism in this matter with a mingling of dread and contempt. But to begin a discussion of the matter here would lead us too far afield in philosophy. I myself hold to the possibility of an universal ethical principle. But of matters strictly philosophical, this is no place to speak.

Yet all the while I feel the great difficulty of giving much practical aid to teachers, especially in this country, and at the present time, by demanding of even the more learned class of them an universal attention to theoretical ethics. The call to become conscious of one's moral ideals, both for the sake of one's own salvation, and for the sake of teaching others, is a call that comes to men in very different degrees and forms. Most commonly men feel the call in religious form, and for reasons closely connected with their faith. Our clergymen are our principal ethical advisers in this country; and, on the whole, it is well that this should be the case. Yet the religious is not the scientific spirit, although there is indeed no proper hostility between the passion to be holy, and the disposition to scrutinize scientifically what holiness is. I should be glad indeed if more of our teachers were early possessed of a share of the latter interest. We should have less philistinism in our schools, less hoodwinking of the childish conscience, less cowardice, less prudery, and more purity. But when I begin to ask who shall teach the teachers ethics, or how a critical and yet a truly reverent study of the great ideals and passions of humanity shall be popularized among them, I confess that I often see how philistinism is indeed far better than moral indifference, and how we might easily exchange the unwisdom of a portion of our customary clerical teaching of morality in this country for a kind of superficial reflection upon ethics, whose outcome would be very evil not only for our teachers, but for their pupils. As a dear friend of mine loves to say: Better strenuousness of devotion even to a false moral ideal, than a well-defined ideal but no strenuousness. In short, it is in the world of devotion to ideals that loyal instinct is most often the securer guide as against science.

Yet, despite all this, I am impelled to insist that the pedagogy of the future will have, as one of its duties, the encouragement of a reasonable ethical reflection among our teachers. I care indeed little, whether or not this reflection is generally pursued under a constant theological supervision. Theology is but the eternal religious passion of humanity, limited (and sometimes, indeed, even enchained) by the historical forces that have formed our relative and often transient imaginings about the world beyond sense. I believe in the passion, and in its true and eternal objects, too deeply not to love even its more transient forms. I do not find its ministers all equally wise guides as to ethical matters; and no wonder—since they do not find one another so. But they have done so much for us in this country that we can safely trust them in the future also to awaken higher reflective thought concerning ethical matters whenever the time clearly calls upon them to lead in this direction. And if ever an age showed signs that such a time was soon coming, surely the present age does so. I desire, then, to see more efforts, both within and without the churches, to train young teachers to a clear consciousness about duty and about its meaning. And I desire the study of ethics, without ceasing to be truly devout, to become also, as time goes on, more and more scientific in spirit and in content. Of the difficulties in the way of such a study in this country, in so far as they immediately concern the educator's business, the present widespread controversy concerning secular and religious instruction in the public schools gives a sufficient hint. In short, it is here the very value of ethical insight itself, both for the teacher and for his pupils, that renders a truly scientific treatment of moral questions, and a truly scientific training of teachers, especially difficult.

IV.

The teacher, I say, should furthermore be a naturalist, and the department of natural history which directly concerns him is called psychology. The great successes of this infant science of late years have been indeed, of themselves, not without certain drawbacks for the practical teacher. Psychology is constantly growing as a whole more complex, and therefore more difficult to survey in its entirety; while, on the other hand, there have been recently developed within its field several very attractive, very special, and therefore very limited lines of research, which have drawn the public attention to themselves in such a fashion as to endanger, through hasty and one-sided generalizations, the proper sense of the magnitude and the difficulty of the whole science. In two directions, therefore, teachers who have looked to psychology for light as to the "science of education," have found their vision confused. Did they undertake to study psychology as one doctrine, they soon found themselves unable to grasp its manifold aspects. It confused them with the multiplicity of its researches. They were fain to go back to some older textbook, wherein, as in Spencer's *Psychology* all the "principles," as they used to be, were "unified." Hence the antiquated character of most of the compendious treatises on "pedagogical psychology." These may or may not be useful. Nearly all of them are very highly inadequate. But did the teacher, on the contrary, study his psychology only in monographs, then, of late years, certain attractive topics, such as hypnotism, for example, made themselves too prominent from among the mass of researches, and psychology seemed a wonderland of singular and one-sided generalizations. I have not yet seen a "system," or a "science of pedagogy," founded solely or mainly on the principle that the teacher ought to be primarily a hypnotizer; but I daily expect to find such a treatise announced. It would hardly be more one-sided or crude in its own way and day than Spencer's book on "Education" was in its time and environment. I doubt if it would have the same success; but it might succeed in bringing the "science" into a little fresh discredit. For the rest, to speak of more serious matters, I know of persons who have struggled with Preyer's admirable monograph on the *Mind of the Child*, in a vain endeavor to extract from its pages an infallible rule of procedure in dealing with very young children. The scientific monograph, even where it is of the best in itself, is in general dishearteningly limited as to its immediately practical outlook. Let me, then, in view of this difficulty, suggest what the direction is in which the study of psychology, as adapted to the use of teachers, ought to progress.

First, then, let the young teacher remember that it is not the "system" of a psychological science, not the exhaustive theory of the "powers of the human mind" that he needs, but rather the psychological spirit: that is, the love and the skill that are required for the purposes of mental diagnosis. When I said that the teacher should be a naturalist, I meant that he should be in the habit of observing the mental life of children for its own sake, and of judging the relative value of its moods and tendencies. For such observation of the live child his study of published psychological researches ought primarily to be meant to prepare him. Preyer's monograph on the *Mind of the Child* is, indeed, from one point of view, little more than a dry mass of details, with a few generalizations of a sort that no teacher will be able to use without much personal experience and skill. All this is necessary. It was not Preyer's first object to be pedagogical, but to contribute facts to his science. But see how useful just this collection of dry facts may become to the teacher if he reads the book, not for the pedagogical rules that he may have vainly hoped to find in it, but for the acquirement of the habit of observation that the book exemplifies. . . . For as teacher you will always be watching minds, yes, watching even more than judging them. And the habit of merely judging minds as good or evil, without observing what state it is, what mental coloring, what inner live process, that makes them good or evil; this habit, I say, is so ingrained in most of us that it is always hard to learn to substitute diagnosis for mere estimation, and a loving study of the process for mere external liking or disliking of the person. Yet just such study of the inner process is the larger part of a teacher's theoretical business. And that is why I counsel him to use his psychological reading rather to train his power of diagnosis, than to equip him with abstract pedagogical rules. The teacher who can make out what the child's actual state of mind is, has developed the true sort of psychological insight. . . .

As for the cure itself, pedagogical formulas will seldom prove sufficient for the case. . . .

This first method in which theoretical psychology can be of service to the teacher having been disposed of, I can speak very briefly, and only by way of illustration, as I close, of two sorts of inductions in modern psychology which seem to me to have especial pedagogical importance.

1. The growth of the intelligence is subject to certain still very imperfectly formulated laws, which, in a vague and general fashion began to be recognized in the last century, and which have been already much employed for pedagogical purposes. The higher processes of the intelligence are begun, and continually supported throughout our lives, by fitting sensory experiences. Upon a more or less accurate analysis of these, and of the perceptive processes that are dependent on them, has been founded the theory of object-teaching. Herbart's principle, since widely stated and applied, that involuntary attention not only precedes voluntary attention, but should always be employed by the teacher as a basis for the latter whenever that is possible, is another example of a pedagogical use of a psychological induction. This principle is embodied in that whole body of pedagogical doctrine about finding and appealing to a child's actual interest, which, in combination with the doctrine that sense-experience should always be used, when that is possible, as a basis for abstract thinking, and that perceptions must prepare the way for higher apperception, has done so much to revolutionize the practice of the modern teacher. The relation of attention and memory, of interest and retention, has again suggested to teachers a relatively scientific basis for much of their work. These are examples of the direct influence of psychology upon the theory of method. Their importance no one will deny. The imitation of the "science of teaching" in these directions is, however, quickly suggested by the story of the numberless pedagogical "fads" that, on the basis of a hasty assimilation of this or that psychological induction concerning the processes of the intelligence, have lived or are living their day, doomed to an untimely death. Object-teaching, too, has had its absurdities; such recent "fads" again as the proclaiming of "manual training" as the one true way of salvation for our schools, will suggest what happens when the single induction pretends to take the place of the whole science, when the single device tries to crowd out nearly all the rest of the art, when one little idea that is most admirable in its place and time, like this very idea of "manual training" assumes a barbarous foreign name to give itself a loftier dignity, and presents itself as the one latest result of "science." Let us study the inductions of psychology; but let us finally anathematize the "fads," and all who trust in them. Science does not counsel individual, unchangeable, and infallible "methods." She corrects our errors; but she also shows that there is no royal road to the true method, which must vary

with the particular educational problem that we have to solve. The devices of the pedagogue should take counsel of science; but they should be modest in their pretensions even after they have done so. Not every one who says "Psychology! Psychology!" shall be saved, nor is every deviser of a new fashion of appealing to the involuntary attention of childhood, or of strengthening its apperceptive processes, a prophet. Whenever we come to see that the possible devices of educational method are endlessly numerous, and that scientific psychology criticises but does not create them, while they themselves are the product of the practical experience and art of the educator, this part of our program for the training of teachers will be more wisely carried out than nowadays it often is. Study, then, the psychology of the intelligence, apply it as best you can to your methods of teaching, but beware of the "infallible methods." Such is my advice to teachers in this realm of their work.

2. A still more recent series of psychological inductions is suggested to us by what Dilthey has said of the typical growth of the human character from the chaotic state of the "primitive impulses" to the organized "teleological" unity of mature conduct. I need not dwell upon the general significance of the whole evolutionary point of view in modern psychology. I will venture, by way of illustration, to mention one aspect of it. I refer to the inductions as to the relations between the phenomena of mental growth and those of mental disease. Readers of Preyer will remember the analogies that he draws between the defects of childish speech, and the diseases of language in the adult. The phenomena of the will contain still more interesting analogies. The naughtiness of the child is indeed very often similar to what would constitute the symptoms of some form of criminal lunacy in the adult. The child shows you at times pathologically insistent impulses, as well as instances of pathological aboulia, or apathy of will, and many volitional derangements, too, of the explosive type, such as the violent outbursts of childish fury and malice in those who, when adults, will show little sign of burdens of this sort. The difference between the childish chaos of impulses and the derangements of mental disease, will usually lie in the fact that the childish defect, as such, is more frequently *merely* chaotic, so that you get what would be individual pathological symptoms in the adult, while you seldom get the whole context of any diseased type, unless, indeed, your child is actually diseased. But the analogy between childish defect and pathological symptoms is interesting; and science is making it constantly more so. I wish, therefore, that teachers who are looking for scientific light as to the care of childhood, would take counsel, more frequently than they yet do, of the more enlightened expositors of modern mental pathology.

Once more, the analogy in question must be used with caution, but the study of the nervous patient, who is, after all, in some fashion or other a child, cannot fail to suggest something to the cautious teacher. If it suggests nothing else, it will suggest to him just that humanity in mental diagnosis which the alienists learn to practice, and which unenlightened teachers so seldom possess. Study, then, the psychology of human evolution, and study it, too, in intimate connection with the psychology of mental defect and disease. Notice the analogy, and use the hints that the wise alienist gives as aids in your examination and training of children. Remember that the chaos of unreason in childhood is itself, in some measure, an incapacity of a relatively diseased sort, and that the wise teacher is a sort of physician who is to help the child toward getting that kind of health which we call maturity.

In the foregoing I have tried only to suggest, and, in the most inadequate fashion, to illustrate a very few of the relations between theoretical study and the teacher's business. To sum it all up in one word: Teaching is an art. Therefore there is indeed no science of education. But what there is, is the world of science furnishing material for the educator to study. If he seeks in that world for exact and universally valid direction, he will fail to get it, and deservedly fail, because science is not there to win anybody's bread, nor yet to furnish short and easy roads to even the noblest callings. But, on the other hand, if the teacher wants aid from the scientific spirit, and counsel from scientific inductions, there stands ready to his hand such assistance as, above all, psychology has to offer to the educator who desires to become a loving observer of the minds of children, and such assistance, too, as ethics may suggest to the man who is strong enough to grapple with deeper problems. I have had no space to give a fair account of what either of these departments can offer to the teacher. Perhaps my one or two illustrations may serve to indicate my purpose.

From: Charles De Garmo, "The Herbartian System of Pedagogics" (1891)

CHARLES DE GARMO (1849–1934) was born in Muckwonago, Wisconsin. He graduated from Illinois State Normal University in 1873. In 1886 he received the Ph.D. degree from the University of Halle, Germany, where he was influenced by the Herbartian movement. In the various positions he held—as principal of public schools in Naples, Illinois, assistant training teacher (1876–1883) and professor of modern languages (1886–1890) at Illinois State Normal University, professor of psychology at the University of Illinois (1891–1898), president of Swarthmore College (1891–1898), and professor of the science and art of education at Cornell University (1898–1914)—he contributed to disseminate and strengthen the Herbartian philosophy of teaching in this country.

The attention of American teachers is invited to a brief consideration of the pedagogical system of Johann Friedrich Herbart, who was born at Oldenburg in the year of American independence, 1776, and who died in the university town of Göttingen, in 1841. He was one of those enthusiastic students who gathered about Fichte at Jena at the time when German philosophy was at its zenith, and was himself destined to strike out a new line of development from the Kantian basis. Herbart was, after Krug, Kant's successor in the chair of philosophy at Königsberg, and was afterward professor at Göttingen. He was the friend of Pestalozzi, some of whose work he scientifically extended. The subject of pedagogics early claimed his attention and interest, and it may safely be said that more than any other man he deserves the distinction of having reduced the subject of education to a science. For its sake he destroyed an old and created a new psychology. In originality and logical consistency in working out pedagogics as a system, Herbart is unrivaled. His influence is growing with increasing rapidity, for his followers have made concrete the thoughts that with him were abstractions. No other system of pedagogics can approach Herbart's in scientific completeness, and although he has many opponents among thinking men, yet all acknowledge his great service. His school is represented in Germany by the *Verein für wisenschaftliche Pädagogik*, which has branches in all parts of the country.

290

Though no American is likely to accept in their completeness all the results at which Herbart arrives, yet I know of no other system which contains half so much that is of direct and suggestive value. The rigid scientific character of Herbart's work makes it particularly valuable for all teachers whose minds are not yet freed from the ruling empiricism of the present time.

Herbart is the first great philosopher who devoted his main attention to pedagogics, and whose system in all its parts stands in close relation to this as an end. With him metaphysics, psychology, ethics, and pedagogics form a system, each of whose parts is essential to the others. The tendency among contemporary adherents of Herbart is to ignore very largely his metaphysics, and to develop the more strictly pedagogical phases of this thought. It will therefore be the aim of this outline to exhibit so much of the Herbartian psychology and ethics as will suffice to give the proper interpretation of pedagogical doctrines. It will not be advisable to attempt an explanation of all the points touched upon, for such an explanation would involve writing an introduction to philosophy in general.

There are two diametrically opposite schools of pedagogy, one of which is best represented by Fröbel, the other by Herbart. The one doctrine may be described as the germ or plant theory, the other as the forming or art theory. The germ or plant theory presupposes germs of power implanted in the soul which are to be developed. The forming or art theory presupposes that education is a matter of outward influence, not dependent upon an inner working power or faculty. It is only the body of man, says Herbart, which, like the germ of a plant, brings its future form with it into the world. Education is with him a giving and drawing out (*geben und entziehen*) and by no means a mere caring for and waiting (*Aussicht und Wartung*). "Man, who may become a wild beast or a personified Reason, needs the art which builds, which constructs him, that he may have the right form."

Herbart stands in an intimate relation to the great leaders of pedagogical thought, both ancient and modern. With Socrates he accepts the building of moral character as the great end of education; with Plato he holds that intellectual culture is a necessary means to this end; and with Aristotle, as we have seen, he regards education as a supplement to the experience derived from nature and the mingling with men in society. His relations to preceding philosophers are quite as complicated in the field of metaphysics. An extender of one side of Kantianism, he returns to the Eleatics for a correct notion of being, to the Atomists for the notion of multiplicity of being, to Wolff for "clear notions and well-grounded proofs," and to Kant for a "science out of notions."

HERBART'S PEDAGOGICS

This is the necessary end and aim of education, but subordinated to this as its conditions we find a number of possible ends of education. These are determined, not by the teacher or by the pupil, but by the aims, the desires, the needs of the future man. Education must make these possible to him. It must think of the "activity of the ongrowing man in general, the quantity of his direct inner life and activity," not so much as the many-sided business but as a many-sided mental receptivity. "All must be lovers of all, each a master of one thing." This leads to one of the most interesting and valuable departments of Herbart's work, his demand for *gleichschwebende Vielseitig-keit des Interesse*, *i.e.*, a harmonious many-sidedness of interest.

We have seen that, with Herbart, the building of moral character is the great end and aim of education, but character building is the building of the will, so that the real worth of instruction is measured by its influence upon the will. One need not go far to find examples of great learning combined with great weakness of moral character. The reason for this is to be found in the fact that learning has been imparted in such a way that interest has not been aroused. The word interest is used in a double sense. The common conception of its function in school is that it is desirable as a means to an end. Pupils should have their interest aroused that they may the better impress upon their minds the matter to be learned. This is receptive interest. But this does not of itself make it certain that a range of thought will be produced out of which will proceed an energetic will. Herbart's conception of interest, however, includes the foregoing and much more; it is of interest not merely as a transient means in education, but as an end, that he speaks. Interest shall not be merely a temporary thing, but continuous, "far following." It shall be something that takes hold of the whole soul of a child, that passes through the stages of pleasure, desire, will, and action. It means in general "the kind of mental activity that instruction should incite, in that it does not stop with mere knowledge, for one thinks of knowledge as a store which might be lacking, without the owner being another than he is. Whoever, on the contrary, holds fast to something known and seeks to extend it, he has interest for this thing."[9] Again, the interest which instruction should excite is direct and not indirect. It should not arise from emulation, or hope of good marks, or a fine position in life. It proceeds from pure love for a subject, finding its reward in the study itself. It is not impelled by selfishness, or fear, or ambition. It is therefore the duty of the teacher to

9. Herbart, *Umriss pädagogischer Verlesungen,* §62.

avoid all those means which arouse the indirect interest, for this may hinder the excitation of the direct interest which is the very aim and end of instruction itself.[10]

But the idea of the direct interest needs a further determination. Does not one constantly see about him narrow, barren lives; men and women whose whole existence is bound up in some one ruling idea? Does he not see men whose only thought is money, or notoriety, and women whose life is summed up in the word fashion, or pride, or ambition? Is it not clear that all the most sacred and valuable possibilities and duties of life are neglected or despised, that life itself is likely to become barren and worthless even to the possessor when its one prop and support is taken away? Such limited, one-sided lives must be avoided through the arousing of a many-sided interest. ''In a many-sided interest,'' says Kern, ''the pupil should find a moral support and protection against the servitude that springs from the rule of desire and passion. It should protect him from the errors that are the consequence of idleness; it should arm him against the fitful chances of fortune; it should make life again valuable and desirable, even when a cruel fate has robbed it of its most cherished object; it should enable one to find a new calling if driven from the old; it should elevate him to a standpoint from which the goods and successes of earthly striving appear as the accidental, by which his real self is not affected, and above which the moral character stands free and sublime.''[11]

To specify more particularly, one may divide these many-sided interests into two groups or classes, namely, interests arising from knowledge, and interests arising from association with others, as in the family, the church, the school, society.

Of interest as related to knowledge we may distinguish:

1. The empirical interest, or the pleasure excited in the mind by the change and novelty which arise from a presentation of the manifold and variegated. This is the starting point in education, and supplies the *raison d'être* of the kindergarten and all the concrete work of observation in the primary school.

2. The speculative interest, or the search for the causal connection of things to which the dark, or problematical, or mysterious impels the mind. ''He who rejoices upon looking into the starry heavens has the empirical interest; he who reflects upon the conditions of their origin has the speculative interest.''[12] It is the speculative interest to which we appeal when we

---

10. Comnare Ziller, *Grunollegung zur Lehre vom erziehenslen Unterricht*, p. 247.
11. Kern, *Grundriss der Pädagogik*, § 12.
12. Ufer, *Vorschule der Pädagogik Herbart's*, p. 46.

teach pupils to see and look for the reasons of things; when we teach them to look beyond the facts to the laws that unify them and make them appear in their rational connection. It pertains to the stage of generalization in instruction.

3. The aesthetic interest, or that which is aroused by regarding, not the manifoldness and variety of things or their causal connection, but their relations to each other, whether in the world of sense or of thought. It is the interest aroused by the beautiful in nature, in art, or in morals.

The interest which arises from association with others is of a sympathetic nature, in which the following points may be distinguished:

1. The sympathetic interest, or that which is aroused by the joy or sorrow of others. It is one of the beautiful things in the kindergarten that it cultivates so exquisitely the sympathetic interest between child and child.

If this feeling of individual sympathy is extended by a knowledge of the greater relations of society into feeling respecting the welfare of large numbers, we have:

2. The social interest. This is, of course, a cultivation of the great institutional interests of the Anglo-Saxon race. It lies at the basis of patriotism and its kindred virtues. When, finally, the interest is directed to the history and destiny of mankind, when it is as clear to the understanding as to the feelings that the ordering of the history of man involves something more than mere human power, and that therefore the history of each individual does not lie entirely in his own hands, then fear and hope gather in the heart.'' This we call

3. The religious interest.

Finally, just as one-sidedness of interest must be avoided, so must an unsymmetrical development be prevented. The growth of interest must be harmonious (*gleichschwebend*).

"Interest is the light with which Herbart, once for all, has brought the dark and tortuous course of dialectics into the clearness of day. It is the charmed word which alone gives power to instruction to call the spirit of youth and to make it serve the aim of the master. It is the lever of education, which, lightly and joyfully moved by the teacher, can alone bring the youthful will into the desired activity and direction.''[14]

Charles De Garmo.
University of Illinois,
Champaign, Ill.

14. Dr. R. Staude, *Pädagogische Studien, Hrsg. von W. Rein,* Heft II.

From: Arnold Tompkins, *The Philosophy of Teaching* (1894)

ARNOLD TOMPKINS (1849–1905) was born on a farm eight miles south of Paris, Illinois. He attended local schools and later the Indiana State Normal School at Terre Haute, from which he graduated in 1888. He was superintendent of schools in Worthington and in Franklin, Indiana (1880–1884). In 1885 he was called to take charge of the Department of English in the normal school of DePauw University, and four years later he became dean. In 1890 he became head of the Department of English in the Indiana State Normal School. In 1893, he withdrew from that position and entered the University of Chicago, where he studied until 1895. From 1895 to 1899 he was professor of pedagogy at the university, and in 1899 he was chosen president of the Illinois State Normal University. The following year he was called to the presidency of the Chicago Normal School, a position he held until his death. Besides *The Philosophy of Teaching* (1894), some of his works, widely read by teachers and used in training schools, were *The Science of Discourse* (1889), *The Philosophy of School Management* (1895), and *Literary Interpretation; or a Guide to the Teaching and Reading of Literature* (1896).

INTRODUCTION.

The term "philosophy of teaching" places the accent on the process of teaching, while the term "philosophy of education" emphasizes the system of principles as such. The philosophy of education will not be attempted; the theme being restricted to the application of philosophic principles to the teaching process. Not that the application of principles is a more worthy object of attention than the system of principles themselves, but because I feel moved to show how helpful in practice, daily and hourly, are the universal principles which philosophy announces.

I have no sympathy with the sneer at mere theorists—those who seek principles for their own sake. What should we do without the light they throw upon our pathway! The practical teacher is not always conscious of, and thankful for, the great service rendered by the speculative philosopher. Universal truth seems so remote from the immediate, concrete details of school work that we do not suspect its presence and controlling power. Hegel well protests against the thought that philosophy deals with another world;

asserting its subject to be the concrete and ever present facts of life. The practical teacher must sooner or later learn that inspiration and guidance through the daily routine of duty must be sought in universal truth; that specific rules and recipes, which seem to be so helpful because of their easy and immediate application, are really impractical and confusing because they have no germinant power and breadth of application; that his bearings must be taken from the fixed stars, and not from the shift in scenes and lights of the lower atmosphere.

The application of universal principles to teaching presupposes a philosophy of education; and the existence of such a philosophy is not always admitted. Even that there is a science of education has been denied; and for stronger reasons may its philosophy be questioned, it being a higher generalization of principles. A distinguished writer, in the *Educational Review*, discusses at length the question, "Is there a science of education?" and concludes in these words: "To sum all up in a word, teaching is an art. Therefore there is indeed no science of education."

That there is not yet a fairly well organized and complete system of educational principles may be readily admitted. But the impossibility of such a science is affirmed on the ground that teaching is an art. This conclusion, however, taken apart from the reasoning on which it is based, does not represent the writer fairly. The drift of the article shows him to mean this: There is no science whose generalizations will fit the concrete case in every act of teaching; that there are special conditions and individual peculiarities that no principle can anticipate. But there is no science of any kind whose generalizations exactly fit the concrete case. The individuals brought into scientific system retain their individuality. We doubt not that there is a science of vertebrates; or think the science of them the less perfect or the less valuable because each vertebrate has countless characteristics which the generalizations must ignore. In fact, it would not be a science without such differences. In order to have a science, the general fact, or law, must be seen as manifesting itself in diversity of individuals. Generalizations of science are not abstractions; but, to be generalizations, must retain their hold on the individuals.

While no other teaching act is just like the one in which that individual teacher instructs that individual pupil, yet that act has essential marks and common elements with every other teaching act. It is the divine skill of the born teacher's instinct that seizes the peculiarity, which seems to annul the law; yet the law is there, and must also be discerned, or the peculiarity could not be known as such. The tact and personal insight of the teacher required in every act of teaching is not to be guided by the immediate consciousness of general principles; but this does not prove that there is no science of teaching, or that such a science is not of supreme value, even to the divinely gifted teacher.

If, in order to be a science, generalizations must be made which shall blot out all peculiarities of each teaching act, so that the teacher needs to apply only monotonous rules, which require no personal insight into the peculiarities of the immediate case, then indeed there is no science of teaching possible; then not even desirable. The science of teaching must leave room for the individual element; as does, without question, any other science. It must ever be remembered that the individual case is not wholly peculiar; that the most essential thing in it is that which is found in every other case. The peculiarity may be so prominent as to thrust the universal element into the background; but the universal element gives law to the act of teaching. The science of education brings diversity under law. It must enable the teacher to bring into consciousness the essential elements of all teaching in every particular act of it.

The philosophy of teaching, as distinguished from the science, gives distinct emphasis to the universal element, showing its controlling power in all that the teacher does. It is the explanation of the teaching process by means of universal law. By it the separate acts are brought, not only into unity among themselves, which constitutes merely the science of teaching, but they are brought into the unity of the complete system of means of spiritual growth. Science expains a group of phenomena by a principle, or law, oc-extensive [*sic*] with the group explained. At least, emphasis is given to such a principle. Philosophy explains a group of phenomena by some principle, or law, which extends beyond the group explained to all other groups. The science of grammar brings all sentences into their own unity; that is, into unity among themselves; while the philosophy of grammar brings the unity established by science into the unity of the universe. It is this larger unity alone which illumines the whole pathway of the teacher, and yields assured guidance to the goal of his labor.

Dignity of work does not depend on what one does, but on being consciously controlled, in the doing, by universal law. The teacher who is conscious only of the individual process before him, is on the lowest possible plane of unskilled labor; he is the slave of recipes and devices. As by degrees he comes under the controlling power of higher and still higher generality of law, he rises from the automatic action of a mere operative to the plane of rational insight and self-direction. The highest plane is that in which universal law guides the hand and inspires the heart. The whole sky of truth bends over each recitation; and the teacher needs but climb Sinai to receive the divine law. All the laws of thought and being pervade the teaching process; all philosophy is back of it. At first, Aristotle, Kant, Hegel, and Spencer seem remote from the immediate work of the teacher. This remoteness must be made to disappear; the ends of the earth must be brought together; the universal laws of spiritual life must become native atmosphere to the teacher. We harm ourselves and degrade our work in holding philosophy to be of another world: that the philosophy of education is one thing, and the practice of educating another thing; that the philosophy of education belongs to the professional philosophizer on great educational problems, rather than to the day-laborer in the vineyard. It is said that philosophy can bake no bread, but that she can secure to us God and immortality. This ought to be sufficient. But she can bake bread, and must do so or miss God and immortality. To secure heaven she must mix with the daily affairs of earth; and while searching out God and immortality, must bring counsel and comfort to the day-laborer in the school-room. . . .

THE TEACHING PROCESS.

. . . The consciousness of manipulating machinery instead of conducting a spiritual process, an experience of growth on the part of the learner, is the main root of all school errors, and has its origin in the belief that knowing itself is a mechanical process,—a belief that the mind is a receptacle called memory, to hold what is put into it; and that learning is receiving and retaining something foreign to the self. The mind being a receptacle, the teacher is, by means of contrivance of lever, wheel, and rope, to transfer some ponderable, external stuff into it. The machinery by which this is done becomes the important factor, and the manipulation of it the chief process involved; for knowing, as usually conceived, is not a process, and the mind is something other than that which it knows.

It is a long step toward freedom when the teacher awakens to the fact that teaching is a spiritual process below the form; that it is the vital touch of the teacher's mind with the mind in which the knowledge is born, and not that of external relation of transferring something to it manufactured elsewhere than in the mind learning. The wind may bear the fecundating pollen to the stigma; but the process of flowering and fruiting is another matter. Some phase of the bondage to the formal and mechanical has been the object of attack of all education reformers; and must continue to receive their attention, for each generation falls into the bondage anew. Every teacher, in learning his art, must strive earnestly from the first to live in consciousness of the spiritual movement below the form; and to hold the form as the mere varying surface play of that movement.

It has been said that teaching is a mental process, in which the mind of the teacher comes in vital touch with the mind of the learner. The mind of the teacher moves forward in the same line of thought, feeling, and volition with the mind of the one taught. The teacher cannot produce in the learner a given experience without having first produced in himself that experience. If the teacher is to cause the pupil to think the position, form, size, cause, and effects of the Gulf Stream, the teacher himself must think each of these relations while stimulating the pupil to think each of them. If patriotism is to be aroused by teaching ''Barbara Frietchie,'' the teacher himself must be stirred by that feeling while causing the pupil to experience it. Thus the two minds are always one in the mental steps required to learn an object; and, also, in the emotion to be cultivated and the resolution to be strengthened. The teacher passes into some act or state of experience, and the pupil rises, at the touch of the teacher, into the same experience.

An important inference from the foregoing should be noted. It is an old saying that as the teacher so the school. The best meaning for this is, that the pupil's mind, in the act of learning, becomes like the teacher's mind; it takes on the tone and coloring of the teacher's thought. The teacher builds his own thought structure into the mind of the pupil; begets him with his own purity, strength, and sweep of emotional life; breathes into him the breath of his own ethical nature. The teacher may resolve to train to accurate, thorough, and methodical habits of thought; but unless these are habits of his own mind his efforts will be unavailing. The stream cannot rise higher than its source. If the teacher thinks loosely and slovenly he cannot hope to realize anything better in the pupil, so far as the teaching goes. The narrow pedant and dogmatist can never secure scholarly habits and liberal culture. The teacher who has not a rich and full range of emotional life can expect nothing but a withered soul born of his teaching. The man who has not strength and purity of character cannot strengthen and purify character. The teacher builds his life into that of his pupil; and it is absolutely essential that his life be all that he expects his pupil to become. The quality of a teacher's life is a part of his professional equipment.

Particular Nature.—1. While the teacher's mind and that of the pupil take the same steps in the process of teaching and of learning, there must be the essential difference which makes the one teaching and the other learning. The difference lies here: while the pupil thinks the object under consideration, the teacher thinks the pupil's process of thinking the object. For example, there are a certain number of fixed mental steps necessary on the part of the pupil to gain the idea adjective: (1) he perceives, (2) imagines, (3) compares and contrasts, (4) reasons, and (5) generalizes. The pupil must move through these forms of activity, but he is not conscious of the movement. His whole conscious effort is expended on the object studied. He says, I find this and this and this in the object; not that now I am perceiving, imagining, etc. The teacher must be conscious of the process of the pupil in knowing the object in the act of producing that process; for how else could he rationally produce it? The difference is between thinking the object and thinking the process of thinking the object. The pupil, in the study of geography, is thinking the earth; but in teaching geography the teacher must think the pupil's thinking of the earth. It follows that the steps of the teacher, which are identical with those of the pupil, as before explained, must be represented steps; the knowledge must be old knowledge. The teacher has before taken the steps in knowing the adjective; so that in teaching he is relieved from any conscious effort in learning it, and may put his whole attention to the pupil's process of learning it. This suggests the necessity for the teacher's familiarity with the subject-matter of instruction.

One phase of a teacher's professional knowledge of a subject is obvious from the foregoing. An academic knowledge of grammar enables the student to think the subject of grammar; while the teacher's knowledge of that subject enables him to think grammer into the processes of the learning mind. As a basis for this the teacher must know the subject of grammar and the mind learning it; but the professional aspect of the work appears when the teacher resolves grammar into the mental processes of the pupil; or, brings the pupil's processes into the form of grammar. All professional treatment of subject-matter resolves it into the mental experience of the learner. . . .

3. Thus far, teaching appears to be the conscious act of producing mental experience in the pupil; and that there is in the process two conscious elements, making the act complex: consciousness of the experience in the act of producing it, and consciousness of the means by which to produce it. The third, and last, factor of which the teacher is conscious is that of the effect of the experience produced on the character of the pupil. In fact, the experience is produced because a certain end in life is to be reached. The rational teacher says to himself that the pupil's spiritual growth requires a given course of experience, and then he proceeds to adjust means to secure that experience. It is impossible to conceive how one can conduct a process without being conscious of the aim in the process. All the steps must be brought into the unity of the aim. If to-day the teacher is to cause the pupil to think Westminster Abbey and to arouse certain emotions by that object, he should be able to state how the knowledge, and how such thinking and feeling, helps the child to realize the aim of life. . . .

It thus appears that teaching is a conscious process having three organic elements: (1) consciousness of the mental experience in the act of producing it, (2) of the means of stimulating the experience in the pupil, and (3) of the value, or purpose, of the experience in the unfolding life of the pupil. Put in the form of a definition: *Teaching is the conscious process of producing mental experience for the purpose of life development;* or, to rid this of its tautology, *Teaching is the process by which one mind, from set purpose, produces the life-unfolding process in another.*

The subjective process above described is not teaching till its counterpart is realized in the objective process of the recitation. The triple idea in the mind of the teacher realizes itself in the external process with the pupil, having the three elements corresponding with those in the subjective process. The elements, however, are reversed as the process held in the mind of the teacher realizes itself in the class taught.

In observing a recitation, the thing noted first in order of time, and first as logical condition, is the external means employed by the teacher; such as directions, questions, statements, illustrations, etc. The second element in time, and in logical relation, is the experience produced; and the last is the good resulting to the learner. But the process in the mind of the teacher has a reverse order. The good of the child must be first in mind; then, and not before, the experience necessary to that good may be considered; and the experience to be produced necessarily precedes in thought the stimulus to that experience.

From: Col. Francis Wayland Parker, *Talks on Pedagogics*: *An Outline of the Theory of Concentration* (1894)

FRANCIS WAYLAND PARKER (1837–1902) was born in Piscataquog, New Hampshire. He studied in rural New Hampshire and attended an academy in Mount Vernon. He began to teach in his home state at sixteen. He taught at Carrollton, Illinois, from 1858 to 1861, when he enlisted in the Union Army. After the war he served as principal of the grammar school in Manchester, New Hampshire (1865–1868), and the district schools in Dayton, Ohio (1868–1871), where he began to put into practice his radical and experimental methods of teaching reflective of the influence of Edward A. Sheldon's *Object Lessons*. In 1871 he went to Europe and studied, at the University of Berlin, the theories of John Amos Comenius, Johann Heinrich Pestalozzi, Johann Friedrich Herbart, and Friedrich Froebel, as well as Carl Ritter's and Arnold Guyot's new methods of teaching geography. In 1875, after returning to the United States, he was appointed superintendent of schools at Quincy, Massachusetts. From 1880 to 1883 he served as supervisor of schools at Boston, from 1883 to 1896 as principal of the Cook County (Illinois) Normal School, and from 1896 to 1899 as principal of its successor, the Chicago Normal School (later, Chicago State University). In 1899 he became president of the Chicago Institute. When the institute became affiliated with the University of Chicago, Parker became the first director of its School of Education. John Dewey referred to Parker, who founded the progressive education movement, as the father of modern education.

I. THE CHILD.

I propose in this and the following talks to present a general exposition of the theory of CONCENTRATION.

The least that can be said for this theory is that it presents to some extent an outline of a rounded educational doctrine for the study and criticism of teachers.

In the beginning of these discussions, the question of all questions, and indeed the everlasting question, is: what is the being to be educated? What is the child? What is this little lump of flesh, breathing life and singing the song of immortality? The wisdom and philosophy of ages upon ages have asked this question, and still it remains unanswered. It is the central problem

302

NOTES

OF

TALKS ON TEACHING,

GIVEN BY

FRANCIS W. PARKER,

AT THE

MARTHA'S VINEYARD SUMMER INSTITUTE,
July 17 to August 19, 1882.

REPORTED BY

LELIA E. PATRIDGE.

FOURTH EDITION.

NEW YORK:
E. L. KELLOGG & CO.
1883.

Yours truly
Francis W. Parker

of the universe. The child is the climax and culmination of all God's creations, and to answer the question, "What is the child?" is to approach nearer the still greater question, What is the Creator and Giver of Life?

I can answer the question tentatively. It is a question for you and for me, and for the teachers of the present and the future, to answer; and still it will ever remain the unanswered question. We should study the child, as we study all phenomena, by its actions, and by its tendencies to act. The child is born, we are told by scientists, deaf, dumb, and blind, yet, in design, possessing marvellous possibilities for development. It is well for us to stand by the cradle of a little child who has drawn his first breath, and is ready to be acted upon by the external energies which surround him.

One hypothesis we can accept as true: the inherited organism of bone, muscle, and brain determines exactly the limits or boundaries of the baby's development. Each nerve-fibre or convolution of the brain says: "Thus far shalt thou go and no farther;" and it is well to say in the same breath that no human being ever had the external conditions for growth by which the full possibilities, predetermined and fixed by the organism, have been realized. The organism itself determines the external conditions for development. Every muscle, every nerve, every fibre, every convolution of the brain, their nature and power, are in themselves possibilities for the reception of those external energies which act upon the body of the child, and make their way to the brain through the sensorium. The child itself is a central energy; or complex of energies, upon which and through which certain external energies act. No simple energy can enter a child's brain except by first touching the child's body (the end-organs), and countless energies touch the child's body which do not enter the brain at all; others enter, but lie below the plane of consciousness.

II. THE CENTRAL SUBJECTS OF STUDY.

Design is a fundmental premise in all that exists. There is a design in each individual being. Another term for design is possibilities to be realized. The working out of the design of a human being into character is education; the realization of all the possibilities of human growth and development is education. In the presentation of conditions for the working out of that design, or the realization of possibilities, consists the art of educating. All mental and moral development is by self-activity. Education is the economizing of self-effort in the direction of all-sided development. Economy of energy is the instrinsic mark and sign of all progress in nature and in art. Apply this fact to education: the individual being is developed by immutable laws, the fundamental law of which is self-activity; all the past, with its vast treasures, has brought us consists of better conditions for human growth, and a better knowledge of the adaptation of those conditions to each stage of development. The study of the science of education gives us a higher knowledge of the human being, and a better knowledge of the conditions to be applied. The art of teaching is the scientific, economical, adaptation of conditions for educative effort. . . .

The common saying that reading is getting the thought of an author is not scientifically correct. Strictly, no one can ever have any thought but his own. The mental value of reading, or intense reading (the study of text), depends entirely upon the ideas which lie below the plane of consciousness; upon the individual concepts that have formerly been in consciousness, and up-on personal experiences, inferences, comparisons, and generalizations. Upon the richness, fulness, and quality of one's own mind depends the action of printed words. Sentences recall former concepts, unite new ones, and arouse the power to understand or to draw original inferences. The quality of all imaginative acts is determined by the quality of previous acts of observation. Thus we see that reading is not the key to knowledge; it is rather the corridor beyond the broad door swung open by observation. . . .

IX. READING AND ITS RELATIONS TO THE CENTRAL SUBJECTS.

Reading is a mental process. It consists of a sequence of mental activities immediately caused or induced by the action of written or printed words arranged in sentences. I propose to discuss the psychology and pedagogics of reading as a mode of attention. Oral reading is a mode of expression, and comes under the head of speech. Many of the grossest errors in teaching reading spring from confounding the two processes of attention and expression. Reading in itself is not expression any more than observation or hearing-language is expression. The custom of making oral reading the principal and almost the only means of teaching reading has led to the many errors prevalent to-day.

Observation is thinking; hearing-language is thinking; reading is thinking; and in anything like a reasonable discussion of the psychological nature of reading the subject of oral reading must be referred to its proper place as a mode of expression.

Reading in itself has no educative value; it does not give rise to a succession of educative acts any more than does seeing, hearing, or touching. The value of reading in education depends entirely upon the educative subject presented, and upon the intensity of the conscious acts. Ordinary reading, then, is not educative. It may consist of a succession of conscious states without any appreciable degree of intensity; it may consist of intense immoral states degrading to the mind: in a word, reading in itself is not moral, neither does it necessarily induce educative action. Reading may lead to the pollution of the soul; or, under the right conditions, it may be made the means of its highest development and elevation. The educative value of reading, then, depends (1) upon what is read; (2) upon how it is read.

With these very important modifications in view it is readily seen that reading in itself may be made, next to observation, the greatest factor in education. Reading opens all the historical records of the past, all the discussions and discoveries that have been made throughout the ages. By reading, poetry and literature may become essential means of human growth. Here I wish to repeat what I have already said in discussing attention: a reader does not think the thought of an author, he simply thinks his *own* thought. By the action of words upon the mind ideas arise above the plane of consciousness; individual concepts and judgments that have formerly been in consciousness reappear, and are recombined and associated; new units are formed and fresh judgments suggested; but the mental results of written or printed words upon the mind are predetermined by the mind itself. If it were true that reading is "getting the thought of an author," then we should have to suppose that the reader has the power to think as the author thinks, the same power of imagination, the same power of inference, of generalization; in fact the power to follow the same processes of reasoning.

Reading is thinking, and thinking depends utterly upon the individual power of the mind. The difference between reading, and studying books consists entirely in the fact that the latter action is more intense than the former. In ordinary reading, waves or states of consciousness are held under the action of the will. In reading, a sentence arouses a thought which is immediately succeeded by another, and another, and so on; in study, the thought aroused by the sentence is delayed or hemmed in, more distinctly presented to the *ego*, and therefore intensified by the action of the will. The result of this hemming in and intensification is a more vivid imagination, and consequently more valuable inferences. Ordinary reading is the essential preparation for study, as the exercise of the senses is for observation.

The psychology of reading, and at the same time of study, plays such an immense part in education that its comprehension is a prime necessity. . . .

No one can observe the work of pupils from the primary grades to the university without being amazed at the impotency of many to think by means of the printed word; the ability to really study text is rare, the ability to merely memorize words is common.

The study of text differs from common reading in the intensity of those acts of the will that hem the flow of consciousness. Now if the child early forms the habit of believing that he reads when he pronounces words,—and by the tricks of the phonic and phonetic methods he can acquire great facility in mere pronunciation,—there is great danger that he will never acquire the fixed habit of thinking by means of words. He will suppose that the pronunciation of words is reading, and afterwards, in studying, he will suppose that learning a lesson means committing words verbatim. This is one of the most terrible evils in all teaching—this habit of pronouncing and learning words disassociated from the thought.

The great benefit of the method of concentration in teaching reading here presented, is that the child will never fancy that he is reading unless he has the thought aroused by the words; if the words do not arouse the thought, he will struggle to that end, willl never read aloud without the closest thinking, and will never study without the most intense thinking. . . .

Most school reading is desultory, promiscuous, and unrelated to the subjects taught; some of it is in a good sense educative; much of it void of sense, and of no literary value whatever. The proposition of the theory of unification is to concentrate directly all reading—first, last, and at every step—upon the central subjects of study in hand: it proposes that geography shall be enhanced by descriptions of countries, travels, and stories; that interest in science shall be kept aglow by delightful accounts of research and discoveries; that history shall be illuminated by the most precious literature, and explained by the mythical treasures of the ages. When, for instance, the intensely interesting story of the first battle of the Revolution is studied, the pupils shall hear "a hurry of hoofs in a village street," shall see "a shape in the moonlight, a bulk in the dark, and beneath, from the pebbles, in passing, a spark" which "kindled the land into flame with its heat." Or when the wonderful story of the Greeks is told, it shall be accompanied by the glorious lyrics of Homer. Literature is the flood-tide of national growth, and loses its power when not immediately related to the peoples who made it possible. . . .

The demand here made is, that from beginning to end the child shall think; that the action of his mind shall be upon that thought which he most needs for his own growth and development; that symbols shall act upon his mind immediately, attracting to themselves the least possible attention; that he shall early form fixed habits of thinking when he reads, and of never fancying that he is reading unless he is thinking. Thus reading may be made, next to observation, the greatest, means of mental and moral development.

I need not describe at any great length what the method of quantity is: it is the prevailing method of today—of text-books, pages, word-cramming and word-recitation; of learning, believing, and conforming; the method of pedantry; the method that limits the mental horizon; the method that keeps the mind from looking outside of a certain definite circle; the method of implicit belief. It is the last ditch of the rule of the few-forced by necessity to give the people education, but still acting to keep the people from the highway of freedom. The method of quantity is almost absolute in its influence; not quite so, for there have been in every age geniuses who, given a stone, would transform it into the bread of life.

In order to explain this method, I must contrast it with the true method, the method of quality,—quality of mental action. I have said that education is self-effort toward freedom by the shortest line of resistance, self-effort in finding and applying the truth; and this is what I mean by quality of mental action—that action of the mind which makes original inferences, which goes through consecutive reasoning processes based upon exact data. The most precious gift of God to man is choice; free choice is the dividing line between man and man, and man and the brute. All progress consists in the discovery and application of truth; man was created to contribute his personal mite of self-choice to the great body of discovered truth. Education consists in presenting the right conditions for personal choice.

If the quality of mental action is right, the quantity will take care of itself. The reason why most students have after long years of painful, arduous drudgery so little mental power, is that their whole ideal is the acquisition of a quantity of facts: they have never had any exercise in quality of action; their minds are simply passive receptacles, taking without resistance that which comes from supposed authorities; self-reliance buried past all resurrection by sixteen years of persistent word-cram.

The products of this method of quantity may be so-called scholars, learned savants, pedants, walking cyclopedias; but have not the inventions of the ages, the newer discoveries of the truth, been met by the opposition of just this class of pedants? The common people have always heard the truth gladly; but the pedant, whose belief in himself is absolute, whose imagination never catches a glimpse beyond the fixed barrier of his own fixed belief, has ever rejected it. Pedants and bigots are the worst outcome of quantity teaching. They have stood as the mighty barriers of progress in all ages; they drove Galileo to prison. It was not one sect alone, but all the learned men, both Protestant and Catholic, of Europe who opposed him, because they had not the power to investigate the truth he presented. . . .

The methods of the few, in their control of the many, still govern our public schools, and to a great degree determine their management: the method of the prison, torture, police, and standing army survives in corporal punishment; the method of bribery,—in reward and prize giving. Both of these immoral methods are absolutely useless; they are the outcome of quantity teaching and the makeshifts of unskilled teachers. Given devoted trained teachers, together with right surroundings and the right educative work, there is absolutely no necessity for either corporal punishment or the bribery of rewards.

The method of mystery still exercises its fearful power,—the inoculated belief that there is something occult and mysterious in knowledge. The height of art is its simplicity, and the same can be said of the art of teaching. What I mean by the control of mystery is illustrated by the attitude of the people toward education. Let a teacher in a country school teach that which a farmer most needs upon the farm,—practical chemistry; let him teach soil, physics, meteorology, zoology of the insects that infest his crops; let him teach arithmetic sensibly by measuring and weighing,—and the farmers would call an indignation meeting and put out a man holding and teaching such newfangled notions. By learning they mean some mysterious process foreign to them. It does not readily enter their minds that that which is most practical is most logical, and that the old teaching of quantity, the mysterious pedantry of the schoolteacher, who is supposed to know so much, is a relic of barbarism, and should hold the same place in the world of affairs as the sickle and the scythe. . . .

The strongest indication that quantity teaching is in the ascendancy is the profound disbelief of the people in anything like a science of education. I have not time to prove that there is a science of education. If, however, there is no such science, then all the other sciences are myths and delusions. Science is organized knowledge of law; and to deny that there is a science of education is to deny that the development of human beings is governed by law.

Robert Lowe (Lord Sherbrooke), while at the head of the English Privy Council, and Chairman of the Education Committee, was asked to support a movement for the establishment of chairs of pedagogics in universities. "There are no principles of education," said this child of tradition. Less than fifteen years ago a distinguished head of a great university declared that all there is to pedagogics could be learned in an hour and a half! It is well for me to say here, that the gentleman has changed his mind most decidedly; indeed, he is a prominent leader in the so-called new education. Colleges did not recognize this science until within a few years. The first Professor of Pedagogics in America, Miss Bibb, was appointed in the University of Missouri within a few years.

The substantial disbelief in a science of education, and the almost universal indifference in regard to it, has one cause, and that cause is quantity teaching; the stimulus to the drudgery is the strap, or, worse, rewards and prizes. A teacher with a conscience, an artist teacher, cannot do such menial service: it would be like requiring a Raphael to paint a board fence. If quantity teaching is ideal teaching, then the plainest deduction is, there is no science of education.

By far the greatest barrier to making the common school what it should and can be, by no means springs from active opposition to the system or from the patronage and pulls of pot-house politicians: *the greatest barrier is the profound indifference of the most intelligent people in regard to the possibilities of radical improvement.* This indifference has been enhanced until within a few years by the influence of colleges and universities, in which quantity instruction has had full swing.

From: Emile Durkheim, "The Nature and Method of
Pedagogy," *Education and Sociology* (1895); Sherwood D.
Fox, translator (1956)

EMILE DURKHEIM was born in Epinal, Lorraine, France, in 1858. He was educated at École Normale, Paris (from which he graduated in 1882), and studied under German psychologist Wilhelm Wundt (1885–1886). A teacher and
a theorist of teaching, Durkheim taught philosophy in provincial lycées
(1882–1885), was lecturer in education and sociology (1887–1896) and professor of sociology (1896–1902; first professorship in sociology in France) at
the University of Bordeaux, and professor of sociology and education at the
University of Paris, Sorbonne (1902–1917).

This excerpt is from *Education and Sociology*, composed in 1895 but published posthumously in 1922, and again in 1956.

The two words "education" and "pedagogy" have often been confused;
they must, however, be carefully distinguished.

Education is the influence exerted on children by parents and teachers.
This influence is always present and it is general. There is no period in social
life, there is not, so to speak, even a moment in the day when the young
generations are not in contact with their elders and when, therefore, they are
not receiving from them some educational influence. For this influence does
not make itself felt only in the very brief moments when parents or teachers
are consciously, and by explicit teaching, communicating the results of their
experience to those who come after them. There is an unconscious education
that never ceases. By our example, by the words that we utter, by the actions
that we perform, we constantly mold our children.

It is quite otherwise with pedagogy. This consists not of actions, but of
theories. These theories are ways of conceiving of education, not ways of
practicing it. Sometimes they are distinguished from practices in use to the
point of being opposed to them. The pedagogy of Rabelais, that of Rousseau
or of Pestalozzi, are in opposition to the education of their times. Education
is, then, only the subject of pedagogy. The latter consists of a certain way of
reflecting on the phenomena of education.

This is what makes pedagogy, at least in the past, intermittent, while education is continuous. There are peoples who have not had pedagogy, properly speaking; it appears, too, only at a relatively advanced period in history. It is found in Greece only after the time of Pericles, with Plato, Xenophon, and Aristotle. It hardly existed in Rome. In the Christian societies, it is only in the sixteenth century that it produces important works; and the progress that it makes then slows down in the following century, to resume its full vigor only during the eighteenth century. This is because man does not always reflect, but only when it is necessary to reflect, and because the conditions for reflection are not always and everywhere given.

This being established, we must find out what are the characteristics of pedagogical reflection and of its products. Must we see in it properly scientific theories, and should we say of pedagogy that it is a science, the science of education? Or is it appropriate to give it another name, and what? . . .

In order to make things quite clear, we must distinguish carefully two different kinds of speculation. Pedagogy is something other than the science of education. What is it, then? To make a reasoned choice, it is not enough for us to know what it is not; we must show what it is.

Shall we say that it is an art? This conclusion would appear to be obvious; for ordinarily one does not see any intermediate step between these two extremes and one gives the name ''art'' to any product of reflection which is not science. But this is to stretch the meaning of the word ''art'' to the point of including in it very different things.

Indeed, one also calls ''art'' the practical experience acquired by the teacher in contact with children and in the exercise of his profession. Now, this experience is manifestly a very different thing from the theories of the pedagogue. A fact of current observation makes this difference very apparent. One can be a fine teacher and yet be quite unsuited for the speculations of pedagogy. The skillful teacher knows how to do what must be done, without always being able to give the reasons that justify the procedures that he employs. Conversely, the pedagogue may lack all practical ability; we would have entrusted a class neither to Rousseau nor to Montaigne. Even of Pestalozzi, who, moreover, was himself an educator, one can say that he was probably not much of a teacher, as his repeated failures prove. The same confusion is found in other fields. One calls ''art'' the skill of the statesman, expert in the handling of public affairs. But one also says that the writings of Plato, of Aristotle, of Rousseau, are treatises on the art of politics; and we can certainly not see in them truly scientific works, since their object is not to study the real, but to construct an ideal. However, there is a wide gap between the mental processes that a book like the *Social Contract* implies and those that the administration of the State presupposes; Rousseau would very likely have been as poor a minister as an educator. It is thus, too, that the best theorists on medical matters are not the best clinicians, by far.

There is an advantage, then, in not denoting by the same word two forms of activity that are so different. It is necessary, we think, to reserve the name of art for everything that is pure practice without theory. It is this that everyone understands when one speaks of the art of the soldier, the art of the lawyer, the art of the teacher. An art is a system of ways of doing which are oriented to special ends and which are the product either of a traditional experience communicated by education, or of the personal experience of the individual. One can acquire them only by coming into contact with the things on which the action is to be performed and by dealing with them oneself. No doubt, it is possible that art may be illuminated by reflection, but reflection is not an essential element of it, since it can exist without reflection. Also, there is not a single art in which everything is reflected upon.

But between art so defined and science properly speaking, there is a place for an intermediate mental attitude. Instead of acting on things or on beings in a determinate way, one reflects on the processes of action which are thus employed, not to understand and explain them, but to appreciate what they are worth, if they are what they should be, if it is not useful to modify them, and in what way, and even more, to replace them completely with new procedures. These reflections take the form of theories; they are combinations of ideas, not combinations of acts, and in this they become closer to science. But the ideas which are so combined have, as their object, not to express the nature of things as given, but to direct action. They are not actions, but are closely related to actions which it is their function to orient. If they are not actions they are at least programs of action, and in this respect they are like art. Such are theories of medicine, politics, strategy, etc. To express the mixed character of these kinds of speculations, we propose to call them practical theories. Pedagogy is a practical theory of this type. It does not study systems of education scientifically, but it reflects on them in order to provide the activity of the educator with ideas to guide it.

III. But pedagogy, thus understood, is exposed to an objection the importance of which cannot be dissimulated. No doubt, it may be said, a practical theory is possible and legitimate when it can rest upon an established and undisputed science, of which it is only the application. In this case, indeed, the theoretical notions from which the practical consequences are deduced have a scientific value which is imparted to the conclusions that one draws from them. It is thus that applied chemistry is a practical theory which is only the putting into practice of the theories of pure chemistry. But a practical theory is worth only as much as the sciences from which it borrows its fundamental notions. Now, on what sciences can pedagogy rest? First there should be the science of education. For in order to know what education should be, it would be necessary, before anything, to know what its nature is, what are the diverse conditions on which it depends, the laws according to which it has evolved historically. But the science of education hardly exists except in embryonic form. There remain, on the one hand, the other branches of sociology which could aid pedagogy to fix the end of education, with the general orientation of method; on the other hand, psychology, the teachings of which could be very useful for the determination in detail of pedagogical procedures. But sociology is only a new science; it has only a very few established propositions, assuming that there are any at all. Psychology itself, although it was established earlier than the social sciences, is the object of all sorts of controversies; there are no psychological questions on which the most contradictory propositions are not still asserted. Consequently, what can practical conclusions be worth which rest on scientific data that are at the same time so uncertain and so incomplete? What can be . the value of a pedagogical speculation which has no bases, or the bases of which, when they are not totally lacking, are so weak?

The fact that is thus invoked to discredit pedagogy is in itself indisputable. To be sure, the science of education has yet to be fully established, sociology and psychology are still not very well developed. If, then, we could wait, it would be prudent and methodical to be patient until these sciences would have made progress and would be able to be used with more assurance. But the problem is precisely that we may not be patient. We are not free to pose the problem to ourselves or to put it off; it is put to us, or rather imposed by phenomena themselves, by facts, by the necessity to live. This is not the whole story. We have begun, and we must go on. At many points our traditional system of education is no longer in harmony with our ideas and our needs. We have a choice, then, only between the following two alternatives: either try to preserve the practices that the past has left to us, anyway, even though they no longer answer the exigencies of the situation, or to undertake resolutely to reestablish the disturbed harmony by finding out what the necessary modifications are. Of these two alternatives, the first is not realizable and can come to nothing. Nothing is so fruitless as these attempts to give an artificial life and apparent authority to obsolete and discredited institutions. Failure is inevitable. One cannot stifle the ideas which these institutions contradict; one cannot silence the needs with which they clash. The forces against which one thus undertakes to fight cannot fail to win out.

We can only, then, set to work courageously, inquire into the changes which are indicated, and realize them. But how to discover them if not through reflection? Only the thinking mind can fill in the gaps in the tradition, when the latter has been faulty. Now, what is pedagogy if not reflection applied as systematically as possible to the phenomena of education, with the aim of regulating its development? No doubt, we do not have at our disposal all the elements that would be desirable for resolving the problem; but that is no reason for not seeking to resolve it—because it must be resolved. We can only do our best, collect as many instructive facts as we can, interpret them as methodically as we can, in order to reduce to a minimum the chances of error. Such is the role of the pedagogue. Nothing is so vain and sterile as that scientific puritanism which, under the pretext that science is not fully established, counsels abstention and recommends to men that they stand by as indifferent witnesses, or at least resigned ones, at the march of events. Beside the sophism of ignorance, there is the sophism of science which is not less dangerous. No doubt, to act under these conditions, one runs risks. But action never proceeds without risks; science, as advanced as it may be, would not know how to eliminate them. All that can be asked of us is to put all our science, as imperfect as it may be, and all our mental ability into the anticipation of these risks, as well as we can. And this is precisely what the role of pedagogy is. . . .

When the educator takes account of the methods that he employs, of their end and their reason for being, he is in a position to judge them and thus he keeps himself ready to modify them if he becomes convinced that the end to pursue is no longer the same or that the means to employ should be different. Reflection is the force *par excellence* antagonistic to routine, and routine is the obstacle to necessary progress. . . .

IV. But in order that pedagogical reflection may be able to produce the useful effects that one has a right to expect of it, it must be properly cultivated.

(1) We have seen that pedagogy is not education and could not take its place. Its role is not to substitute for practice, but to guide it, enlighten it, help it, if necessary, to fill the gaps which have been produced in it, to remedy its inadequacies. The pedagogue, then, does not have to construct a whole new system of education as if there were none before him; but he must, on the contrary, apply himself above all to knowing and understanding the system of his time; it is on this condition that he will be in a position to use it with discernment and to judge what is defective in it. . . .

The pedagogic culture, then, should have a largely historical basis. It is on this condition that pedagogy will be able to avoid a criticism that has often been made of it and which has strongly prejudiced its influence. Too many pedagogues, including the most outstanding, have undertaken to erect their systems without considering what had existed before them. The treatment to which Ponocrates submits Gargantua before initiating him into new methods is significant on this point: he cleanses his brain ''with Anticyrian hellebore'' in such a way as to make him forget ''everything that he had learned under his former teachers.'' That meant, in an allegorical form, that the new pedagogy was to have nothing in common with that which had preceded. But it meant by the same token that he was ignoring actual conditions. The future cannot be evoked from nothing; we can build it only with the materials that the past has bequeathed to us. An ideal that one constructs taking the reverse of the existing state of affairs is not realizable since it has no roots in reality. Besides, it is clear that the past had its reasons for being; it would not have been able to last if it had not answered legitimate needs which would not disappear completely overnight; one cannot ignore the past so completely without disregarding vital necessities. That is how it comes about that pedagogy has too often been only a form of utopian literature. We would pity children to whom the method of Rousseau or that of Pestalozzi would be rigorously applied. No doubt, these utopias have been able to play a useful role in history. Their very simplicism has allowed them to impress men more vividly and to stimulate them to action. But first, these advantages are not without drawbacks; further, for this everyday pedagogy which each teacher needs to illuminate and guide his daily practice, less emphatic and unilateral training is necessary and, on the contrary, more method, a keener awareness of reality and of the multiple difficulties which must be faced. It is this awareness that a well-understood historical culture will give.

From: Charles Alexander McMurry and Frank Morton McMurry,
  The Method of the Recitation (1897)

CHARLES ALEXANDER MCMURRAY (1857–1929) was born in Crawfordsville, Indiana. He received his elementary, high school, and first professional training in the training school of the Illinois Normal University (later Illinois State University). He attended the university and was graduated in 1876. From 1876 to 1880 he attended the University of Michigan. He did graduate studies at the University of Halle, Germany, then went to Jena, Germany, to study Herbartian pedagogy with William Rein. He received the Ph.D. degree in 1887. When he returned to the United States, he held different teaching positions: he was head of the training school and teacher of education at Winona Normal School (Minnesota) and was on the faculty of Illinois State Normal School (1900) and Northern Illinois Normal School at De Kalb (1899–1915). In 1915 he became professor of elementary education at George Peabody College for Teachers in Nashville, Tennessee, where he remained until his death (1929). With his brother, he was one of the most enthusiastic and knowledgeable proponents of the Herbartian philosophy of education. For eight years he was secretary of the National Herbartian Society, which he organized in 1892. The author of numerous publications on teaching methods, he became known for his type studies in geography.

FRANK MORTON MCMURRY (1862–1936) was born in Crawfordsville, Indiana. Like his older brother he studied at the University of Michigan as well as at the universities of Halle and Jena (Germany). He received the Ph.D. degree from Jena University in 1889. When he returned to the United States he served as principal of a school in Chicago, where he was influenced by Francis W. Parker. He was professor of pedagogics at the State Normal School in Normal, Illinois (1891). After another year in Europe, he taught at the University of Illinois (1893–1894), served as principal of the Franklin School in Buffalo, New York (1894–1895), was appointed professor of pedagogics and dean of the teachers' college at the University of Buffalo, and from 1898 to 1926 he was professor of elementary education at Teachers College, Columbia University. He was a founder of the National Herbart Society for the Scientific Study of Education (later, National Society for the Study of Education) in 1895.

PREFACE

The Method of the Recitation has sprung out of school-room work, and is designed to be a practical application of the principles of method to the various problems of class-room instruction. It is an effort to bring together and to organize the various principles that control skilful teaching.

It is based fundamentally upon the inductive-deductive thought movement in acquiring and using knowledge.

This organized plan of laying out recitation work was first projected by the thinkers of the Herbart school in Germany. For more than thirty years they have been developing and applying it under the title "The Formal Steps of Instruction" *(Die formalen Stufen des Unterrichts)*. Formerly Dr. T. Ziller at Leipzig was a leader in the movement, and more recently Dr. W. Rein at Jena. They worked out their theory and applied it with proficiency to a large variety of topics in different studies, thus showing the flexibility of leading principles under various forms of application.

The Method of the Recitation is based upon the principles of teaching which were expounded and illustrated in the work of Herbart, Ziller, and Rein. At the same time, the authors hope to have shown in the body of the work that we have to do here with principles recognized by teachers in every land, and that there is no thoughtless imitation of foreign methods and devices. While out debt to German thinkers for an organization of fundamental ideas is great, the entire discussion, as here presented, springs out of American conditions; its illustrative materials are drawn exclusively from lessons commonly taught in our schools. . . .

Our pedagogy seems to have fallen into a condition similar to that in which philosophy found itself in the time of the Sophists. Each man's judgment was counted as good as another's. Each man was the measure of all things, and though two men differed radically, both might be right in their judgments. The Sophists were sceptical of any universal standard of truth.

But Socrates, who followed the Sophists, sought in the individual's thinking, when properly guided, a universal principle of truth, so that all men when they think logically and soundly must agree. He was in search of a uniform mode of thinking which would have universal validity. Pedagogy likewise is in search of universal principles of method in learning, based not upon the subjective whim of the teacher, but upon the common law of mental action which is universal with children and students, in fact with all human beings. And the extent to which such universal principles of method are discovered, determines the extent to which there is a science of education.

The question is this: Is there any essential, natural process upon which a uniform method of treating the varied school subjects can be based? As already said, to outward appearance there seems to be no such process; there seem to be no principles that may serve as a guide for all persons in teaching all subjects. But we should not be discouraged by appearances. The fact that even good teachers show an infinite variety of individual and personal traits, and that studies differ greatly in subject-matter, is no proof that there is not a common mode of procedure for instruction. We remember that everywhere in nature and in society is variety and apparent confusion; fundamental laws do not stand out so as to be easily detected by careless observers. They lie deep and must be searched out by patient examination and labor. In the study of trees and flowers no scientist is deceived by the multiplicity and variety of forms. It is the habit of his mind to reduce all varieties to common structural forms and simple classes.

Hence, while there is a large element in teaching that is always variable, according to the branch of study and the differing personality of teacher or pupils, may there not be essential uniformity; some great underlying principles of method?

Could these principles be discovered, no one would deny their value; we are not so enamoured of individual freedom as to refuse submission to rational, regulated processes.

Definite and valuable principles of action, while they check one's freedom along foolish lines, guide effort into the channels of efficiency. Too much freedom becomes positively oppressive. Whether travelling over a continent or through a field of thought, erecting a mansion, or developing a high moral character, whoever would keep his bearings and work forward to an important end, must have a guide. Whether it be a compass, a model, or an ideal, he must look to it continually for direction. Any one engaged in a work so important and difficult as teaching is much in need of fixed principles which outline for him the ideal of method. If convinced that no one method is right, that no ideal can be set up, he is like a sea captain who is persuaded that whatever course he may choose for his vessel is at least possibly good. He acknowledges the possession of no standard of excellence, and sees chiefly fog in his chosen course. He is subject, therefore, to halfhearted action, for energy and encouragement are not born of uncertainty and confusion.

No one, therefore, will object to a search for the unity that may underlie the variety of good methods in teaching.

Our text-books supply us with a definite formulation of methods of teaching. They are generally constructed out of the experience of the better teachers and in conformity with those traditional ideas and practices which are common to the great body of instructors. The examination and comparison of our most widely used text-books in grammar, arithmetic, history, geography, reading, etc., will show a uniformity in at least one very important respect. . . .

If now we find that the ground for this uniformity is really a scientific idea, not only widely recognized, but valid in psychology, we may fix a starting-point for a sound pedagogy. The mastery of the general truths of a study must remain the direct purpose of instruction in each branch of knowledge. These truths are what are known in psychology as general notions or concepts. They are the centres around which the knowledge of any subject is grouped and classified. It is the mastery of these rules and principles, and the ability to apply them, that are constantly aimed at in all the best school work. From an examination of the psychologies we detect that the treatment of the precept and the concept (the particular and the general notion) furnishes two leading chapters of mental science. The process of learning as explained by all the psychologies culminates in the general notion or concept. Psychology supplies, therefore, a strong support to our conclusion as to the basis of scientific method.

It would not be difficult to show that all the higher studies, as history, science, language, medicine, law, etc., become organized under general notions or principles; in fact, the definition of science is ''generalized, classified knowledge.''

In the history of philosophy also the general notion plays a role not less important than in these other subjects. From the days of Socrates and Plato on, inductive and deductive reasoning have set the general notion as the centre of all thinking—as the thing aimed at in induction, and as the basis of all true deduction. When Herbert Spencer, therefore, calls his most fundamental book ''First Principles,'' he has in mind those general truths which lie at the basis of his entire system of thought. . . .

In the main, most subjects are treated according to one of *three methods;* namely, according to the lecture, the text-book, or the developing method.

1. The *lecture method* is followed extensively in college and university work, and to some extent in high schools. According to that plan, the teacher imparts knowledge directly, or tells the facts which the students are expected to learn. . . .

2. *Text-books* have long been in vogue and are probably as popular to-day as ever. Recent years, however, have brought very great improvement in their use. There was a time when it was customary for children to learn verbatim the text in grammar and geography. It is needless to say that that

work was destructive of the best qualities of mind. Subject-matter was often committed to memory that failed entirely to be understood, although a pretence to the contrary was made. In the main, it was the memory that was appealed to, rather than the ability to under stand and appreciate.

In more recent years a better class of teachers has required pupils to memorize only the substance of the thought, neglecting the form of expression in the book. They have often even discouraged similarity between the language of the child and that of the book, hoping thus to throw the chief emphasis upon the thought itself.

A third class of teachers also require only the gist of the lesson, but instead of employing the recitation period for a mere reproduction of the thought, they occupy a good part of that time with discussion, so that the ideas presented in the book may be comprehended and appreciated. . . .

3. The *developing plan of teaching* is one radically different from the lecture and the text-book methods. The teacher who employs it lectures but little to her class, although it is important to remember that she does tell some things outright; neither does she allow the facts that are to be learned to be first presented through a text-book; she prefers to develop facts and conclusions by conversation with the pupils. . . .

Lecturing ordinarily consists simply in offering or telling. The instructor regards the mind as a granary or storehouse, and pours into it the desired knowledge. The learner is not the central thought of the teacher, but the latter directs his attention primarily to the knowledge that he is imparting. Consequently there is little tendency to adjust the new knowledge to what is already present in the pupils' minds. . . .

The text-book plan is essentially like the preceding. The difference lies in the fact that books appeal to the eye by the printed page, while the lecturer, or the one who tells, appeals to the ear. So far as the adjustment of the new to the old is concerned, there is less of it in the text-book than in the lecture. . . .

The third method of using the book, according to which the substance of the text is studied, and then carefully discussed in class, greatly remedies this defect; conversation affords opportunity for calling up related past experiences, correcting misconceptions, etc., and thus the new becomes adjusted to the old. . . .

The third method . . . makes both problems and answers prominent, and it puts the questions to the child before their answers have been presented. More than that, the child is expected to *conceive these answers himself;* he is systematically required to make discoveries, to judge what might reasonably follow from a given situation, to put two and two together and declare the result. Often, too, he finds it possible to *discover the leading questions* involved, as well as their answers; he must often state what should be the next question to be considered, and by practice in such thinking he becomes skilled in *conceiving both problems and their solutions*. Thus provision is made for adjustment of the new to the old by the large amount of self-activity allowed.

Another valuable feature of the developing method is the fact that it provides for a *close sequence of thought*. Text-books ordinarily omit many of the necessary connecting links of thought. . . .

A careful examination of the developing method convinces us that the right kind of conversation is the best means of thoroughly welding new thoughts and feelings to those already in the child's possession, and an examination of text-books shows that they tell many things that could far better be discovered by the children without the aid of any book. Hence, conversation for the sake of developing facts should be prominent in all school instruction; and since text-books, if used to introduce the topics, would often deprive this conversation of its point, their perusal should in such cases *follow* rather than *precede* the discussion itself. . . .

Since discussion is to play so prominent a part in all good teaching, it is well to realize that the skill required in conducting it is shown first of all in the value of the questions asked. It is necessary, therefore, for the ambitious teacher to become a careful student of the *art of questioning*. Especially must she consider the purpose of the questions. Ordinarily they aim merely to test the presence of knowledge supposed to be already acquired in the lesson assigned, as map questions in geography. But those necessary in the developing method cannot aim primarily to test memory in this way; they must provoke thought first of all. Hence, instead of catechetical questions, or others that can be fully answered by a yes or a no, or by memorized statements in the book, those are to be put which are suggestive enough to arouse thought and broad enough to call for even a series of thoughts.

From William James, *Talks to Teachers on Psychology: and to Students on Some of Life's Ideals* (1899)

WILLIAM JAMES (1842–1910) was born in New York City. His formal school-ing was irregular, in part because of his parents' travels, and in part because of his father's regard for the genius of his children and his desire that they develop whatever talent they had been endowed with. In 1861, he entered the Lawrence Scientific School where he spent three years studying chemis-try under Charles W. Eliot, anatomy and physiology under Jeffries Wyman, and zoology with Louis Agassiz. In 1864, he entered the Harvard Medical School. In 1867 he traveled to Germany, where he spent the next eighteen months studying experimental physiology and German language and litera-ture and trying to cure his unstable physical health and his depression. In 1868 he returned to Cambridge and the following year he obtained his medi-cal degree. After recovering from another period of ill health and mental depression, in 1872 he began teaching physiology, comparative anatomy, and hygiene at Harvard and continued doing so for the next ten years. In 1875 he announced in the Department of Natural History a course for graduates on the "Relationship Between Physiology and Psychology," and in the follow-ing year he added an undergraduate version of it. In 1877 the courses were transferred to the Department of Philosophy where, the next year, James became assistant professor. In 1878 he had contracted with H. Holt & Co. a book on psychology, which finally appeared in 1890 as *The Principles of Psy-chology*. The period during which he composed this book was rich with con-tacts with European philosophers and travels to Europe. Before he had completed his task James became weary of it and turned to philosophy, al-though he never completely abandoned psychology. In 1899, when his repu-tation as a psychologist was at the highest, he published his *Talks to Teachers*, a book that had tremendous influence in disseminating the conceptualization of pedagogy as art. The year 1907 saw the publication of his famous *Pragma-tism*. This controversial book epitomizes James's attempts to stress the im-portance of an empirical study of human nature and its application to human affairs; of the significance of the experience of religion and its convergence with science; and of the play of will and feeling in the formation of belief.

323

Imitation. Man has always been recognized as the imitative animal *par excellence.* And there is hardly a book on psychology, however old, which has not devoted at least one paragraph to this fact. It is strange, however, that the full scope and pregnancy of the imitative impulse in man has had to wait till the last dozen years to become adequately recognized. M. Tarde led the way in his admirably original work, "Les Lois de l'Imitation"; and in our own country Professors Royce and Baldwin have kept the ball rolling with all the energy that could be desired. Each of us is in fact what he is almost exclusively by virtue of his imitativeness. We become conscious of what we ourselves are by imitating others—the consciousness of what the others are precedes—the sense of self grows by the sense of pattern. The entire accumulated wealth of mankind—languages, arts, institutions, and sciences—is passed on from one generation to another by what Baldwin has called social heredity, each generation simply imitating the last. . . .

Imitation shades imperceptibly into *Emulation.* Emulation is the impulse to imitate what you see another doing, in order not to appear inferior; and it is hard to draw a sharp line between the manifestations of the two impulses, so inextricably do they mix their efforts. Emulation is the very nerve of human society. Why are you, my hearers, sitting here before me? If no one whom you ever heard of had attended a 'summer school' or teachers' institute, would it have occurred to any one of you to break out independently and do a thing so unprescribed by fashion? Probably not. Nor would your pupils come to you unless the children of their parents' neighbors were all simultaneously being sent to school. We wish not to be lonely or eccentric, and we wish not to be cut off from our share in things which to our neighbors seem desirable privileges.

In the schoolroom, imitation and emulation play absolutely vital parts. Every teacher knows the advantage of having certain things performed by whole bands of children at a time. The teacher who meets with most success is the teacher whose own ways are the most imitable. A teacher should never try to make the pupils do a thing which she cannot do herself. "Come and let me show you how" is an incomparably better stimulus than "Go and do it as the book directs." Children admire a teacher who has skill. What he does seems easy, and they wish to emulate it. It is useless for a dull and devitalized teacher to exhort her pupils to wake up and take an interest. She must first take one herself; then her example is effective as no exhortation can possibly be.

Every school has its tone, moral and intellectual. And this tone is a mere tradition kept up by imitation, due in the first instance to the example set by teachers and by previous pupils of an aggressive and dominating type, copied by the others, and passed on from year to year, so that the new pupils take the cue almost immediately. Such a tone changes very slowly, if at all; and then always under the modifying influence of new personalities aggressive enough in character to set new patterns and not merely to copy the old. The classic example of this sort of tone is the often quoted case of Rugby under Dr. Arnold's administration. He impressed his own character as a model on the imagination of the oldest boys, who in turn were expected and required to impress theirs upon the younger set. The contagiousness of Arnold's genius was such that a Rugby man was said to be recognizable all through life by a peculiar turn of character which he acquired at school. It is obvious that psychology as such can give in this field no precepts of detail. As in so many other fields of teaching, success depends mainly on the native genius of the teacher, the sympathy, tact, and perception which enable him to seize the right moment and to set the right example. . . .

Unquestionably, emulation with one's former self is a noble form of the passion of rivalry, and has a wide scope in the training of the young. But to veto and taboo all possible rivalry of one youth with another, because such rivalry may degenerate into greedy and selfish excess, does seem to savor somewhat of sentimentality, or even of fanaticism. The feeling of rivalry lies at the very basis of our being, all social improvement being largely due to it. There is a noble and generous kind of rivalry, as well as a spiteful and greedy kind; and the noble and generous form is particularly common in childhood. . . .

The wise teacher will use this instinct as he uses others, reaping its advantages, and appealing to it in such a way as to reap a maximum of benefit with a minimum of harm; for, after all, we must confess, with a French critic of Rousseau's doctrine, that the deepest spring of action in us is the sight of action in another. The spectacle of effort is what awakens and sustains our own effort. No runner running all alone on a race-track will find in his own will the power of stimulation which his rivalry with other runners incites, when he feels them at his heels, about to pass. When a trotting horse is 'speeded,' a running horse must go beside him to keep him to the pace. . . .

As imitation slides into emulation, so emulation slides into *Ambition;* and ambition connects itself closely with *Pugnacity* and *Pride*. Consequently, these five instinctive tendencies form an interconnected group of factors, hard to separate in the determination of a great deal of our conduct. The *Ambitious Impulses* would perhaps be the best name for the whole group. . . .

We have of late been hearing much of the philosophy of tenderness in education; 'interest' must be assiduously awakened in everything, difficulties must be smoothed away. *Soft* pedagogics have taken the place of the old steep and rocky path to learning. But from this lukewarm air the bracing oxygen of effort is left out. It is nonsense to suppose that every step in education *can* be interesting. The fighting impulse must often be appealed to. Make the pupil feel ashamed of being scared at fractions, of being 'downed' by the law of falling bodies; rouse his pugnacity and pride, and he will rush at the difficult places with a sort of inner wrath at himself that is one of his best moral faculties. A victory scored under such conditions becomes a turning-point and crisis of his character. It represents the high-water mark of his powers, and serves thereafter as an ideal pattern for his self-imitation. The teacher who never rouses this sort of pugnacious excitement in his pupils falls short of one of his best forms of usefulness.

The next instinct which I shall mention is that of *Ownership,* also one of the radical endowments of the race. It often is the antagonist of imitation. . . .

In education, the instinct of ownership is fundamental, and can be appealed to in many ways. In the house, training in order and neatness begins with the arrangement of the child's own personal possessions. In the school, ownership is particularly important in connection with one of its special forms of activity, the collecting impulse. An object possibly not very interesting in itself, like a shell, a postage stamp, or a single map or drawing, will acquire an interest if it fills a gap in a collection or helps to complete a series. Much of the scholarly work of the world, so far as it is mere bibliography, memory, and erudition (and this lies at the basis of all our human scholarship), would seem to owe its interest rather to the way in which it gratifies the accumulating and collecting instinct than to any special appeal which it makes to our cravings after rationality. . . .

The teacher who can work this impulse into the school tasks is fortunate. Almost all children collect something. A tactful teacher may get them to take pleasure in collecting books; in keeping a neat and orderly collection of notes; in starting, when they are mature enough, a card catalogue; in preserving every drawing or map which they may make. Neatness, order, and method are thus instinctively gained, along with the other benefits which the possession of the collection entails. . . .

But the wise education takes the tide at the flood, and from the kindergarten upward devotes the first years of education to training in construction and to object-teaching. I need to recapitulate here what I said awhile back about the superiority of the objective and experimental methods. They occupy the pupil in a way most congruous with the spontaneous interests of his age. They absorb him, and leave impressions durable and profound. Compared with the youth taught by these methods, one brought up exclusively by books carries through life a certain remoteness from reality: he stands, as it were, out of the pale, and feels that he stands so; and often suffers a kind of melancholy from which he might have been rescued by a more real education. . . .

Of course, the proper pedagogic moment to work skill in, and to clench the useful habit, is when the native impulse is most acutely present. Crowd on the athletic opportunities, the mental arithmetic, the verse-learning, the drawing, the botany, or what not, the moment you have reason to think the hour is ripe. The hour may not last long, and while it continues you may safely let all the child's other occupations take a second place. In this way you economize time and deepen skill; for many an infant prodigy, artistic or mathematical, has a flowering epoch of but a few months. . . .

Attention. Whoever treats of interest inevitably treats of attention, for to say that an object is interesting is only another way of saying that it excites attention. But in addition to the attention which any object already interesting or just becoming interesting claims—passive attention or spontaneous attention, we may call it—there is a more deliberate attention—voluntary attention or attention with effort, as it is called,—which we can give to objects less interesting or uninteresting in themselves. The distinction between active and passive attention is made in all books on psychology, and connects itself with the deeper aspects of the topic. From our present purely practical point of view, however, it is not necessary to be intricate; and passive attention to natively interesting material requires no further elucidation on this occasion. All that we need explicitly to note is that, the more the passive attention is relied on, by keeping the material interesting; and the less the kind of attention requiring effort is appealed to; the more smoothly and pleasantly the class-room work goes on. I must say a few more words, however, about this latter process of voluntary and deliberate attention.

One often hears it said that genius is nothing but a power of sustained attention, and the popular impression probably prevails that men of genius are remarkable for their voluntary powers in this direction. *But a little introspective observation will show any one that voluntary attention cannot be continuously sustained,—that it comes in beats.* When we are studying an uninteresting subject, if our mind tends to wander, we have to bring back out attention every now and then by using distinct pulses of effort, which revivify the topic for a moment, the mind then running on for a certain number of seconds or minutes with spontaneous interest, until again some intercurrent idea captures it and takes it off. Then the processes of volitional recall must be repeated once more. Voluntary attention, in short, is only a momentary affair. The process, whatever it is, exhausts itself in the single act; and, unless the matter is then taken in hand by some trace of interest inherent in the subject, the mind fails to follow it at all. The sustained attention of the genius, sticking to his subject for hours together, is for the most part of the passive sort. The minds of geniuses are full of copious and original associations. The subject of thought, once started, develops all sorts of fascinating consequences. The attention is led along one of these to another in the most interesting manner, and the attention never once tends to stray away.

Voluntary attention is thus an essentially instantaneous affair. You can claim it, for your purposes in the schoolroom, by commanding it in loud, imperious tones; and you can easily get it in this way. But, unless the subject to which you thus recall their attention has inherent power to interest the pupils, you will have got it for only a brief moment; and their minds will soon be wandering again. To keep them where you have called them, you must make the subject too interesting for them to wander again. And for that there is one prescription; but the prescription, like all our prescriptions, is abstract, and, to get practical results from it, you must couple it with mother-wit.

The prescription is that *the subject must be made to show new aspects of itself; to prompt new questions; in a word, to change.* From an unchanging subject the attention inevitably wanders away. You can test this by the simplest possible case of sensorial attention. Try to attend steadfastly to a dot on the paper or on the wall. You presently find that one or the other of two things has happened: either your field of vision has become blurred, so that you now see nothing distinct at all, or else you have involuntarily ceased to look at the dot in question, and are looking at something else. But, if you ask yourself successive questions about the dot,—how big it is, how far, of what shape, what shade of color, etc.; in other words, if you turn it over, if you think of it in various ways, and along with various kinds of associates,—you can keep your mind on it for a comparatively long time. This is what the genius does, in whose hands a given topic coruscates and grows. And this is what the teacher must do for every topic if he wishes to avoid too frequent appeals to voluntary attention of the coerced sort. In all respects, reliance upon such attention as this is a wasteful method, bringing bad temper and nervous wear and tear as well as imperfect results. The teacher who can get along by keeping spontaneous interest excited must be regarded as the teacher with the greatest skill.

There is, however, in all schoolroom work a large mass of material that must be dull and unexciting, and to which it is impossible in any continuous way to contribute an interest associatively derived. There are, therefore, certain external methods, which every teacher knows, of voluntarily arousing the attention from time to time and keeping it upon the subject. Mr. Fitch has a lecture on the art of securing attention, and he briefly passes these methods in review; the posture must be changed; places can be changed. Questions, after being answered singly, may occasionally be answered in concert. Elliptical questions may be asked, the pupil supplying the missing word. The teacher must pounce upon the most listless child and wake him up. The habit of prompt and ready response must be kept up. Recapitulations, illustrations, examples, novelty of order, and ruptures of routine,—all these are means for keeping the attention alive and contributing a little interest to a dull subject. Above all, the teacher must himself be alive and ready, and must use the contagion of his own example.

But, when all is said and done, the fact remains that some teachers have a naturally inspiring presence, and can make their exercises interesting, while others simply cannot. And psychology and general pedagogy here confess their failure, and hand things over to the deeper springs of human personality to conduct the task. . . .

The genius of the interesting teacher consists in sympathetic divination of the sort of material with which the pupil's mind is likely to be already spontaneously engaged, and in the ingenuity which discovers paths of connection from that material to the matters to be newly learned. The principle is easy to grasp, but the accomplishment is difficult in the extreme. And a knowledge of such psychology as this which I am recalling can no more make a good teacher than a knowledge of the laws of perspective can make a landscape painter of effective skill. . . .

If the topic be highly abstract, show its nature by concrete examples. If it be unfamiliar, trace some point of analogy in it with the known. If it be inhuman, make it figure as part of a story. If it be difficult, couple its acquisition with some prospect of personal gain. Above all things, make sure that it shall run through certain inner changes, since no unvarying object can possibly hold the mental field for long. Let your pupil wander from one aspect to another of your subject, if you do not wish him to wander from it altogether to something else, variety in unity being the secret of all interesting talk and thought. The relation of all these things to the native genius of the instructor is too obvious to need comment again.

From: Burke Aaron Hinsdale, *A History of the University of Michigan* (1906); Isaac N. Demmon, editor

BURKE AARON HINSDALE (1837–1900) was born in Wadsworth, Ohio. He studied at the Western Reserve Eclectic Institute at Hiram, Ohio, where he became a close friend of his teacher, James A. Garfield—a friendship that lasted until the president's assassination (1881). He taught in several schools in Ohio, then returned to Hiram, where he taught throughout the Civil War. Between 1865 and 1868 he entered the ministry of the Disciples of Christ, preaching to small congregations. Then he again returned to Hiram as professor of history, English literature, and political science (1868) and was president of Hiram College from 1870 to 1882. He was superintendent of schools in Cleveland from 1882 to 1888, and from 1888 to 1890 he succeeded Payne as chair in the science and art of teaching at the University of Michigan. He edited President Garfield's papers, wrote extensively on history, politics, and education, and was active in professional associations. In 1897 he was president of the National Council of Education and in 1900 of the Michigan State Teachers' Association.

Methods of instruction have undergone important changes. In the first period of the University history teaching followed the customary text-book lines; with the coming of Dr. Tappan there was some talk about, but little practice of, the German methods, and it was not until near the close of the next administration that the lecture became firmly established as a means of teaching. Once more, that the teachers of the academical youth should be investigators and discoverers of truth is the first of the twin ideas relating to instruction that Germany has done so much to propagate; the other is that students also should engage in investigation. From the two ideas taken together with the teacher's function a third one naturally follows; namely, that teachers should teach their pupils to conduct research work. This is the origin of the well-known German invention, The *Seminar*. This mode of teaching was first introduced into the University by Professor Charles K. Adams, then the head of the Department of History. He was led to take this step by his study, on its native ground, of the *Historische Gesellschaft*. That was in the year 1871–1872. A little later, Professor Moses

330

Coit Tyler, of the English Department, followed the example. In time other Professors fell into line, and for the last fifteen or twenty years the seminary, so called, has formed an important part of the machinery of teaching. ''Seminary,'' however, was slow in finding its way into the catalogue, perhaps because the authorities were afraid of the word in such a connection. There is good reason to think that the University was the first American institution to naturalize this product of the German soil. But however this may be, the introduction of seminary methods in humanistic studies, and the great extension of laboratory methods in the sciences, has been followed by the happiest results. . . .

All in all, 1877–1878 is the most important year in respect to internal changes in the University that has been seen since President Tappan's arrival in 1852. In 1882 the ''University system'' was established. Under the rules constituting this system, students who had completed the required work of the first two years were no longer held to complete a fixed number of courses, but were permitted to select, subject to approval, three lines of study to be pursued under the direction of a Committee composed of the Professors having these studies in charge, and to graduate at the end of the course, receiving the appropriate degree, provided they passed the prescribed examinations in a satisfactory manner. The object of this system was to secure the advantages of such specialization as can be given to students at this stage of advancement, to students who should elect them, subject to approval. It looked to a still greater degree of liberty than the new rules of 1877–1878 afforded. In a sense, the University system was intended to be the counterpart of the credit system. The rules of 1882, more or less modified, are still in force, but the system, for reasons that are not perhaps altogether plain, has never met the expectations of its founders; the vast majority of students have always preferred to take their work on the credit system. These rules, it may be added, constituted for a time the constitutional basis of the Graduate School, in so far as that School had any real existence.

Another innovation, one not less important and more novel than those made in 1877–1878, came the next year, namely, the establishment of a Professorship of the Science and the Art of Teaching. The duty of the University to provide society with teachers is one of its main functions, and it naturally attracted the attention of Dr. Tappan. In his report to the Board of Regents for 1856 President Tappan said the highest institutions were necessary to supply the proper standard of education, to raise up instructors of the proper qualification, to define the principles and methods of education, to furnish cultivated men to the profession, to civil life, and to the private walks of society, and to diffuse everywhere the educational spirit.

In 1858–1859, probably owing to Dr. Tappan's initiative, an advanced class in the ancient languages was announced for teachers in the union and high schools, and the next year Frieze's Virgil was named as the particular text-book to be used. Nor was this all; Dr. J. M. Gregory, then State Superintendent of Public Instruction, about the year 1860 gave a course of lectures occupying several weeks, two lectures a week, to the Senior class and such others as saw fit to attend on the principles and philosophy of education, and the organization, management and instruction of schools. The announcement relative to the class in Frieze's Virgil was repeated year by year until 1874–1875, when any member of the Senior class who pursued courses of study with reference to preparation for teaching, and who, by special examination, showed such marked proficiency as qualified him to give instruction, was promised a diploma signed by the President and Professors who had charge of the studies he had taken, with this object in view. The next year notice was given that a special examination in the Ancient and Modern Languages and Mathematics would be held before the spring vacation, and that those who passed such examinations would receive a diploma designed to be a certificate of qualification, which would be the only form of recommendation that would be given by the Professors in charge of these studies. The teachers' course in Latin was now expanded so as to include exercises in exegesis and Latin prose composition. A teachers' class in Greek was also offered, embracing prose composition and exercises in syntax. No other teachers' courses are named in those years.

It had long been the custom in the Universities of Germany for Professors of Philosophy to lecture on Pedagogy, to use a word of their own invention. The Bell Chairs of the Theory, History and Art of Education had been established in the University of Edinburgh and St. Andrews in 1876. Systematic instruction in the Science and the Art of Teaching was one of the features of the New System which President Wayland introduced into Brown University in 1850, but which, unfortunately, did not prove to be permanently successful; while Horace Mann made the same subject an elective study in Antioch College, organized in 1853. The subject was agitated, too, in connection with Columbia College, once in 1858, and again in 1881 and 1882; while some tentative efforts had been made to teach education in the Universities of Missouri and Iowa before 1870. These facts show conclusively that the idea of giving instruction in the subject of education, or teaching, in Colleges and Universities had begun to stir men's minds in various part of the country. In fact, brief courses of lectures on the Theory and Practice of Teaching, in the Colleges, at least of the West, was in no way uncommon.

When Dr. Angell came to Ann Arbor, he found himself called upon to certify to the competency of students to teach in the union and high schools, and he felt the need of some source of information that was more definite and positive than any that was then open to him. He reflected, also, upon the value of instruction in the subject of teaching to the students who were intending teachers. He therefore brought the matter to the attention of the Board in his report for 1874.

"It cannot be doubted that some instruction in Pedagogics would be very helpful to our Senior class. Many of them are called directly from the University to the management of large schools, some of them to the superintendency of the schools of a town. The whole work of organizing schools, the management of primary and grammar schools, the art of teaching and governing a school,—of all this it is desirable that they know something before they go to their new duties. Experience alone can thoroughly train them. But some familiar lectures on these topics would be of essential service to them."

Four years later he again brought the subject forward, urging that the new system that had been inaugurated in 1877–1878 would easily yield a place for such instruction. "Perhaps for a time, at least, a non-resident lecturer occupying a part of the year might meet the wants of our students," he said, "and might afford us an opportunity to test the value of such a course as is here suggested." In June 1879, the Faculty adding its recommendation to that of the President, the Regents took the desired action, creating and filling at the same time the Chair of the Science and the Art of Teaching. The objects of this chair, as stated in the official circular sent out in August following, were these: (1) To fit University students for the higher positions in the public school service; (2) To promote the study of educational science; (3) To teach the history of education and of educational systems and doctrines; (4) To secure to teaching the rights, prerogatives, and advantages of a profession; (5) To give a more perfect unity to our state educational system by bringing the secondary schools into closer relations with the University. Referring to the subject in his next annual report, the President said he was not aware that there was at the time a chair exclusively for this work in any other American College.

The Board of Regents made a happy choice in selecting its first Professor of Education. William H. Payne, who was called the new chair, was recommended for the position by his studies of the general subject, his contributions to educational literature, his experience as Editor of an educational journal, and his varied and successful work as a practical teacher and Superintendent of schools. Neither too radical nor too conservative, he pursued a course that steadily and surely commanded the confidence of teachers, educators and enlightened citizens of the state. He began with a modest programme of but two courses for the year, "one practical, embracing school supervision, grading, courses of study, examinations, the art of instructing and governing, school architecture, school hygiene, school law," etc., two lectures each week; and "one historical, philosophical and critical," also two hours a week. The work expanded as time went on, and at the time of Professor Payne's withdrawal from the University in February 1888, he offered seven distinct courses embracing twenty-one hours of instruction. Not only by his instruction and the administration of the department, but also by his writings he established the chair in the respect and confidence of the University constituency and of many prominent educators in the country.[1]

In 1899–1900 the Department of the Science and the Art of Teaching was strengthened by the addition of a Junior Professor, who was also to serve as inspector of high schools. Additional courses were now added, making a total of twenty-five hours in the subject of Education.

The action of 1879 made it necessary to adjust the Teacher's Diploma to the new Professorship of the Science and the Art of Teaching. The rule was now promulgated that any one who pursued one of the courses in this department, and some one other course of study with reference to teaching, and who by special examination showed such marked proficiency as qualified him to give instruction, might receive a special diploma signed by the President and Professors who had charge of the studies he had taken with this object in view. This diploma has always been strictly limited to students who have taken degrees at the University, and the requirement has been increased until it now includes eleven hours of pedagogical work. In 1891 the Legislature passed an Act empowering and instructing the Literary Faculty to give students who received this diploma a certificate, which should serve as a legal certificate to teach in any of the schools of the state.

1. *Harper's Weekly,* July 26, 1879, signalized the establishment of the Chair of Education in a brief article entitled "Teaching How to Teach." The University of Michigan, this journal said, was one of the most progressive as well as efficient of our great schools of learning; the most striking fact in its recent annals was the establishment of a Chair of The History, Theory and Art of Education, "the value of which will be seen at once from the fact that the public schools of Michigan generally fell under the control of graduates of the University." It was the first chair of the kind established in the country, and the University again justified its position as the head of the educational system of the state. "This action will promote," the article ran, "the highest interests of education, not only by tempting future teachers to the training of the University, but by apprising the public that teaching is itself an art and that the knowledge how to teach may make all the difference between school money well or uselessly spent in a community."

From: Felix Emanuel Schelling, *Pedagogically Speaking: Essays and Addresses on Topics More or Less Educational* (1929)

FELIX EMANUEL SCHELLING (1858–1945) was born in New Albany, Indiana. Because of poor health, he was taught by private tutors and by his mother. He entered the University of Pennsylvania with sophomore standing and received the A.B. (1881), LL.B (1883), and A.M. (1886) degrees. He practiced law in Philadelphia and in 1886 became a teacher of English at the University of Pennsylvania. In 1893 he became John Welsh Centennial Professor of History and English Literature, and department head in 1895. In 1929 he was appointed Felix E. Schelling Professor and continued in that position until he retired (1934). He was creator of the modern English Language and Literature Department at the University of Pennsylvania and was one of the foremost scholars of the Elizabethan drama in America.

PREFATORY

Pedagogically speaking, somebody else ought to have written this book, somebody who has acquired the right to sign after his name in conscious superiority that potent word "educator." But in that case, this book would never have been written at all: or, written, it would emphatically not have been this book. The writer of these papers came too early into this much be-educated world to have ever been taught how to teach anybody anything. He has never studied "educationally" "the child," or anyone else professionally. He has never prepared a chart of pedagogical statistics. Above all, he has never measured anything. In short, the gatherer of these, some of his papers that touch on the subjects of his trade, is neither a "pedagogist," an "educator," nor anything else difficult and technical. He is merely a teacher who has loved his work in his day and delighted in the companionship of his students; one who has put down from time to time the thoughts that occasion has demanded of him in the exercise of his vocation; one who feels assured that just as there are a hundred different ways in which to write a novel, all of them good, so there are innumerable enchanting paths threading the luxuriant meadows, gardens and jungles of knowledge, all of them safe and of happy outcome, however we may seek to run a supererogatory concrete boulevard of pedagogic method through their diversity and beauty.

As I reread these papers, originally devised as they were for different occasions and separated as to time, I am struck by the iterations in them of certain ideas which I have hammered on I trust with not too tiresome a monotony. Perhaps the likeness of pedagogy to pugilism is one of the things not set down in even the more meticulous works in the former exhaustless subject. And possibly the teacher, be he heavyweight or bantam, may hope to produce some effect, if he will hit in the same place only sufficiently hard and sufficiently often.

THE TEACHER OF ENGLISH

I am a teacher and pride myself upon that title. I rather object to being described as "an educator": the word is new-fangled and suggests, like "pedagogue," someone more interested in how to do it than in doing it, one admirable in his criticism of the work of other people, not quite so successful in his own—when he does any. I am even shy of the honorable title "Doctor," which is worth while only when it has been earned in course by diligent study; and I regret the convention that gives any of us of American birth a title, even such as the perfunctory and much abused "Professor." For, call us by what formal or hard names you may, the glory of our profession is in the process, the art, the very subtle craft of teaching, about which you may theorize until you become incomprehensible, and, when all has been said, humbly confess: a teacher is one who has shown that there is in him or her a certain quality of guidance, persuasion and restraint that makes him capable of leading others along the paths of learning, to the end that their minds may expand and the qualities that make men modest and honorable may not suffer in the process. Perhaps you are a little disappointed at this tame ideal which differs considerably from a current conception of the blaring trumpets of a valiant and denunciatory army making war on ignorance and hunting error into dark corners, there to do execution upon it with flaming swords, accompanied by pæans of victory. It differs, too, from another current notion of the process in which we are engaged when we teach: that it consists mainly in the shoveling in of information, the accumulation and feeding—crowding, stuffing in—of facts, dates, things that *are,* things that you can see, hear, touch, taste and button up, as Carlyle once put it, into the breeches pocket. Let me repeat that the teacher seems to me less a warrior or a heaver of facts into the coal-bins that supply the intellectual fuel of the world, than a guide, who, having gone the path before, may help others upon it, finding something new along the way, no matter how often he has traversed it, and having a correction of the wayward trend of his followers ever more in mind than any thought of his own importance or glory.

Having suggested to you thus at the outset what I conceive we who are teachers ought to be, let us drop, as far as the skylark from the clouds, to the ground on which, be it remembered, after all, like the larks, we must build our nests. I am not oblivious of facts, which are often ugly customers to reckon with; nor do I ignore the obstacles along the glorious paths that I have just been prating about. This is a bold and daring experiment of ours, this popular American education; and it bids fair to reach a logical end in the slogan—and what would we be without slogans?—''Teach Everybody Everything.'' I listened to a somewhat disheartening discourse the other night in which a competent zoologist and anthropologist told us that something like one American in every five of us is mentally incapable of progressing to anything like the successful conclusion of a high-school education; and to those of us who have not any minds is to be added another, if smaller, percentage, those who have lost what little they once had. He went further to disclose that mentally and physically there is no animal, wild or domesticated, that offers so many departures and deteriorations from the standards of its species as does mankind; and he finds, as is obvious to us all who keep up with the times, that the human race has not only interfered with natural selection but appears almost perversely intent some day to realize a complete reversal of that law by a substitution of one which shall read: ''Let us see to it that the unfit and the unfit alone shall survive.''

Of course we cannot smother our incompetents; though possibly some day we shall be completely smothered by them, as we are even now to a degree. And I am not unaware of the honest efforts that are in the making to solve this all important problem. I know of no one who so quickly awakens my sympathies as the wide-eyed innocent who has not yet been able to find out just what it is all about, who perhaps never may. He needs all the care we can give him; but should we as teachers diminish our value to his brothers and sisters who *can* profit by our teaching, and encumber our onward way with what the Latins aptly called *impedimenta,* in brutal English, luggage. Every teacher knows this perplexity. It is a question of the head versus the heart. In pruning, with the thought of the health of the tree in view, we cut back sometimes the living shoot. We can emulate nature in arboriculture; but are tender to do so in education. I am theoretically one of the severest disciplinarians in the University of Pennsylvania; and we have martinets among us. But, alas, my practice does not conform invariably to my theory, as perhaps, whose does in this imperfect world? And yet it is a serious responsibility—this of being a teacher, for the nonce a species of deity determining who shall be and who not, "thus far shalt thou go and no further." Depend upon it, judging from what we still get into college somehow, it is an important matter, this weeding out of the unfit from among the fit. And unless we contrive to do it somehow more effectively than it has been done often in the past, we must look to a further settling down of even that dull level which we now call mediocrity.

As I think of the teacher, my first thought is of the enormous weight of responsibility that is ours, each and every one. This guidance of others is a serious business, especially if we are none too competent in the guidance of ourselves. First of all we must take our work as a vocation, not as an avocation, not as something merely to beguile the time until something better turns up. Teaching, with all our reforms in that respect, is still so poor a means to a livelihood that only the inferior-minded can look upon it from that point of view. And while I wish that every one of you were far better paid than you are, and I feel sure that you would all deserve it, it would be a pity if our profession should ever come to be so well paid that it would attract especially for that reason. For then the call, the vocation, the spirit of sacrifice and devotion would go out of it to the loss of all. I like to think of teaching as a profession, not a trade, and a profession, let us remember, involves the traffic in a commodity not to be estimated in terms of barter and trade. Not that I think for a moment that we teachers should assume an attitude of superiority to those who make honest livings in the business workshops of the world; but if the teacher takes so low a view of his vocation as to regard it merely a means to feed and clothe him, he will lose the spirit of that calling and in so doing impair the nature and the quality of his work. For, be it remembered, the focus, the center, the heart of our work as teachers is inevitably the student, and what we can do for him, to the end that he understand more fully that which it is our business to impart to him, and gain, in the process of our teaching, a wider and more liberal attitude of mind.

Continuing with this idea of our responsibility, how important it becomes that our teachers shall be genuinely well equipped, first with that larger culture that is at the foundation of all specialization, and secondly with a very specific mastery of the subject which each is told off to teach. I came into this world too early to be submitted to the processes of the educational expert. I have studied a certain variety of subjects in my day; and I have taught perhaps a greater number of them than I had then any too thoroughly studied. . . . Variety of experience is better than mere specialization after a given pattern. The standardizing of the processes of the teaching of almost any subject seems to me as idle as an attempt to teach a terrier how to pick up a rat. . . .

It is not enough to create good teachers on the basis of what they are born to; *we must keep them good*. And here it seems to me we run afoul of one of the current obsessions of our age. Because we can manufacture automobiles and a thousand other objects best for all concerned by a standardized process, we assume that there is nothing to which such a process does not apply. . . . Mouth-filling word that it is, standardization is not an evidence of advanced thinking. To standardize, to make alike, to level, this is among the most primitive of instincts: the pack tears to pieces the white wolf—for being white; the small boy is persecuted by other small boys if he is less freckled, more red-headed, too small, or too lanky. The process of standardizing is the process of leveling, it makes for mediocrity and deterioration. There is no such ally in standardizing our teaching as overwork. . . . True education, for student and for teacher alike, is a never-ending process, devoted to an emphasis of whatever natural aptitude or talent the individual man or woman may possess. True education makes for inequality; the inequality of individuality, the inequality of success, the glorious inequality of talent, of genius; for inequality, not mediocrity, individual superiority, not standardization, is the measure of the progress of the world.

It is high time now for me to justify the title of this paper, "The Teacher of English." I feel as to teaching as I feel as to work, that what particularly you happen to be teaching is unimportant, provided that you are teaching it well. There is only one thing that is really dignified, and that is work; and there is only one true aristocracy, that of brains in employment to make the world somewhat more approaching what it should be. On the basis of such doctrine, we ought to pride ourselves on being teachers, for we at least are on the path, whatever the wanderings of others in the jungles about us. I have already told you that I have had occasion to teach many things in my day. In my own English department at the University, I have trailed the pike of composition work and directed the small-sword play of debate. I have carried the musket on the long historical trail from Beowulf to Browning, and now, after many years of happy duty in the pleasant Elizabethan country, I am still serving, with such effect as may be, the big guns of Shakespeare. I am glad that I have had so diversified an experience, for I never weary of repeating the paradox that the best specialist is the man who knows and has had the most experience about many other things. Peculiarly true, this seems to me to be as to the teacher of English, who holds a singular position in these days of the twilight, the *Götterdämmerung,* so to speak, of ancient Greek and Latin learning.

But before I come to this, let me note the most serious of our responsibilities as teachers of English, a responsibility best designated in the phrase: *our duty to stamp out illiteracy*. Without the solid foundation of a reasonable degree of literacy, whether hewn out of the rock or poured in liquid concrete, there is no superstructure. . . .

This arduous, uninteresting, laborious task is the first, the most essential, of all our duties as teachers of English; I repeat: Stamp out, wipe out, destroy and away with, as far as possible, inability, clumsiness, ineptitude in the ordinary use, in speaking and writing, of our English mother tongue.

Another of our tasks, whether provided for in the curriculum as such or not, is to create somehow in the minds of our students a respect for that beautiful mother tongue which is ours, by getting them to realize somewhat the dignity of its origins, its long development, the lithe and adaptable instrument that is has become in the hands of those who have been masters in the use of it. . . .

While it is one of the fundamentals of my creed as a teacher that it is not the nature of any subject that makes it what we call a liberal subject, but the manner, better the spirit, in which it is taught, I cannot but feel that we who are engaged somewhat in the teaching of literature—the more particularly when our teaching is in our own tongue—enjoy a position somewhat peculiar in the educational process of which our work is of course only a part. I do not suppose that you who are teachers in the schools hear much any more nowadays of what used to be so much aired under the old shibboleth, the humanities. When you hear the word it connotes in your minds doubtless a something about which there seems still to linger a certain superstitious belief. The humanities, O yes, a species of pedagogical dinosaur, traces of whose uncouth existence cannot be successfully denied, but whose embodied reality we should be very much afraid to have anything to do with. But studies that make men human—and what else are the liberal studies—must not perish from the face of the earth, even if we substitute the civics of Harrisburg for *The Republic* of Plato. Gone is our Greek and going our Latin, and so confirmed in prejudice and unrepentant am I, that I have still a tear to shed for their departure. Except for the few, we have lost here in America that conversancy with the classics that make them a veritable liberalizing element in our education. But when the liberalizing, the enlightening and enfranchising quality goes out of education, it will cease to function. With vocational, technical, utility and business topics surging into the curriculum, it is we who teach literature in English who maintain to a large degree the struggle for liberal studies, studies not clogged with immediate deadening ends and aims, which, however useful, cannot at the same time be expected to radiate artistic, moral and spiritual light. English literature, with its contact with the choicest of human thought and the most precious of human experience, its touch with the novelists and dramatists who have depicted the ways of the human kind, its converse with the poets who have looked out beyond for us and shown us the stars—it is English literature which remains the last stronghold of the humanities. That stronghold we must maintain, if primeval darkness is not to overwhelm us. A race that continues the intellectual continuity of mankind in a knowledge and love of the best of the past linked onto the best of the present, a race that preserves that sense of continuity by means of an acquaintance with the loftiest ideals, the wisdom and prophecy of the past, need not fear the charge of illiberality. Depend upon it, fellow teachers, to the degree in which we, each of us, bears his part in this liberalizing, humanizing process, whatever your topic or mine, are we worthy to be enrolled in the noble, the honorable brotherhood of those who guide forward their fellow men.

Notes

Works Cited

Notes

Introduction: Chronicle of a Search

1. For a rigorous critique of Lusted's call for pedagogy, see Richard E. Miller's Ph.D. unpublished dissertation, "Representing the People: Theoretical and Pedagogical Disjunctions in the Academy" (University of Pittsburgh, 1993).

2. The production and publication (and the reception) of Lentricchia and McLaughlin's *Critical Terms for Literary Study* can be read as a validation of the issues I am raising here.

3. In earlier stages of my work, I proposed the adoption of Italian philosopher Giovanni Gentile's definition of pedagogy as "philosophical science" (cf. "Towards a Hermeneutics of Difficulty," "Pedagogy: From the Periphery to the Center," and "On Behalf of Pedagogy." See also the Italian dictionary entry on pedagogy in this volume). But because *philosophy* and, even more so, *science* in Gentile's definition are culturally coded in different ways than they are currently in the U.S., I have more recently opted for a definition of pedagogy as "reflexive praxis." I want to acknowledge Kathryn Flannery's contribution to coining this phrase. We used it for the title of a panel we proposed at the 1989 Conference on College Composition and Communication.

4. I am not suggesting that redefining pedagogy will erase the effect of its past and present negative constructions. I am arguing that although the term is deployed in many contexts as if it were common and ordinary and made common sense, its meaning is neither ordinary nor common, and it does not make common sense (as in agreement). What Lentricchia and McLaughlin say of the terms that are the subject of the essays collected in *Critical Terms for Literary Study* is applicable to pedagogy: "terms have a history . . . they shape how we read . . . they engage larger social and political questions." And, they add, invoking Raymond Williams,

> [the] point is not simply that the meanings of the terms change, but that their history impinges on their current use, and that the radical changes that terms undergo suggest that there is no stable and reliable meanings for any terms. Terms cannot be used as though they were neutral instruments. Terms such as "culture" and "race" have been put to so many uses in so many different social and interpretive settings that no use of them can be innocent. Using a term commits you to a set of values and strategies that it has developed over the history of its use. It is possible to use a term in a new way, but it is not possible to escape the term's past. (1990, 3–4)

It is true that in the United States the dominant past that *pedagogy* cannot escape constructs it in negative or limiting ways. But another past, the one I have tried to reconstruct in part one, is also a past that, once reactivated, pedagogy cannot escape, and one that hopefully will complicate negative and limiting definitions of it.

5. This theoretical impulse and commitment animates Patricia Donahue's and Ellenn Quandahl's *Reclaiming Pedagogy* 1989. See also Donahue 1987.

6. In *Anti-intellectualism in American Life,* Hofstadter suggests that the unenviable situation of the (American) teacher

> can be traced back to the earliest days of our history. The educational enthusiasm of the American people was never keen enough to dispose them to support their teachers as well. In part it seems to have reflected a common Anglo-American attitude toward the teaching function, which was sharply different from that prevailing on the European continent. (1963, 312)

Hofstadter footnotes this statement with revealing comments by English observers of the North American schools:

> Presumably the labor market was somewhat different in England in the early nineteenth century, but the social and economic conditions of teachers in public education seem less enviable than that of the Americans (See Asher Tropp: *The School Teachers.* London, 1957). Somewhat revealing in this connection was the remark of one of Her Majesty's Inspectors, H. S. Tremenheere, on a visit to the United States in the 1850's. He wrote: "Any one from England visiting those schools would be also greatly struck with the very high position, *considering the nature of their employment,* of the teachers, male and female . . ." *Notes on PUblic Subjects Made During a Tour in the United States and Canada* (London, 1852, pp. 57–58). I believe the phrase I have italicized here would have been intelligible to English and American readers and quite mystifying to most readers on the Continent. For another English observer, who found the status of American teachers high, though their pay was equally bad as in England, see Francis Adams: *The Free School System of the United States* (London, 1875), especially pp. 176–8, 181–2, 194–5, 238. (Hofstadter 1963, 312, n. 2)

I find it difficult to generalize on the difference between Anglo-American and Continental (I use Hofstadter's term with some unease) status and the reputation of teachers. Continental economic and political conditions vary so drastically from one country to another (in spite of their geographic proximity), within one country, within one city, and within one district that Hofstadter's "contrast" might not be so sharp. And it might be even less accurate now than at the time he wrote his book. Nevertheless, insofar as the status of pedagogy as a university discipline is concerned, and insofar as that status is connected to the status of teachers, the "Continent" seems to tell a different story. But to define the extent and the nature of that difference falls for the moment outside the parameters of the present study.

7. But Walter S. Monroe, in *Teaching-Learning Theory and Teacher Education, 1890 to 1950,* suggests that the characterization of normal schools as eminently professional was not accurate:

> Criticism of normal schools during the seventies and eighties as being mainly academic institutions indicates that this program was widely prevalent. However, it was opposed by a number of normal-school leaders who maintained that "reviews" of the academic type and instruction in higher branches similar to that provided in the high schools and academies of the time did not result in the sort of knowledge a teacher needed. They argued that the subject matter should be

professionalized, i.e. selected and organized with the needs of the teacher in mind, and that the instruction should also be directed to his end. The extent to which this point of view was exemplified in practice is uncertain. No widely accepted technique for professionalizing subject matter and instruction had been developed and what was accomplished depended largely upon the insight and ingenuity of individual instructors. However, it appears that by 1890 professional treatment of subject-matter was being attempted in a number of normal schools, especially in the better ones. Where there was effective professional treatment, there was also an integration of subject-matter study and pedagogical study. In contrast with these two positions, both of which emphasized the teacher's understanding of the subjects to be taught, there were some normal school leaders who advocated that the normal school should be a "strictly professional" institution. . . .

The crucial weakness of the "strictly professional" normal school was in the implicit assumption that a person's common school experience would result in an adequate knowledge of the subjects to be taught. (1952, 174–75)

Monroe's assessment of normal schools prompts reflection on several points: insofar as the treatment of the subject matter came to be identified as the fundamental feature of normal schools, attempts to regularize what was meant by that were only made at the end of the century. Considering that it was around that time that normal schools began to set themselves in open competition with colleges, the need to define their distinguishing feature must be carefully examined in terms of its various complex causes and consequences. Worthy of attention are Monroe's distinction between "professional"—as the *integration* of subject matter and pedagogical study (his use of the term *pedagogical* means "practical")—and the "strictly professional," which was used as an indictment of the work of normal schools by proponents of "liberal education." Insofar as "the strictly professional" ideal rested on the assumptions that "a person's common-school experience would result in an adequate knowledge of the subjects to be taught," it is important that we do not blind ourselves to the similarity between this position and that held by those who opposed the study of pedagogy on the premise that "scholarly" knowledge of subject matter would "teach" the teacher to teach it. I also mean to point out the use of the term *academic*, and the nuances of superfluity it accrues in Monroe's text. Traces of this meaning reappear, I believe, in some pejorative commonplace uses of the term *academic* as a synonym for university person not in touch with the "real world."

8. This is not to argue that faculty in English departments do not care about teaching. Many do. This is to point out that "to care about" does not necessarily mean to know how to teach others to teach. Moreover, as long as teaching and the teaching of teaching do not get more widespread institutional support in all university departments, caring about teaching will not be recognized and sustained as a scholarly activity: the most telling sign of this is, of course, that caring about and being good at teaching do not help in tenure cases and promotions in major research universities.

9. Dismissive attitudes toward pedagogy are not exclusive to departments of English. In many departments of languages, for example, pedagogy is regarded as the work of "teachers of language" (part-time instructors, teaching assistants) rather than of "professors of literature."

10. I am thinking of the deconstructive move in the terms suggested by Barbara Johnson—as a tactic that posits the necessity for a reader-thinker, and for a teacher, to expose a text's fissures ("text" as both the text being read, and the hidden but not invisible text of a teacher's theory of teaching and learning). As Johnson argues, these fissures ought to be examined and studied less as symptoms "of flaws and imperfections" in the theoretical system that has produced the text, than as indications of "that system's possibility" (Barbara Johnson quoted in Salvatori 1988).

11. The understanding of pedagogy responsible for my early opposition to and interrogation of cultural constructions that identify it with "just teaching" is one of the most resilient traces of my foreignness. It is an understanding to which I was exposed throughout the years of my formal education in Italy, both at the high school *(liceo classico)* and university level. Although at the time I wasn't aware of it (since it was so pervasive, at least in my cultural milieu), one of its most authoritative theoretical sources is Giovanni Gentile's *Sommario di Pedagogia Come Scienza Filosofica* (1912). Philosopher Giovanni Gentile thought it necessary for him to address and to eliminate the prejudice

> solidified in the term *pedagogy* whose Greek etymos indicates the education of
> the child rather than the education of man. It is true that the Greek term desig-
> nating what we call *education* was formed by adding a suffix to the word of *child*
> (paideia). But to conceive of pedagogy as a branch of *pedology* is a prejudice that
> results from the non-empirical idea that only children, and adolescents, need to
> be educated. (135, my translation)

For persistent traces of the "prejudice," see Robert Somers's "Working with the Adult Learner: Applied Andragogy for Developmental Programs" (*Review of Research in Developmental Education* 5, no. 5 [1988]: 1–5). In this article, Somers proposes the term "andragogy" to refer to "our consolidated knowledge about adult development which justifies our treating adult learners as adults." He suggests the adoption of this term as a substitute for " 'pedagogy,' which is of course the business of teaching children." To get a sense of how differently the term *pedagogy* is currently being used, even by its proponents, see Clifford 1991; Donahue and Quandahl 1989; Giroux 1988, 1992; Gore 1993; Morton and Zavarzadeh 1991; Shor and Freire 1987; Smyth 1987.

12. For a sense of how the difference between pedagogy and education can and does matter in other cultural contexts, consider Emile Durkheim's definition of the term (see part three). Consider, also, what can be gleaned out of William Payne's "Translator's Preface" to Gabriel Compayré's *Histoire de la Pedagogie*. Payne writes:

> The reader will observe the distinction made by Monsieur Compayré between
> *Pedagogy* and *Education*. Though our nomenclature does not sanction this distinc-
> tion, and though I prefer to give to the term *pedagogy* a different connotation, I
> have felt bound by moral grounds to preserve Monsieur Compayré's use of
> these terms wherever the context would sanction it. It seems mere squeamish-
> ness to object to the use of the word *pedagogy* on account of historical associa-
> tions. The fact that this term is in reputable use in German, French, and Italian
> educational literature, is a sufficient guarantee that we may use it without danger.
> With us, the term *pedagogics* seems to be employed as a synonym for *pedagogy*.
> It would seem to me better to follow continental usage, and restrict the term

Pedagogy to the art or practice of education, and *pedagogics* to the correlative science.

It has taken me considerable time to understand that the historical associations Payne refers to might be the normal schools (see part three). Payne's understanding of continental uses of the term ought to be complicated by the definitions Durkheim and Gentile provide for it.

13. I would like to call attention to the semantic aura that dictionaries construct around each of the terms they list. In the case of *pedagogue,* the presence or the absence of words like *peculate, peculiar,* and *pecuniary* in the spaces above *pedagogue,* and *pedant, pedate, pederast,* and *pedophile* in the spaces below, must somehow affect the meaning that a reader constructs as she focuses on the term in question. (Gallop 1982 acknowledges the links between pedagogy, pedophilia, and pederasty.) When one scans a dictionary page for a definition, the proximity of one term to another, the highlighted characters, and the discernible grouping of words by first syllables can make it difficult to block peripheral words out of one's vision and mind. See part one for how dictionaries and encyclopedia's might have contributed to the marginalization of pedagogy and pedagogues.

14. I focused on French, Italian, and Spanish because of their cultural links with Greek and Latin, the "roots" of *pedagogue* and *pedant* respectively. I also looked at Brazilian sources to check possible antecedents for Paulo Freire's concept of pedagogy. As I had expected, these sources suggest their culture's awareness of the difference between *education* and *pedagogy* and of the history of pedagogy as a discipline and subject of study, rather than as a synonym for practice or teaching. Because of German influence on U.S. constructions of pedagogy, I consulted German dictionary and encyclopedia entries, for one of which I offer a partial translation.

Part One: Of Pedagogues and Pedagogy, Pedants and Pedantry

1. In *Dictionaries: The Art and Craft of Lexicography,* Sidney I. Landau provides important and interesting information about the industry—scholarly or commercial—of dictionary and encyclopedia making; the influence that this industry exercises on culture; and the different function of dictionaries and encyclopedias and the awareness of that different function readers are supposed to have. Landau specifies that although

> dictionaries and encyclopedias are closely linked and are sometimes considered interchangeable . . . they are essentially different kinds of reference works with different purposes. A dictionary is a book that lists words in alphabetical order and describes their meanings. . . . An encyclopedia is a collection of articles about every branch of knowledge. Although the articles are usually arranged alphabetically, and though they often include definitions, their descriptions go far beyond the information given in a dictionary. . . . Dictionary definitions are usually confined to information that the reader must have to understand an unfamiliar word. The emphasis is on the word, and all the information given bears directly on the meaning, pronunciation, use, or history of the word. Encyclopedic articles are essentially topical, dealing with the entire subject represented by the article's title. (5–6)

Landau is careful to point out that one cannot expect of a dictionary what one can expect of an encyclopedia. Moreover, he points out the considerable difference between scholarly dictionaries (which appeal to and construct a vertical market) and commercial dictionaries (whose market is horizontal). The primary purpose of the scholarly dictionary is to describe data and communicate knowledge; a secondary purpose may be to promote the name of the supporting institution or to acquire prestige for it by publishing a major work. The primary purpose of a commercial dictionary is to make money, although to the people writing it the day-to-day purpose is usually indistinguishable from that of a scholarly dictionary (11).

Commercial dictionaries, because they address a broad, nonspecialized spectrum of the population, tend to be synchronic: they

> deal with a narrow band of time and attempt to represent the lexicon as it exists or existed at a particular point in time—not necessarily the present. . . . As a rule, *archaic and obsolete words are the first to go when a dictionary is abridged.* Thus in synchronic dictionaries etymology is less important, and the representation of current slang and technological terms is more important than in diachronic works. (31, emphasis added)

As he gives a detailed account of the complexities, pressures, and demands imposed on commercial lexicographers—he is one—Landau seems to want to make sure that readers do not impose unreasonable expectations on the function of dictionaries. He is quite adamant in representing their function as *descriptive* rather than *prescriptive,* though he recognizes the inevitability of their being deployed in prescriptive ways. "*Dictionary* is a powerful word," he writes. "Authors and publishers have found that if they call a reference book a dictionary it tends to sell better than it would if called by another name because the word suggests authority, scholarship, and precision" (5). It is this power, or more precisely, some possible consequences of this power, that my project problematizes. Although, as Landau states, commercial dictionaries function within certain limiting parameters; although they report *common usages* the "commonality" of which is documented through complicated and carefully recorded systems of citation files; and although they cannot satisfy specialized demands, the fact remains that, much more than scholarly dictionaries and encyclopedias, they are consulted and used as sources of "authority, scholarship, and precision"—a fact that subtly complicates the problematic differentiation between descriptive and prescriptive.

2. As Landau points out, the question of what counts as a definition is a thorny one, addressed by ancient and modern philosophers, especially by logicians and semanticists:

> Although the distinction is not always made, and when made not always observed, logical definition is not the same as lexical definition. Logical definition—Richard Robinson calls it real definition, because it attempts to analyze things in the real world, as distinguished from words—has been the chief preoccupation of philosophers. . . . The traditional rules of lexical definition, based on Aristotle's analysis, demand that the word defined (called in Latin the *definiendum*) be identified by *genus* and *differentia*. . . . Among other rules sometimes promulgated for definition are that a definition be equivalent to or capture the essence of the thing defined, that the definiendum be included in any form among the words (called the *definiens*) used to define it, and that the DEFINITION BE POSITIVE RATHER THAN NEGATIVE [editor's emphasis]. Philosophers are not ignorant

of the nature of linguistics or dictionary making, but it is remarkable how little attention they pay to users of dictionaries. By contrast, lexicographers—all of them—pay a great deal of attention to the needs of their readers. For lexicography is a craft, a way of doing something useful. It is not a theoretical exercise to increase the sum of human knowledge but practical work to put together a book that people can understand. . . . Every lexicographer, like any good author, has his readers very much in mind. Whereas philosophers are concerned with the internal coherence of their system of definition, lexicographers are concerned with explaining something their readers will understand. The methods each uses to achieve his goals only incidentally coincide. (1984, 120–21)

When the lexicographic rules of definition are combined with the rules on brevity, considerable problems may emerge, problems that Landau would call "characteristics" of the genre. This is what he writes on "brevity" in the section on "definition": "The need to save space in dictionaries leads naturally to the injunction: 'Be brief.' Dictionary definitions should not waste words. The art of defining depends not only on the ability to analyze and understand what words mean, but equally on the ability to express such meanings succinctly. Robinson writes, 'A lexical definition could nearly always be truer by 'being longer.' A good definer learns how to lose the least measure of *truth* with each shortening of a definition" (137, emphasis mine). Consequently, then, the most general of the general dictionaries, the abridged ones, the college editions, the paperbacks—the ones, that is, that reach the least specialized audience, the audience that is least apt at or interested in discriminating on the accuracy and fairness of certain definitions, are potentially the disseminators of the least *true* definitions.

3. But as a counterexample, see the *Dictionnaire Langue Francaise,* A. Beaujean's abridgment of E. Littré's dictionary.

4. In support of my argument, let me cite Laurence Urdang, former editor in chief of *The Random House Dictionary of the English Language.* In *The Dictionary of Confusable Words,* Urdang enters pedant/pedagogue as a set of contrastive terms that are ordinarily confused in U.S. culture. He writes that the terms once meant the same thing, i.e., "teacher," but

while *pedagogue* (also spelled *pedagog* in the U.S.) has retained that sense, *pedant* has become an opprobrious term meaning someone who is entirely concerned with what can be found in books and who places far too much emphasis on niggling details. The adjective *pedantic* means "exhibiting a boring and unfeeling obsession with the slavish observance of inconsequential rules and minutiae." *Pedagogical,* or, less often, *pedagogic,* means "having to do with teaching"; it is usually reserved for rather formal contexts, and it would sound pompous to say of someone who wanted to become a teacher that "He wished to follow a pedagogical career." *Pedantic* suggests *pedantry,* which implies all the unfavorable associations people may have with school: the stuffiness of some teachers; the excessive showing-off of knowledge and an attempt to put down those who do not possess it; the strict adherence to rules set forth on paper without regard to common sense; the attitude of superiority of many teachers, and so on. Although these words may seem to be related, they are not: *pedagogical* (referring to *pedagogy* or to a *pedagogue*) come ultimately from the Greek word (via Latin) for a "boy's tutor"; it is made from the same initial element used in *ped(iatricts)* and ped(iatrician), meaning "child," and the same final element appearing in dem(-agogue), meaning, in these instances, "leader." Pedantry, pedantic, by contrast, are traced to the ped of ped(al) and ped(icure), meaning foot. The semantic notion is of one who follows in the footsteps of others, who engages in (to use an older term) footling activities, and whose thinking is, so to speak, pedestrian. (1988, 246–47)

5. Toward the end of this project, as I was perusing the section on pedagogy and education in a bookstore in Italy, I picked up and started leafing through Mario Alighiero Manacorda's Storia Illustrata dell'Educazione. In it I found startling visual support (which I had planned to make available to my readers, but could not because of production cost) for my argument in this chapter and throughout this book. Each page of Manacorda's learned text is enlivened by a collage of pertinent and extraordinary illustrations which he told me he has accumulated over many years. The linguistic and conceptual corruption of pedagogue and, by extension, of pedagogy that I had been tracing through dictionary and encyclopedia entries came to life for me as I looked at and established a link among the following illustrations: Greek terracottas (p. 44, figs. 3, 4, 5) representing, respectively, a stocky pedagogue leading two children to school (one seemingly willing to go, the other recalcitrant), the other two representing the pedagogue reading to, or writing for, or talking to an eight- to ten-year-old child who leans trustingly on him; a scene of pederasty from the inside of a 480–470 B.C. kylix representing a teacher fondling a visibly adoring slightly older (thirteen? fourteen?) child (p. 48, fig. 3); the frontispiece of the play Il Pedante (p. 130, fig. 1); the maschera of Dottor Belanzone (p. 130, fig. 4), a Bolognese comic character.

What I find striking in this sequence of images is the function of the pedagogue's hand, which suggests a complicated and provocative story, one that deserves much more attention than a footnote can give it. Let me just mention at least three strands of such a story, which I would like to further investigate in the future. One strand would suggest (and explore the consequences of) the connection between the loving, protective gesture of the Greek pedagogue's hand and the hand of the woman (teacher, mentor, mother, madonna) extended to touch or embrace children, on many covers of North American Readers. Another strand might suggest a connection between the hand that strokes and the hand that strikes the child (see, for example, the illustration David Lusted chose for the Screen issue on pedagogy where the teacher's hand holds a ferule about to descend on the student). Given the always asymmetrical power relationship between teacher and student, what kind of love/power nexus does either relationship represent and exploit, and to which "educational" end? Yet another strand might link the self-absorbed affectation and empty knowledge conveyed by Belanzone's hand to American scenes of pedagogic incompetence wherein a self-absorbed and oblivious Ichabod Crane is depicted as being more interested in sharpening the nib of a pen (a material "tool" of education whose function is represented as suspended in the air) than in the students who should learn to use it to produce knowledge.

6. In Education in Ancient Rome, Bonner writes:

Generally, the "pedagogue" (though he did sometimes have a rather foreign accent) appears to have been a sturdy fellow, as he needed to be, and, though prone to err on the side of severity rather than leniency, often concealed a kind heart under a rough exterior. Greek terracottas depict him as an oldish man, stockily built, heavily bearded, and with rather unpreposterous features, some-times he rests his right hand on the little boy's head as they stand together . . . and sometimes tweaks his ear, as Cato's slave, Chilo, used to do, when he has done something wrong. It was natural for parents who had an intelligent "pedagogue" to expect that he would not only conduct the children to and from school, but also see that they learnt their lessons properly. He might well remain present at these himself (as did Palaemon in Roman times), and on returning home would test the children and make them repeat to him what they were supposed to know by heart. The more literate he was himself the better, but, in general, he was primarily engaged to supervise rather that to teach, and often, in both Greek and Roman times, the "pedagogue" was clearly differentiated from the "teacher" or "master" (didaskalos, preceptor, magister). Nevertheless it did also happen, certainly in the Hellenistic period, and probably earlier, that he was able to give primary instruction himself. (Bonner, 39)

7. Bonner writes:

It may perhaps seem rather surprising that Roman parents should have become so readily accustomed to entrust their children to slaves who were not born within the household, but were of foreign origin and might, at first, not even speak the same language. But there were several reasons why they found such an arrangement acceptable. In the first place, the Greeks had a long tradition of child-protection, and the Greeks at Rome, as a rule, seem to have performed this essential duty well. Such protection became increasingly necessary in the last half-century or so of the Republic, with all the turbulence and strife caused by embittered political factions, when the streets were frequently the scene of dis-order and bloodshed, and the home itself was not secure. . . . "Pedagogues," like nurses, were often remembered with affection, as Cicero says, in later years. . . . There were, of course, cases in which a "pedagogue" might come under suspicion, but the penalty for any kind of serious misconduct was severe. (40–41)

Part Two: Early Articulations of Pedagogy

1. *Mutatis mutandis,* that is, given the amount and sophistication of theoretical knowledge available in the past. The different kind of language we use to discuss these issues can blind us to the fact that early pedagogues were interested in understanding how one knows, can be said to know, can enable others to know. They might have made assumptions about knowledge formation remarkably different from ours; they might have studied instead the genesis of ideas in *man;* they might have stressed the individual's power to shape that social context; they might have had excessive faith in the individual's will to perfect his or her own nature; but these are the theories of knowing that were then in circulation, and we need to understand what these theories have to do, for example, with the fact that so many believed so strongly in the project of common schools, in the appropriateness of "moral education," and in the theory that a "good student" makes a "good citizen" makes a "good nation."

2. Not all authors in this section use the term *pedagogy* to refer to the theory and practice of teaching. Some call it *education* and differentiate it from *instruction.* Others,

possibly influenced by German scholarship on the subject, call it *pedagogy*. Since they don't make an evaluative distinction between the two terms, I have retained the use of *pedagogy* in my commentary upon their work.

3. I capitalize *Academy* as a synonym for *university* to distinguish it from teachers' academies, early centers for the preparation of teachers. The capitalization, however, is not meant to suggest a hierarchy of values, as far as teacher preparation is concerned.

4. I have suggested elsewhere that we should call this understanding of teaching and learning *didactics*, a term that in U.S. culture has been and is used as a synonym for *pedagogy*, of which it is part, but which it cannot totally encompass (Salvatori 1988, 1989, 1991).

5. In this case, "subject matter" indicates knowledge of the specific subjects a teacher is supposed to teach: for example, *The Canterbury Tales, A Doll's House,* "the Victorian era."

6. In *The Signification of Chalk: The Teacher/Student-in-the-Classroom Dynamic and Progressive Pedagogies of 20th Century American Education* (Ph.D. diss., University of Pittsburgh), Paula Kristofik writes:

> *Pedagogy,* a term whose etymology reveals a two-person relationship of a different order, was defeated by *education* in the 1890's contestation over a name for the study of learning. This defeat may have something to do with the rootedness of language: pedagogy calls forth an image of persons in the labor of learning. Meanwhile *educare* or *educere* indicates an acting upon: raising up; leading out. In any case, the old term has returned. Pedagogy can re-introduce the activity of knowing/learning in light of a teacher/student dynamic.

7. For a shocking and sobering reminder of the disparity between aspirations, plans, ideals—spiritual and intellectual—and the actual conditions within which many teachers had to perform, see "A New Jersey Teacher's Contract" (1848) and "1872 Rules for Teachers," both collected in this volume.

8. As Merle Borrowman states:

> Formal, highly self-conscious efforts to create a profession of teaching, with the elaborate artifacts of formal training, credentials, organization, and internal propaganda, began in Western Europe in the seventeenth century and accelerated rapidly in conjunction with the growth of nationalistic systems of universal state-supported schooling in the early nineteenth century. Formal training for the professions of statesmanship, scholarship, and the priesthood had emerged long before, and novices in these older professions had been educated and trained in literature and techniques later to be appropriated by those attempting to professionalize the teaching of children and youth. But in the United States as a whole in 1839, in regions of the United States as late as 1920, and in the minds of many Americans as late as 1940, a moderately schooled older sister or mother, working in a homelike environment, functioned in what was considered an adequate manner as a teacher of children. ("History of Teachers' Education," *The Encyclopedia of Education,* 71)

Ignoring, for the moment, the undoubtedly unintentional condescending remark about women teachers, who were no less prepared for the profession of teaching than men, I want to suggest that Borrowman's comments record a "tradition" that was to have lasting consequences for pedagogy. As far as the teaching of children and youth (which to many is all that pedagogy meant) was concerned, the borrowing of techniques and methods from professions that capitalized on lectures, declamations, recitations, and other kinds of "performance" might account for the didacticism of early approaches to teaching. (See, above, my comments about two of the most problematic and widely circulated representations of pedagogy.)

9. To indict the common school and the normal school (also modelled after the Prussian system) educational projects for trying to inculcate *homogenous* cultural and moral values is to focus on a shortcoming that is too obvious, and perhaps, given the times, inevitable. (I would not make the same argument about similar cultural projects today, given our awareness of the silencing effects of authority.) A more instructive and profitable critique of the American turn to militaristic Prussia, I believe, would have to focus on a less obvious shortcoming: the fact that such borrowing *ignores* (that is, does not posit as theoretically valid) or *silences* (that is, makes it impossible to engage) these fundamental questions: what constitutes learning, for whom, under what circumstances, and the inseparable correlative questions of teaching. Having noticed this much, we have the responsibility to determine whether at the time theories of learning were available that made it possible to raise such questions. My intention is not to minimize the consequences of past top-down, morally dogmatic, educationally co-optive approaches to education—the danger of doing so is to become obtuse to their recurrence in the present. My intention is to point out how in the passion of indicting we can become less sensitive to some of the representations we construct and disseminate, and their effect on nonspecialized audiences. In an entry on the history of the education of teachers, Merle Borrowman constructs a rather uninviting—to a prospective teacher—representation of the beginnings of professionalization. (Elsewhere, in his more extended writings, he offers a much more balanced critique.) Here is a representative excerpt:

> The drive to professionalize primary and secondary teachers was begun in the Northeastern United States in the first half of the nineteenth century. Its leading exponents were such people as James G. Carter, Horace Mann, Henry Barnard, and Calvin Stowe. As a group these men were largely trained for the law and the ministry, and although several are well known as educational statesmen, few ever spent any considerable amount of time as actual teachers. Their concern as ministers and statesmen was to ensure an orderly society by creating a stable, conservative corps of dedicated and self-effacing people who would, in turn, inculcate habits of obedience, loyalty, morality, and economic efficiency in the young. The dominant instrument adopted to create the teaching profession was an American version of the Prussian normal schools. Its American exponents, sometimes hard pressed by charges of un-Americanism, were quick to assert that the American normal school served a republican rather than a monarchical system. Nevertheless, one suspects they would have been less than candid had they not admitted some sympathy for the Prussian monarch Frederick William IV, who charged in 1848 that he had trusted the normal school graduates to prepare loyal citizens and that they had instead produced a revolution. Implicit in the campaign for a system of universal publicly controlled schooling was the assumption that the primary group—the family and the face-to-face commu-

nity—could no longer be relied upon to maintain orderly and efficient social action through familial tutelage, private schooling, apprenticeship, and communal ritual. Later in the nineteenth century, John Dewey, Francis W. Parker, and others would explicitly define the ideal school as a simplified and purified home and community, and they could talk about the teacher's maternal, paternal, and community leadership roles. These models have undergirded the earlier movements. (1971, 72)

10. Hofstadter points out the "persistent, intense, and sometimes touching faith in the efficacy of popular education," that was characteristic of a people

who would create a common-school system, but would balk at giving it adequate support. They would stand close to the vanguard among the countries of the world in the attempt to diffuse knowledge among the people, and then engage drifters and misfits and offer them the wages of draymen.

The history of American educational reformers often seems to be the history of men fighting against an uncongenial environment. The educational jeremiad is as much a feature of our literature as the jeremiad in the Puritan sermons. That this literature should have been one of complaint is not in itself surprising, for complaint is the burden of anyone who aims at improvement; but there is a constant undercurrent of something close to despair. (1963, 301)

Hofstadter's comments refer to the establishment and support of the common schools. His comments are equally apt at describing the response to the establishment of normal schools and to the speeches and appeals of their proponents which were also marked by despair.

11. This is a charge that needs to be thoughtfully examined and equitably assessed. It is plausible to suggest that, for example, early educators' strong reliance on religion, and later, theorists of reading and writing who place and need to keep a reader's or a writer's "creativity" beyond the reach of analysis, might be responsible for approaches to teaching and learning that foster and propagate particular manifestations of anti-intellectualism (see Caleb Atwater).

12. To argue that early pedagogists' conceptualizations of pedagogy could afford to be reflexive because of the more limited body of knowledge available to them, and to the teachers they taught, would be specious. Though the difficulty of reflexivity increases with the intricacy of the knowledge to be reflected upon, a reflexive enactment of pedagogy has more to do, I believe, with a particular theoretical understanding of learning and the *forma mentis* it depends on and fosters than with quantity of knowledge to reflect on.

13. Before he was twelve years of age he had read Watt's *The Improvement of the Mind* and Mason's *Self-Knowledge* and shortly afterward read Locke's *Human Understanding*. This latter volume was read and reread by the youth and its influence on Hall is not hard to see. Hall also taught himself the rudiments of Latin. These books were all part of his father's library and were afterward treasured by the educator (Hall's *Lectures on School-Keeping*, "Introduction," 11).

14. As Hall writes:

One of the first convictions that fastened itself on my mind after I became a teacher was that the whole system of education in the country was defective and that the time of the scholars was, in great measure, lost. I determined therefore to do what I could to reform abuses and correct evil. My efforts were appreciated and services sought *at my own prices*. (1929, Hall's *Lecture on Schoolkeeping*, 13; emphasis added)

15. This is not to suggest that Hall, for the sake of (apparently) fairly remunerated teaching, slighted his duties as minister. After founding Concord Academy, his frail health notwithstanding, he conducted the school unassisted for three years while simultaneously attending to his religious duties. He also started a family and wrote on educational and religious issues. On Hall's other achievements, see excerpts in this volume.

16. Hall's insistence on this point must be understood within the conditions of the time. Many were the teachers who knew little more than their students.

17. To be prepared and to be able to tell the why and wherefore in every intellectual move we make as teachers, to be accountable for and to make manifest what we profess to know, is a daunting but inescapable responsibility. Undoubtedly, the greater and the more intricate that knowledge production becomes, the more difficult for a teacher to originate or to recuperate rules and to expose their why and wherefore to intellectual scrutiny. But this, I suggest, is the most important aspect of any teacher's education, in every department of knowledge, though one that has been and is still not much valued. The more intricate does knowledge become, the more does a teacher need this kind of preparation. Paradoxically, instead, the relation between a theorist's or scholar's complexity of knowledge and his or her "teacher preparation" has been constructed as inversely proportional. The higher the status of a theorist-scholar, the more implausible to expect of him or her a commitment to reflexive teaching. No less than in the case of unprepared and defensive teachers, this situation breeds dogmatism and mechanical transmission of knowledge among "scholars."

18. Almira Phelps's *Lectures to Young Ladies*, capitalizing on Willard's work, could bluntly define as *absurd* the idea, "a favorite one with the poet and the novelist, that in the shade of domestic life, and under the care of a wise mother, a young female would blossom into maturity, lovely and intelligent and fitted for discharge of various duties, which may hereafter devolve upon her" (1833, 33).

19. Let me hasten to clarify that the feminization of pedagogy that a muse would suggest is a consequence of the fact that *pedagogia*, in Italian, is a feminine noun, like *filosofia*, *storia*, *tecnologia*, *chimica*, *algebra*, and *chirurgia*. In Italian both science *(la scienza)* and art *(l'arte)* are feminine nouns.

20. It would be tempting to read Fowle's story as an ironic parable, a cautionary tale. The fact is, however, that Fowle's language is not unique. Most early writers on education defined the "ideal teacher" in quite extraordinary terms. See, for example, Page's description.

Part Three: Pedagogy in the Academy

1. In *Ontogeny and Phylogeny*, Stephen Jay Gould writes about the popularity of recapitulatory curricula in America:

I do not think that the Zellerian Herbartians ever achieved a majority position. But they were certainly no fringe movement and the lives of millions of school children were directly influenced by their practices. I have tried to survey primers and instructional manuals of 1880–1915 and have discovered a strong influence for recapitulation in the establishment curricula. The leading pundits at traditional universities said little (indeed, most of these schools provided no formal training in education). But the principals of normal schools and the heads of boards of education told a different tale—and these were the people who did the practical job of educating, even though their writings are ignored by traditional historians of ideas. (151)

2. Clifford and Guthrie argue that these self-interests were shaped by universities' need to modernize themselves into institutions that could offer instruction to just anybody (Ezra Cornell conceived of universities as "institutions in which any person can find instruction in any study" [Bledstein 1976, 286]), as well as by their need to appease various populist demands and to increase enrollments (1988, 123–28). One of the consequences of such policies was that the classics, philosophy, and other liberal arts fields attracted unprecedented numbers of women—a change that disturbed many liberal arts faculty fearful that women's presence would push male students into social and physical science, business, and engineering. Apparently, "female students became scapegoats for faculty frustration in a time of transition when the release of students from a required, set curriculum gave professors and administrators less control over students' academic direction." Ironically, however, though the relation between pedagogy and the feminization of the student population was perceived as a problem, it was also seen as a solution: "By admitting women, and by assisting their plans to teach, a college might double its potential pool of applicants—more than double it, in fact, because girls were two-thirds of high school graduates at the turn of the century" (125–26). The extent to which this policy might have constructed or confirmed or disseminated an understanding of pedagogy as a feminine occupation, as crafty and emotional rather then theoretical and scientific, as intellectually not very reputable, is worth reflecting on.

3. I choose Harvard as an exemplary case because very early in my research, when I began to formulate the argument central to this section—the progressive weakening of pedagogy in the university milieu and its reduction to just "techniques" or "practice" (or to "theory")—the much-cited Josiah Royce essay, "Is There a Science of Education?" led me to Paul Hanus, to Charles Eliot, and to William James, whose textbook on pedagogy I had previously read but could not quite contextualize. The different versions of pedagogy that Hanus, Royce, and James represent seemed to me important issues to investigate. I am now in the process of researching and trying to understand William Payne's position at Michigan University. Though his appointment was hailed as an educational milestone, his writings, as I argue later, betray considerable unease if not anger about his position as a university professor of pedagogy. Another site might be Duke University, which began as a normal college (see L. E. Blauch's "An Early Normal College in the South," in *Peabody Journal of Education*, 1931). I am interested in finding out and making manifest the various rationalizations that justified this institution's move "beyond pedagogy" (see Beck, 1980).

4. Insofar as from his perspective pedagogy constitutes the "technical" preparation of teachers (i.e., the art, the practice of teaching), Borrowman, an advocate of "liberal" education, is not very invested in reclaiming a more complex conceptualization of pedagogy.

5. In *Teaching-Learning Theory and Teacher Education, 1890 to 1950*, Walter Monroe argues that although following 1890 the "normal school idea" of teacher education was generally accepted, "provisions for the professional training of teachers were at the level of 'small beginnings.' " On the basis of information he gathers from a *Report for 1889–90* from the United States commissioner of education, and from G. W. A. Luckey's *The Professional Training of Secondary Teachers in the United States*, he points out that in 1890, 114 out of 415 colleges and institutions offered "teachers' courses." These courses, also called departments, were not much different from normal schools.

> At this time most institutions classified as "colleges and universities" maintained a "preparatory department" and this characterization presumably meant that "with a few exceptions" the pedagogical work for teachers was offered in this department and was designed for the preparation of elementary teachers. (1952, 308)

Monroe notes that whereas normal schools were essentially dedicated to the education of elementary school teachers, and considered any other function incidental or even extraneous, the development of professional education for secondary teachers in colleges and universities

> seems to have originated with scholars and professional men who had become impressed by the great waste and inefficiency of college graduates that obtained employment as teachers, mainly in secondary schools. . . . A more significant difference is that the colleges and universities were established institutions devoted to certain recognized functions and committed to academic ideals and practices which had developed over a long period. Their attitude toward new lines of work was highly conservative. This attitude was accentuated in the case of the proposed professional training for teachers. The offering of pedagogical work in preparatory departments and the reputation of the normal schools of the time contributed to the opinion that professional courses for teachers would not be of college grade. Furthermore, teaching was thought of as an art and hence pedagogical instruction was not needed for secondary teachers, except possibly a departmental teachers' course. (308–09).

For an explanation of what "normal" originally meant, see Calvin Stowe in part 2.

6. In his account of the founding of Teachers College, James Earl Russell writes that in 1892, the trustees of Teachers College, despondent about the future of that institution, asked Columbia University Council to take it over. Their request was rejected, the decision having been made on the grounds that "there is no such subject as Education and *moreover it would bring into the University women who are not wanted*" (1937, 26).

The opposition to pedagogy that in 1892 so shocked Russell was actually not a new phenomenon at Columbia University. In the 1800s, Russell discovered, President Barnard had already repeatedly reported "the want of attention in Columbia College to what he declared was its own most important business, vis., the study of education as a science"; but to no avail. His "exposition, supported by incisive argument and wealth of illustration" had been buried "without decent consideration in the archives of the board" (26). By 1903, Russell notes, the university's acceptance of and relation to the college had not improved much:

Within a year our loyalty was questioned by the Columbia Trustees; the head professor of mathematics had denounced the appointment of a normal school man to a professorship; the head professor of history had publicly warned President Butler that the reputation of the University would be jeopardized by further coddling of this parvenu institution; the head professor of Latin aired his opposition to women students by dubbing 120th street "hairpin alley." (64–65)

Because the consequences of universities' oppositions to pedagogy affect the whole educational system, documents like these—accounts of disturbing, offensive, but also, fortunately, self-indicting postures—ought to be more widely circulated and carefully analyzed.

7. Throughout this chapter, I have tried to record, as accurately as possible, this terminological substitution. As will become evident, the old term—pedagogy—often crops up, though the reasons are not necessarily stated. This undoubtedly causes some confusion about what it designates and how it was used—a confusion I thought was important to document. As far as my use of the term is concerned, I continue to use it as a valorizing term to identify understandings of the teaching of teaching that posit the interconnectedness of theory and practice. Sometimes the term is used in this chapter to refer to constructions of pedagogy that limit it only to "practice," to mechanical application of theory, or to an automatic or natural enactment of knowledge of subject matter. I also use the phrases *pedagogy as art* and *pedagogy as science* to refer to the two positions in the academic debate that, I claim, can be seen as the historical antecedents of current reductive conceptualizations of pedagogy.

8. Payne was well aware of the specific conditions that had led to the expediency of relying on exact method as an essential part of a teacher's professional preparation in normal schools. But because he sensed that present conditions could lead to the same expedient, he repeatedly warned his audience about the disenabling consequences of divorcing method "from the principle that is its justification":

Contrasted with a principle, a rule is undiscriminating, narrowing, unfruitful; and it must be confessed that systematic training in method has a tendency to rob the teacher of his freedom, his versatility, and his personal power. Method has incomparable value when it directs capitalized energy, wisdom, and culture; but method is taught at some sacrifice of scholarship and culture when it accompanies a teacher's instruction in subjects and is made a characteristic element in his course of study. (1886, viii)

I am not sure, I must admit, whether Payne's argument is that method can only benefit those who have already "capitalized energy, wisdom and culture"—which would imply that method's "incomparable value" can*not* be taught (not at least to normal school students whose education Payne sees as "vocational" rather than "liberal"); or that it is, though it need not be, taught reductively (supposedly, again, in normal schools) through "undiscriminating, narrowing, unfruitful" procedures. Perhaps this is one of Payne's ways to debunk normal schools and their disciplines.

9. It is in terms of practice that Payne most sharply and vehemently demarcates the differences between the study of pedagogy at the university from the study of it in normal schools. He argues that the appreciation normally bestowed on normal schools for their valorization of practice is actually "begotten of false analogies":

Of the great categories of employments, the manual and the mental, teaching falls clearly within the second; and the art of teaching is distinguished from most employments of its class by the circumstance that in it there is a maximum of mental and a minimum of the manual. In the learning of every part, knowing precedes doing, and in a mere manual art, the major part of the learning process must consist on making experiments on brute matter that will not resent clumsy manipulation; but in an art like teaching the major part of the learning process is mental, and almost the whole preparation consists in informing clear conceptions of the processes that constitute that art. The forming of these conceptions I hold to be the almost exclusive aim of the strictly professional part of the normal instruction, and for this purpose there is not need of a school of children on whom experiments are to be wrought by apprentice teachers. (1886, 304)

That Payne, in his long career as superintendent of schools, might have witnessed prima facie questionable "practices" does not seem to constitute sufficient reason for him to conclude that there is no need for practice schools. What might have been, and might still be, profitable to investigate are the conditions under which an educational site instituted to implement responsible teaching became an implement of irresponsibility—at least in his opinion.

10. The *Educational Review* at once became the leading educational magazine of the United States and "held that position until the differentiation of education interests led to a demand for departmental periodicals, each ministering to the special needs of teachers of English, history, mathematics, and the rest, or to the specialized interests of elementary-school teachers, secondary-school teachers, superintendents of schools, college professors, etc." (Hanus 1937, 113).

11. In *Adventuring in Education* (1937), Paul Hanus writes:

I did not learn until after the college year began in September that many members of the faculty were doubtful about the value of the new department and that some of them looked on such department with little more than contempt. Quite in harmony with this attitude, and doubtedless as a concession to that minority, the faculty, while voting in favor of establishing the new department, *also* voted that the courses in the history and art of teaching should not be allowed to count toward any degree without special permission of the faculty. . . . What finally caused the faculty to vote for the new department was the persuasive cogency of President Eliot . . . and the fact that, as President Eliot told the faculty, a number of prominent secondary-school men of Boston were agitating for the establishment of a state institution for the training of secondary-school teachers. . . . I think that much of the opposition to the new department was due to the name attached to it in faculty discussions. It was called the "normal" department; and the name "normal" suggested the practice of the normal schools at the time for the training of elementary-school teachers. While very few of the members of the faculty had any real knowledge of normal schools, nearly all of them knew in a general way that those schools were devoted very largely to the rather rigid inculcation of current methods of teaching elementary school subjects and that consequently their work was circumscribed and definitely elementary. (110–11)

Like Payne, though less bitterly, Hanus carefully distinguishes the work of normal schools from the work of university departments of education. This excerpt, but even moreso the whole book, as well as *Educational Aims and Educational Values* (1902), suggests how difficult it was for aspiring *university* professors of pedagogy to define the importance of their work without scaling down the importance, and generalizing the poor performance, of normal schools.

12. Hofstadter had pointed out the American *public*'s incredible trust in education and its ignorance about it. I believe this contradiction has marked and continues to mark representatives of the *academy*. Burton J. Bledstein, in *The Culture of Professionalism*, writes that in 1873, President Charles Eliot of Harvard University noticed a "grevious fact" that would "cast uncertainty" upon Harvard's future. Bledstein quotes Eliot as saying: "Scholars like Asa Gray, Benjamin Pierce, Jeffries Wyman, and Louis Agassiz are all going off the stage and their places cannot be filled with Harvard men, or any other men that I am acquainted with. This generation cannot match them. These men have not trained their successors" (1976, 277). I am intrigued by the use of "stage," as well as the "mould" and "template" metaphors implicit in the expressions "their places cannot be filled" and "this generation cannot match them." These metaphors imply a version of pedagogy very similar to the one that Eliot would encourage Josiah Royce and William James to train Paul Hanus in—pedagogy as a sharing, a display, a performance of knowledge that posits an already appreciative audience (or more precisely, an audience already capable to appreciate). What I find striking about this is Eliot's emerging acknowledgment that Harvard could not count on a student population that could make the "passing over" of scholarship possible. That acknowledgment, however, does not lead Eliot to ask why the educational approaches he so valued could do so little to remedy the lack he so lamented. The educational approach he favored, he *did not* realize, would not make possible for a changed student population to "receive" that "passing over."

13. According to Bledstein (1976), Eliot exerted enormous control over younger faculty, even to the point of checking their marital status and the suitability of their wives (see *The Culture of Professionalism*, 300–309).

14. Hanus does repeatedly notice the limitedness of his mentors' view of pedagogy. About one of his first epistolary exchanges with Royce, he writes: "Royce's reply to my inquiries was very cordial but once more conveyed very definitely the tentative and experimental character of the enterprise on which the Faculty of Arts and Sciences had embarked, and especially the faculty's idea that the work of the new department must consist chiefly of introduction in methods of teaching" (1937, 117–18).

15. It is significant, I think, that the student testimonials Barzun quotes in his representation of James's "gifts" as a teacher should come from people like Woodbridge (a philosopher of note), Gertrude Stein, W. E. B. Du Bois, Leo Stein, and Walter Lippman. It is also significant that James should refer to "the teacher part" of his *Talks to Teachers* (his lectures on psychology to the teachers of Cambridge, undoubtedly more "ordinary" as students than the ones mentioned above) as "incarnate boredom." What is also worth noticing is Barzun's uncritical stance on James's views of teaching ("The Genius," *A Stroll with William James*, 279). An insightful commentary on the consequences of views of teaching similar to those of James and Barzun is Mike Rose's *Lives on the Boundary: The Struggles and Achievements of America's Underprepared.*

16. We often talk about "practice" interrogating "theory." This, I think, is an exem-

plary case when one, in practice, can discern the consequences of a too "rigorous" enactment of theory. A logical enactment of James's theory makes *mute* the question of whether or not his theory takes into account the student population that universities are now serving. But this is a question that today's educators cannot silence; and this is a question that could and should lead to a revision of theory.

17. In *The End of Modernity,* Gianni Vattimo provides an interesting angle on this issue. In his discussion of models of historicity, he suggests that a particular reading of Kant might lead to differentiating between "normal" and "revolutionary" models. "Normal historicity," he writes, "is that which is constituted by those 'mechanical heads'—as Kant terms them—which 'although they are not epoch-making, with their intellect that progresses every day a little further by leaning on the canes and props of experience' have perhaps made 'the greatest contribution to the growth of the sciences and [technical] arts' " (*Anthropology,* para. 50). On the other hand, "revolutionary historicity" is that which is constituted by geniuses, about whose ways of knowing Kant has this to say:

> Thus we can readily learn all that Newton has set forth in his immortal work on the *Principles of Natural Philosophy,* however great a head was required to discover it, but we cannot learn to write spirited poetry, however express may be the precepts of the art and however excellent its models. The reason is that Newton could make all his steps, from the first elements of geometry to his own great and profound discoveries, intuitively plain and definite as regards consequences, not only to himself but to everyone else. But a Homer or a Wieland cannot show how his ideas, so rich in fancy and yet so full of thought, come together in his head, *simply because he does not know and therefore cannot teach others.* (Kant in Vattimo, 93, emphasis added)

As Kant sets the genius in opposition to the mechanical head, he justifies, and glorifies, the particular kind of not-knowing characteristic of geniuses. When Barzun describes James's reputation as a teacher, even what to others might appear James's shortcomings are presented as worthy of praise. In other words, Barzun, and James, seem to believe with Kant that there is a not-knowing that is a marker of greatness. In the case of Kant, the fact that Newton is taken as a representative of "mechanical heads" provocatively complicates the opposition. In the case of Barzun, also of James, however, there is no sense that those who are not born teachers, those who are not geniuses, have much to offer. Without lingering much longer on what's questionable about this way of categorizing mental abilities and contributions, I want to call attention to how this theory "frames" pedagogy.

18. To read Tompkins's preface to *The Philosophy of Teaching* is to acknowledge a disturbing imbalance. Tompkins's engagement of his opponent's position, though limited by the space allotted and the audience addressed, makes it necessary for him to mention their *names* and to demonstrate that he not only understood that their philosophical orientations are responsible for their views of pedagogy but that those philosophical orientations might not necessarily lead to those conclusions. Critics of pedagogy, amply represented in this volume, instead, consistently resort to derision and contribute to making their opponents invisible by rarely mentioning their names.

19. One of the ways by which early university professors or proponents of pedagogy believed they would accrue status and power to pedagogy as a discipline was by

billing it as a "mixed science." Their intention, I believe, was to emphasize the capaciousness of pedagogy, but that intention might have been pedagogy's coup de grace because it presupposed a breadth of knowledge, an understanding of the various disciplines, that institutions of higher learning had not been put in a position to provide for future teachers. It is plausible to suggest a parallel between pedagogy and composition. Insofar as to establish itself as a field of study composition has looked to other disciplines and has borrowed their speculative instruments and methods, we might consider learning from pedagogy's past history so as to avoid some of the fated steps it took.

20. I believe these conventions are *not* known to many students, graduates as well as undergraduates. For a teacher to assume that they are is arbitrary and counterproductive. The fallaciousness of this assumption is amply demonstrated by the fact that critical debates are often mistaken and conducted in classrooms and elsewhere as personal attacks, or as manifestations of academics' perverse pleasure in ripping apart somebody's argument, as licenses to dismiss (as incongruous, or too theoretical, or anti-intellectual) different perspectives. The more we allow, as we should, the classroom to become a critical site wherein to investigate issues of difference, the more attention we should pay to teaching, spotlighting, and reflecting on and critiquing the presuppositions of knowledge that govern these conventions.

Works Cited

Adams, Francis. 1875. *The Free School System of the United States.* Reprint 1969. New York: Arno.

The American Heritage Dictionary. 1969. Ed. William Morris. Boston: American Heritage Publishing Co.

The American Heritage Dictionary, paperback ed. 1970. Ed. Peter Davies. New York: Dell Publishing Co., Inc.

Atwater, Caleb. 1841. *Essay on Education.* Cincinnati: Kendall and Henry.

Barnard, Henry. 1851. *Normal Schools and Other Institutions, Agencies, and Means for the Professional Education of Teachers.* 2 vols. Hartford: Case, Tiffany, and Co.

The Barnhardt Dictionary of Etymology, ed. Robert K. Barnhardt. 1988. Bronx, N.Y.: H. W. Wilson.

Barzun, Jacques. 1983. *A Stroll with William James.* New York: Harper and Row.

Beck, Frederick A. G. 1964. *Greek Education.* New York: Barnes and Noble.

Beck, Robert H. 1980. *Beyond Pedagogy: A History of the University of Minnesota College of Education.* St. Paul: North Central.

Bersani, Leo. 1985. "Pedagogy and Pederasty." *Raritan* 5 (1): 14–21.

Blauch, L. E. 1931. "An Early Normal College in the South." *Peabody Journal of Education* 8 (March): 294–304.

Bledstein, Burton J. 1976. *The Culture of Professionalism: The Middle Class and the Development of Higher Education in America.* New York: Norton.

Bonner, Stanley F. 1977. *Education in Ancient Rome.* Berkeley: University of California Press.

Bordieu, Pierre. 1988. *Homo Academicus.* Trans. Peter Collier. Stanford: Stanford University Press.

Borrowman, Merle L. 1956. *The Liberal and Technical in Teacher Education.* New York: Teachers College, Columbia University Press.

———, ed. 1965. *Teacher Education in America: A Documentary History.* New York: Teachers College Press.

———. 1971. "History of Teachers' Education." *The Encyclopedia of Education.* New York: Macmillan.

Bové, Paul. 1990. "Theory as Practice." *Work and Days* 16 (fall): 11–28.

Brackett, Anna C., trans. 1872–1874. *Pedagogics as a System,* by Karl Rosenkranz. Published in three installments in the *Journal of Speculative Philosophy.* 1972 (Oct.): 6: 4, 290–312; 1973 (Jan., Apr., July, Oct.): 49–71, 40–67, 1–23, 1–27; 1974 (Jan.): 49–73.

Bush, George Gary. 1889. "The Education of the Freedmen." In *History of Education in Florida.* Washington: Government Printing Office.

Calvino, Italo. 1981. *If on a winter's night a traveler.* Trans. William Weaver. New York: Harcourt Brace Jovanovich.

Carter, James Gordon. 1825. *Essays upon Popular Education with an Outline of an Institution for the Education of Teachers.* Reprint 1969. New York: Arno.

The Century Dictionary: An Encyclopedic Lexicon of the English Language. 1899. 8 vols. Ed. William Dwight Whitney. New York: Century.

Chambliss, J. J. 1968. *The Origins of American Philosophy of Education: Its Development as a Distinct Discipline, 1808–1913.* The Hague: Martinus Nijhoff.

Clifford, Geraldine Jonçich, and James W. Guthrie. 1988. *Ed School: A Brief for Professional Education.* Chicago: University of Chicago Press.

Clifford, John, ed. 1991. *The Experience of Reading: Louise Rosenblatt and Reader-Response Theory.* Portsmouth, N.H.: Boynton-Cook.

Cmiel, Kenneth. 1990. *Democratic Eloquence: The Fight Over Popular Speech in Nineteenth-Century America.* New York: Walter Morrow.

Cohen, Sol, ed. 1974. *Education in the United States: A Documentary History.* 5 vols. New York: Random House.

Compayré, Gabriel. 1886. *The History of Pedagogy.* Reprint 1971. New York: AMS Press.

———. 1910. "Pedagogy." Trans. Stephen Brett Sutherland. In *La Grande Encyclopédie Inventaire Raisonné des Sciences, des Lettres et des Arts par une Société de Savants et de Gens de Lettres.* 24 vols. Paris: Société Anonyme de la Grande Encyclopédie.

Conant, James B. 1963. *The Education of American Teachers.* New York: McGraw Hill Book Co.

Cremin, Lawrence Arthur. 1951. *The American Common School: An Historic Conception.* New York: Bureau of Publications, Teachers College, Columbia University.

———. 1961. *The Transformation of the School: Progressivism in American Education, 1876–1957.* New York: Knopf.

———. 1966. *The Genius of American Education.* New York: Vintage.

———. 1980. *American Education: The National Experience, 1783–1876.* New York: Harper and Row.

———. 1988. *American Education: The Metropolitan Experience, 1876–1980.* New York: Harper and Row.

De Garmo, Charles. 1891. "The Herbartian System of Pedagogics." *Education Review* (Jan.): 33–45.

DeVoto, Giacomo e Gian Carlo Oli. 1971. *Dizionario della Lingua Italiana.* Firenze: Felice Le Monnier.

Diccionario Enciclopedico Abreviado. 1975 (no editor given) Madrid: España-Calpe, S.A.

Diccionário Enciclopédico Brasilero. 1946. Organizádo sob a direção do Professor Alvaro Magalháes. São Paulo: Edição Da Livraria do Globo.

A Dictionary of Education. 1981. Ed. Dereck Rowntree. Totowa, N.J.: Barnes and Noble.

Dictionary of Philosophy and Psychology. 1928. Ed. James Mark Baldwin. New York: Macmillan.

Dictionnaire Langue Francaise. 1922. Abrégé du Dictionnaire de É. Littré le L'Academie Française. Par A. Beaujean. Paris: Librarie Hachette.

Donahue, Patricia, 1987. "Misreading Students' Texts." *Reader,* no. 17 (Spring 1987): 1–12.

Donahue, Patricia, and Ellen Quandahl. 1989. "Reading the Classroom." *Reclaiming Pedagogy: The Rhetoric of the Classroom.* Carbondale and Edwardsville: Southern University Press. 1–18.

———. "Freud and the Teaching of Interpretation." *Reclaiming Pedagogy.* 49–59.

Durkheim, Emile. 1958. *Education and Sociology.* Trans. Sherwood D. Fox. First published in France, 1895. New York: Free Press.

Eby, Frederick and Charles Flinn Arrowood. 1940. *The History and Philosophy of Education Ancient and Medieval.* New York: Prentice Hall.

Education Report. 1888–1889. 274–318. University of Pittsburgh Microfilms.

Encyclopedia Britannica; or, a Dictionary of Arts and Sciences. 1761. 3 vols. Edinburgh: A. Bell and C. Macfarquhar.

The Encyclopedia and Dictionary of Education, a Comprehensive, Practical and Authoritative Guide on All Matters Connected with Education, Including Educational Principles and Practice, Various Types of Teaching Institutions, and Educational Systems Throughout the World. 1922. 4 vols. Ed. Foster Watson. London: Sir Issac Pitman and Sons.

The Encyclopedia of Education. 1971. 10 vols. Ed. Lee C. Deighton. New York: Macmillan and Free Press.

The Encyclopedic Dictionary. 1896. Ed. Robert Hunter and Charles Morris. Philadelphia: Syndicate.

Ferguson, Margaret. 1988. "Teaching and/as Reproduction." *Yale Journal of Criticism.* vol. I, 2 (Spring): 213–22.

Flannery, Kathryn T. 1995. *The Emperor's New Clothes: Literature, Literacy and the Ideology of Style.* Pittsburgh and London: University of Pittsburgh Press.

Foucault, Michel. 1972. *The Archaeology of Knowledge and The Discourse on Language.* Trans. A. M. Sheridan Smith. New York: Harper and Row.

———. 1973. *The Order of Things: An Archaeology of the Human Sciences.* New York: Vintage.

Fowle, William B. 1866. Reprint 1873. *The Teacher's Institute; or, Familiar Hints to Young Teachers.* New York and Chicago: A. S. Barnes.

Freire, Paulo. 1968. *The Pedagogy of the Oppressed.* Trans. Myra Bergman Ramos. New York: Seabury.

Funk and Wagnalls New Practical Standard Dictionary of the English Language. 1946. 2 vols. Ed. Charles Earle Funk. New York: Funk and Wagnalls.

Gadamer, Hans-Georg. 1975. *Truth and Method.* New York: Continuum.

———. 1976. *Philosophical Hermeneutics.* Trans. and ed. David E. Linge. Berkeley: University of California.

Gallaudet, Thomas H. 1825. "Plan of a Seminary for the Education of Instructors of Youth." Reprint 1831. *American Annals of Education,* vol. I (Jan.): 25–26.

Gallop, Jane. 1982. *The Daughter's Seduction: Feminism and Psychoanalysis.* Ithaca: Cornell University Press.

———, ed. 1995. *Pedagogy: The Question of Impersonation.* Bloomington and Indianapolis: Indiana University Press.

Gentile, Giovanni. 1912. *Sommario di Pedagogia Come Scienza Filosofica.* 2 vols. Reprint 1982. Firenze: Sansoni.

Giroux, Henry A. 1988. *Schooling and the Struggle for Public Life: Critical Pedagogy in the Modern Age.* Minneapolis: University of Minneapolis Press.

———. 1988. *Teachers as Intellectuals: Toward a Critical Pedagogy of Learning.* New York: Begin and Garvey.

———. 1992. *Border Crossings: Cultural Workers and the Politics of Education.* New York: Routledge.

Goleman, Judith. 1995. *Working Theory: Critical Composition Studies for Students and Teachers.* Westport, Connecticut and London: Bergin and Garvey.

Gordy, J. P. 1891. *Rise and Growth of the Normal-School Idea in the United States.* Washington: Government Printing Office.

————. "Chairs of Pedagogy." In *Rise and Growth of the Normal-School Idea in the United States.*

Gore, Jennifer. 1993. *The Struggle for Pedagogies: Critical and Feminist Discourses as Regimes of Truth.* New York: Routledge.

Gould, Stephen Jay. 1977. *Ontogeny and Philogeny.* Cambridge: Harvard University Press.

Graff, Gerald. 1987. *Professing Literature: An Institutional History.* Chicago: University of Chicago Press.

Graff, Gerald and Michael Warner, eds. 1989. *The Origins of Literary Studies in America: A Documentary Anthology.* New York: Routledge.

Grande Dizionario Enciclopedico. 1954. Torino: Unione Tipografico-Editrice Torinese.

La Grande Encyclopédie Inventaire Raisonné des Sciences, des Lettres et des Arts par une Sócieté de Savants et de Gens de Lettres. 1910. 24 vols. Paris: Société Anonyme de la Grande Encyclopédie.

Grande Larousse Encyclopédique. 1963. Paris: Librairie Larousse.

Gray, Thomas. 1891. "The Normal-School Idea as Embodied in the Normal School at St. Cloud." In *Rise and Growth of the Normal-School Idea in the United States,* ed. J. P. Gordy. Washington: Government Printing Office.

Hall, Baynard Rush. 1848. *Teaching, a Science: The Teacher, an Artist.* New York: Baker and Scribner.

Hall, Samuel R. 1829. *Lectures on School-Keeping.* Boston: Richardson, Lord, and Holbrook. Reprint 1929. *Hall's Lectures on School-Keeping.* Ed. Arthur D. Wright and George E. Gardner. Hanover, N.H.: The Dartmouth Press.

Hanus, Paul. 1891. "The New Department of Pedagogy at Harvard University." *Educational Review* (Oct.): 252–54.

————. 1902. *Educational Aims and Educational Values.* New York: Macmillan.

————. 1937. Adventuring in Education. Cambridge: Harvard University Press.

Harris, William T. 1882. Reprint 1883. "Chairs of Pedagogics." In *Education: An International Magazine.* Ed. Thomas W. Bicknell. Boston: New England Publishing Co.

————. 1891. "Letter of Transmittal." In *Rise and Growth of the Normal-School Idea in the United States,* ed. J. P. Gordy. Washington: Government Printing Office.

————, ed. 1866. *The Philosophy of Education,* by Karl Rosenkranz. Trans. Anna C. Brackett. Vol. I of the Appleton Series on Education. New York: Appleton.

Hart, Albert Bushnell. 1893. "The Teacher as a Professional Expert." *School Review* I, no. I (Jan.) 4–14.

Henderson, E. N. 1913. "Pedagogy." In *A Cyclopedia of Education.* 5 vols. Ed. Paul Monroe. New York: Macmillan.

Hinsdale, Burke A. 1906. *History of the University of Michigan.* Ed. Isaac N. Demmon. Ann Arbor: University of Michigan Press.

Hofstadter, Richard. 1963. *Anti-intellectualism in American Life.* New York: Knopf.

James, William. 1899. *Talks to Teachers on Psychology: and to Students on Some of Life's Ideals.* New York: Henry Holt.

Johnson, Walter R. 1825. "Observations on the Improvement of Seminaries of Learning." In *Education in the United States: A Documentary History*. Ed. Sol Cohen. Vol 2.

Judd, C. H. 1909. "The Department of Education in American Universities." *The School Review: A Journal of Secondary Education* 17, no. 9: 593–608.

Kecht, Maria-Regina. 1992. *Pedagogy Is Politics: Literary Theory and Critical Teaching*. Urbana and Chicago: University of Illinois Press.

Knight, E. W., ed. 1930. *Reports on European Education*. New York: McGraw-Hill.

Knoper, Randall. 1989. "Deconstruction, Process, Writing." In *Reclaiming Pedagogy: The Rhetoric of the Classroom*. Carbondale and Edwardsville: Southern Illinois University Press. 128–43.

Landau, Sidney I. 1984. *Dictionaries: The Art and Craft of Lexicography*. New York: Cambridge University Press.

Landy, Marcia. 1991. "Socialist Education Today: Pessimism or Optimism of the Intellect?" *Re-Thinking Marxism* 4, no. 3 (fall): 9–23.

Lather, Patti. 1991. *Getting Smart: Feminist Research and Pedagogy With/in the Postmodern*. New York: Routledge.

Lentricchia, Frank, and Thomas McLaughlin. 1990. *Critical Terms for Literary Study*. Chicago: University of Chicago Press.

Lodge, R. C. 1947. *Philosophy of Education: Plato's Theory of Education*. London: Kegan Paul.

Luckey, G.W.A. 1903. *The Professional Training of Secondary Teachers in the United States*. New York: Macmillan.

Lusted, David. 1986. "Why Pedagogy?" *Screen: Incorporating Screen Education* (Sept./Oct.): 2–15.

Lyte, Eliphalet Oram. 1904. *The State Normal Schools of the United States*. *Education Report* (May): 1103–30.

McMurry, Charles A., and Frank M. McMurry. 1897. Reprint 1912. *The Method of the Recitation*. Reprint, New York: Macmillan.

Marrou, Henri Irénée. 1956. *A History of Education in Antiquity*. New York: Sheed and Ward.

Mayo, A. D. 1889. "The Training of the Teacher in the South." *NEA Proceedings*: 597–607.

Meyers Grosses Konversations Lexicon. 1943. "Pedagogy," Trans. Thomas Ernst. Leipzig und Wien: Bibliographisches Institut.

Miller, Richard. 1993. "Representing the People: Theoretical and Pedagogical Disjunctions in the Academy." Ph.D. diss., University of Pittsburgh.

Monroe, Walter S. 1952. *Teaching-Learning Theory and Teacher Education, 1890–1950*. Urbana: University of Illinois Press.

Morton, Donald, and Mas'ud Zavarzadeh, eds. 1991. *Theory/Pedagogy/Politics: Texts for Change*. Urbana and Chicago: University of Illinois Press.

The New Century Dictionary of the English Language, Based on Matter Selected from the Original Century Dictionary and Entirely Rewritten, with the Addition of a Great Amount of New Material, and Containing the Great Mass of Words and Phrases in Ordinary Use. 1959. Ed. H. G. Emery and K. G. Brewster. New York: Appleton-Century-Crofts.

"A New Jersey Teacher's Contract (1841)." *History of Education in New Jersey*. Ed. David Murray. Washington. Reprint 1976 in *Education in the United States: A Documentary History*. Ed. Sol Cohen. New York: Random House.

Ohles, John. F., ed. 1978. *Biographical Dictionary of American Educators.* 3 vols. West-port, Conn.: Greenwood.

Oxford American Dictionary. 1980. Ed. Eugene Ehrlich, Stewart Berg Flexner, Gorton Carruth, and Joyce M. Hawkins. New York: Oxford University Press.

The Oxford Dictionary of English Etymology. 1966. Ed. C. T. Onions. Oxford: Clarendon.

Oxford English Dictionary. 1888–1928. 1st ed. Ed. Sir James A. H. Murray. Oxford: Clarendon Press.

Page, David P. 1847. *Theory and Practice of Teaching; or, The Motives and Methods of Good School-Keeping.* Ed. William H. Payne. 1885. New York: American Book Company.

Parker, Col. Francis Wayland. 1894. *Talks on Pedagogics: An Outline of the Theory of Concentration.* New York and Chicago: A. S. Barnes.

Payne, William H. 1886. *Contributors to the Science of Education.* New York: Harper and Brothers.

———. 1901. *The Education of Teachers.* Richmond: B. F. Johnson.

———. 1971. "Translator's Preface." Gabriel Compayré, *The History of Pedagogy.* Trans. William Payne. New York: AMS Press.

Phelps, Almira Hart Lincoln. 1833. *Lectures to Young Ladies: Comprising Outlines and Applications of the Different Branches of Female Education for the Use of Female Schools, and Private Libraries.* Boston: Carter, Hendee.

Putnam, Daniel. 1895. *Manual of Pedagogics.* Cambridge: University Press.

The Random House Dictionary of the English Language. 1967. Jess Stein, Ed. in Chief. Lawrence Urdang, Managing Ed. New York: Random House.

The Random House Dictionary, paperback ed. 1980.

"Report of the 'Chicago Committee' on Methods of Instruction, and Courses of Study in Normal Schools." 1889. Thomas J. Gray, chairman. *NEA Proceedings:* 570–78.

Rose, Mike. 1989. *Lives on the Boundary: The Struggles and Achievements of America's Underprepared.* New York: Free Press.

Rowntree, Derek. 1981. *A Dictionary of Education.* Totowa, New Jersey: Barnes and Noble.

Royce, Josiah. 1891. "Is There a Science of Education?" *Educational Review* (Jan.–Feb.): 15–25; 121–32.

"Rules for Teachers." 1872.

Russell, James Earl. 1937. *Founding Teachers College: Reminiscences of the Dean Emeritus.* New York: Bureau of Publications, Teachers College, Columbia University.

Salisbury, Albert. 1889. "Discussion: Normal School Work Among the Colored People." *NEA Proceedings:* 594–97.

Salvatori, Mariolina. 1988. "Towards a Hermeneutics of Difficulty." In *Audits of Meaning.* Ed. Louise Z. Smith. Portsmouth, N.H.: Boynton-Cook.

———. 1989. "Pedagogy: From the Periphery to the Center." In *Reclaiming Pedagogy: The Rhetoric of the Classroom.* Ed. Patricia Donahue and Ellen Quandahl. Carbondale and Edwardsville: Southern Illinois University Press.

———. 1991. "On Behalf of Pedagogy." In *The Experience of Reading: Louise Rosenblatt and Reader-Response Theory.* Ed. John Clifford. Portsmouth, N.H.: Boynton-Cook.

Schelling, Felix E. 1929. *Pedagogically Speaking: Essays and Addresses on Topics More or Less Educational.* Philadelphia: University of Pennsylvania Press.

Seely, Levi. 1903. "The Relation of Theory to Practice in the Training of Teachers." In *The Second Year-Book of the National Society for the Scientific Study of Education.* Chicago: University of Chicago Press.

————. 1901. *The Foundations of Education*. New York: Hinds and Noble.

Shipley, Joseph T. 1945. *Dictionary of Word Origins*. New York: Philosophical Library.

Shor, Ira, and Paulo Freire. 1987. *A Pedagogy for Liberation: Dialogues for Transforming Education*. South Hadley, Mass.: Bergin and Garvey.

Simon, Roger I. 1992. *Teaching Against the Grain: Texts for a Pedagogy of Possibility*. South Hadley, Mass.: Bergin and Garvey.

Skeat, Walter W. 1910. *An Etymological Dictionary of the English Language*. 1879–1882. Reprint, Oxford: Clarendon.

Smyth, John, ed. 1987. *Educating Teachers: Changing the Nature of Pedagogical Knowledge*. New York: Palmer.

Somers, Robert L. 1988. "Working with the Adult Learner: Applied Andragogy for Developmental Programs." *Review of Research in Developmental Education* 5, no. 5: 1–5.

Spivak, Gayatri Chakravorty. 1987. *In Other Worlds: Essays in Cultural Politics*. New York and London: Methuen.

————. 1993. *Outside the Teaching Machine*. New York and London: Routledge.

State Normal University Faculty (Normal, Illinois). 1903. "The Relation Between Theory and Practice in the Training of Teachers." In *The Second Year-Book of the National Society for the Scientific Study of Education*. Chicago: University of Chicago Press.

Steele, A. J. 1889. "Normal School Work Among the Colored People." *NEA Proceedings*: 588–97.

Stowe, Calvin Ellis. 1838. "Normal Schools and Teachers' Seminaries." Reprint 1851. In *Normal Schools and Other Institutions, Agencies, and Means for the Professional Education of Teachers*. 2 vols. Ed. Henry Barnard. Hartford: Case, Tiffany, and Co.

"The Substance of Two Reports of the Faculty of Amherst College to the Board of Trustees with the Doings of the Board Thereon." 1827. Amherst: Carter and Adames Printers. (Rollins College, Fla.: Microfilms).

Tompkins, Arnold. 1894. *The Philosophy of Teaching*. Boston: Ginn and Co.

Urdang, Lawrence. 1988. *The Dictionary of Confusable Words*. New York: Ballantine.

Vattimo, Gianni. 1985. *The End of Modernity*. Baltimore: The Johns Hopkins University Press.

Webster, Noah. 1806. *A Compendious Dictionary of the English Language*. New Haven: Sidney's Press.

Webster's New Dictionary of Synonyms. 1968. 1st ed. 1942. Reprint, Springfield, Mass.: Merriam.

White, Emerson E. 1886. *The Elements of Pedagogy*. New York: American Book Company.

————. 1901. *The Art of Teaching: A Manual for Teachers, Superintendents, Teachers' Reading Circles, Normal Schools, Training Classes, and Other Persons Interested in the Right Training of the Young*. New York: American Book Company.

Willard, Emma. 1819. *An Address to the Public; Particularly to the Members of the Legislature of New York, Proposing a Plan for Improving Female Education*. Middlebury: J. W. Copeland, Printer.

Williams, Raymond. 1983. *Keywords: A Vocabulary of Culture and Society*. Revised ed. New York: Oxford Universty Press.

Worcester, Joseph E. 1846. *A Universal and Critical Dictionary of the English Language*. Boston: Wilkins, Carter, and Co.

Library of Congress Cataloging-in-Publication Data

Pedagogy : disturbing history, 1819–1929 / Mariolina Rizzi Salvatori, editor.
      p. cm.—(Pittsburgh series in composition, literacy, and culture)
    Includes bibliographical references and index.
    ISBN 0-8229-3922-3 (cl : alk. paper)
    1. Education—Study and teaching (Higher)—United States—
    History—19th century. 2. Education—Study and teaching (Higher)—
    United States—History—20th century. 3. Teachers—Training of—
  United States—History—19th century. 4. Teachers—Training of—
  United States—History—20th century. 5. Teaching—United States—
  History—19th century. 6. Teaching—United States—History—20th
  century. I. Salvatori, Mariolina Rizzi. II. Series.
  LB1715.P35 1996
  370.71'0973—dc20   96-11938